LEVEL ONE

SCOPE ENGLISH ANTHOLOGY

Literature and Reading Program

Edited by
Katherine Robinson
Editorial Director, Scope Magazine

SCHOLASTIC INC.

The Scope English Story

In 1964, when Scholastic first published it, SCOPE Magazine was a near-revolutionary publication: a magazine designed to bring good literature and reading, and useful skills, to young people. Now, after more than twenty years, SCOPE is the most widely used magazine in junior and senior high school Reading and English programs—reaching nearly 40 percent of all secondary schools in the United States.

Teachers have found SCOPE Magazine so useful in motivating readers that they have asked for a more permanent resource containing the high quality reading selections and activities found in every issue of SCOPE. So we developed SCOPE ENGLISH—a complete English program including both reading and literature as well as a comprehensive writing and language program. Teachers all over America are finding in SCOPE ENGLISH precisely those qualities that made SCOPE Magazine so popular: It makes English easier to learn, more motivating, more teachable. We've included selections from the magazine that are of high interest to students—stories, poems, plays, TV scripts, articles and more—as well as tried-and-true teacher favorites that create a basic curriculum framework. The reading levels of these selections are accessible to all junior and senior high school students, grades 6–12, yet the ideas are challenging and provocative. SCOPE ENGLISH includes an *Anthology* at each grade level, organized by themes, authors, or genres, and a *Writing and Language* text, written in clear, conversational style.

SCOPE ENGLISH contains eye-catching photos and illustrations that actually aid in students' understanding of the important events in a selection. An illustration is provided every three to five pages of text, to make the reading experience less threatening for the students. All the materials motivate secondary students to read more and write better.

More than twenty years after SCOPE Magazine first brought the SCOPE philosophy to the English classroom, we're proud to be able to reach you with the SCOPE ENGLISH program. We hope you will find these materials just as useful and helpful as you've found SCOPE Magazine to be in making English learning easier and more satisfying.

LITERATURE CONSULTANTS

Jane Yolen
Author

Theodore Hipple, Ph.D.
Department Chair
Curriculum and Instruction
University of Tennessee
Knoxville, Tennessee

LEVEL ONE READERS

Charlene Couvillon
Teacher
Max Bruner Junior High School
Fort Walton Beach, Florida

Allen Gill
Teacher
Harding Junior High School
Philadelphia, Pennsylvania

Helene Steinbuck
Language Arts Coordinator, District 4
New York, New York

CURRICULUM CONSULTANTS

Barbara Coulter
Director of Language Education
Detroit Public Schools
Detroit, Michigan

Nora Forester
Reading Coordinator
North Side School District
San Antonio, Texas

William Horst
Secondary Section Committee
National Council of Teachers of English

Barbara Krysiak, Ed.D.
Principal
North Hampton Elementary School
North Hampton, New Hampshire

Nancy McHugh
Teacher
Grant High School
Van Nuys, California

READING CONSULTANT

Virginia B. Modla, Ph.D
Reading Curriculum Associate
School District of Cheltenham Township
Elkins Park, Pennsylvania

COVER: *A Sunday Afternoon on the Island of La Grande Jatte* (detail), by Georges Seurat (1884-1886). Courtesy of the Art Institute of Chicago.

ACKNOWLEDGMENTS

Grateful ackowledgment is made to the following authors and publishers for the use of copyrighted materials. Every effort has been made to obtain permission to use previously published material. Any errors or omissions are unintentional.

T. D. Allen, Institute of American Indian Arts, a Bureau of Indian Affairs School at Santa Fe, New Mexico, for "Grandfather" by Shirley Crawford, copyright © 1969 by the University of South Dakota.

Larry Bortstein for the adaptation of "African Battle" from *Muhammad Ali's African Battle*, copyright © 1976 by Larry Bortstein

Curtis Brown, Ltd. for British Commonwealth rights to "The Panther," "The Canary," "The Shrew," and "The Termite" by Ogden Nash. The adaptation of "Priscilla in the Pond" by John Savage, copyright © 1966 Curtis Publishing Company.

J. S. F. Burrage for the adaptation of "The Waxwork" from *Someone in the Room* by Alfred McLelland Burrage. All rights reserved.

Hugh B. Cave for the adaptation of "Two Were Left" by Hugh B. Cave, copyright 1942 by The Crowell-Collier Publishing Company.

Creativity, Inc. and Eyre Methuen, Ltd. for British Commonwealth rights to the adaptation from *The Good Earth* by Pearl S. Buck.

(Acknowledgments continue on page 512)

ISBN 0-590-34967-8

Copyright © 1988, 1983, 1979 by Scholastic Inc. All rights reserved. Published by Scholastic Inc.

12 11 10 9 8 7 6 5 4 3 2

8 9/8 0/9 1

Printed in the U.S.A.

LEVEL ONE

Contents

Skills Lessons

Note: Each page number indicates the first time a skill is taught or practiced. In most cases, each skill is tapped several times in this book.

READING COMPREHENSION

VOCABULARY/WORD ATTACK

ORAL LANGUAGE DEVELOPMENT

PROCESS OF WRITING

WRITING ABOUT THE SELECTION

RESEARCH AND STUDY SKILLS

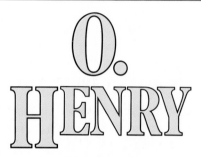

O. HENRY

*O. Henry had
seen the Old West, the inside of a
prison, and the streets of New York.
Nothing could surprise him — but his
stories surprised the world.*

Biography

O. Henry

O. Henry is one of the most popular writers who ever lived. The story of his life is as interesting as some of the stories he wrote. But it doesn't have the one thing that his stories are famous for — a surprise ending.

His real name was William Sydney Porter. He was born in North Carolina during the Civil War. After his mother died, he was raised by his grandmother and his Aunt Lina.

At 15, Porter started working in his uncle's drugstore. While learning to be a pharmacist, he started drawing cartoons.

He also learned a lot about the people who came into the drugstore. He watched their actions and listened to their talk. Later in his life, he used what he learned when he wrote his stories.

The West

When he was 19, Porter visited a ranch in Texas. He stayed there for two years, doing some of the ranch work. But he spent most of his time reading, drawing, and writing. He saved up more material for stories he would write later. The play you will read, "Pancakes," is based on one of the stories that O. Henry wrote about cowboy life in Texas.

Porter moved on to Austin, the capital of Texas. He was married at age 24 and became a teller in Austin's First National Bank. He also started a comic newspaper, *The Rolling Stone*. He wrote most of it himself. It lasted a year, and lost a lot of money.

Porter borrowed money to keep *The Rolling Stone* going. He also seems to have taken money from the bank. He may have planned to pay it back later. But he fixed his account books to hide the "borrowing."

A U.S. bank examiner saw that the money was missing. Porter quit his bank job. The case was brought to a grand jury. The grand jury decided that Porter would not have to go on trial.

Porter went to Houston to work on a newspaper. But the bank examiner kept his case open. Porter was arrested and taken back to Austin for trial.

Instead of waiting for his trial, Porter left the country. He went to Honduras, in Central America. There he met other Americans who had run away from the U.S. law. As always, he picked up material that he used later in his stories.

Then he heard that his wife was dying. He went back to Texas, knowing he would have to go on trial.

Prison

His wife died before the trial began. Porter was charged with taking $5,500 from the bank. He was also charged with running away from the law. The jury found him guilty. He was sentenced to five years in a U.S. prison.

At first, he was very unhappy in prison. He wanted to kill himself. And he kept away from the other prisoners.

Then he worked as a prison druggist. This left him with time to write. As usual, he picked up plenty of material. Jimmy Valentine — in the story "The Safe-cracker" — is based on a prisoner that Porter knew.

He started selling stories to important magazines. He also started using the pen-name "O. Henry." He did not want his readers — or anyone else — to know about his past life. Later, he would try to keep people from knowing that O. Henry, the famous writer, was William Sydney Porter, an ex-convict. Even his young daughter did not know that his letters to her came from prison.

Porter's pen-name may have come from a cowboy song he heard in Texas. The song is called "Root, Hog, or Die." Part of it goes:

Along came my true lover at 12 o'clock
Saying Henry, O Henry, what sentence have you got?

In 1901, Porter left prison. With time off for good behavior, he had been in prison for three years.

New York City

Most American magazines were published in New York City, so Porter went to live there. He liked the big city. In a small town, someone who knew about his past might spot him. In New York, he could get lost in the crowds of people.

He also liked talking to the different kinds of people in the city. Among them were store clerks, artists who had to get by on very little money, and vagrants. His sympathy for them is shown in stories like "A Service of Love" and "The Cop and the Anthem."

Not all of his stories are about city people, though. In "Pancakes," the main characters are a cowboy and a sheep rancher. And here the author shows a humorous side of human nature.

Porter wrote and sold hundreds of stories. For a while, he wrote a story every week for a Sunday newspaper. Sometimes he would write a story in just one hour.

His stories became very popular. They showed a good deal of understanding of the problems, hopes, weaknesses, and strengths of ordinary people.

Porter made a lot of money. But he always spent more than he made. He married again, but the marriage did not work out. He sometimes drank as much as two bottles of whisky a day. This ruined his health.

Porter was asked to turn the story of Jimmy Valentine (see "The Safecracker") into a play. Instead, he sold his rights to the story for $250.

The play was called *Alias Jimmy Valentine*, and it was a big hit. The man who wrote it made $100,000. But Porter never got another cent for it.

His Stories Live On

Porter died in 1910. He was 47. His stories became even more popular after he died. Books of his work are still in homes and libraries all over the world. Many of the stories have been made into plays, movies, and TV shows.

People who study writers have not always liked O. Henry's stories. Some say that the stories are too tricky, and do not deal seriously with real life. The things that happen in the stories, they say, could not happen in real life.

Other people like O. Henry's stories because they *do* seem to show what life was like in the late 1800's and early 1900's. They also enjoy the surprise endings. Most of O. Henry's stories end with a sad or funny surprise for the characters — and for the reader.

Will Jimmy Valentine try to save a little girl's life — only to lose everything that's valuable to him? The ending of "The Safecracker" may surprise you.

When Joe and Delia Larrabee run short of money, will their love run short, too? Find out in "A Service of Love."

Jud Lomax and Jackson Bird are both determined to marry Wilella Learight. To see how much depends upon a *recipe*, read "Pancakes."

Will Soapy find a warm place to spend the winter? The answer takes a surprising turn in "The Cop and the Anthem."

The Safecracker

by O. Henry

Imagine that only you can save some other people's lives. But if you do, you will lose everything that makes your own life worthwhile. That's the choice "The Safecracker" had to make. And he proved what kind of man he really was.

A guard brought Jimmy Valentine to the warden's office. The warden handed Jimmy his pardon. "The governor signed it this morning," the warden said.

Jimmy had served 10 months of a four-year sentence. He had never thought he would stay more than three months. He had many important friends on the outside.

"Now, Valentine," the warden said, "make a man of yourself. Stop cracking safes. Begin to live straight."

"Me?" said Jimmy. "Why, I never cracked a safe in my life."

"Oh, no." The Warden laughed. "Of course not. Then how was it you got sent up for that Springfield job?"

"Why, I never was in Springfield in my life."

"Fix him up with some clothes," the warden told the guard. "Better think over my advice, Valentine," he said.

Mr. James Valentine walked out into the sunshine. He headed straight for a restaurant. There he tasted the first sweet joys of freedom in a broiled chicken and a bottle of white wine.

Then he took a train to a little town near the state line. He went to the cafe owned by Mike Dolan. He shook hands with Mike, who was behind the bar.

"Sorry we couldn't make it sooner," Mike said. "We had those people in Springfield to worry about. The governor almost backed down. Feeling all right?"

"Fine," said Jimmy. "Got my key?"

He took his key and went upstairs. Everything in his room was the way he left it. There on the floor was Ben Price's shirt button. It was torn off when the famous detective arrested Jimmy.

Jimmy opened a panel in the wall. He took out a dusty suitcase. Inside the suitcase was the finest set of burglar's tools in the East. Jimmy had paid a lot to have them made.

In half an hour, Jimmy went downstairs. He was dressed in his own good clothes. He carried his suitcase.

"Got anything on?" Mike asked

"Me?" Jimmy said. "I don't understand. I'm a salesman for the New York Biscuit Company." Mike laughed.

A week after Jimmy left prison, there was a neat job of safecracking in Richmond, Indiana. There were no clues. The burglar took $800. Two weeks later, a burglar-proof safe in Logansport was opened. Only cash was taken — $1,500. Then a bank safe in Jefferson City — $5,000.

The losses were now high enough to bring Ben Price into the case. Ben Price went to the scene of one of the robberies. He said, "That's Jimmy Valentine's signature. He's back in business. Look at that combination knob. It was pulled out as easy as pulling up a radish in wet weather. He's got the only tools that can do it. Yes, I guess I want Mr. Valentine."

One afternoon, Jimmy Valentine and his suitcase arrived in Elmore, a little town in Arkansas. He saw a young lady going into the Elmore Bank. Jimmy Valentine looked into her eyes and became another man. She blushed.

Jimmy asked a boy on the street, "Isn't that Miss Polly Simpson?"

"Naw," the boy said. "She's Annabel Adams. Her pa owns this bank."

Jimmy went to the hotel. He took a room as Ralph D. Spencer. He said to the

clerk, "I'm looking for a place to go into business. How is the shoe business in Elmore?"

The clerk was impressed by Jimmy's clothes and way of speaking. "Well," he said, "there isn't any shoe store. If you decide to settle in Elmore, Mr. Spencer, you'll find it a pleasant town."

"Well, I'll stay for a few days and look it over," Jimmy said. "No, don't bother. I'll carry my suitcase myself. It's rather heavy."

That day, Mr. Ralph Spencer rose from Jimmy Valentine's ashes—ashes left from the flame of sudden love.

Mr. Spencer stayed in Elmore. He opened a shoe store. He made many friends. And he got his heart's wish. He met Miss Annabel Adams.

At the end of a year, Mr. Ralph Spencer's shoe store was doing very well. He and Annabel were engaged to be married in two weeks. That was when Jimmy wrote this letter to an old friend:

Dear Old Pal,

I want you to be at Sullivan's place in Little Rock, next Wednesday night. I want you to take care of some business for me. And I want to give you my kit of tools.

Billy, I've quit the old business. I'm making an honest living. I'm going to marry the finest girl on earth two weeks from now. It's the only life, Billy — the straight one. I wouldn't touch a dollar of another man's money now for a million.

After I get married, I'm going to go west. There won't be so much danger there of having old scores brought up against me.

Your old friend,
Jimmy

On the Monday night after Jimmy wrote this letter, Ben Price came into Elmore. From across the street, he got a good look at Ralph D. Spencer.

"Going to marry the banker's daughter, Jimmy?" said Ben to himself. "Well, I don't know!"

The next morning, Jimmy had breakfast at the Adams home. He was going to Little

Rock that day, to buy his wedding suit and a present for Annabel.

The Adams family went downtown with Jimmy. There were Mr. Adams, Annabel, and Annabel's married sister with her two little girls, aged five and nine. First, they stopped at Jimmy's hotel. Jimmy got his suitcase.

Then they all went into the bank. Annabel picked up Jimmy's suitcase. She said, "How heavy this is, Ralph! It feels like it's full of gold bricks."

"It's a lot of metal shoe horns," Jimmy said. "I'm returning them. I thought I would save money by taking them myself."

The Elmore Bank had just put in a new vault. Mr. Adams was very proud of it. He took everyone to the back room. He showed them the steel bolts and the time-lock. The two children, May and Agatha, liked the shiny metal and the funny knobs.

Ben Price walked into the bank. He told the teller that he was waiting for a friend.

Suddenly, there was a scream from the women. They hadn't noticed the two girls playing. May, the nine-year-old girl, had shut Agatha inside the vault. Then she had turned the knob.

Mr. Adams pulled at the handle. "The door can't be opened," he said. "The clock hasn't been wound in the time-lock. The combination wasn't set."

Agatha's mother screamed again.

"Hush," said Mr. Adams. "Let's all be quiet for a moment." He called, "Agatha! Can you hear me?"

In the silence, they could hear the child. She was screaming.

"My little darling!" the mother cried. "She'll die of fright! Open the door! Break

it open! Can't you men do something?"

"There isn't a man closer than Little Rock who can open that door," Mr. Adams said, in a shaky voice. To Jimmy he said, "Spencer, what shall we do? That child can't stand it for long. There isn't enough air."

"Use dynamite," someone said.

Annabel turned to Jimmy. "Can't you do something, Ralph?" she said.

Jimmy looked at her with a strange smile on his lips. "Annabel," he said, "give me that rose you are wearing."

She gave him the rose. Jimmy put it into

his pocket. With that act, Ralph D. Spencer passed away, and Jimmy Valentine took his place.

"Get away from the door, all of you," he said.

He opened his suitcase. He worked quietly with the tools. The others watched him as if they were under a spell.

In a minute, Jimmy's drill was biting into the steel door. In 10 minutes — breaking his own record — he opened the door.

Agatha's mother took the child in her arms.

Jimmy walked out toward the front door. He heard a voice behind him calling, "Ralph!" But he did not stop.

A man was standing at the door.

"Hello, Ben," Jimmy said. "You got around at last, did you? Well, let's go. I don't know that it makes any difference now."

But Ben Price acted rather strangely.

"I guess you're mistaken, Mr. Spencer," Price said. "I don't believe I know you."

Then Ben Price turned and walked down the street.

READING COMPREHENSION

Summarizing. Choose the best phrase to complete each sentence. Then write the complete statements on your paper.

1. Jimmy Valentine became Ralph Spencer because he _____ (planned to commit more burglaries, fell in love with Annabel, disliked his old name).

2. If Jimmy hadn't opened the bank vault, _____ (Agatha would probably have died, Ben Price would never have found Jimmy, Annabel would probably have run away).

3. Ben Price did not arrest Jimmy because he _____ (saw that Jimmy had changed, did not recognize him, was afraid to).

Interpreting. Write the answer to each question on your paper.

1. How could Ben Price tell that Jimmy was guilty of several recent burglaries?

2. Why did Jimmy have his burglar's tools with him when Agatha was locked in the bank vault?

3. Why did Jimmy open the bank vault when he expected to be arrested for doing so?

For Thinking and Discussing

1. Can people change their lives as much and as suddenly as Jimmy did?

2. Did Ben Price do the right thing by letting Jimmy, a known criminal, escape?

UNDERSTANDING LITERATURE

Plot. Every story has a *plot*. The plot is a sequence of events that makes a point, or brings out a reaction in the reader.

Here are some events about "The Safe-cracker." But they are out of order. On your paper, write them in the correct order. Look back in the story if you want.

"Jimmy Valentine looked into her eyes and became another man."

"The losses were now high enough to bring Ben Price into the case."

" 'I guess you're mistaken, Mr. Spencer,' Price said. 'I don't believe I know you.' " now.'"

"The warden handed Jimmy his pardon."

Jimmy quit the old business.

Here are some headlines that might have appeared in a newspaper. Write the headlines in the correct order.

Logansport Safe Not Very Safe

Governor Pardons Valentine

Child Rescued From Elmore Safe

Elmore Woman to Wed Businessman

Ben Price Called Into Safecracking Case

WRITING

Imagine you are Jimmy Valentine. Write a letter to your friend, Mike Dolan. Explain the important events in your life from the time you arrived in Elmore through the day you rescued the girl from the safe.

A Service of Love

by O. Henry

O. Henry liked to write about artistic young people trying to make names for themselves in New York City. Joe and Delia were talented, ambitious, and in love. But like many of O. Henry's characters, they were also poor. And poverty put their love to a real test.

Joe Larrabee found out that he was an artist when he was only six years old. It was a windy day, and the mayor of the little Midwestern town rushed past Joe's house. Joe drew a picture of the mayor, looking as if the wind were driving him down the street. Everybody thought it was wonderful. It was framed and hung in the window of the one drugstore on Main Street.

By the time Joe was 20, there was a whole row of his pictures in the window. He was expected, of course, to go to New York and become famous.

Delia Caruthers could play the piano. Everyone in her pine-tree Southern village agreed that she would have a great future. When she was 18, all her relatives chipped in to send her North to study music.

Joe and Delia met in a cafeteria where penny-counting students ate cheap meals. The two young people smiled at each other over the franks and beans. Over the rice pudding, they fell in love. And they got married.

They found a tiny furnished apartment. It was five flights up, and shabby. But they loved it, and each other. Every morning Joe kissed Delia good-bye and went to art class. The great Magister, whose pictures hung in museums all over the world, was his teacher. Delia left the breakfast dishes for Joe to wash, and hurried downtown. There she was studying under a famous concert pianist named Rosenstock.

They knew that Joe's pictures would soon sell for thousands. They knew that Delia, dressed in white, would soon be walking out onto a stage to the tune of wild applause. But a problem began to develop.

The kind relatives who took up a collection for Delia had been thinking of life in a sleepy Southern town. Life and music lessons in Manhattan ate up the money in a third of the time they had planned for. And Joe's savings melted like a frozen custard under a New York summer sun. Rosenstock and Magister began to hint that students were supposed to pay.

"I will simply have to give music lessons," Delia said. "I'll put an ad in the Greenwich Village paper. After I get two or three pupils, I will go back to my classes with Herr Rosenstock."

"But what about me?" Joe said. "I can't let you give up your lessons to pay for mine. I'll have to find a job, too."

"You will not," said Delia firmly. "After all, it's different with me. While I teach, I learn. I'm never away from music. We'll manage just fine. You are going on with Mr. Magister."

Two or three days later, Delia met Joe at the door, her eyes shining.

"I've got a pupil!" she said. "And guess who? General A. B. Pinkney's daughter! Her name is Clementina. They live in the most beautiful house on East 71st Street. And the General didn't even ask how much I charged. He said he'd pay $15 a lesson. Three times a week! Just a few more pupils and I can go back to Herr Rosenstock. Don't look so serious. I'm going to love teaching. Two of your pictures are hanging in that shop window down on 8th Street. One of them is sure to sell soon."

"I know, but I don't like the idea of my wife supporting me," Joe said.

All week Delia came home bubbling with stories about the Pinkneys. "Sometimes," she said, "Clementina seems a little slow. She doesn't practice enough. But the General is the dearest old man! He comes in and listens while I'm teaching. I wish you could meet him."

She described the furnishings in the Pinkney flat, and Clementina's clothes. She imitated the General's accent. And at the end of the week, she tossed two $20 bills and one five on the table.

But Joe was not to be outdone. He took out his wallet, and threw two $20 bills on the table beside Delia's money.

"Sold that watercolor of the Washington Square Arch to a man from Peoria," he said, trying to sound casual.

"Joe!" Delia gasped. "A man from Peoria, of all places?"

"Heavy man dressed in a checked suit. Wouldn't have thought he was an art lover. But he saw my sketch in the window and went in and bought it. And — the best is yet to come. He asked me to make him a sketch of the Flatiron Building. Guess how much he's going to pay for that? Fifty dollars!"

On the following Saturday, Joe got home first. He put $50 on the table. Then he went into the kitchen and washed his hands for a long time. He seemed to have been using a very dark paint.

Half an hour later, Delia came in. Her right hand was tied up in a bundle of bandages.

"Darling," Joe cried. "What happened? Are you hurt?"

"It's better now," Delia said, but there were traces of tears on her face. "Clementina wanted some hot chocolate after her lesson. The General was there, and he said he'd make it. With all their servants! But he went out, and a while later came back with a big silver pot and china cups. He poured out a cup and handed it to me — and somehow it spilled all over my hand. It was really *hot*. Boiling. Oh, the General

and Clementina were almost crazy. The old man rushed downstairs and sent somebody — the furnace man, I think — out to the drugstore for oil and bandages."

Joe took the tied-up hand tenderly. He pulled at some white strands under the bandages.

"What's this stuff?" he said.

"Oh, something soft that had oil on it," Delia said. She looked at the table. "Joe! The man from Peoria paid for the sketch!"

"Yes. And he thinks he wants a picture of the skating rink in Central Park and then a view of the Hudson. Delia, what time this afternoon did you burn your hand?"

"It must have been about five," Delia said. "The iron — I mean the General brought the silver pot in about then. You should have seen him, Joe, when he — "

"Delia, sit down," Joe interrupted. He pushed her gently into a chair. "What have you really been doing these past two weeks?" he asked.

Delia's face turned red. She tried to say something about "General Pinkney." But she saw that it was no use.

"I couldn't get any pupils," she said. "Nobody answered my ad at all. And I couldn't let you give up your lessons. So I took a job ironing shirts in a laundry. This afternoon, a girl in the laundry set a hot iron down on my hand. All the way home I practiced that story about the General and the hot chocolate. You're not angry, are you, Joe? If I hadn't gone to work, you might not have sold those pictures to the man from Peoria."

"He wasn't from Peoria," Joe said slowly.

"Who cares where he was *from*? Joe — what made you suspect I wasn't giving music lessons to Clementina?"

"I didn't," Joe said, "until tonight. I believed every word you said. But this afternoon, I sent up this cotton and oil from the furnace room for a girl whose hand had been burned with an iron. I've been working in the basement of that laundry for the last two weeks."

"Joe!" Delia said. "Then — the man who bought the pictures — "

"Was just as real as General Pinkney and Clementina," Joe said.

They looked at each other. And soon the next-door neighbors began to wonder what the young Larrabees had found to laugh about so long.

READING COMPREHENSION

Summarizing. Choose the best phrase to complete each sentence. Then write the complete statements on your paper.

1. It was very important to Joe and Delia to _____ (earn a lot of money, compete with each other, develop their talents in art and music).

2. After Delia found work and brought home some money, Joe _____ (was angry, told Delia to quit her job, said he had sold a painting).

3. Joe knew that Delia's story about burning her hand wasn't true because

_____ (he had sent up the bandages himself, Delia loved to make up stories, Joe knew General Pinkney).

4. Delia and Joe lied to each other about their jobs because they _____ (wanted to help each other feel better, often lied to each other, didn't think they'd get caught).

Interpreting. Write the answer to each question on your paper.

1. Why didn't Delia give piano lessons instead of working in a laundry?

2. Why did Joe begin working in the furnace room?

3. What is the first clue for Joe that Delia has been lying about her job?

4. Why did Delia and Joe laugh at the end of the story?

5. Joe and Delia loved their artistic goals and loved each other. Which love proved more important?

For Thinking and Discussing

1. Most people believe that lying is wrong. Yet Joe and Delia both lied, thinking they were being helpful. Were they doing something wrong? What would have happened if they had told the truth?

2. Could Joe and Delia have taken turns working? Can you think of other ways they might have solved their problem?

3. What do you think they learned about lying and telling the truth?

UNDERSTANDING LITERATURE

Plot. In some stories, there is a *surprise ending*. The story does not turn out the way you expected. A surprise ending occurs when the reader, or the characters in the story, are surprised by what happens.

O. Henry's stories often have surprise endings. In "A Service of Love," the surprise is shown in stages, or parts. Each stage is important to the surprise, but the whole surprise is not shown until the end of the story.

The following events are clues to the surprise at the end of the story. Write the clues on your paper in the correct order. Look back in the story if you need to.

Delia explains to Joe that she took the job in the laundry to pay for his painting lessons.

Delia realizes that Joe had made up the story about selling his paintings to a man from Peoria.

Joe recognizes the soft cloth with oil under Delia's bandages.

Delia tells Joe that the accident happened about five o'clock.

Joe explains to Delia how he found out about her working in the laundry.

WRITING

Imagine that you are Delia. You realize that Joe probably knows you are making up the story about Clementina and the General. Write what you would say.

Pancakes

a play based on a story by O. Henry

There's an old saying: "All's fair in love and war." The cowboy hero of "Pancakes" believed it. But he forgot that two people can play the same game. (Note: "gastronomical" means "having to do with food.")

CHARACTERS

Jud Lomax, a cook who was once a cowboy
Pete, a cowboy
Aunt Emma Telfair, a storekeeper
Willella Learight, her niece
José, a customer
Jackson Bird, a sheep rancher

Scene One

A camp during roundup time in cattle country. Jud is sitting next to the cook wagon. Pete comes over. He walks with a limp.

Jud: Good afternoon to yer, Pete. How's the ankle?
Pete: Getting better. Are you waiting for the men to ride in?
Jud: Oh, there's a bit of time before I have to cook their supper.
Pete *(sitting):* Jud, can you make pancakes?
Jud *(suspiciously):* What?
Pete: Pancakes. Can you make 'em?

Jud: Do you mean that straight, feller? Or did the boys tell you about that pancake business?
Pete: No, Jud. I mean it. Sitting here all day, a kind of craving came over me. I'd swap my pony for a stack of hot pancakes and sweet syrup.
Jud: Oh, I thought maybe you had another meaning.
Pete: Is there some story about pancakes?
Jud: No, not a story. *(He takes some bags from the cook wagon.)* Just a few facts in the case of me — and that sheepherder — and Miss Willella Learight. I don't mind telling you. You see, I was punching then for old Bill Toomey, on the San Miguel Ranch. One day I had a craving something like yours. . . .

Scene Two

The porch outside Aunt Emma's store in Pimienta. Jud, eight years younger, comes out of the store. He holds four open tin cans and a spoon. Aunt Emma comes out after him.

Emma: My word, Jud. I'm happy to sell you some grub. But why do you want to eat apricots, pineapple, cherries, and plums — all at the same time?

Jud *(eating the fruit):* I couldn't help myself, Emma. I had to ride in here today. It was time for a change in my dining habits. I just had to taste something that never went "moo" or "baa" or "oink."

Willella *(coming up the stairs to the porch):* Good morning, Aunt Emma.

(Jud's mouth drops open.)

Emma: Hello, child. Did you have a nice walk around town?

Jud *(grabbing Emma's arm):* Who is this, Emma?

Emma: This is my niece, Miss Willella Learight. She's down from Paradise on a visit.

Jud *(grinning):* Well, that's where the angels come from. Howdy, Miss Willella.

Emma: This here is Jud Lomax, Willella.

Willella: How do you do? I see you have a liking for apricots and plums.

Jud: It was apples that got some other folks sent out of Paradise, Miss Willella. Is that what brings you to Pimienta?

Willella: No, Mr. Lomax. I'm just visiting my aunt. This hot climate is good for my health.

Emma: And I'm an old devil down here. Well, I think you young people are likely to get even sillier. I ain't staying around to see it. *(She goes into the store.)*

Willella: What do you do when you're not eating fruit, Mr. Lomax? Are you a sheepherder?

Jud: I heard the words. But I don't believe 'em. Is there something wrong with your pretty blue eyes? Do I look like a scrawny, pink-livered wool-catcher?

Willella: Then you must be in the cattle business.

Jud: Now you are improving in judgment, Miss Willella. I knew your mind had to be as excellent as your outward appearance.

Willella: Why, thank you, Mr. Lomax.

Jud *(with a big grin):* Why don't you call me Jud?

Scene Three

Aunt Emma comes out of the store with José, a customer.

Emma: It's good to see you again, José. I hope your wife likes that cloth. *(She sits in a rocking chair and lights her pipe.)*

José: I'm sure she'll like it, Aunt Emma. How is your niece?

Emma: Oh, her health is real good. The climate agrees with her. *(A horse is heard riding up.)* She's made some friends, too.

José: Who is this riding up here?

Emma: One of Willella's friends. A darn fool.

José: Well, adiós, Aunt Emma.

Emma: Adiós, *(José goes.)*

Jud *(offstage):* Hold on there, Sally. I won't be more than two or three hours. *(He walks onto the porch.)* Howdy, Emma.

Emma: Howdy, Jud. You come by more regular than the Houston stage. What brings you here today? Apricots or peaches?

Jud: None of your jokes, Aunt Emma. You know why I've been packing my range-weary bones over here twice a week. It ain't to watch you smoke that corncob of yours.

Emma: Ain't it? Well, you're no gentleman then, Jud Lomax. I wouldn't let you see my niece, even if she was here.

Jud: She ain't? Well, where is she?

Emma: She went riding with Jackson Bird, the sheep man from Muddy Mule.

Jud: No! *(Shouting to his horse)* Did you hear that, Sally? She's gone riding with Birdstone Jackbird, the hired mule from

Muddy Sheep! Don't that make you weep, old cow pony?

Emma: Calm down, Jud.

Jud: You said a sheep man, didn't you?

Emma: I said a sheep man. You must have heard tell of Jackson Bird. He's got 4,000 head of the finest merinos south of the Arctic Circle. He's called here a few times, same as you.

Jud: How can this happen to me, Aunt Emma? What can I do? I never believed

30

in hurting a sheep man. I always let them go their ways, just as you would a skunk. I always been kind and let them live. And look what happens! Gosh durn it!

Emma: Well, you can curse all day if you want to, Jud. I got some accounts inside that need to be added up.

(She goes inside. Jud sits on the porch stairs.)

Jud: Sally, ain't life a mystery? I saw a sheep man once, carrying an umbrella in a little thunderstorm. And I vowed to protect all sheep men. I wouldn't so much as *spit* on one of them. And here comes a sheep man, riding off with Miss Willella Learight!

(Horses are heard riding up. Willella enters with Jackson Bird. Jackson wears fancy clothes. Jud stands up.)

Jackson: And then I put a rope around that old ram —

Jud: Howdy, Miss Willella!

Willella: Why, hello, Mr. Lomax. This is —

Jud: How are you today, Miss Willella?

Willella: Just fine, Mr. Lomax.

Jackson: I don't think —

Jud: Your aunt is waiting for you, Miss Willella.

Willella: Well, thank you, Mr. Lomax. Excuse me, Mr. Bird. *(She goes inside. Jackson holds his hand out to Jud. Jud doesn't shake it.)*

Jackson: I don't think I've had the pleasure, Mr. —

Jud *(stepping up close to Jackson)*: The name is known as Dead-Eye Jud — on account of the way I shoot. When I want a stranger to know me, I always introduce myself before the draw. I never did like to shake hands with a *ghost*.

Jackson: I see.

Jud: My, that's a pretty silk handkerchief you got around your neck. Where's yer umbrella?

Jackson: I'm glad to know you, Mr. Dead-Eye. I'm Jackson Bird, from the Muddy Mule Ranch.

Jud: Hey!

Jackson: Yes?

Jud: You see that rabbit-hawk up there?

Jackson *(looking up)*: Yes. *(Jud draws his gun and shoots. The bird drops down near the porch.)*

Jud: *Birds* just seem to draw my fire, Mr. Birdstone.

Jackson: Nice shooting. Say, wasn't that a fine rain last week for the young grass?

Jud *(grabbing Jackson's necktie)*: Birdstone, let's stop analyzing the weather. You seem to have a bad habit of riding with young ladies. I've known birds that were stuffed and roasted for less than that. Now, Miss Willella don't want any nest made out of sheep's wool from a Muddy Mule. Are you going to quit? Or do you wish for to measure yourself against my title of Dead-Eye? Step right up. My offer is good for a peck of birdseed and a real pretty gravestone.

Jackson *(laughing)*: Why, Mr. Dead-Eye. You've got the wrong idea. I've called on Miss Learight a few times. But not for the reason you think. My aim is simply a gastronomical one.

Jud *(reaching for his gun)*: You coyote! To talk that way about Miss Willella!

Jackson: Wait a minute. Let me explain. What would I do with a wife? If you ever saw that ranch of mine! I do my own cooking and mending. My only pleasure in life is from cooking. Mr. Dead-Eye, did you ever taste the pancakes that Miss Learight makes?

Jud: No.

Jackson: They're golden sunshine. I'd give two years of my life to get the recipe. That's what I came to see Miss Learight for. But she won't give it up.

Jud: That's all you want?

Jackson: The recipe's been in the family for 75 years. They don't give it away to outsiders. If I could get that recipe, I'd be a happy man.

Jud: Are you sure that you ain't after the hand that mixes the batter?

Jackson: Sure. Miss Learight is a mighty nice girl. But I tell you my interest in her is gastro —

Jud: Watch yer language.

Jackson: My interest is in owning a copy of that recipe.

Jud: You know, you ain't such a bad little man. I was thinking of making orphans of your sheep, but I'll let you fly away this time. But you stick to them pancakes. Or they'll be singing hymns at your ranch, and you won't hear 'em.

Jackson: To prove that I mean it, I'll ask you to help me. Miss Learight is your close friend. Maybe she'll give the recipe to you. Get me a copy of that pancake recipe, and I'll never call on her again.

Jud: That's fair. (He shakes hands with Jackson.) I'll get it for you.

Jackson: I'll be off in a minute. First, I must pay my respects to Miss Emma. (He goes into the store.)

Jud: Yippee! You hear that, Sally? Miss Willella is safe from the big bad sheep! And I didn't even have to shoot this Mr. Birdstone. (Willella and Jackson come out of the store.)

Jackson: Good day, Miss Willella.

Willella: Good-bye, Mr. Bird.

(Jackson starts walking off. As he passes Jud, he winks. Jud winks back. Jackson goes.)

Jud: Take care of yourself, you sweet little lamb! (Jackson's horse is heard riding off.)

Willella: Did you and Mr. Bird get to know one another, Mr. Lomax?

Jud: Now, look here, Willella. You know me good enough to call me Jud.

Willella: Yes, Jud. Did you have a pleasant talk with Mr. Bird?

Jud: Oh, sure. We understand each other right well.

Willella: I'm glad of that. Oh, look at that rabbit-hawk flying around up there. Do you see it?

Jud: Sure.

Willella: What does it make you think of?

Jud: Pancakes.

Willella: Oh, no! (Nervously) Did you say pancakes?

Jud: There's nothing I like better than a nice hot pancake under some molasses.

Willella: Tell me, Jud — how are your cows?

Jud: My cows? They're fine. They're as peaceful as a stack of pancakes. You know what I mean? (He winks.)

Willella: I think so.

Jud: Come on now, Willella. Let's hear how you make 'em. Pancakes are spinning around in my head like wagon wheels.

Willella *(afraid):* Pancakes?

Jud: Pancakes!

Willella *(calling inside):* Aunt Emma! Aunt Emma!

Jud: Are you going to give me the recipe?

Willella: Aunt Emma!

Emma *(coming out, holding a shotgun):* Here I am, child. Don't you worry none.

Jud: What's going on? All I did was ask about Willella's pancakes —

Emma: All right, Jud. Calm down. Try to think about something else. No one's going to hurt you.

Jud: What's that shotgun for, Aunt Emma?

Emma: Oh, there's a coyote around here. I don't want him taking after my chickens.

Jud: At four in the afternoon? You're both loco — making such a deal out of those pancakes.

Willella: Oh, Aunt Emma! *(She runs into Emma's arms.)*

Emma: Jud, you've upset this poor child something fierce. You better get back to your ranch.

Jud: But all I did was ask about those pancakes — *(Emma points the shotgun at him.)* All right. I'm going.

(He leaves. His horse is heard riding off. Emma leads her niece into the store.)

Scene Four

Jackson Bird comes out of the store. A horse is heard riding up. Jud enters, carrying a bunch of flowers.

Jud: Howdy, Jackson! Got the secret of them flapjacks yet?

Jackson: No, I don't seem to have any luck. Did you get a chance to ask?

Jud: I did. But it's like trying to dig a prairie dog out of his hole with a peanut shell.

Jackson: I'm almost ready to give up.

Jud: You keep trying, and I'll do the same. It's a real dilemma. But one of us will get a rope over its horns before too long.

Jackson: I hope so. Well, good-bye, Jud.

Jud: Good-bye, Jackson. (*Jackson goes. His horse is heard riding off.*) Poor feller. (*Calling into the store*) Aunt Emma!

Emma (*coming out*): What is it, Jud? It's sure busy with one of you fellers after

Look, Aunt Emma. Do you know how to make them pancakes?

Emma *(worried):* Look here, Jud. You've been riding in the sun. Do you want a drink of water? Cool off your brain a little.

Jud: There you go — always changing the subject. Can't you urge Willella a little? Tell her to give me that pancake recipe. *(Willella opens the door.)* Howdy, Willella!

Willella: Jud Lomax, are you talking about that subject again?

Jud: I'll stop, Willella.

Willella *(coming out):* Then I'm happy to see you. You promise you'll stop?

Jud: If you give me the recipe — please! *(The two women rush into the store and slam the door shut.)* Sally, some folks are crazy around these parts! *(He throws the flowers down.)* Gosh durn it!

Scene Five

Aunt Emma is sitting on the porch, smoking her pipe. Jud enters.

Jud: Howdy, Aunt Emma. How's my favorite storekeeper?

Emma: Fit as a mountain lion, Jud. Say, have you heard the news?

Jud: What?

Emma: Willella and Jackson Bird was married in Paradise two days ago. I just got a letter this morning.

Jud: No!

Emma: That's what they said.

Jud: My hearing is wrong, Aunt Emma. You must have said that the price of steers is down.

another calling on Willella. I wish I had as many customers.

Jud: Shut the door, Emma. I don't want Willella to hear.

Emma: All right. *(She closes the door.)*

Jud: You got to help me. And you won't just be helping me. You'll be helping one of the nicest sheep men in these prairies.

Emma: Married yesterday. Didn't you see none of the signs all along? Jackson Bird has been courting Willella ever since that day he took her out riding.

Jud: Then what was all the sassafras he gave me about pancakes?

Emma: Oh, no Jud! Keep a cool head on.

Jud: Tell me, Emma! Does Willella make pancakes?

Emma: She never made one in her life, Jud. That wound in your head is upsetting your brain. Try not to think about pancakes.

Jud: Aunt Emma, I'm not wounded in the head. But I figure I *have* been awful stupid. Jackson Bird told me he was calling on Willella so he could find out her pancake recipe.

Emma (*chuckling*): Well, well.

Jud: He asked me to help him. I done so, with the results as you see. Have I been fleeced by a fancy-dressed sheepherder?

Emma: It looks that way, Jud. That day he went riding with Willella, he came back in the store. He told us to watch out if you got to talking about pancakes. He said you was in camp once, and they was cooking flapjacks. A feller, Jackson said, cut you over the head with a frying pan.

Jud: Oh, no!

Emma (*chuckling*): He said when you get excited or hot, the wound hurts you. You go kind of crazy, and you keep going on about pancakes. He said to get you to change the subject. Then you wouldn't be dangerous. So we did the best we knew how. Well, that Jackson Bird is sure one clever sheep man.

Jud (*sadly*): He sure is, Aunt Emma. He sure is. Gosh durn it! (*He goes.*)

Scene Six

At the roundup camp.

Jud: Well, that's the story. Here.

(*He gives Pete a tin plate of pancakes and syrup.*)

Pete: How long ago did these things happen?

Jud: Eight years ago this August. They're living on the Muddy Mule Ranch now. But I haven't seen neither of 'em since.

Pete: That low-down sheepherder.

Jud: Oh, I got over it. But the boys kept the racket up. All over the state. They still do.

Pete: These pancakes are good, Jud. Did you make them by the famous recipe?

Jud: Didn't I tell you there wasn't no recipe? But the boys kept hollering, "Pancakes." Making fun of me got them hungry for pancakes. So I cut this recipe out of a newspaper. How do they taste?

Pete: They're delicious, Jud. Why don't you have some?

Jud: Not me. I don't never eat 'em.

READING COMPREHENSION

Summarizing. Choose the best phrase to complete each sentence. Then write the complete statements on your paper.

1. Jackson told Jud that his aim with Willella was to _____ (marry her, learn her recipe for pancakes, teach her to cook pancakes).

2. When Jud talked about pancakes, Wil-

lella believed he was _____ (joking, dangerous, hungry).

3. Jud didn't get the recipe for Jackson because _____ (Jackson got it first, Jud hated pancakes, Willella didn't have one).

4. Jud found out he had been tricked _____ (while Jackson was courting Willella, after he became a cook for other cowboys, after Jackson and Willella were married).

5. Later, Jud would not _____ (speak to Emma, eat pancakes, cook pancakes).

Interpreting. Write the answer to each question on your paper.

1. Where did Jud finally get a recipe for pancakes?

2. Before that, why did he try to get a recipe for pancakes from Willella?

3. How did Jackson trick Jud?

4. Did Jud do anything to deserve being tricked?

For Thinking and Discussing

1. In this play, sheep ranchers and cattle ranchers didn't get along together. Can you think of a reason for this?

2. Jackson and Jud tried to keep each other away from Willella. What was the main difference between their methods? Which worked best?

3. Does cleverness usually win out over physical threats? Or is it usually the other way around?

UNDERSTANDING LITERATURE

Plot. In most stories and plays, the plot follows a plan. The plan can be divided into three parts. The first part is called the *rising action*. In this part, the action builds up and a problem or a situation develops. The second part is the *turning point*. This is usually an event that shows how the problem will be solved. The third part of the plot is called the *resolution*. This is the part where the problem is solved.

Write three headings on your paper: *rising action, turning point,* and *resolution.* Then read the list of events from "Pancakes" below. Under each heading, write the events that belong with that part of the plot.

Jud meets Willella and falls in love.

Jud finds out that Willella has married Jackson.

Jud finally learns how Jackson tricked him.

Jud agrees to help Jackson get a pancake recipe from Willella.

Jud threatens Jackson.

In "Pancakes," the plot includes a *flashback*. The play begins in the present and then flashes back to tell about the events that happened in the past. Which scenes in the play are part of the flashback?

WRITING

Pretend you are Jud Lomax. Explain why you don't like pancakes.

The Cop and the Anthem

by O. Henry

Soapy had a sure-fire way of getting a warm place to stay for the winter — warmer than the park bench he was now using as "home." Little did he know that he was in for a series of surprises.

On his bench in Madison Square, Soapy moved uneasily. When women without fur coats grow kind to their husbands, and when Soapy moves uneasily on his bench in the park, you know that winter is near at hand.

A dead leaf fell on Soapy's lap. That was Jack Frost's card, giving fair warning of his annual visit. Soapy realized that the time had come for him to find a warm place to stay during the winter.

Soapy's ambitions were not great. He wasn't dreaming of cruises or beaches. Three months on the Island — in Blackwell's Prison — was what he wanted. Three months of food, a bed, and good company was his desire.

For several years the prison had been his winter home. In Soapy's opinion the Law was kinder than Charity. The gifts of charity hurt his proud spirit. For every bed of charity he had to take a bath; for every meal of charity he had to answer all kinds of personal questions. It was better to be a guest of the law, which did not pry too much into a gentleman's private affairs.

There were many easy ways of getting to the Island. The best way was to eat at an expensive restaurant, then say you couldn't pay the bill. A policeman would take you away quietly. A judge would do the rest.

Soapy left his bench and walked up Broadway. He stopped before a fancy restaurant.

Soapy had confidence in himself. His face was shaved, his coat was clean, and his tie had been given to him by a lady missionary on Thanksgiving Day. He just hoped he could reach a table before the head waiter could see how ragged his shoes and trousers were.

Roast duck, thought Soapy, was just the thing — with a bottle of wine, and then some coffee and a cigar. But as Soapy stepped inside the restaurant, the head waiter spotted his frayed trousers and ancient shoes. Strong hands turned him back out to the sidewalk.

Soapy turned off Broadway. This did not seem to be the way to get arrested. He'd have to think of another route.

At the corner of Sixth Avenue a shop window glowed with electric lights. Soapy picked up a stone and hurled it through the glass. People came running around the corner, with a policeman in the lead. Soapy stood with his hands in his pockets, and smiled at the sight of brass buttons.

"Where's the man who did that?" asked the policeman.

"Don't you think I might have had something to do with it?" said Soapy in a friendly way.

The policeman paid no attention to

him. Men who smash windows don't stick around to chat with cops. The policeman saw a man down the block, running to catch a cab. With club in hand, he ran after the man. Soapy walked on, disgusted.

On the opposite side of the street was a simple restaurant. Here you could get plenty to eat for not much money. The bowls were thick and the soup was thin, but no one stared at Soapy's old shoes and trousers when he went in. He sat at a table and ate beefsteak, pancakes, doughnuts, and pie. Then he admitted to the waiter that he and money were like strangers.

"Now call a cop," said Soapy. "And don't keep a gentleman waiting."

"No cop for you," said the waiter. "Hey, Joe!"

Two waiters tossed Soapy onto his left ear on the sidewalk. He got up painfully and beat the dust from his clothes. Arrest seemed a mere dream. The Island seemed very far away.

Soapy walked five blocks before he tried again. A pretty young woman was standing before a shop window, looking with interest at some shaving mugs. Two yards away stood a tough-looking policeman.

It was Soapy's plan to pretend to make a pass at the well-dressed young woman. She would be shocked and frightened, and the policeman would take him away.

Soapy straightened his tie, set his hat at an angle, and walked over. He made eyes at her. He smiled and smirked and made fresh remarks. He saw that the policeman was watching. The young woman moved away a few steps. Soapy boldly followed.

"Come on, cupcake," he said. "Don't you want to take a walk with me?"

The woman faced him and winked. "Sure, sport," she said, smiling. "I'd have spoken sooner, but the cop was watching."

Soapy couldn't shake her off until the next corner. Then he ran until he came to the theater district. Here, women in furs and men in overcoats moved gaily in the cold air.

When Soapy saw a policeman, he decided to try for "disorderly conduct." He began to yell drunken nonsense. He danced and he howled.

The policeman remarked to a citizen, "It's one of those college boys celebrating a football victory. He's noisy, but no harm."

Soapy stopped yelling. Wouldn't he ever get to the prison on the Island? He buttoned his thin coat against the chilling wind.

Then he saw a well-dressed man buying a cigar in a cigar store. The man's silk umbrella was set by the door. Soapy stepped inside, took the umbrella, and walked off with it slowly. The man with the cigar followed quickly.

"That's my umbrella," he said sternly.

"Oh, is it?" said Soapy "Then why don't you call a policeman? There's one on the corner."

The policeman looked at the two men.

"Well," said the umbrella man, "you know how these mistakes happen. If it's your umbrella, I hope you'll excuse me. I found it this morning in a restaurant. But if it's yours —"

"Of course it's mine," said Soapy.

The policeman left to help a woman across the street. Soapy stamped off in a rage. He hurled the umbrella into a gutter and headed back to his park bench in Madison Square.

Soapy stopped when he came to an old church. Through a stained-glass window a soft light glowed, and sweet music drifted out to Soapy's ears. The church organ was playing an anthem that he had known in his younger days. He had known it when his life contained such things as mothers and roses and ambitions and friends and clean collars.

Suddenly Soapy had a change of heart. He viewed with horror the pit into which he had tumbled. He wanted to be decent again. He would pull himself out of the mud. There was still time. He wasn't too old. The anthem had changed him completely. Tomorrow he would get a job. He would —

Soapy felt a hand on his arm. It was the hand of a policeman.

"What are you doing here?" asked the officer.

"Nothing," said Soapy.

"Then come along," said the policeman.

"Guilty of vagrancy and loitering," said the judge the next morning. "Three months on the Island."

READING COMPREHENSION

Summarizing. Choose the best phrase to complete each sentence. Then write the complete statements on your paper.

1. Soapy was planning to spend the winter _____ (near a warm beach, in a shelter for homeless people, in prison).

2. Soapy ate in a restaurant without being able to pay for the meal, hoping to get _____ (a job washing dishes, a free meal, arrested).

3. When Soapy walked off with a man's umbrella, the man _____ (admitted it wasn't really his, grabbed it back, called a policeman).

4. When Soapy heard the church anthem, he decided to _____ (join the church, get married, get a job).

5. At that point, Soapy _____ (got a job, was arrested, found a fortune).

Interpreting. Write the answers to each question on your paper.

1. What three things would the Island provide for Soapy during the winter?

2. When Soapy entered the fancy restaurant, why was he turned away?

3. When he was finally arrested, was he trying to get arrested?

For Thinking and Discussing. What do you suppose Soapy's childhood was like? Why might he have become homeless?

UNDERSTANDING LITERATURE

Plot. A story is often made up of a series of events. What happens is sometimes different from what was expected. This is called an *ironic turn of events*. For example, in "The Cop and the Anthem," Soapy thought the best way to get arrested was to eat at an expensive restaurant, then say he couldn't pay the bill. Yet when he entered an expensive restaurant, he was turned away before he could order a meal.

Here are some ironic turns of events in "The Cop and the Anthem." But they are out of order. On your paper, write them in the correct order.

Soapy couldn't pay for a meal at a simple restaurant. When he told the waiter to call a cop, he was thrown out on his ear.

When Soapy took a man's umbrella and suggested he call a policeman, the man admitted he had "found" the umbrella.

When Soapy heard an anthem, he had a change of heart — but was arrested.

Soapy acted disorderly, but a policeman thought he was harmless.

Soapy pretended to make a pass at a young woman, thinking she'd make a fuss and he'd be arrested, but she didn't mind at all.

WRITING

Put yourself in Soapy's shoes. The judge has just sentenced you to three months in prison. Write what you would say in your defense.

Section Review

VOCABULARY

Comparisons. One way to describe something is to compare it to something else, or to say what it is *like*. Comparisons add emphasis to reading.

In "Pancakes," for example, Aunt Emma could have told Jud, "You've been coming by here a lot lately." Instead she said, "You come by more regular than the Houston stage." She compared Jud's visits to the stops made by the stagecoach.

Read these comparisons from the selections in Section 1. Then answer the questions on your paper.

1. Ben Price in "The Safecracker" said, "Look at that combination knob. It was pulled out as easy as pulling up a radish in wet weather." What did Ben think was *like* pulling up a radish?

2. In "A Service of Love," Joe's savings "melted like a frozen custard under a New York summer sun." What did his savings melt *like*?

3. Jud Lomax in "Pancakes" said getting the pancake recipe was "like trying to dig a prairie dog out of his hole with a peanut shell." What was getting the pancake recipe *like*?

4. In "The Cop and the Anthem," Soapy and "money were like strangers." What were Soapy and money *like*?

READING

Main Idea and Details. The *main idea* of a paragraph tells what the paragraph is mostly about. In the paragraph below, the main idea is written in italics.

Some people don't like O. Henry's stories. They say that the stories are too tricky. They think that the stories do not deal seriously with real life.

The *details* in the paragraph tell you more about the main idea. For example, "They say that the stories are too tricky. They think that the stories do not deal seriously with real life." These details tell *why* some people don't like the stories.

Number your paper from 1 to 4. After the number of each paragraph below, write the main idea. Then write the details that tell more about the main idea.

1. Porter learned a lot about people who came into the drugstore. He watched their actions and listened to their talk.

2. Mr. Adams was proud of the new vault. He showed everyone the steel bolts and special timelock.

3. Joe was running out of money. Life in the city was expensive. The music and art teachers began to hint that students were supposed to pay.

4. Soapy's ambitions were not great. He wasn't dreaming of cruises or beaches. Three months on the Island was what he needed.

WRITING

The Writing Process. Most writers use a process, or series of steps, to help them write. A good plan to follow involves four steps: (1) Set your goal, (2) make a plan, (3) write a first draft, and (4) revise. You will follow this plan to complete the writing assignment in each Section Review.

Step 1: Set Your Goal

In Step 1, you choose a topic and decide on your purpose. You also identify your audience.

First, choose one of the following topics:

☐ **a.** Willella's marriage to Jackson Bird in "Pancakes."

☐ **b.** The relationship between O. Henry's own life and Soapy's life in "The Cop and the Anthem."

Now decide what you want to say about the topic, or what your purpose is. Suppose you were writing about this topic: the ending in "The Safecracker." You might decide that your purpose was to tell why the ending was a surprise — or why it wasn't really such a surprise after all.

Write down your topic and purpose like this:

TOPIC: the ending of "The Safecracker."

PURPOSE: to tell why the ending is a surprise.

Finally, decide who is going to read what you write, or who your audience is.

Do you plan to have only your teacher and classmates read the story? Or will you share it with family members and other friends? If your readers have not read the story you're writing about, you will have to include more information.

Write a sentence telling who your readers are below your topic and purpose.

Step 2: Make a Plan

Now it is time to decide what you're going to say. Go through the story you plan to write about looking for events and statements that relate to your topic. If you were writing about why the ending of "The Safecracker" is a surprise, you would look for places where O. Henry threw you off the trail. You might note the parts of the story that showed how badly Ben Price wanted to arrest Jimmy Valentine, for example.

Step 3: Write the First Draft

Your first draft is not supposed to be a finished piece of writing. As you work on it, remember you are free to change anything later on. Use the list of points you made when you were planning, but don't feel bound by it. If something you planned doesn't work, discard it. If you think of other points you want to make, add them. You might try starting with a statement of your purpose or with the idea that interests you most. Here is an example of how you could begin a paper about the ending of "The Safecracker."

I was sure that Jimmy Valentine would never crack another safe. When he did, I was even more sure that Ben Price would arrest him on the spot.

You could follow this opening with examples from the story that tell why you were so sure.

Step 4: Revise

If possible, wait a day or two before you revise your paper. Then read it over, looking for ways to make it clearer and more effective. This may involve changing the order in which you present the information. It may mean rewriting sentences so that they are clearer. It may also mean adding or taking out certain ideas or details.

You should check to be sure that you have used complete sentences throughout. You should also watch for unnecessary words and cross them out.

You will probably have to go over your paper a number of times before you are satisfied. You may find that reading it aloud helps you find the spots that sound rough.

After you have revised your paper, proofread it. Look for mistakes in sentence structure, grammar, punctuation, and spelling. Finally, type your paper or copy it over neatly.

QUIZ

The following is a quiz for Section 1. Write the answers in complete sentences on your paper.

Reading Comprehension

1. O. Henry is famous for his short stories, especially the endings. What kind of endings did he often write?

2. In "The Safecracker," Jimmy Valentine did not plan to follow the warden's advice after he left jail. What proves that this statement is true?

3. In "A Service of Love," name the people Joe and Delia made up.

4. Although he was a cook, Jud never ate pancakes. Why not?

5. In "The Cop and the Anthem," how was Soapy's wish at the beginning different from his wish at the end?

Understanding Literature

6. In O. Henry's biography, find five events that were important in his life. Write the events in order.

7. What event is the turning point in the plot of "The Safecracker"?

8. What event is the turning point in the plot of "A Service of Love"?

9. Explain the trick that Jackson Bird played on Jud Lomax.

10. What event is the turning point in the plot of "The Cop and the Anthem"?

ACTIVITIES

Word Attack

1. Some of the words in the story below are written with their phonetic spellings. These words all appear in Section 1. Use the pronunciation key in the glossary (page 478) to help yourself "decode" the words. Write the words on your paper. Then write a sentence telling what all the words have in common.

My (nā′ bərz) have a (dô′ tər), named Isabel, who (thôt) she was a bird for about a week. It all started when her father (bôt) a canary for Isabel. The girl went (strāt) to the cage and started flapping her "wings." Her father had a terrible (frīt) when he saw Isabel standing on top of the refrigerator poised for (flīt). He grabbed the bird cage and (brôt) it — and the bird — back to the pet store, where he traded in the bird for a puppy.

2. The words below all appear in Section 1. Each one contains a *root word*. A root word is a word to which you can add one or more prefixes and suffixes to make other words. For example, if you add the prefix *re-* to the root word *pay*, you get *repay*. If you then add the suffix *-ment*, you get *repayment*. Find the root word in each of the following:

signature   uneasily   disorderly
combination   missionary   loitering

Speaking and Listening

With a group of your classmates, act out the scene in "The Safecracker" in which Jimmy Valentine opens the back vault to free Agatha. You will need people to play these characters: Ben Price, Jimmy Valentine, Mr. Adams, May, Agatha, Annabel, and Annabel's sister. Prepare to perform the scene for the entire class.

Researching

1. The entire plot of "Pancakes" depends on a recipe for pancakes, which is never given. Find out how to make pancakes by looking in a cookbook. Read the recipe and answer these questions:
   a. How much milk should you use?
   b. Which ingredients are sifted?
   c. How do you know when it's time to turn the pancakes?

With your family's permission, make pancakes for them, following the directions in the recipe.

2. Both "A Service of Love" and "The Cop and the Anthem" take place in New York City. List some of the places mentioned in the two stories. Find a map of New York City in an atlas. Find the story locations on the map.

Creating

The illustration on pages 20 and 21 of "The Safecracker" shows an almost burglar-proof bank vault. (Only Jimmy Valentine could break in.) Note all the locks and bolts on the door. Design a bank vault that even Jimmy can't conquer. Draw a diagram of the vault, showing the various parts. Then write instructions for locking and opening it.

47

DISCOVERY

Discoveries are made every day. Some change the world. But some change just one person. Could these discoveries be the most important?

Discovery

The theme of this section is discovery, not of new places, but of who you are and what other people are like.

Why is it important for you to know who you are? It is rewarding, and it is useful. The more you know about your strengths, the better you feel about yourself. The more you know about your shortcomings, the better you can overcome them or live with them. And the more in tune you are with your thoughts and feelings, the better you can handle problems that arise.

Why bother discovering what other people are like? This, too, is both rewarding and useful. It can be comforting, for instance, to learn that certain people share your hopes or your fears or your sense of humor. At the same time, it can be fun to learn about new "worlds" from people whose interests or backgrounds are very different from your own.

The stories and poems in this section are about young people who make discoveries about themselves — and others. The main characters have different backgrounds and goals. The situations they face vary a good deal. But they all discover important truths about themselves by interacting with other people.

In "The Sound of Annie's Silence," a high school student feels uncomfortable baby-sitting for a girl her age who doesn't talk. The baby-sitter's feelings change, though, when she finds out what they both have in common.

The narrator of "Thumbprint," a poem, has discovered that her fingerprints are like no one else's in the world. And if something as small as a thumbprint is special, think how special an entire human being is!

In "President Cleveland, Where Are You?" a boy wants nothing more than to win a baseball glove. Along the way, he learns that by giving up something important to a rival, he can obtain something even more important for his brother.

In "Ta-Na-E-Ka," a girl faces a test of survival. The way she handles it surprises her grandfather — and herself.

The narrator of "Grandfather," a poem, learned the traditions of her people from her grandfather. But who will now learn them from her? Is it possible to pass along old traditions in today's world?

Dealing with a sudden death in the family is the subject of "The Shirt." The younger brother of the victim discovers that grieving takes different forms. And he is finally comforted by the very person he has been resenting the most.

As you read these selections, watch for the discoveries the characters make. Perhaps you will make some discoveries of your own.

The Sound of Annie's Silence

by Phyllis Fair Cowell

A young girl's discomfort with Annie turns to love as she learns that all people have feelings — even when they can't say them aloud.

When I answered the ad, I had no idea what I was getting into. It sounded simple enough.

Wanted: Someone to stay with my daughter Mon.–Fri. afternoons 3:30–5:30. High school student preferred. $25/wk.

I called the number listed with the ad. The next day I met Mrs. Walters and her daughter, Annie.

Meeting Annie was a shock. Mrs. Walters led me to a girl sitting in the living room. I stood there, staring.

The girl I was supposed to watch was no child at all. Annie was my age!

"Hello," I finally muttered.

"Annie doesn't talk," Mrs. Walters said.

I realized that Annie was staring, too, but not at me. I wasn't sure if she was really looking at anything. I couldn't even tell if she knew I was there.

"What's wrong with her?" I asked.

Mrs. Walters tried to explain, but the long words were lost on me. I did understand that Annie went to a special school. In a few months, she would go to live

there. Until then, Mrs. Walters needed help with Annie.

"Someone has to watch Annie until I get home from work," she explained. "She likes being around people her own age. So I thought a student would be good for the job. Are you still interested?"

I thought for a second. Annie didn't seem to do much of anything. Watching her would be easier than babysitting.

"Sure," I said.

Mrs. Walters described the job. I would pick up the house keys at a neighbor's house. Annie's school bus would bring her home by 3:45. All I had to do was watch Annie until Mrs. Walters got home. If I had any problems, I could call on the neighbor for help.

I couldn't believe it. I could study or watch TV — and get paid for it. The job would be a breeze.

That's what I thought then.

That was before I heard the sound of Annie's silence.

I can't say just what it was like. At first

I thought she was watching me. That was silly. Annie stared, but I never knew what she saw with those eyes. It made it hard to ignore her.

I began doing things for her. I put her chair next to a window so she could stare at different things. I turned on the TV for her. Mostly, though, I tried not to think about her.

Annie had her good days and her bad days. On good days, she just sat. On bad days, she rocked back and forth. The chair legs would slam on the floor. Annie's head would bang on the wall behind her.

On one of Annie's bad days, I started talking to her. "Come on, Annie!" I said crossly, "Cut it out!"

I slammed my history book shut, but Annie kept rocking. I moved her away from the wall so she wouldn't hurt her head.

The rocking stopped. Now there was her silence again — and her staring. That was almost worse than the rocking and the banging. Suddenly, I couldn't stand it any longer. I grabbed my jacket and headed for the door.

Then I realized I couldn't just leave Annie there. But I had to get away from the walls that echoed her silence.

I shoved Annie's arms into her coat, and I pulled her outside with me. As soon

as Mrs. Walters got home, I decided, I was going to quit this crazy job.

Crazy was the word for it. Here I was, trying to get away from Annie. But instead, I was walking with her, and I was even holding her hand. I had to. If I didn't she would just stand there.

Crazier than that, I was still talking to her. "It's much better out here, isn't it?" I asked. Even though I knew she couldn't answer, I went on. "There's a lot more to see here than indoors. That's the new playground over there. And over there is the corner where I catch my bus home."

We got back to the house late. Mrs. Walters was already home. I wanted to tell her I was quitting, but she started talking first.

"It was so nice of you to take Annie for a walk," she said. "You don't have to do that, you know. You're so good with her. I appreciate that."

She kept saying things that made it hard to quit right then. I decided to quit the next day.

The next day came and went, and I said nothing about quitting. The whole week went by without my bringing it up.

Almost every day, I took Annie for a walk. If the weather was bad, I sat and looked out the window with her. All the time, I kept talking to her. It made her silence easier to bear.

I pointed out cars and people and buses. I talked about trees, birds, and even umbrellas. Every day I thought about quitting, but I did nothing about it.

My last day of work finally arrived. Annie would begin living at her school from now on. I could tell that Mrs. Walters was sad that Annie was moving away, but she tried not to show it.

"Annie's school runs a day camp during the summer," she told me. "They hire teenagers to help out. I've told them about you, and I'm sure you could get a job there."

Oh, no, I thought. I don't want to work with a lot of Annies.

Out loud I said, "Thank you, Mrs. Walters, but I already have a summer job." That was a lie.

When I left the house, I felt relieved. But I didn't feel as happy as I thought I would. When I missed my bus, I didn't care, I just felt numb.

I stood at the bus stop, wondering why I felt so bad. I had said good-bye to Annie quickly and without emotion. Then I had left as fast as I could.

Now I tried to look for something to cheer me up. I noticed the kids in the playground across the street. They all seemed happy — except for one girl. She was older than the others, and she stood outside the playground.

When I looked at her closely, I could see it was Annie. As I ran toward her, I wondered how she had gotten outside. She had never wandered away before. Maybe she felt my good-bye wasn't enough.

I threw my arms around her and gave her a hug. Then I took her hand, and we headed back to the house.

I began to feel happier. I knew what I would be doing this summer. My job with Annie hadn't been so bad, once I started treating her like the human being she was.

READING COMPREHENSION

Summarizing. Choose the best phrase to complete each sentence. Then write the complete statements on your paper.

1. At first, the narrator thought she would like the job because _____ (Annie would be fun, it would be easy, she liked taking care of people).

2. The narrator began talking to Annie because _____ (she wanted someone to listen to her, she wanted to fill the silence, Annie asked her to talk).

3. After she said good-bye to Annie, the narrator felt _____ (very happy, unhappy, worried about a new job).

4. The narrator realized she cared about Annie when _____ (Annie started talking to her, she said good-bye to Annie, she sensed Annie had feelings).

Interpreting. Write the answer to each question on your paper.

1. Why didn't Annie's mother watch her daughter on weekday afternoons?

2. Why did Annie need someone to watch her?

3. How did the narrator treat Annie at first? How did she treat her later?

For Thinking and Discussing

1. Would the narrator of this story be a good friend? Why or why not?

2. Do you think Annie could be saying something in her silence?

UNDERSTANDING LITERATURE

Characterization. The author often tells you about the characters, or the people in a story, by writing about what they do. The things characters do are called their *actions*. If you read a story in which a girl takes a stray dog, sets a rabbit free from a trap, and helps a sick bird get better, you would know that this person loves animals. The author wouldn't have to say, "She loved animals." You would know she loved animals from her actions.

There are two main characters in "The Sound of Annie's Silence." Answer the following questions about their actions.

1. The narrator of the story keeps saying she is going to quit her job. Instead, she does things for Annie. What does she do?

2. Does the narrator of the story seem kind? Does she seem to like Annie? Why or why not?

3. The narrator says that Annie never wandered away before. Why do you think Annie went to the park alone?

4. The narrator never says how she feels about Annie. What does she do at the end that shows how she feels?

WRITING

In this story, you never really know how Annie feels about the narrator. Write two things Annie might have done to show how she felt about her friend. Let Annie's actions speak for her.

Thumbprint

by Eve Merriam

In the heel of my thumb
are whorls, whirls, wheels
in a unique design:
mine alone.
What a treasure to own!
My own flesh, my own feelings.
No other, however grand or base,
can ever contain the same.
My signature,
thumbing the pages of my time.
My universe key,
my singularity.
Impress, implant
I am myself,
of all my atom parts I am the sum.
And out of my blood and my brain
I make my own interior weather,
my own sun and rain.
Imprint my mark upon the world,
whatever I shall become.

1. What do the police use fingerprints for? Why does the poet call her thumbprint "my signature"?

2. What does she mean by "my own interior weather"? Does she think she creates her own feelings, or are they imposed on her by others?

3. Does she believe that her life is ruled by fate? Or does she think she has some influence upon her life?

4. The poet often takes two or more words that begin with the same sound, and places them closely together. An example from this poem is "my blood and my brain." What other examples can you find?

5. Can you find lines that rhyme?

President Cleveland, Where Are You?

by Robert Cormier

Both Jerry and Rollie need only one more trading card to win the baseball glove. Jerry could win, but he has another problem — a brother who has always thought of others first.

That was the autumn of the cowboy cards. The cards came in those five-cent packs of bubble gum. You couldn't blow good bubbles with that gum, but it didn't matter. The cowboy cards mattered.

After school, we met in front of Lemire's Drugstore and traded the cards. Ken Maynard was the most popular movie cowboy of all. One of his cards was worth at least 10 of any other kind.

Rollie Tremaine had the most cards. He wouldn't trade his Ken Maynard cards, unless the other kids threatened not to trade with him at all.

You could almost hate Rollie Tremaine. First, he was the only son of a store owner. He did not live in a tenement like the rest of us. He lived in a big, white, birthday cake of a house.

Second, he was no good at football. So he couldn't help the Frenchtown Tigers — our team — beat the North Side Knights.

Worst of all, he made us aware that he always had money. He would walk into Lemire's and buy a quarter's worth of cowboy cards. The rest of us would watch with envy.

Once in a while, I earned a nickel or a dime by running errands for Mrs. Belander. Sometimes I found pieces of metal at the dump and sold them to the junkman. Then I'd race to Lemire's and buy a cowboy card or two.

One week I was especially lucky. I had gotten a quarter from Mrs. Belander. My father had worked a full week at the factory, so he gave each of us children a dime. With my 35 cents, I planned to put Rollie Tremaine to shame on Monday.

Monday was the best day to buy cards. That was when Lemire's got a new collection. That Monday, I ran home from school and changed my clothes. But when I tried to run outside, my brother Armand blocked my way.

He was 14, three years older than I. He was no longer interested in things like cowboy cards and the Frenchtown Tigers.

59

"Wait a minute, Jerry," he said. "How much money have you got?"

"Are you in some kind of trouble?" I asked.

"No. It's Pa's birthday tomorrow. I think we kids ought to chip in and buy him something."

"Here," I said, handing him a nickel.

He looked at me with disgust. "Your sisters each gave me 15 cents. I'm throwing in a quarter. Paul gave me a dime — all he had left of his birthday money. Is a nickel all you can do?"

"I haven't got a Ken Maynard left," I said. "I was going to buy some cards today."

He asked, "Who's more important — Ken Maynard or your father?"

His question was unfair. He knew I had to answer, "My father."

I took a dime from my pocket and handed it to him.

"Thanks, Jerry," he said. "I hate to take your last cent."

"That's all right," I said. I didn't feel too bad because I still had 20 cents left.

When I got to Lemire's, Roger Lussier was outside. Rollie Tremaine was, too. They both looked glum.

"Save your money," Roger said.

"There aren't any more cowboy cards," Rollie explained.

"They're going to have President cards," Roger said. He pointed to the store window. "Look!"

A sign in the window said: "Watch for the new series. Presidents of the U.S. free in each five-cent package of Caramel Chew. Collect a complete set and win an Official Imitation Major League Baseball Glove."

The thought of owning a new baseball glove excited me. But I wondered who could become excited about Presidents. As I jingled the coins in my pocket, I felt guilty. I thought of how I had betrayed Armand and my father.

"I'll see you later," I said, and I hurried home. When I got there, I learned that Armand had already left to buy the present.

I raced my bike through the streets. Finally I saw Armand walk out of a shop, holding a thin package.

"Did you buy the present yet?" I asked, although I knew it was too late.

"Yes," he said. "It's a blue tie."

He looked at me for a long moment. Then he smiled sadly and touched my arm. I turned away from him because he knew the truth.

"It's all right," he said. "Maybe you've learned something."

A week before Christmas, everyone in my class got a high mark on a history essay. Our teacher didn't know we had become experts on the Presidents because of the cards we bought at Lemire's. Each card had a picture of a President on one side. On the other side was a biography. We looked at the cards so often that we knew the facts by heart.

The President cards were a success. In the first place, caramel candy came with the cards. We learned to stuff the candy into one side of our mouths. This made us look as if we were chewing tobacco, like a baseball star.

In the second place, competition for the cards was fierce. Everyone wanted to win the baseball glove. Certain cards, though, did not show up at Lemire's. Sometimes the deliveryman left boxes filled with cards of only one President.

One week, Roger Lussier and I rode our bikes to the North Side. We traded cards with some boys there, and we got five new Presidents. That made us heroes in Frenchtown.

Then the card company sent a sample glove to Mr. Lemire. He placed it in the window. I was sick with longing for it. But so was Rollie Tremaine.

Once Rollie spent 50 cents on cards. They all turned out to be Calvin Coolidge, and he threw them on the ground. Then he pulled some dollar bills from his pocket and said, "I'm going to buy that glove!"

"Look at what it says at the bottom of the sign," Roger said.

We all looked, although we knew the words by heart. It said: "This glove is not for sale."

Rollie picked up his cards from the sidewalk. After that, he never showed us his cards.

To me, the cards had become a comfort in a world that was suddenly gloomy. There was a layoff at the factory, and my father stopped getting a salary. The only money we got was from Armand's after-school job at the grocery store. But he lost his job when business went down because of the layoff.

My father kept saying he'd get his job back sooner or later. But he seemed to grow old before our eyes.

When he finally went back to work, another disaster took place. Armand fell in love.

I found this out by accident. I picked up a piece of paper from the floor of the bedroom we shared. I started to read the writing on it.

"Dear Sally, When I look into your eyes —"

The paper was pulled out of my hands before I finished reading.

"What's the big idea?" Armand demanded. "Can't a guy have any privacy?"

"It was on the floor," I said. "I didn't know it was a letter. Who is Sally?"

"If you tell anyone, I'll murder you. She's Sally Knowlton."

Nobody in Frenchtown had a name like Knowlton. "Is she from the North Side?" I asked, amazed.

"What's wrong with that?" he said angrily. "Do you think she's too good for me? I'm warning you, Jerry, if you tell anybody . . ."

"Don't worry," I said. Love seemed like a waste of time to me. But I was curious. "Why are you writing to her? Did she move?"

"No. I wasn't going to mail it. I just felt like writing to her."

I was glad I had never been involved with love. Love made you upset. It made you write letters you didn't plan to send.

I did not give away Armand's secret. I felt sorry for him, especially when he wouldn't eat much at supper. But I had other things to worry about.

I couldn't earn any more money from Mrs. Belander because she had moved away. And I needed only one more President to win the baseball glove. So did Roger Lussier and Rollie Tremaine. Each of us had a complete set of cards — except for Grover Cleveland. Each time a box of cards arrived at Lemire's, it never contained a Grover Cleveland. Was the card company playing fair?

Roger Lussier brought up a terrible thought. Grover Cleveland had been the 22nd and the 24th Presidents. Did we need two Grover Clevelands to complete the set?

We complained to Mr. Lemire. He became annoyed and said he'd never carry a new series again. But he went through his papers and found a list of rules.

"All right," he announced. "It says here you need only one Grover Cleveland. Now get out, unless you've got money to spend."

Outside the store, Rollie Tremaine said, "Boy, I'd give five dollars for a Grover Cleveland."

When I got home, Armand was sitting on the porch steps. He looked as unhappy as I was. I sat beside him and asked if he felt sick.

He finally told me what the matter was. There was going to be a big dance at Sally's high school next week. She had asked him to be her date.

"What's so bad about that?" I wanted to know.

"How can I take Sally to a dance?" He asked sadly. "I can't buy her a corsage. My shoes are falling apart. Pa's got too many worries to give me money for shoes or flowers."

"Yeah," I said. "Look at me. Baseball time is almost here. I need a new glove, but I can't find a Grover Cleveland card."

"They've got Grover Cleveland cards on the North Side," he said. "Some kid told me. He said they're looking for Warren G. Harding."

"I've got an extra Warren G. Harding!" I shouted.

I ran to my bike, swung onto the seat, and found that the front tire was flat. But Armand helped me fix it.

Within half an hour, I was at the North Side Drugstore. Several boys were trading cards outside. I said to myself, "President Cleveland, here I come!"

Next week, Armand went to the dance. He was all dressed up as if it were Sunday. He wore new shoes, and he carried a corsage in a florist's box.

After he left, I sat on the porch railing. I remembered the silly look on his face when he had looked in the mirror. I thought that love was really dumb.

I turned at the sound of footsteps. Roger Lussier appeared, looking angry.

I said, "I thought you were at baseball practice."

"I was," he said, "but I couldn't stand Rollie Tremaine. Why did he have to be the one to get a Grover Cleveland? You should see him showing off. He won't let anybody even touch that glove."

I felt like a traitor. I had to confess what I had done.

"I got a Grover Cleveland card on the North Side," I said. "I sold it to Rollie for five dollars."

"Are you crazy?"

"I needed the five dollars. It was an emergency."

"Why did you have to do a thing like that?" He turned and began to walk away.

"Hey, Roger!" I called.

He looked back at me as if I were a stranger. "What?" he asked.

"I had to do it!"

He didn't answer. He walked to the fence behind our house, moved a loose board, and slipped through.

I felt betrayed. Wasn't I supposed to feel good about doing something fine and noble?

A moment later, Roger's face appeared over the top of the fence. "Was it a real emergency?" he yelled.

"Yes! It was really important!"

His face dropped from sight, and I heard him call, "All right!"

"See you tomorrow!" I yelled.

It was beginning to get dark. The darkness made the edges of the fence and the rooftops look softer. I sat there a long time, waiting for the good feeling to come.

READING COMPREHENSION

Summarizing. Choose the best phrase to complete each sentence. Then write the complete statements on your paper.

1. When Armand wanted to buy the birthday present, Jerry _____ (gave him all his money, wouldn't give him any money, kept most of his money for himself).

2. Jerry needed a Grover Cleveland card to _____ (trade with Roger, get a job at Lemire's, win a baseball glove).

3. Armand was able to take Sally to the dance because _____ (he got a new job, Jerry sold the Grover Cleveland card to Rollie, Rollie lent him the money).

Interpreting. Write the answer to each question on your paper.

1. Why couldn't Rollie buy the baseball glove in Lemire's window?

2. How did Jerry finally get a Grover Cleveland card?

3. Was Jerry generous with his money at the beginning of the story? At the end?

For Thinking and Discussing

1. The narrator said, "The cards had become a comfort in a world that was suddenly gloomy." What did he mean?

2. Have you ever done something selfish and felt guilty later? Did you try to make up for it by being generous?

UNDERSTANDING LITERATURE

Characterization. It is important to pay attention to the author's *description* of the characters in a story. A description includes all the words an author uses to tell you how a character looks, speaks, and acts. A description of a character helps you make a picture of the person in your mind.

Read the following descriptions from "President Cleveland, Where Are You?" In your mind, try to make up a picture of each character. Then answer the questions.

> You could almost hate Rollie Tremaine. First, he was the only son of a store owner. He did not live in a tenement like the rest of us. He lived in a big, white, birthday cake house. Second, he was no good at football.

1. How do you picture Rollie's house?

2. Does this description help you picture Rollie himself? How do you think Rollie looks? How do you think he dresses?

> My father kept saying he'd get his job back sooner or later. But he seemed to grow old before our eyes.

3. Can someone grow old before your eyes? What do you think this expression means?

4. How do you picture Jerry's father?

> Next week, Armand went to the dance. He was all dressed up as if it were Sunday. He wore new shoes, and he carried a corsage in a florist's box.

5. Write two or three sentences about what you think Armand is wearing. How do you think Armand's face looks?

The *dialogue*, or words the characters say to each other, can also tell you a lot about them. Read the following dialogue taken from the story. Then answer the questions.

> Mr. Lemire said, "It says here you need only Grover Cleveland. Now get out, unless you've got money to spend."

6. What do these words tell you about Mr. Lemire?

> Armand said to Jerry, "It's all right. Maybe you've learned something."

7. How do you think Armand feels toward his brother? Is Armand an understanding person?

> Roger said about Rollie, "Why did he have to be the one to get a Grover Cleveland? You should see him showing off. He won't let anybody even touch that glove."

8. What does this say about Rollie?

9. Do you think Rollie would be a good friend? Why? What is Roger's opinion of Rollie?

WRITING

When Jerry gave Armand the money he got for the Grover Cleveland card, the author does not tell you what the brothers said to each other. What do you think they said? Write a short dialogue between Jerry and Armand. Use what you know about the characters to make their words sound real.

Ta-Na-E-Ka

by Mary Whitebird

*To be a Kaw Indian woman was a privilege. A Kaw woman
was the equal of any man. But she had to prove it — by
taking the same endurance test as the future warriors.*

*The test was called Ta-Na-E-Ka. According to tradition, it
was time for Mary to go through it. But Mary had some
untraditional ideas of her own.*

My birthday drew close, and I had awful nightmares about it. I was reaching the age at which all Kaw Indians had to participate in Ta-Na-E-Ka.

Well, not all Kaws. Many of the younger families were beginning to give up the old customs.

But my grandfather, Amos Deer Leg, was devoted to tradition. He still wore beaded moccasins instead of shoes. He still kept his gray hair in tight braids.

He could speak English, but he spoke it only with white men. With his family, he used a Sioux dialect.

Grandfather was one of the last living Indians who fought against the U.S. Cavalry. He was wounded in a battle at Rose Creek. At the time, my grandfather was only 11 years old.

Eleven was a magic word among the Kaws. It was the time of Ta-Na-E-Ka, the "flowering of adulthood." It was the age when a boy could prove himself to be a warrior, and a girl took the first steps to womanhood.

"I don't want to be a warrior," my cousin, Roger Deer Leg, told me. "I'm going to become an accountant."

"None of the other tribes make girls go through the endurance ritual," I told my mother.

"It won't be as bad as you think, Mary," my mother said. "Once you've gone through it, you'll never forget it. You'll be proud."

I even complained to my teacher, Mrs. Richardson. I felt that a white woman would side with me.

She didn't. "All of us have rituals of one kind or another," Mrs. Richardson said. "Besides, how many girls get to compete equally with boys? Don't look down on your heritage."

Heritage, indeed! I would not live on a reservation for the rest of my life. I was a good student. I loved school. My fantasies were about knights in armor. I didn't think that being an Indian was very exciting.

But I've always thought that the Kaw started the women's liberation movement. No other Indian tribe treated women more "equally" than the Kaw.

The Kaw allowed men and women to eat together. A Kaw woman always had the right to refuse a future husband. This was true even if her father had arranged the marriage.

The wisest old women often sat in tribal councils. Plus, most Kaw legends revolve around "Good Woman." She was a kind of super-squaw. Good Woman helped Kaw warriors win battle after battle.

And girls as well as boys had to go through Ta-Na-E-Ka.

The ceremony was different from tribe to tribe. But Ta-Na-E-Ka was a test of survival.

"Endurance is the highest quality of the Indian," my grandfather said. "To survive, we must endure. When I was a boy, Ta-Na-E-Ka was more than it is now.

"We were painted white with the juice of a sacred herb. We were sent naked into the wilderness without a knife. We couldn't return until the white had worn off. It took almost 18 days.

"We trapped food, and we ate insects and roots and berries. We watched out for enemies. Our enemies were the white soldiers and the Omaha warriors.

"These warriors were always trying to capture Kaw boys and girls during the endurance test. It was an exciting time," Grandfather said.

"What happened if you couldn't make it?" Roger asked. He was born only three days after I was. We were being trained for Ta-Na-E-Ka together. I was happy to know he was frightened, too.

"Many didn't return," Grandfather said. "Only the strongest and smartest. Mothers were not allowed to weep over those who didn't return."

"How stupid," Roger whispered. "I'd give anything to get out of it."

"What choice do we have?" I asked.

Roger gave my arm a little squeeze. "Well, it's only five days."

Five days! Maybe it was better than being sent out naked for 18 days. But not much better.

We were to be sent, barefoot and in bathing suits, into the woods. Our parents put their foot down when Grandfather suggested we go naked.

For five days, we'd have to live off the land. It was May. But the days were chilly on the northern banks of the Missouri River. The nights were freezing cold.

Grandfather was in charge of the month's training for Ta-Na-E-Ka. One day he caught a grasshopper. He showed us how to pull its legs and wings off. Then we were supposed to swallow it.

I felt sick, and Roger turned green. "It's a darn good thing it's 1947," I told Roger. "You'd make a terrible warrior."

I knew one thing. This Kaw Indian girl wasn't going to swallow a grasshopper. And then I had an idea. Why hadn't I thought of it before? It would have saved nights of bad dreams about squooshy grasshoppers.

I headed straight for my teacher's house. "Mrs. Richardson," I said, "would you lend me $5?"

"What for?" she asked.

"You remember the ceremony I talked about?"

"Ta-Na-E-Ka? Of course. Your parents asked me to excuse you from school for it."

"I need some things for the ceremony," I said. "I don't want to ask my parents for the money."

"It's not a crime to borrow money, Mary. But how can you pay it back?"

"I'll baby-sit for you 10 times."

"That's more than fair." She handed me a new $5 bill. I'd never had that much money at once.

A few days later, the ritual began with a long speech from my grandfather. All our friends and relatives made jokes about their own Ta-Na-E-Ka experiences.

They told us to have a large dinner. For the next five days, we'd be eating crickets. But Roger and I weren't very hungry.

"I'll laugh about this when I'm an accountant," Roger said, trembling.

"Are you trembling?" I asked.

"What do you think?"

"I'm happy to know boys tremble, too," I said.

At six the next morning, we set off for the woods.

"Which side do you want?" Roger asked.

Roger and I were supposed to stake out

separate territories. We weren't allowed to talk to each other.

"I'll go toward the river. That okay with you?" I asked.

"Sure," Roger said. "What difference does it make?"

To me, it made a lot of difference. There was a small harbor a few miles up the river. There were boats there. At least, I hoped so. I'd rather sleep in a boat than under a pile of leaves.

"Why do you keep holding your head?" Roger asked.

"Oh, nothing. Just nervous," I told him. I was afraid I'd lose the $5 bill. I had tucked it into my hair with a bobby pin.

As we came to a fork in the trail, Roger shook my hand. "Good luck, Mary."

"N'ko-n'ta," I said. It was the Kaw word for courage.

The sun was shining, and it was warm. But my bare feet began to hurt.

I saw one of the berry bushes Grandfather had told us about. The berries were orange and fat. I popped one into my mouth.

Argh! I spat it out. It was awful and bitter. Even grasshoppers were probably better tasting.

I sat down to rest my feet. A rabbit hopped out from under the berry bush. He looked at me, twitching his nose. I watched a woodpecker bore into an elm tree.

All of a sudden, I realized I was no

longer frightened. Ta-Na-E-Ka might be more fun than I had thought. I got up and headed toward the harbor.

"Not one boat," I said to myself.

But the restaurant on the shore was open. I walked in, feeling silly in my bathing suit.

The man at the counter was big and tough-looking. He had only three fingers on one of his hands. He asked me what I wanted.

"A hamburger and a milk shake," I said.

"That's a pretty big breakfast," he said.

"That's what I always have for breakfast," I lied.

"Forty-five cents," he said, bringing me the food. (Back in 1947, hamburgers were 25 cents, and milk shakes were 20 cents.)

"Delicious," I thought. "Better than grasshoppers. Grandfather didn't say I couldn't eat hamburgers."

While I was eating, I had a great idea. Why not sleep in the restaurant? I went to the ladies' room and made sure the window was unlocked. Then I went back outside and played along the riverbank.

The restaurant closed at sunset. I watched the three-fingered man drive away. Then I climbed in the unlocked window. There was a night-light on, so I didn't turn on any lights.

But there was a radio on the counter. I turned it on to a music program. It was warm in the restaurant, and I was hungry. I helped myself to a glass of milk and a piece of pie.

I planned to leave money for what I'd eaten. I also planned to get up early and sneak out the window.

I turned off the radio and wrapped myself in the man's apron. The floor was hard, but I soon fell asleep.

"What the heck are you doing here, kid?"

It was the man's voice.

It was morning. I'd overslept. I was scared.

"Hold it, kid. I just wanna know what you're doing here. You lost? You must be from the reservation. Your folks must be worried sick about you. Do they have a phone?"

"Yes, yes," I answered. "But don't call them." I was shivering.

The man — Ernie — made me a cup of hot chocolate. I explained about Ta-Na-E-Ka.

"Darnedest thing I ever heard," Ernie said. "Pretty silly thing to do to a kid."

That was just what I'd been thinking for months. But when Ernie said it, I became angry.

"No, it isn't silly. It's a custom of the Kaw. We've been doing this for hundreds of years," I said. "It's why the Kaw are great warriors."

"Okay, great warrior," Ernie laughed. "Suit yourself. And if you want to stick around, it's okay with me." Ernie went to the broom closet and tossed me a bundle.

"That's the lost-and-found closet," he said. "Stuff people left on boats. Maybe there's something to keep you warm."

The sweater fitted loosely, but it felt good. I felt good. I'd found a new friend. Most important, I was surviving Ta-Na-E-Ka.

My grandfather had said that the experience would be filled with adventure. I was having my fill. Grandfather had never said we couldn't accept hospitality.

I stayed at the restaurant for the whole five days. In the mornings, I went into the woods and watched the animals. I picked flowers for each of the tables in Ernie's.

I had never felt better. I was up early enough to watch the sun rise on the river. I went to bed after it set. I ate everything I wanted. I insisted Ernie take all my money for the food.

I was sorry when the five days were over. I'd enjoyed every minute with Ernie. He taught me how to make western omelets and chili.

I told him all about the legends of the Kaw. I hadn't realized I knew so much about my people.

Ta-Na-E-Ka was over. I came home at about 9:30 in the evening. I was nervous all over again. What if Grandfather asked me about the berries and the grasshoppers?

My feet were hardly cut. I hadn't lost a pound, and my hair was combed.

"They'll be so happy to see me," I told myself. "They won't ask too many questions."

I opened the door. My grandfather was in the front room. He was wearing the ceremonial shirt which had belonged to his grandfather. "N'g'da'ma," he said. "Welcome back."

I embraced my parents warmly. I let go only when I saw my cousin Roger. He was lying on the couch. His eyes were red and swollen.

He'd lost weight. His feet were a mass of blood and blisters. He was moaning, "I made it, see? I made it. I'm a warrior. A warrior."

My grandfather looked at me strangely. I was clean, well-fed, and healthy. My parents got the message. My uncle and aunt looked at me angrily.

Finally, my grandfather spoke. "What did you eat to keep you so well?"

I sucked in my breath and told the truth: "Hamburgers and milk shakes," I said.

"Hamburgers!" my grandfather growled.

"Milk shakes!" Roger moaned.

"You didn't say we *had* to eat grass-hoppers," I said.

"Tell us all about your Ta-Na-E-Ka," my grandfather commanded.

I told them everything.

"That's not what I trained you for," my grandfather said sadly.

I stood up. "Grandfather, I learned that Ta-Na-E-Ka is important. I didn't think so during training. I was scared stiff of it. I handled it in my way.

"And I learned I had nothing to be afraid of. There's no reason in 1947 to eat grasshoppers when you can eat a hamburger."

I was shocked at my own nerve. But I liked it. "Grandfather, I'll bet you never ate one of those rotten berries yourself."

Grandfather laughed! He laughed aloud! My mother and father and aunt and uncle couldn't believe it. Grandfather never laughed. Never.

"Those berries — they are terrible," Grandfather said. "I could never swallow them. I found a dead deer on the first day of my Ta-Na-E-Ka. He kept my belly full for the whole time!"

Grandfather stopped laughing. "We should send you out again," he said.

I looked at Roger. "You're pretty smart, Mary," Roger groaned. "I'd never have thought of what you did."

"Accountants just have to be good at arithmetic," I said. "I'm terrible at arithmetic."

Roger tried to smile, but couldn't. My grandfather called me to him.

"You should have done what Roger did," he said. "But I think you realize what is happening to our people today. I think you would have passed the test at any time. You know how to exist in a world that wasn't made for Indians. I don't think you're going to have any trouble surviving."

Grandfather wasn't entirely right. But I'll tell about that another time.

READING COMPREHENSION

Summarizing. Choose the best phrase to complete each sentence. Then write the complete statements on your paper.

1. Mary didn't want to take part in Ta-Na-E-Ka because she was _____ (afraid, too busy, ashamed of being a Kaw Indian).

2. When Ernie called Ta-Na-E-Ka silly, Mary _____ (agreed, was silent, was insulted).

3. After Ta-Na-E-Ka, Mary told her grandfather that she _____ (wanted to take the test again, had learned not to be afraid, had not learned anything).

4. At the end, Grandfather felt that Mary _____ (knew how to survive, was like her cousin, was a failure).

Interpreting. Write the answer to each question on your paper.

1. What did Grandfather expect Mary to eat during Ta-Na-E-Ka? What *did* she eat?

2. Why did Grandfather laugh at the end?

3. Why didn't Grandfather tell Mary to take the test over again?

For Thinking and Discussing

1. Do you think Mary passed the test fairly, or did she cheat?

2. Have you had to prove that you are no longer a child? Did you have to give up anything, or help others more?

UNDERSTANDING LITERATURE

Characterization. *Action, description,* and *dialogue* can help you understand the characters in a story. Give examples of action, description, or dialogue from the article to support the statements below about the characters in "Ta-Na-E-Ka."

Grandfather kept the old traditions in many ways.

Grandfather knew how to stay alive in the wilderness.

Mary was glad to know boys feel as frightened as girls at times.

Ernie was a large man who looked as if he could take care of himself.

Roger suffered during Ta-Na-E-Ka.

What do the following examples of action, description, and dialogue tell you about the characters in the article?

Grandfather spoke English with white people, but only Sioux with his family.

Ernie thought Ta-Na-E-Ka sounded silly until Mary explained it. Then he let her stay there for the five days.

Mary told Grandfather that there was no need to eat grasshoppers in 1947.

WRITING

In the article, Kaw boys and girls carry on the tradition of Ta-Na-E-Ka. Have you carried on any traditions? Write about a tradition you know and describe it in one paragraph. Draw pictures if you want.

Grandfather

by Shirley Crawford

Grandfather sings, I dance.
Grandfather speaks, I listen.
Now I sing, who will dance?
I speak, who will listen?

Grandfather hunts, I learn.
Grandfather fishes, I clean.
Now I hunt, who will learn?
I fish, who will clean?

Grandfather dies, I weep.
Grandfather buried, I am left alone.
When I am dead, who will cry?
When I am buried, who will be alone?

1. Shirley Crawford is an American Indian. In this poem, she talks about traditions. Grandfather passed the traditions on to her. She wonders whom she will pass them on to. Why do you think she asks this question? Is it hard for American Indians to keep their old ways of living?

2. Have you heard any other people ask this question? If so, why did they ask it?

3. How do the feelings in this poem compare to the feelings of Mary Whitebird in "Ta-Na-E-Ka"?

The Shirt

by Susan E. Kirby

Hank's older brother Rodge had died a year ago, and Hank was still grieving. Didn't anyone else in the family care as much about Rodge as Hank did?

Hank Griffith's mother was busy fixing Sunday dinner. She glanced at him and said, "Change that shirt. It's too worn out."

That wasn't what she really meant. The old denim shirt had belonged to his older brother, Rodge. She didn't want to be reminded of Rodge. But the Griffiths were not good at saying what they meant.

"The whole family will be here," she said. "So change that shirt."

Hank went outside. Her voice carried through the screen door.

"Melody will be here, too."

"Again?" he growled.

"She was Rodge's wife, so she's part of the family."

"Rodge is gone, so she isn't family anymore!" Hank crossed the yard and got into the pickup truck.

"You aren't going anywhere," his mother called from the porch. "You were

awfully late getting home from the movies last night.

Hank slumped over the steering wheel. He thought of all the times he had ridden in this truck with Rodge. Rodge would drive as fast as the truck would go. Hank could almost hear the gravel flying, the motor screaming, and Rodge laughing. Rodge was always laughing.

Melody had thought she could tame him. But after a year of marriage, she hadn't. Rodge had died as he had lived — recklessly. The accident report had said: "Driving too fast."

The family wasn't surprised, but they were deeply grieved. Melody didn't cry, though, when they buried Rodge.

Two days later, she threw Rodge's things into the yard and set them on fire. Hank managed to grab the denim shirt from the flaming heap. He didn't understand why he had done this. He didn't understand why Melody had burned Rodge's things, either.

A station wagon of cousins pulled up behind Hank. He left the truck and followed his cousins to the porch. But he didn't go inside.

More family members arrived. Hank ignored them.

Then Melody came up the walk with her quick, light step.

"Hello, Hank," she said.

He gave her a scornful look.

Melody was outspoken, unlike the Griffiths. She said, "It's been a year since Rodge died."

"Really?" he said sarcastically.

"I saw you outside the theater last night," she said. "You could see I had a date. If you've got something to say, say it."

"It's none of my business."

"Then don't judge me."

Hank's mother opened the screen door and called, "Dinner's ready." Then she welcomed Melody, and Melody followed her into the house. Hank stayed outside.

Soon Hank's oldest brother, Greg, came out and said, "Come in and eat."

Hank ignored him.

"We have company," Greg said.

"You mean Melody?" Hank said.

"Yes, Melody!"

Hank made no move to rise. Greg said, "Hank, you're upsetting Mom by being rude to Melody."

Then Greg noticed the shirt for the first time. "You shouldn't have worn that," he added. "It reminds Melody —"

"Of Rodge?" Hank finished the sentence for him. "Well, she needs remind-

ing. Did you know she had a date with John Miles last night?"

Greg didn't seem surprised. He said, "Rodge is dead, Hank. Life goes on."

Hank got up and started to walk away. Greg followed him, saying, "Don't you think she ever gets lonely?"

Hank didn't answer. Greg reached out and jerked him back by his shirt. As he did, Hank heard the rotten material rip. Angrily, he ripped it the rest of the way off and threw it on the ground.

"Are you happy now?" he asked Greg. "Or do you want to burn it, so Melody won't be reminded?"

"Look, Hank," Greg said, "I didn't mean to do that."

Hank walked away. He didn't stop until he came to the old pond where he and Rodge used to swim.

Melody followed him there, carrying the denim shirt. She held it out to him, but he wouldn't take it.

"Do you think you're the only one who misses Rodge?" she asked. "Do you think you're the only one who ever loved him?"

"I'm the only one who ever understood him," Hank said.

Melody shook her head. "No one understood Rodge. Rodge didn't even understand himself. He did things without thinking. He was wild and free and thoughtless."

Hank could not deny it. What she said was true. But it hurt not having Rodge alive.

"I miss him, too," Melody said softly. "Every day that goes by, I think of him a thousand times."

"You went to the trouble of burning

his things," Hank sneered. "I'm surprised you're still reminded of him."

She blushed. "I shouldn't have done that. But I was furious with him for dying such a pointless death. Hank, can't you understand that?"

She reached out to touch his arm, but he moved away. Then he saw tears in her eyes. Still, he didn't answer her. The silence grew between them. Finally Melody walked back toward the house.

Hank watched her go. Her steps lacked their usual bounce. She looked small and helpless as she gathered the torn shirt around her shoulders.

Did she find some comfort in the shirt? Hank wasn't sure. He started to run after her. He wanted to say, "Keep the shirt." He wasn't ready yet to say, "I understand."

So he stopped and let her go. If the shirt gave her comfort, it should be hers. He couldn't tell her that, though. The Griffiths were at their worst when it came to putting feelings into words.

READING COMPREHENSION

Summarizing. Choose the best phrase to complete each sentence. Then write the complete statements on your paper.

1. Rodge was killed by _____ (a fire, a hit-and-run driver, driving too fast).

2. Hank was angry at Melody, thinking she _____ (had forgotten about Rodge, wanted Rodge's shirt back, had changed Rodge's wild ways).

3. Melody had burned Rodge's things because _____ (they were useless, she hadn't really loved Rodge, she was furious at him for dying the way he did).

4. Hank finally knew that Melody _____ (missed Rodge a lot, stopped loving Rodge when he died, had never loved Rodge).

Interpreting. Write the answer to each question on your paper.

1. What reason did Hank's mother give for telling Hank to change his shirt?

2. Why did Hank want to remind Melody of Rodge?

3. What did Greg mean when he told Hank, "Life goes on"?

4. Why did Hank let Melody have Rodge's old shirt at the end?

For Thinking and Discussing. Do people who hide their feelings usually feel as strongly as people who express their feelings? Explain your answer by giving examples.

UNDERSTANDING LITERATURE

Characterization. An author often tells you about the characters in a story by describing their actions, or what they do. Characters' actions may include their reactions to memories, events, and other characters.

Here is a list of characters' actions and reactions in "The Shirt." On your paper, explain what each one tells you about the character whose actions or reactions are described.

1. Hank wore Rodge's old shirt when Melody came over for dinner.

2. Two days after Rodge's funeral, Melody burned Rodge's things in the yard.

3. When Hank saw Melody with a date, he didn't speak to her about it.

4. Melody followed Hank to the old pond and held out the torn shirt.

5. Melody reached out to touch Hank's arm, but he moved away.

6. Melody walked back toward the house, her steps lacking their usual bounce.

7. Hank started to run after her, but he stopped and let her go.

WRITING

Think of something you or someone you know values, even if it is in poor condition, such as a ragged pair of jeans or a beat-up old hat. Describe the object and explain why the owner values it.

Section Review

VOCABULARY

Synonyms. Words that have the same meaning, or almost the same meaning, are called synonyms. For example, in "Ta-Na-E-Ka," Mary told Roger, "You'd make a terrible warrior." Some synonyms for *terrible* are *awful, poor, dreadful,* and *pitiful.*

Number your paper from 1 to 6. For each word in italics in the sentences below, choose the correct synonym from the list of synonyms. Write the synonym on your paper.

Synonyms

finish	cold
dreams	feeling
frank	repeated

1. I had said good-bye to Annie quickly and without *emotion.*

2. I had to get away from the walls that *echoed* her silence.

3. Did we need two Grover Clevelands to *complete* the set?

4. My *fantasies* were about knights in armor.

5. But the days were *chilly* on the northern banks of the Missouri River.

6. Melody was *outspoken,* unlike the Griffiths.

READING

Comparing. To compare means to show how people or things are alike and how they are different. An author can help you understand characters by setting up comparisons between them. In "Ta-Na-E-Ka," the comparison between Mary's experience and Roger's shows you how clever Mary is at getting around the rules.

Each of the following statements compares two or more characters. Write *similar* if the statement tells how the characters are alike. Write *different* if the statement tells how they differ. The words in italics will help you decide.

1. Jerry loved baseball *as much as* his friend.

2. Jerry didn't have much, *but* Rollie Tremaine had everything.

3. Jerry is at first selfish, *while* his sisters are generous.

4. Jerry and his brother *both* wanted to do things for others.

5. The young girl could play and laugh; *however,* Annie could do neither.

6. *Like* Grandfather, Mary hated the taste of the wild berries.

7. Mary and Grandfather *both* proved they had courage.

8. Roger's feet had blisters, *while* Mary's feet were hardly cut.

9. Melody was outspoken, *unlike* the Griffiths.

10. The Griffith family had adjusted to Rodge's death, *but* Hank was still grieving.

WRITING

Paragraphs. A paragraph is a group of sentences that all relate to one main idea or topic. When you write, you can use paragraphs to help you organize your ideas. Your paragraphs will help your readers follow your train of thought.

Step 1: Set Your Goal

Choose one of the following topics for a paragraph:

1. Suppose you were Mrs. Walters in "The Sound of Annie's Silence." You decide to write the camp director to tell why you think the girl who took care of Annie would make a good counselor. Write one paragraph telling why you think the girl would be right for the job.

2. In "Grandfather," the poet learned a lot from her grandfather. Think of an older person who has taught you. Write one paragraph telling how this person has helped you.

Step 2: Make a Plan

Once you have decided on a topic, it's time to gather your ideas. Write down all the ideas you can think of about your topic. If you were writing about what Mary in "Ta-Na-E-Ka" learned on her Ta-Na-E-Ka, your list might look like this:

- ☐ how to use her brains to survive
- ☐ people will help if you ask
- ☐ importance of the Ta-Na-E-Ka
- ☐ her grandfather's wisdom
- ☐ the importance of traditions

Once you've written down your ideas, decide what the main idea of the paragraph will be. Then write a topic sentence that states the main idea. A topic sentence for the paragraph about Mary might be, "On her Ta-Na-E-Ka, Mary learned a great deal about herself and other people."

Write a list of ideas about the topic you have chosen. After you have completed the list, decide what your main idea will be and write a topic sentence.

Step 3. Write the First Draft

Begin your first draft with the topic sentence. Each sentence that follows should contain a fact, idea, or incident. All the sentences should support the main idea. The first draft of the paragraph about Mary might look like this:

On her Ta-Na-E-Ka, Mary learned a great deal about herself and other people. She used to think that her grandfather was just old-fashioned, but she learned how wise he was. Mrs. Richardson and Ernie taught Mary that people were ready to help — all you had to do was ask. Mary learned a great deal about herself. She found out that she could use her brains to survive. She also found out that she belonged to a people with traditions and values worth preserving.

As you write your first draft, remember that you will be free to change it any way you want later on.

Step 4. Revise Your Paragraph
Ask yourself these questions when you revise your paragraph: Is the main idea clear? Does the topic sentence work best at the beginning, or should it go elsewhere in the paragraph? Do all the other sentences relate to the main idea? Would additional examples or details make the paragraph more interesting?

QUIZ

The following is a quiz for Section 2. Write the answers in complete sentences on your paper.

Reading Comprehension

1. In "The Sound of Annie's Silence," the narrator wanted to quit her job, but she didn't. How did Annie's mother keep her from quitting?

2. In "President Cleveland, Where Are You?" how did Jerry get the money his brother needed to go to the dance?

3. How did the Kaw Indians of the past survive during Ta-Na-E-Ka?

4. At first, Mary thought Ta-Na-E-Ka was silly. How did she feel after she went through it?

5. In "The Shirt," who was responsible for Rodge's death?

Understanding Literature

6. In "The Sound of Annie's Silence," what does the narrator learn?

7. In the poem "Thumbprint," what does the pattern of whirls on the poet's thumb tell you about the poet?

8. Jerry gave up the baseball glove to send Armand to the dance. What does this tell you about Jerry?

9. In "Ta-Na-E-Ka," why wasn't Grandfather angry with Mary?

10. In "The Shirt," what does Hank finally learn?

ACTIVITIES

Word Attack

1. Many words in "Ta-Na-E-Ka" are from a Sioux dialect. The author has tried to come up with English spellings that will tell you how the words sound.

a. Look through the story for Sioux words. Say the words aloud.

b. Make up some words from an imaginary foreign language. Write them

84

down, using our alphabet to show how they are pronounced. Ask a friend to read your words. Did your friend pronounce the words correctly? If not, try to find ways to improve your spellings. Read the words to another friend. Have the friend write them down as you read. Did your friend spell the words the same way you did? Which spelling makes more sense?

2. Below are some words that appear in the section stories. Use a dictionary to find out what language each word comes from and what the original word meant.

umbrella   knight   corsage

Speaking and Listening

1. In "The Shirt," Hank and his family have trouble talking about what they are feeling. With a classmate, act out the opening scene of the story between Hank and his mother. In your version, have both characters tell each other what they really feel.

2. When a number of people read something aloud at one time, it is called choral reading. With a group of friends, prepare a choral reading of the poem "Grandfather." Practice staying together and reading with expression. Be prepared to perform your reading for the class.

Researching. Use an encyclopedia to learn more about schools and camps for students with special needs, such as Annie in "The Sound of Annie's Silence." Be prepared to report your findings to the class.

Creating. The President cards in "President Cleveland, Where Are You?" were probably like the baseball cards people collect today. They had a picture of the President on the front and some information about him on the back. Decide what information each card would give and how it would be arranged. Then pick three Presidents and make cards for them. Use index cards or cut some cardboard into squares. Write the information on one side on the card. If you would like, draw a picture of the President on the other. You can find the information you need in an almanac.

WILLIAM SAROYAN

*Saroyan's stories
show a special understanding of
people. He knew that life could be
unfair. But he wrote about the
humor, love, and hope in life.*

Biography   William Saroyan

William Saroyan was born in 1908 in Fresno, California. His parents were Armenian immigrants.

When Saroyan was two years old, his father died. His mother was so poor that she had to put her children in an orphanage. Five years later, the children went to live with her again. By then, she had a job in a food-canning factory.

At the age of eight, Saroyan began selling newspapers. Later, he became a telegraph messenger and worked from afternoon until midnight.

As a boy, Saroyan loved to read. He began writing when he was 13. Until he was 25 — when his first story was published — he worked at many different jobs. Then he became a full-time writer.

Saroyan had great compassion, or feeling, for others. One of his goals was to hurt no one. Another was " . . . to cherish fools and failures even more than wise men and saints, since there are more of them." He believed in the worth of every human being.

Saroyan believed that humor was very important. He once wrote: " . . . without humor, there is no hope. And man can no more live without hope than he could without the earth underfoot."

Saroyan wrote novels, plays, and hundreds of short stories. Some of his stories are sad. But they usually show how much he cared about people who have had a hard time in life. "The Telegram," "Laughing Sam," and "The Parsley Garden" are examples.

Some of his stories, like "The Coldest Winter Since 1854," are humorous. Others, like "Where I Come From People Are Polite," show people enjoying life, even when life is unfair.

Much of Saroyan's work was based upon things that happened to him and to people he knew. He died in 1981 at the age of 72.

The Telegram

by William Saroyan

It was a matter of life or death. "In his heart he was saying, 'What can I do? I'm only the messenger.'" But Homer had a job to do. He had to deliver the message.

Homer, the messenger, got off his bike in front of the house of Mrs. Rosa Sandoval. He went to the door and knocked. The woman who opened the door was shocked to see the telegram in his hand.

"Mrs. Rosa Sandoval?" Homer said. He held out the telegram. But the woman would not touch it.

"Are you Mrs. Sandoval?" he asked.

"Please," she said, "please, come in."

He opened the telegram.

The woman said, "Who sent it — my son, Juan Domingo?"

"No, ma'am. It is from the War Department."

"The War Department?"

"Mrs. Sandoval," Homer said quickly, "your son is dead. Maybe it's a mistake. Maybe it isn't your son. Maybe it was someone else. The telegram says it was Juan Domingo Sandoval. But maybe the telegram is wrong."

"Do not be afraid," she said. "Come inside. I will give you candy." She took the boy by the arm and led him to a table.

"All boys like candy," she said. She went into another room and came back with a box. She opened it at the table.

Inside, Homer saw a strange kind of candy.

"Eat this candy," she said. "All boys like candy."

Homer took a piece of candy. He put it in his mouth and tried to chew.

"You would not bring me a bad telegram," she said.

Homer chewed the dry candy while the woman talked.

"It is our candy," she said, "it is made from cactus."

Suddenly she began to make soft breathing sounds. She was trying not to cry.

Homer wanted to get up and run. But he knew he would stay. He didn't know what else to do to make the woman less unhappy. In his heart he was saying, "What can I do? I'm only the messenger."

The woman suddenly put her arms around him. "My little boy," she said. "My little boy."

He didn't know why, but for some reason he felt sick. He didn't dislike the woman. But what was happening to her seemed so wrong.

The woman straightened up. "Let me look at you," she said. And she looked at him strangely.

Homer could not move. He felt great compassion, not for this poor woman alone, but for all people. He felt compassion for the terrible way they endured and died.

He saw the woman as she was years ago. He saw a beautiful young woman sitting beside the crib of her baby son. He saw her looking at the helpless child. And he heard her singing to her baby.

Suddenly, he was on his bicycle, riding fast. Tears were coming out of his eyes. His mouth was whispering crazy young curses.

When he got back to the telegraph office, the tears had stopped. But his anger and sorrow were stronger than ever. He knew there would be no stopping them.

"Otherwise," he said aloud, "I'm as good as dead myself."

READING COMPREHENSION

Summarizing. Choose the best phrase to complete each sentence. Then write the complete statements on your paper.

1. Homer delivered a telegram to Mrs. Sandoval that said _____ (the U.S. had won the war, her son was dead, her son was a war hero).

2. Homer felt sick because _____ (he was tired and hungry, he disliked Mrs. Sandoval, what was happening to Mrs. Sandoval seemed so wrong).

3. Later, Homer realized that sorrow and anger _____ (were part of life, could be avoided, were not as important as he once thought).

Interpreting. Write the answer to each question on your paper.

1. What did Mrs. Sandoval give to Homer?

2. Why did Homer tell Mrs. Sandoval that the telegram might be wrong?

3. In what ways did Mrs. Sandoval treat Homer like a son?

4. Why did Homer think that if his sorrow and anger stopped, he'd be as good as dead?

For Thinking and Discussing. Do you think that Homer helped Mrs. Sandoval through this terrible moment? How did he try to comfort her? How did she try to comfort him? What does this tell you about each character?

UNDERSTANDING LITERATURE

Characterization. The plot of a story depends upon the characters and how they act. In "The Telegram," the plot depends on the way Mrs. Sandoval and Homer react to the telegram. Both characters have strong reactions. If the characters had acted differently, the story would not be the same.

Read the following statements. Then write the answer to each question in a complete sentence on your paper.

1. Mrs. Sandoval would not touch the telegram. What if she had? How would the story have been different?

2. Homer cared about Mrs. Sandoval. What if Homer had cared only about himself? How would the story have been different?

3. Mrs. Sandoval had a terrible shock. But she told Homer, "You would not bring me a bad telegram." What would have happened if Mrs. Sandoval had just ignored Homer?

4. Homer had to leave Mrs. Sandoval alone at the end of the story. What if Homer had stayed? How do you think the plot would have continued?

WRITING

Think about the kind of person Juan Domingo Sandoval might have been. For example, he was probably a loving son and a brave soldier. Write a few sentences describing Juan's character.

The Coldest Winter Since 1854

by William Saroyan

*It was a long, cold winter. First, he hurt his leg. Then he fell
in love with a rich girl. But she wouldn't even look at him.
He knew his leg would heal, but what about his heart?*

It was very cold the year I tore a ligament in my right leg. That was the year I fell in love with Emma Haines. I also got a job as a messenger boy after school. And I sent away for a booklet about how to be a success.

It was the coldest winter since 1854. The newspaper said it was, so I guess it was.

I tore the ligament in my leg playing football. It was the cold. If I hadn't been so cold, I would have kicked the ball right.

Instead, I fell down in great pain. Johnny Cooper came over. He looked disgusted.

"I guess I can't play anymore," I said.

"Why not?" Johnny said.

"I can't stand up."

"You don't have to stand to be a quarterback," he said. "You can call signals while you're on your knees. Your mouth isn't hurt, is it? You can still call signals."

"All right," I said. "But my mind won't be on it. I'm freezing. And something's really wrong with my leg."

"You can still talk," Johnny said.

I called signals, and we beat the other team. I didn't stay long after the game, though. I was too frozen.

I couldn't get up and walk. So I began crawling home. I also began whistling for my little brother, Raleigh.

People on the street asked me to get up and walk. They said it was a disgrace to imitate a crippled person. It was wrong to laugh at people with troubles.

I couldn't tell them I really was hurt. They wouldn't have believed me.

My little brother, Raleigh, heard my special whistle for him. He ran up to me, out of breath.

"Why don't you get up and walk," he said.

"I can't. Something's wrong with my leg."

"Get up," he said. "I'll help you walk on your left leg."

He helped me home. It took us half an hour to go three blocks. I hopped all the way.

I rubbed liniment on my leg.

The liniment burned, and my leg got very red. But in the morning, I couldn't walk. So I didn't go to school.

That day, the mailman brought me a booklet I had sent away for. It was supposed to be about how to be a success. But it didn't say what kind of success.

There was a picture of a young man reading a booklet. There was another picture of another young man leaning on the wall of a poolroom. The young man reading the book was supposed to be the one to admire. But I wasn't sure.

The other young man seemed to be having a better time. He had probably just hit some good shots. And he was probably watching another fellow missing a shot.

The booklet said: "Which of these fellows will be a success?"

Maybe the young man in the poolroom would become the world's champion pool player. Maybe the young man reading the book would end up with a boring job.

I decided not to write away for any more of those booklets.

I wasn't able to ride my bicycle for a week. Even then, I couldn't do much with my right leg. I had to do most of my peddling with my left leg. This looked awkward, and people laughed at me.

"Go ahead, laugh at me," I would say. "My leg is only paralyzed. That's all."

I had always wanted to get a job as a messenger. I wanted to make money to buy a car. But I was always afraid to ask for the job.

I wasn't old enough, for one thing. I was scared, for another thing. But when I could hardly walk, I asked for a job at the telegraph office.

The boss was a big man named Grifford. He said, "But son, you're lame!"

"I'm not lame," I said. "Something's wrong with my right leg. But it will be all right tomorrow."

I got the job. I worked from four in the afternoon till midnight. Those seemed to be the coldest hours of the day and night. My hands would freeze on the handlebars.

Sometimes I thought I would quit. But I didn't. I got used to my hands freezing and dogs chasing me. I even forgot my lameness. And after a while, I was riding my bike in fancy style.

I wouldn't get to bed till one in the morning. I would only get six hours of sleep. I needed twice that amount. But I would race to school because Emma Haines would be there.

I'd be very sleepy all day. Emma Haines sat across from me. But I'd be so tired that I'd start to sleep with my eyes open.

Our teacher, Mrs. Haggerty, would call my name. I wouldn't hear her. I'd be dreaming about Emma Haines. Mrs. Haggerty would pull my ear. She wanted to make my open eyes see.

One day I fell sound asleep in class. My eyes were closed. My head was on my folded arms.

Mrs. Haggerty woke me up. She was angry. I don't blame her, in a way.

"Young man," she said, "this is not a hotel. This is a classroom."

I never felt awake until I got out of school. I would race to town on my bike. I would run into the telegraph office and start working.

It got so I'd fall asleep in school soon after I sat down. One day when I woke up, I noticed Emma Haines looking at me.

After school, I saw her walking with another girl whose father was rich. Emma Haines's father was about the richest man in town. I don't know why I had to fall in love with her. I guess it was because she was so pretty.

I had never talked to her before. Now I figured I would. I caught up with her and her friend. They stopped and waited for me to say something. But when I tried to open my mouth, I couldn't.

The two girls got very angry. They

walked away, saying bad things about me.

It was mighty cold that night. I felt terrible. Emma Haines's opinion of me didn't help. I thought I'd die if she didn't understand what kind of guy I was.

I began to look at her more often at school. But her attitude went from bad to worse. Now she would not even look at me.

One day, I put a love letter on her desk. It said: "Emma, I love you." Under that I wrote my name.

She handed the note to Mrs. Haggerty. Mrs. Haggerty said, "Young man, did you write this note?"

"Yes, m'am," I said.

"Go to the office," she said.

I went to see Mr. Bowler, the principal. He was almost a giant.

"Did you write this note?" he asked me.

"Yes, sir," I said.

"Don't you realize who Emma Haines is?"

"Well," I said, "I know her father is rich."

"And you wrote this note anyway?"

"Yes, sir," I said.

"It's one of the best love letters I've ever seen," he said. "But I must punish you anyway. For the rest of the day, you will be my helper. I'm too tired to give you a whipping."

I was his helper for the rest of the day. He sent me out to buy two sandwiches and two bottles of soda pop. He made me eat one of the sandwiches and drink one of the sodas.

"I have one thing to say to you," he said. "It's my duty to tell you. Stop being in love with Emma Haines."

"Why?" I said.

"She's a rich man's daughter. You're a poor man's son. It won't work."

It was terrible to hear. But maybe he was right.

"Maybe she loves me and doesn't know it," I said.

"There's not a chance of that," he said. "Forget her. Otherwise you'll get into trouble."

The winter was long. The paper said it was the coldest winter since 1854.

I was still in love with Emma Haines. I'd see her riding in fancy cars with boys who had rich fathers. I thought I'd die of sorrow.

One day in the spring, the sun was shining. Everything was warm. That was the day I was cured.

I was riding my bicycle when I saw Emma Haines. She was in a slick car with the worst creep in the world — Everett Rhodes.

Here was a chance for me to put Emma Haines in her place. How could she not love a guy like me when I told her I loved her? How could she go around with a creep like Everett Rhodes?

I caught up with them. I made a very loud noise with my tongue and lips. Then I rode off, doing tricks on my bicycle.

I figured I didn't need to take a course in how to be a success. My leg healed all right. The coldest winter since 1854 ended. And I got over Emma Haines.

I did some mighty fancy bike riding that day. I was celebrating my victories.

READING COMPREHENSION

Summarizing. Choose the best phrase to complete each sentence. Then write the complete statements on your paper.

1. The narrator sent away for a booklet about _____ (playing football, healing lameness, being a success).

2. He became a messenger when _____ (his leg got better, he could hardly walk, he was given a bicycle).

3. He fell in love with Emma Haines, who _____ (fell in love with him, was mean to him, was shy).

4. After a winter of suffering, he _____ (was cured of his lameness and hopeless love, got a raise at his job, threw out the booklet he had sent away for).

Interpreting. Write the answer to each question on your paper.

1. Why was it hard for the narrator to pedal his bike for a while?

2. The booklet on success pictured two young men. Which one was probably meant to be a success? Which one did the narrator seem to like?

3. Why, at the end, did the narrator no longer feel he had to learn how to be a success?

For Thinking and Discussing. The narrator wanted a lot out of life and he worked hard to get it. He didn't even give up even when he failed. Do you think he was realistic?

UNDERSTANDING LITERATURE

Characterization. In "The Coldest Winter Since 1854," Emma treats the narrator like a laughable failure. But the narrator shows us a side of himself that other people don't see. He shows that he had courage, self-respect, and a feeling of success. He is able to overcome all of his problems.

The following passages give hints about how the narrator sees himself. They are hints that are not obvious to the other people in the story. Read the passages and answer each question on your paper.

> I got used to my hands freezing and dogs chasing me. I even forgot my lameness. And after a while, I was riding my bike in fancy style.

1. The picture of a freezing-cold lame boy is sad. But the narrator doesn't feel sad. How can you tell he is enjoying himself?

> Here was a chance for me to put Emma Haines in her place. How could she not love a guy like me when I told her I loved her?

2. What does the narrator think of Emma's opinion? What does he think of himself? How would you describe the narrator?

WRITING

The booklet on how to be a success was no help to the narrator. What would you say if someone asked your advice on the subject of success? Make a list of your suggestions.

Laughing Sam

by William Saroyan

Sam was one of those people who laugh at everything. He wanted to get along with everyone. But he just didn't seem to fit in. No one understood him. Why did he laugh all the time?

There was a boy in my hometown called Laughing Sam. He was one of those people who laugh at everything because they are afraid of everything. This got him into all kinds of trouble. He couldn't do anything without doing it partly wrong.

Several boys in my hometown died before they were 20. Sam was one of them. But he even died wrong. And for all I know, maybe he was laughing at the time.

I was 10 and he was 12 when I first saw him. That was in the office of the *Evening Herald*, a newspaper. He was with Buzz Martin, who hired the newsboys.

"Wait here till the papers come off the press," Buzz told Sam.

Sam looked at all the other newsboys. He looked at the big press. Slowly, he began to be very frightened.

I could tell he was just another poor boy in the world. But he had more than being poor against him. I knew he'd always have a lousy time.

I felt bad about him. I wanted to say, "Take it easy. There's nothing to it."

I couldn't say anything, though. I saw something like horror and sorrow in his eyes. I thought he would start to cry. He laughed instead.

He was small and nervous. His skin was broken out, and he had foolish-looking ears. His arms were short. His fingers were stubby. He had hardly any shoulders at all, and he had big feet. He looked underfed and overworked. But there was something noble, as well as sad, about him.

I didn't talk to him that first day. I was a little afraid of him. I was afraid of what he stood for — all the helpless victims of life.

But I watched him, I could see he was lost. He didn't fit in with the world around him. He never would. And he seemed to know it.

I heard him try to talk to Buzz Martin. But he couldn't at first. When his mouth began to shape a word, it froze. You could see him trying to say something, but you couldn't hear anything.

Finally he asked Buzz, "Where shall I wait?"

Buzz Martin was a great guy. He was tough on boys who got out of line. But he was never tough on a scared kid. So he wasn't unkind to Sam. But he was a little confused by Sam's question.

"Just wait where you're standing," Buzz said. "The paper will be out in about five minutes. I'll give you 10 papers and tell you what to holler."

Sam laughed and stood where he was. Then he looked around for someone to talk to. He picked out Nick Kouros.

"How do you sell papers?" Sam asked. Then he laughed.

"I don't know," Kouros said. He did not laugh. He was probably the saddest newsboy in town. He hated everything and everybody. Now and then, we would see him crying, for no reason at all.

"I ain't never sold papers," Sam said. "Do I have to holler?" He laughed again.

Kouros said, "No."

"Do you holler?" Sam said. He laughed even more. Kouros scowled at him.

"Yes," Kouros said.

"How do you do it?" Sam said.

"I just open my mouth and holler."

"What do you holler?"

"Paper, paper!" Kouros said. "*Evening Herald!* And then I holler the headline."

"I ain't never sold papers," Sam said. "My mother said we need money. Ha, ha, ha! So I came down here. Do you make much money?"

"No," Kouros said.

"Do you make any money at all?" Sam said.

"If you sell two papers, you make a nickel."

"How many do you think I can sell if I try hard?"

"Maybe 10," Kouros said.

"That's 25 cents, ain't it?" Sam said.

"Yes."

Then the press began to work. "Look!" Sam said. "Ha, ha, ha!"

"What's the matter?" Kouros said.

Sam laughed again, "Look at it!" he said.

Soon we got our papers and ran to town. I had the corner near the post office. The better you are at selling papers, the better the corner you got. My corner was sixth from the best.

If you were new, you had to walk around town and do the best you could. Sam didn't walk around town — he ran. He was hollering and laughing. He wanted to please Buzz Martin. And he wanted to take home some money to his mother.

But he looked and sounded funny. So the newsboys began to make fun of him. Some kids asked him questions — just to hear him laugh when he answered. After awhile, they got a kick out of pushing him over backward to hear him laugh.

They couldn't understand him. They thought he would fight or cry. But all he did was laugh.

One day, they smeared press ink all over him. He stood in the middle of the crowd of crazy kids. He tried to get the ink off — and laughed.

"You put ink on me," he said. "Ha, ha, ha! It won't come off."

I felt terrible. I could tell how hurt he was. I knew how much he wanted to get along with people.

For about a week, the newsboys got a big kick out of him. Then his laughter began to annoy them. It wasn't right to laugh at everything.

One day, he came running down into the press room. He tripped and fell down the cement steps. Everybody ran over to help him. Even the toughest kids wanted to be kind.

Sam's coat was torn, and his arm was bleeding. But he jumped up and began to laugh.

"I fell downstairs," he said. "Ha, ha!"

Everybody thought he was crazy. And after awhile, nobody would talk to him.

One day, the newspaper headline was about a crash on the highway. Five people were killed. Two of them were kids.

Sam went running around town, hollering the headline — and laughing. I heard him when he came around my corner.

"Five killed in highway accident!" he hollered. "Ha, ha, ha!"

I stopped him, "Wait a minute," I said. "That's nothing to laugh about."

"I ain't laughing," he said.

Then I knew what was going on. He wasn't laughing, he was crying. He was doing it by laughing.

"Listen," I said. "You're not glad those people were killed, are you?"

"No," he said.

"You're sorry, aren't you?"

"I'm sorry, all right."

"That's all I wanted to know," I said.

He sold papers until he was 15. Then he got a job in a warehouse. I don't know what his job was. Maybe he was supposed to run the freight elevator now and then. But I guess the other workers made him do it because he was so afraid of the thing. And I guess he did it to try to get along. I guess he laughed, too.

I don't know how it happened. But one day, I read in the paper that he was smashed by the elevator and killed.

Everybody said it was his own fault. He panicked when the elevator didn't stop where it was supposed to stop. The other workers were laughing at him. He tried to get out of the elevator while it was moving. He didn't quite make it.

He lived 16 years in this world. He laughed all the time. Like all helpless victims, he cried from the beginning of his life.

READING COMPREHENSION

Summarizing. Choose the best phrase to complete each sentence. Then write the complete statements on your paper.

1. Sam seemed to know that he would _____ (be good at selling papers, be happy someday, never fit in).

2. Sam's laughter _____ (made people like him, got him into all kinds of trouble, helped him sell papers).

3. After the narrator heard Sam laugh about a highway accident, he realized that Sam _____ (was really crying, enjoyed suffering, had no feelings).

4. To the narrator, Sam stood for all _____ (poor people, helpless victims, people without feelings).

Interpreting. Write the answer to each question on your paper.

1. How old was Sam when he died?

2. Did the narrator sympathize with Sam's situation?

3. What did the narrator mean when he said that Sam, "like all helpless victims. . .cried from the beginning of his life"?

For Thinking and Discussing

1. Were you surprised to learn that when Sam laughed, he was really crying.

2. The narrator felt that Sam would never fit in with the world around him. Do you think that was true?

UNDERSTANDING LITERATURE

Characterization. In some stories, you know right away what a character is like. This is the case in "Laughing Sam." Sam is a tragic character. The fact that he is treated cruelly is only part of what makes Sam tragic. The other part is that Sam never understands that he is a victim.

Read the following passages and answer each question on your paper.

> He was one of those people who laugh at everything because they are afraid of everything. This got him into all kinds of trouble.

1. Why did the narrator think Sam laughed at everything?

> I could tell he was just another poor boy in the world. But he had more than being poor against him. I knew he'd always have a lousy time.

2. Why did the narrator know that Sam would always have a bad time?

> One day, they smeared press ink all over him. . . . I felt terrible. I could tell how hurt he was. I knew how much he wanted to get along with people.

3. What does this passage tell you about Sam?

4. Why did he want to get along with people who were cruel to him?

WRITING

What do you think of Sam at the beginning of this story? How did you feel about him by the end? Write a few sentences telling how your reaction changed.

Where I Come From People Are Polite

by William Saroyan

Joe had always wanted to buy a motorcycle. Now he had a chance to buy one. He could keep his job and earn enough money. But Mrs. Gilpley would have to be fired. . . . What would you do?

When I walked into the office, Mrs. Gilpley, the bookkeeper, was putting on her coat. Tears were coming out of her eyes.

It was Friday, and I had been whistling. Tomorrow I would take a train to the shore. I'd be free until Monday.

But when I walked into the office, I stopped whistling. The door to Mr. Wylie's office was partly opened. I knew he was at his desk.

"Good morning, Joe," she said.

It was Mrs. Gilpley. Nobody liked her. I had worked with her from September to April. I wasn't exactly crazy about her. But she was good-hearted. And I felt I should find out why she was crying.

"Mrs. Gilpley," I said, "is something the matter?"

She pointed at Mr. Wylie's office. Then she put her finger to her lips. She didn't want Mr. Wylie to hear.

"Mrs. Gilpley," I said, "you haven't lost your job, have you?"

"I've resigned," she said.

"No, you haven't," I said. "You can't fool me."

Mrs. Gilpley had worked there for years. Her salary was $27.50 a week. They had taught me to do her work. My salary was $15 a week. So, Wylie was letting the lady go. He wanted to pay someone a smaller salary to do her work.

Well, I was pretty lucky to have a job. I felt fine in a new pair of shoes and a new hat. But I didn't like the idea of making Mrs. Gilpley cry.

"Mrs. Gilpley," I said, "I came in this morning to quit my job. I've got an uncle in Oregon who has opened a grocery store. I'm going to work for him. I'm not going to work in this cemetery company all my life."

"Joe," she said, "you don't have an uncle in Oregon."

"You'd be surprised at all the uncles I've got," I said. "I'm through keeping track of dead people's addresses."

"Joe," she said, "if you quit, I'll never speak to you again."

102

"I don't need a job in a cemetery company," I said.

"You've got no friends in this town, Joe. You need this job."

"I can't take your job. It isn't right. You've been working here for 20 years or more."

I walked into Mr. Wylie's office. He was tall, and he was mean.

"Mr. Wylie," I said, "I'm quitting my job."

"What are you quitting for?" he asked.

"I'm not getting enough money," I said.

"How much do you want?"

I was surprised. "I want $30 a week."

"But you're only 18," he said. "You seem a little young to earn so much. But maybe we can arrange it."

If I had simply asked for a raise, it never would have worked. I thought about getting $30 a week. That would be enough to buy all the stuff I always wanted. Why, I'd be able to buy a motorcycle.

"No," I said. "I'm quitting."

"I thought you liked your work."

"I used to like it. But I don't like it anymore. Mr. Wylie, why did you fire Mrs. Gilpley?"

He looked angry. "Young man, a check for your salary will be made out this morning. Come back for it in an hour."

I was angry, too. "I want my check now!"

"Then wait outside," he said.

I left his office. I said to Mrs. Gilpley, "I quit. He'll have to give you your job back. He hasn't got anyone else to do your work."

"Joe," she said, "you've hurt me very deeply."

"Where I come from," I said, "a young man doesn't take a lady's job."

"Joe, suppose you can't find another job?"

I snapped my fingers. "I can get another job just like that."

Mr. Wylie came to the doorway of his office. He nodded at Mrs. Gilpley. She went into his office. Later, she came out, carrying a check.

"Here's your check, Joe," she said. "I tried to get him to pay you $15. But he said you were insolent. He's paying you $13."

"Did he give you your job back?" I asked.

"Yes."

"I'm glad about that. What did he say I was?"

"He said you were insolent," she said.

"What does that mean?'

"It means impolite."

"I'm not impolite," I said. "Where I come from, people are polite."

I walked into Mr. Wylie's office. "You can't call me impolite," I said. "Where I come from, people are polite."

"Where do you come from?" he asked.

"Chicago."

"Well, you've got a lot to learn. You must learn that you can't bite the hand that feeds you."

"I didn't bite any hand," I said.

"You quit your job, didn't you?"

"Yes, sir. But I didn't bite anybody."

"Well, what do you want now?" he asked.

"I just want to say good-bye. I just want you to know I have good manners."

"All right," he said. "Good-bye."

"Good-bye."

I went out and said good-bye to Mrs. Gilpley. Mr. Wylie came out while I was speaking to her. She got nervous, but I went on talking.

"Mrs. Gilpley," I said, "I've always wanted to buy a motorcycle. I guess I could have done it if I had wanted to keep my job here. But where I come from, a man doesn't keep a job and get someone fired."

"Why do you want a motorcycle?" Mr. Wylie asked.

"I want to travel," I said.

"That's no way to travel," he said.

"It's one of the best ways in the world. Mrs. Gilpley, if I ever get a motorcycle with a side-car, I'll take you for a ride."

"Thank you very much, Joe," she said.

We all said good-bye. I walked out of the building and up the street. I don't know how it happened. But I went straight to a place where motorcycles are sold.

The salesman showed me a new model. I asked him if I could try it out for a while. He said I could — if I would leave some money with him. So I gave my check to him.

It was a beautiful machine. I raced down the street to the building where I used to work. I walked into Mr. Wylie's office. He looked surprised.

"Mr. Wylie," I said, "I've got a beautiful motorcycle outside. If you'd like a ride, I'd be glad to take you."

"I don't want to ride a motorcycle," he said.

"I thought maybe you would," I said. I left his office. Then I went back in. "Would you like to see it?" I asked.

"No!" he said.

I went outside and drove away. The motor was great.

When I got on the highway, I remembered my plan to go to the shore. I decided to drive the motorcycle down there and back and start looking for a job.

I drove the motorcycle all the way to the shore. Then I drove it right onto the wet sand of the beach. I scared the sea gulls.

I stopped at a place and had three hamburgers. Then I started back to the city.

I had a great time with that motorcycle. Then I turned it back in.

The salesman said, "Where did you go?"

"To the shore," I said.

"To the shore?" he said. "I didn't know you wanted to go that far. That's 200 miles round trip!"

"Well," I said, "I've always wanted to go there. Can I have my money back?"

"Are you going to buy the motorcycle?"

"How much is it?"

"It's $275."

"I haven't got that much money," I said.

"How much do you have?" he said.

"I have that check for $13," I said. "That's all."

"I thought you were going to buy the motorcycle."

"I would have bought it if I hadn't quit my job," I said. "Can I have my money back?"

"I don't think so," the salesman said. "I'll talk to the manager."

He went into the office and talked. He came out with the manager, who looked angry.

"What do you mean by taking a new motorcycle to the shore and back?" the manager said.

"What?" I said. I didn't know what else to say. What did he mean? I didn't mean anything.

"We thought you wanted to ride it around the block," he said. "We thought you wanted to test the motor or show it to somebody."

"I showed it to a few people," I said. "Can I have my money back?"

"I'm afraid you owe us money," the manager said. "That was a new machine. It was for sale. It's second-hand now — used!"

"Can't I have some of my money back?"

"No!"

"It's a swell motorcycle," I said.

I walked out of the place and down the street. I didn't even think about where I would ever find a job. I was feeling too happy about the ride to the shore and back.

READING COMPREHENSION

Summarizing. Choose the best phrase to complete each sentence. Then write the complete statements on your paper.

1. Mr. Wylie fired Mrs. Gilpley because _____ (she demanded too high a salary, she was not a good worker, Joe could do her work for less money).

2. Joe knew that if he quit, _____ (Mrs. Gilpley would get her job back, he could work for his uncle, he could travel instead of work from then on).

3. After Joe quit his job, he _____ (started looking for another one, took Mrs. Gilpley out to lunch, tried out a motorcycle).

4. When the motorcycle salesman would not return Joe's $13, Joe _____ (got upset, was too happy to get upset, decided to buy the motorcyle).

Interpreting. Write the answer to each question on your paper.

1. Whose salary was bigger — Joe's or Mrs. Gilpley's?

2. What did Mr. Wylie mean when he told Joe, "You must learn that you can't bite the hand that feeds you"?

3. When Joe rode the motorcycle to the shore, was he trying to take advantage of the motorcycle salesman?

For Thinking and Discussing. This story was written in the 1930's, when jobs were hard to find. Was Joe right to quit his job?

UNDERSTANDING LITERATURE

Characterization. Characters in a story are often like people in real life. They can have may different traits, or qualities. This is true of Joe in "Where I Come From People Are Polite." Joe is an easy-going person. He also has strong feelings about what is right. His most outstanding quality is his ability to enjoy life.

Read the following passages and answer each question on your paper.

"Mrs. Gilpley," I said, "I've always wanted to buy a motorcycle. I guess I could have done it if I had wanted to keep my job here. But where I come from, a man doesn't keep a job and get someone fired."

1. How does the passage show that Joe has a strong sense of justice?

I walked out of the place and down the street. I didn't even think about where I would ever find a job. I was feeling too happy about the ride to shore and back.

2. Explain how the passage shows Joe's ability to enjoy life.

3. How does it show that Joe is an easy-going person?

WRITING

Write Mrs. Gilpley's name on one side of your paper. On the other side, write Mr. Wylie. Underneath each name, write one or two sentences telling what each person thinks of Joe. Write the way you think Mrs. Gilpley and Mr. Wylie would.

The Parsley Garden

by William Saroyan

For Al, the parsley garden is a haven of fresh food and cool breezes. But it is also the place where he realizes he is capable of great hatred — a place marked by a loss of innocence. It is, in a sense, his Garden of Eden.

One day in August Al Condraj was wandering through Woolworth's without a penny to spend when he saw a small hammer that was not a toy but a real hammer, and he was possessed with a longing to have it. He believed it was just what he needed by which to break the monotony and with which to make something. He had gathered some first-class nails from Foley's Packing House, where the boxmakers worked and where they had carelessly dropped at least fifteen cents' worth. He had gladly gone to the trouble of gathering them together because it had seemed to him that a nail, as such, was not something to be wasted. He had the nails, perhaps a half pound of them, at least two hundred of them, in a paper bag in the apple box in which he kept his junk at home.

Now, with the ten-cent hammer, he believed he could make something out of box wood and the nails, although he had no idea what. Some sort of a table, perhaps, or a small bench.

At any rate he took the hammer and slipped it into the pocket of his overalls, but just as he did so a man took him firmly by the arm without a word and pushed him to the back of the store into a small office. Another man, an older one, was seated behind a desk in the office, working with papers. The younger man, the one who had captured him, was excited and his forehead was covered with sweat.

"Well," he said, "here's one more of them."

The man behind the desk got to his feet and looked Al Condraj up and down. "What's he swiped?"

"A hammer." The young man looked at Al with hatred. "Hand it over," he said.

The boy brought the hammer out of his pocket and handed it to the young man, who said, "I ought to hit you over the head with it, that's what I ought to do."

He turned to the older man, the boss, the manager of the store, and he said, "What do you want me to do with him?"

"Leave him with me," the older man said.

The younger man stepped out of the office, and the older man sat down and went back to work. Al Condraj stood in the office fifteen minutes before the older man looked at him again.

"Well," he said.

Al didn't know what to say. The man wasn't looking at him, he was looking at the door.

Finally Al said, "I didn't mean to steal it. I just need it and I haven't got any money."

"Just because you haven't got any money doesn't mean you've got a right to steal things," the man said. "Now, does it?"

"No, sir."

"Well, what am I going to do with you? Should I turn you over to the police?"

Al didn't say anything, but he certainly didn't want to be turned over to the police. He hated the man, but at the same time he realized somebody else could be a lot tougher than he was being.

"If I let you go, will you promise never to steal from this store again?"

"Yes, sir."

"All right," the man said. "Go out this way and don't come back to this store until you've got some money to spend."

He opened a door to the hall that led to

the alley, and Al Condraj hurried down the hall and out into the alley.

The first thing he did when he was free was laugh, but he knew he had been humiliated, and he was deeply ashamed. It was not in his nature to take things that did not belong to him. He hated the young man who had caught him, and he hated the manager of the store who had made him stand in silence in the office so long. He hadn't liked it at all when the young man had said he ought to hit him over the head with the hammer.

He should have had the courage to look him straight in the eye and say, "You and who else?"

Of course he had stolen the hammer and he had been caught, but it seemed to him he oughtn't to have been so humiliated.

After he had walked three blocks, he decided he didn't want to go home just yet, so he turned around and started walking back to town. He almost believed he meant to go back and say something to the young man who had caught him. And then he wasn't sure he didn't mean to go back and steal the hammer again, and this time not get caught. As long as he had been made to feel like a thief anyway, the least he ought to get out of it was the hammer.

Outside the store he lost his nerve, though. He stood in the street, looking in, for at least ten minutes.

Then, crushed and confused and now bitterly ashamed of himself, first for having stolen something, then for having been caught, then for having been humiliated, then for not having guts enough to go

back and do the job right, he began walking home again, his mind so troubled that he didn't greet his pal Pete Wawchek when they came face to face outside Graf's Hardware.

When he got home, he was too ashamed to go inside and examine his junk, so he had a long drink of water from the faucet in the backyard. The faucet was used by his mother to water the stuff she planted every year: okra, bell peppers, tomatoes, cucumbers, onions, garlic, mint, eggplants, and parsley.

His mother called the whole business the parsley garden, and every night in the summer she would bring chairs out of the house and put them around the table she had had Ondro, the neighborhood handyman, make for her for fifteen cents, and she would sit at the table and enjoy the cool of the garden and the smell of the things she had planted and tended.

Sometimes she would even make a salad and moisten the flat old-country bread and slice some white cheese, and she and he would have supper in the parsley garden. After supper she would attach the water hose to the faucet and water her plants and the place would be cooler than ever and it would smell real good, real fresh and cool and green, all the different growing things making a green-garden smell out of themselves and the air and the water.

After the long drink of water he sat down where the parsley itself was growing, and he pulled a handful of it out and slowly ate it. Then he went inside and told his mother what had happened. He even told her what he had thought of doing after he had been turned loose: to go back and steal the hammer again.

"I don't want you to steal," his mother said in broken English. "Here is ten cents. You go back to that man and you give him this money and you bring it home, that hammer."

"No," Al Condraj said. "I won't take your money for something I don't really need. I just thought I ought to have a hammer, so I could make something if I felt like it. I've got a lot of nails and some box wood, but I haven't got a hammer."

"Go buy it, that hammer," his mother said.

"No," Al said.

"All right," his mother said. "Shut up."

That's what she always said when she didn't know what else to say.

Al went out and sat on the steps. His humiliation was beginning to really hurt now. He decided to wander off along the railroad tracks to Foley's because he needed to think about it some more. At Foley's he watched Johnny Gale nailing boxes for ten minutes, but Johnny was too busy to notice him or talk to him, although one day at Sunday school, two or three years ago, Johnny had greeted him and said, "How's the boy?" Johnny worked with a boxmaker's hatchet, and everybody in Fresno said he was the fastest boxmaker in town. He was the closest thing to a machine any packing house ever saw. Foley himself was proud of Johnny Gale.

Al Condraj finally set out for home because he didn't want to get in the way. He didn't want somebody working hard to notice that he was being watched and maybe say to him, "Go on, beat it." He didn't want Johnny Gale to do something like that. He didn't want to invite another humiliation.

On the way home he looked for money, but all he found was the usual pieces of broken glass and rusty nails, the things that were always cutting his bare feet every summer.

When he got home, his mother had made a salad and set the table, so he sat down to eat, but when he put the food in his mouth he just didn't care for it. He got up and went into the three-room house and got his apple box out of the corner of his room and went through his junk. It was all there, the same as yesterday.

He wandered off back to town and stood in front of the closed store, hating the young man who had caught him, and then he went along to the Hippodrome and looked at the display photographs from the two movies that were being shown that day.

Then he went along to the public library to have a look at all the books again, but he didn't like any of them, so he wandered around town some more and then around half-past eight he went home and went to bed.

His mother had already gone to bed because she had to be up at five to go to work at Inderrieden's, packing figs. Some days there would be work all day, some days there would be only half a day of it, but whatever his mother earned during the summer had to keep them the whole year.

He didn't sleep much that night because he couldn't get over what had happened, and he went over six or seven ways by which to adjust the matter. He went so far as to believe it would be necessary to kill the young man who had caught him. He also believed it would be necessary for him to steal systematically and successfully the rest of his life. It was a hot night and he couldn't sleep.

Finally, his mother got up and walked barefooted to the kitchen for a drink of water, and on the way back she said to him softly, "Shut up."

When she got up at five in the morning, he was out of the house, but that had happened many times before. He was a restless boy, and he kept moving all the time every summer. He was making mistakes and paying for them, and he had just tried stealing and had been caught at it, and he was troubled. She fixed her breakfast, packed her lunch, and hurried off to work, hoping it would be a full day.

It was a full day, and then there was overtime, and although she had no more lunch, she decided to work on for the extra money, anyway. Almost all the other packers were staying on, too, and her neighbor across the alley, Leeza Ahboot, who worked beside her, said, "Let us work until the work stops, then we'll go home and fix a supper between us and eat it in your parsley garden where it's so cool. It's a hot day and there's no sense not making an extra fifty or sixty cents."

When the two women reached the garden, it was almost nine o'clock, but still daylight, and she saw her son nailing pieces of box wood together, making something with a hammer. It looked like a bench. He had already watered the garden and tidied up the rest of the yard, and the place seemed very nice, and her son seemed very serious and busy. She and Leeza went straight to work for their sup-

per, picking bell peppers and tomatoes and cucumbers and a great deal of parsley for the salad.

Then Leeza went to her house for some bread, which she had baked the night before, and some white cheese, and in a few minutes they were having supper together and talking pleasantly about the successful day they had had. After supper they made Turkish coffee over an open fire in the yard. They drank the coffee and smoked a cigarette apiece, and told one another stories about their experiences in the old country and here in Fresno, and then they looked into their cups at the grounds to see if any good fortune was indicated, and there was: health and work and supper out of doors in the summertime and enough money for the rest of the year.

Al Condraj worked and overheard some of the things they said, and then Leeza went home to go to bed, and his mother said, "Where you get it, that hammer, Al?"

"I got it at the store."

"How you get it? You steal it?"

Al Condraj finished the bench and sat on it. "No," he said. "I didn't steal it."

"How you get it?"

"I worked at the store for it," Al said.

"The store where you steal it yesterday?"

"Yes."

"Who give you job?"

"The boss."

"What you do?"

"I carried different stuff to the different counters."

"Well, that's good," the woman said.

"How long you work for that little hammer?"

"I worked all day," Al said. "Mr. Clemmer gave me the hammer after I'd worked one hour, but I went right on working. The fellow who caught me yesterday showed me what to do, and we worked together. We didn't talk, but at the end of the day he took me to Mr. Clemmer's office, and he told Mr. Clemmer that I'd worked hard all day and ought to be paid at least a dollar."

"That's good," the woman said.

"So Mr. Clemmer put a silver dollar on his desk for me, and then the fellow who caught me yesterday told him the store needed a boy like me every day, for a dollar a day, and Mr. Clemmer said I could have the job."

"That's good," the woman said. "You can make a little money for yourself."

"I left the dollar on Mr. Clemmer's desk," Al Condraj said, "and I told them both I didn't want the job."

"Why you say that?" the woman said. "Dollar a day for eleven-year-old boy good money. Why you not take job?"

"Because I hate the both of them," the boy said. "I would never work for people like that. I just looked at them and picked up my hammer and walked out."

"All right," his mother said. "Shut up."

His mother went inside and went to bed, but Al Condraj sat on the bench he had made and smelled the parsley garden and didn't feel humiliated anymore.

But nothing could stop him from hating the two men, even though he knew they hadn't done anything they shouldn't have done.

READING COMPREHENSION

Summarizing. Choose the best phrase to complete each sentence. Then write the complete statements on your paper.

1. Al Condraj tried to steal a hammer from a store because he _____ (couldn't pay for it, hated the store manager, wanted to see if he could get away with it).

2. When Al left the store manager's office the first time, he felt _____ (proud, relieved, ashamed).

3. Al got the hammer the next day by _____ (stealing it — successfully, working for the store manager, paying for it with his mother's money).

4. When the manager offered Al a full-time job Al _____ (turned it down, was grateful, demanded the minimum wage).

Interpreting. Write the answer to each question on your paper.

1. What did Al's mother do when Al told her he had been caught stealing?

2. Why did he return to the store and work for the manager?

3. Why did he refuse the dollar and the full-time job offered to him?

For Thinking and Discussing. Al knew that stealing was wrong. Why did he hate the two men at the store? Why was it so awful to feel humiliated?

UNDERSTANDING LITERATURE

Characterization. Characters in a story, like people in real life, can experience different emotions — sometimes at the same time. This is true of Al Condraj in "The Parsley Garden."

Read the following passages and answer each question on your paper.

> The first thing he did when he was free was laugh, but he knew he had been humiliated, and he was deeply ashamed.

1. How could he laugh when he felt deeply ashamed?

> It was not in his nature to take things that did not belong to him. . . .Of course he *had* taken the hammer and he had been caught, but it seemed to him he oughtn't to have been so humiliated.

2. What does this tell you about Al's sense of justice?

> . . .Al Condraj sat on the bench he had made and smelled the parsley garden and didn't feel humiliated anymore. . . .But nothing could stop him from hating the two men, even though he knew they hadn't done anything they shouldn't have done.

3. What does this show about his pride?

WRITING

The two men at the store learned that Al was a good worker. They were probably surprised when he turned down the job he was offered. Write a conversation they might have had in which they try to figure out why Al refused the job offer.

Section Review

VOCABULARY

Antonyms. Authors get their meanings across by choosing words carefully. They often used *antonyms*. For example, *love* and *hate* are antonyms. You can often discover the full meaning of a word by learning its antonym(s).

1. In "Laughing Sam," the antonyms *laughing* and *crying* are important to the story. Can you explain why?

2. In "The Coldest Winter Since 1854," the principal said he had to punish the narrator. But instead of whipping him, he gave the narrator a sandwich and a soda. Think of an antonym for *punish*. Write it in a sentence that tells how the principal really treated the narrator.

3. For each word directly below, find the word with the opposite meaning in the list of antonyms. On your paper, write the correct antonym next to the letter for each word.

   a. fired   e. sorrow
   b. serious   f. disgrace
   c. nervous   g. insolent
   d. necessary   h. good-hearted

   ### Antonyms

   cruel   polite
   joy   needless
   hired   calm
   honor   joking

READING

Author's Purpose. Most stories are written for a reason, or purpose. An author writes a story to make a point or to make you feel certain emotions. Some stories are written to be entertaining. In other stories, the author may try to inform you and entertain you at the same time.

1. Read the following statements in the last paragraph of "The Coldest Winter Since 1854." The narrator is speaking. "I did some mighty fancy bike riding that day. I was celebrating my victories." What point do you think Saroyan was making about the narrator? Now think about the whole story. Did Saroyan want this story to be entertaining? Explain your answer.

2. Here is a statement from "Laughing Sam," which is part of a description of Sam: "But there was something noble, as well as sad, about him." Why do you think Saroyan was careful to include this line? How do you think he wanted you to feel about Sam?

3. Saroyan wrote with compassion, or feeling, for people who suffer in life. Which of his stories here fit this description? Give reasons to support your answer.

4. Saroyan also wrote about people who enjoy themselves even when life is hard or unfair. His sense of humor often comes out in this stories. Which of the stories here fit into this category? Give reasons to support your answer.

WRITING

A Social Letter. People write social letters for many reasons. Sometimes they write to say thank you or give an invitation. Often they write simply to share their experiences with someone who is far away. Such letters can be very informal. Even so, the four-step writing process can ensure that they are clear.

Step 1: Set Your Goal

Choose one of the following topics:

a. Pretend you are Mrs. Gilpley in "Where I Come From People Are Polite." Write a social letter to Joe, thanking him for saving your job and telling him what happened in the office after he left.

b. Pretend you are a friend of the narrator of "The Coldest Winter Since 1854." You received a letter from him about how he hurt his leg and about falling in love with Emma Haines. Write a letter to your friend telling him you hope he is better and offering advice about Emma.

Step 2: Make a Plan

To plan your social letter, think about what you want to tell your friend and jot down your ideas. Then organize your ideas, placing those on the same topic together.

Suppose the narrator of "Laughing Sam" were to write a letter to a friend about Sam's death. He might come up with the ideas shown below and organize them in these three groups:

☐ How Sam Died
  accident
  elevator didn't stop
  jumped out

☐ What Sam Was Like
  frightened all the time
  laughed, but sad
  clumsy — tripped on steps
  wanted to be friends

☐ How I felt When Sam Died
  sad
  wished I had been friendlier

Now make a list of the facts and ideas you want to cover in your letter. Arrange the items according to topic.

Step 3. Write Your First Draft

Your letter should contain one paragraph for each topic you want to cover. Each paragraph should have a topic sentence. Other sentences should state the specific points you want to make.

The narrator of "Laughing Sam" might have written the following draft for his letter. Note that each paragraph begins with a topic sentence.

I just read some terrible news. Sam, a boy I knew, died yesterday. He fell to his death in a strange accident. He was in the freight elevator at work. When the elevator didn't stop, Sam jumped out.

Sam was an odd person. He laughed all the time. But he was not happy. His laughter was like other people's tears. He was shy and clumsy, but he wanted to be liked.

I felt terrible when I read about the accident in the paper. It's always sad when somebody so young dies. I felt especially bad because I didn't try harder to make friends with Sam. Maybe I could have helped him.

Step 4. Revise Your Letter

Check your letter to be sure it is well organized and clear. Will your reader know what you think and feel about the topics you covered? Also, correct any errors in grammar, spelling, and punctuation you find. When you copy your letter over, include all these parts:

Heading: Three lines at the upper right-hand corner with your address and the date.

Salutation: A greeting — usually "Dear" — followed by the name of the person you're writing to.

Body: The actual text of the letter.

Closing: Words such as " Yours " or "With love," followed by your signature.

QUIZ

The following is a quiz for Section 3. Write the answers in complete sentences on your paper.

Reading Comprehension

1. In "The Telegram," Homer stayed with Mrs. Sandoval even though he was tempted to run away. Why?

2. The narrator of "The Coldest Winter Since 1854" was not discouraged by failure. Why not?

3. In "Laughing Sam," what finally happened to Sam? Why?

4. In "Where I Come From People Are Polite," what did Joe consider unfair? What did he do about it?

5. In "The Parsley Garden," what happened that Al considered unfair? What did he do about it?

Understanding Literature

6. In "The Telegram," Homer had strong reactions to the death of Mrs. Sandoval's son. Describe his reactions. What do they tell you about Homer?

7. In "The Coldest Winter Since 1854," the narrator fell in love with Emma Haines. What do you think Emma was like?

8. In "Laughing Sam," Sam was a victim. Explain why.

9. In "Where I Come From People Are Polite," Joe ended up without a job when jobs were hard to find. But this is not a sad story. Why not?

10. In "The Parsley Garden," Al's mother didn't punish Al for trying to steal a hammer. Why not? What did she understand about her son?

ACTIVITIES

Word Attack

1. Two of the stories in this section —

"The Telegram" and "The Coldest Winter Since 1854" — are about boys who have jobs delivering telegrams or telegraphs. The words *telegram* and *telegraph* are made from Greek word parts: *tele* (far) and *gram* or *graph* (write). Think of as many words as you can that contain these word parts. Explain what each word has to do with distance or writing. You may use your dictionary to help you.

2. *Principal* is a very troublesome word. It is used in "The Coldest Winter Since 1854" to mean "the person in charge of a school." It can also mean "chief." It sounds like *principle,* which means "rule." Rewrite this sentence, using *principle* or *principal* correctly: "The [head of our school]'s [chief] [rule] is 'study hard and you'll do well.'"

Now write sentences like the one for *principal/principle* for these pairs of homophones:

yoke/yolk
stationary/stationery
muscle/mussel

Feel free to use your dictionary.

Speaking and Listening. If the store manager in "The Parsley Garden" had called the police, Al Condraj might have gone on trial for shoplifting. Get together with some classmates to act out the trial.

You will need the following characters: judge, defense lawyer, prosecutor (the lawyer making the case against Al), the defendant (Al), witnesses (the store manager, the store clerk, Al's mother). When you are ready, act out the trial in front of the class. Let the class be the jury.

Researching. The stories in this section include many details that tell what life was like in the 1930's. For example, you learn that you can buy a hammer for a dime and that messengers delivered telegrams in person, rather than over the telephone. Use the library to find out more about day-to-day life during this period. Perhaps you can find a book with photographs so that you can actually see what it was like. Share what you learn with your classmates.

Creating. The cost of a telegram is determined by how many words are in it. Therefore, people try to use as few words as possible when they send telegrams. Make up telegrams with the following purposes:

☐ To tell the narrator of "The Coldest Winter Since 1854" that Emma Haines has started going steady with somebody else.

☐ To offer Joe in "Where I Come From People Are Polite" a job as bookkeeper in your office.

☐ To tell Al Condraj's mother in "The Parsley Garden" that you, her cousin, will be arriving from Armenia in 10 days.

119

SPORTS

What sets one sports figure apart from all the others? Why are some games remembered forever? The answers can be found in the exciting world of sports.

Sports

Sports and the outstanding athletes who play them are favorite subjects of stories and articles. Why? Here are just three of many reasons.

• Sports are inspiring, whether you take part in them or watch from the sidelines. If you are an athlete, you may spend hours trying to improve your performance. You may then experience the thrill of making a spectacular play or scoring the winning point. And if you are a sports fan, you are sure to admire the athletes who make dazzling performances look easy. Certain athletes may even become heroes to you.

• Sports reflect the real world, whether team is pitted against team, athlete against athlete, or individuals against their own best records. Life is competitive. For every winner, there is usually a loser. But today's loser may be tomorrow's winner.

• Sports demand qualities that most people admire: drive, teamwork, self-confidence, coordination, speed, strength, judgment, endurance. No wonder sports are favorite subjects of literature!

On the following pages, you will find two short stories in which the importance of winning is measured against other values. You will also find two nonfiction pieces about two famous athletes, Cheryl Toussaint and Muhammad Ali.

Two Winners

In the article about Cheryl Toussaint, you will see how a teenager's life took on new meaning as she became serious about a sport. Before she got involved in running, Cheryl had no particular goals, was labeled a "slow learner" in school, and lacked self-confidence. Find out how her love of running turned her life around.

In "Muhammad Ali's African Battle," a sports writer describes one of boxing's most famous matches, held in Zaire, Africa. The contenders were the heavyweight champion of the world, George Foreman, and former heavyweight champion, Muhammad Ali. One was a "puncher," whose main tactic was power, while the other was a "boxer," whose main tactics were speed and cleverness. The style of the man who won the fight suggests why he became a hero to so many people around the world.

Tough Choices

In the short story "There Must Be a Losing Coach," a young football player and his father find themselves in stiff competition. The son wants to win an impor-

tant game, which will help him pursue a career in football. But if his team wins, his father, who is coach of the opposing team, will lose his job. What should the son do? The answer is an eye-opener.

The short story "Winning . . . and Losing!" is similar. Here again, a son is at odds with his father, yet doesn't want to hurt the father. In both cases, the son wonders whether he should try to win or lose an important sports event. There is a difference, though, in the way each one tries to resolve his dilemma.

In all four of these selections, you will find athletes who compete against other athletes. But they also face conflicts of other sorts. As you read about these real and fictional athletes, notice the conflicts they face. Whether you're an athlete or not, you've probably faced similar ones.

Cheryl Toussaint

by Francene Sabin

Nobody praised Cheryl Toussaint. Nobody seemed to care whether she ran or not. She gave up. But the memory of running, of winning, wouldn't leave her.

At last she understood. She was the one who really had to care. And she was on her way to a new life. It's not just a story. It really happened.

In 1967, a group called Youth in Action held a track meet at a field in Brooklyn, New York. Because she had nothing better to do that day, 15-year-old Cheryl Toussaint went to watch the meet.

Sitting in the stands with her friends, Cheryl found it very exciting. She loved the speed of the runners, the yelling, and the cheering.

An "open" race for girls was announced. That meant that any girl could come to the starting line and race, even if she didn't belong to a track team. Cheryl loved to run, and she wanted to enter. Cheryl's friends begged her to give it a try. When one said, "I dare you," Cheryl took the dare.

"It was a 100-yard dash," Cheryl remembered, "and I didn't even know how long 100 yards was. I didn't know how to start. I was standing straight up. Then the man said, 'Take your marks. . . . Set. . . . Go!' and I ran. I got second."

After the meet was over, Cheryl saw some Atoms runners doing exercises on the grass. The Atoms Track Club of Brooklyn was a team of local girls who wanted to run against other teams. Cheryl asked them how she could join. They told her that all she had to do was come to the practices every afternoon.

For a while, Cheryl went to Prospect Park in Brooklyn for the Atoms' daily practice. But when no one paid much attention to her, she began to wonder if she was a good runner.

"I was putting my whole heart into it," she said. "I thought the coach should have done more than tell me to run laps, do exercises, or practice starts."

Cheryl had no way of knowing that Atoms coach Fred Thompson always treated new team members this way. He realized that the long, tough practice sessions were more than many girls would put up with. If they stayed with it, without praise — he would be sure they were ready for real coaching.

After two months as an Atom, Cheryl dropped out of the club. But the memory of her one race kept coming back to her.

She thought of the pounding of her heart before the start, the free feeling of running, the excitement of coming in ahead of others. So, after six months away from the Atoms, Cheryl Toussaint returned to the club. This time, she was there to stay.

Those six months away from track had given her time to think about herself and her goals in life. Cheryl learned that she really cared about track. She went out to the Prospect Park field ready to dig in and work, even if *nobody* paid any attention to her.

Until Fred Thompson came into her life, nobody had ever thought of Cheryl Toussaint as something special. Cheryl was born on December 16, 1952. Soon after, her parents separated.

Cheryl went to live with her grandmother. Her home was in one of the worst parts of Brooklyn. In the crowded schools, Cheryl slipped further and further behind. By junior high, she was in the "slow learner" class.

Then Cheryl joined the Atoms, and everything in her world took on new meaning. Fred Thompson took the part of the father she didn't have at home. He scolded Cheryl when she let up and praised her when she worked hard.

"Freddy always encouraged me and all the girls to try for good grades," Cheryl said. "He'd say, 'When those report cards come in, I want to see them!' He made me feel that he was just as concerned with how I was doing in school as with my running. I couldn't tell him that a C was okay because the teacher had said so — he knew better. My mother and grandmother cared, but Freddy knew what each grade meant. There was no snowing him."

With a new goal, Cheryl set to work. It was tough, but Cheryl gave it everything she had. She began to learn and do well. "When I got my report card," Cheryl said, "not only did I feel good for myself in getting good grades, I felt proud having somebody else to show them to — somebody who really appreciated them. Freddy would say, 'Cheryl, that's darn good. Keep it up.' Then he started to talk about college."

To Cheryl, the idea of college sounded like a wild fairy tale. But she understood, and so did all the Atoms, that Fred meant every word he said. He told them that if they were good enough, being poor would never stop them.

If the girls made the Nationals, no matter where the races were held, he'd see that they got there. Fred would use his own money, or borrow it, or beg for it — but the Atoms never had to worry about how they would pay for track equipment or travel expenses.

Her part of the bargain, Cheryl learned, was to do well in school. (If you flunked, you were off the team.) And you also had to work hard on the track. She stuck with the two-hour practice every day.

As her schoolwork improved, Cheryl began to do better on the track. She began winning races. Cheryl had been running for only about a year when she was picked to run in the U.S. trials for a place on the 1968 Olympic team.

Looking back at that time, Cheryl later said, "I had been doing fairly well. But at that point I didn't think I was ready for the Olympics. It was enough of a thrill to know that I had made it to the trials. I ran and did the best I could, coming in fifth, but I didn't make the Olympic team. I was a little disappointed, but I know now that if I had made the team then, it might have been the ruination of me."

Cheryl was ready to become an outstanding student, however. Fred Thompson helped her to see that she could go to college. He told her that she might even win a scholarship. With that goal in mind, the "slow learner" was soon at the top of her class. In June, 1970, Cheryl graduated from Erasmus Hall High School in Brooklyn. She won a scholarship to New York University.

"It might sound kind of boring," Cheryl said of her teen years, "because my life was a round of sleeping, eating, classes, running, studying, and more sleeping. But I was doing what I loved and what I wanted to do."

Running took Cheryl to Europe many times, and to the U.S. Nationals year after year. Each trip was fun, and each was a challenge. But they were only practice for what Cheryl wanted most — the Olympics.

The teenage runner made the Games the focus of her entire life. Only two things mattered — school and track. This didn't leave much free time for dating. Cheryl went out with boys once in a while, but she felt it was wrong to have a steady boyfriend while she was in training.

During the indoor season of 1971–72, she won every race. She was faster every time out.

Then the outdoor season began. Cheryl had to run fast enough outdoors for the U.S. Olympic team. She began to press too hard, and she lost time on the track.

Coach Thompson tried to calm her. He was sure that she would make the team. Soon she was chosen as a runner on the metric-mile relay team. But she still hadn't been chosen in her individual event, the 800 meters. And the summer was growing short.

Fred took Cheryl to Ohio, where there were to be two meets that would give her the chance she needed. On the day of the first meet, Madeline Manning Jackson, the one woman who might have challenged Cheryl, became sick. With nobody challenging her, Cheryl won the race. But her time still wasn't fast enough.

At the second meet, Thompson was counting on Nancy Shafer, another top American runner, to push Cheryl to go all out. But in the 95-degree heat on the day of the race, Nancy faded away. From the first turn, Cheryl ran alone. She missed out again.

Cheryl went to the Olympic training camp with one last chance to make the team in an individual event. "On the day of the race," Fred Thompson recalled, "I sneaked in, so that Cheryl wouldn't see me. I hid behind a tree and watched her run. When she had done it, I came out and she saw me. Well, we both cried and cried in relief. It was really down to the wire on that one."

Then she was off to Munich and the 1972 Olympics. Her first event was the 800-meter run, her specialty. She followed Fred Thompson's advice never to fall farther back than third — with awful results. Mr. Thompson said afterward, "The girls in her heat went out so fast that Cheryl was thrown off her normal pace and didn't make it. It was my mistake, and I'll never stop blaming myself. If Cheryl had run her usual race, pacing her first quarter more slowly, she'd have made it to the semifinals — and then, maybe, to the finals."

The night after the race, Thompson went looking for Cheryl in Olympic Village. He found her in tears. Fred reminded her that she was the youngest one in the event. He told her that her running career was just beginning. There would be another Olympics for her. Besides, the relay race was yet to come. Cheryl had one more chance to win a medal.

On September 9, 1972, the first women's 4 × 400-meter relay in Olympic history was set to be run. The U.S. team of Mabel Ferguson, Madeline Jackson, Cheryl Toussaint, and Kathy Hammond had to do well in their heat to run in the finals. Cheryl, running the third leg of the relay, waited to be handed the baton from Madeline Jackson.

"I turned," Cheryl said, "and reached for the stick. I was just starting to run with it, when a girl from another team fell in front of me. My first reaction was to rear back, so I wouldn't trip over her — but you never stop. I dashed around her, only to have *another* runner step on the heel of my left shoe. Half my shoe was tied on tightly but the other half was crushed under my heel. 'I can't believe it!' I thought. 'Here I am in the Olympics, and my shoe is coming off!'

"If I had stopped to pull it up, my teammates would have killed me. So I just ran. I'd gone another 10 yards when the shoe flew up in the air. I just kept running — wondering if my shoe had hit anyone, and if the people in the stands and on TV were asking what that girl was doing out there without a shoe.

"There had been two teams ahead of us when I got the stick. Somehow, before I knew it, I had passed their runners. Then I saw where I was, and I felt stunned at getting there. All I'd been thinking was that my shoe had come off, that this was the Olympics, and that these things don't happen. But it did."

She may have done it the hard way — but she'd done it. Cheryl and her teammates had made it to the relay finals. "Nothing more could happen after that shoe thing. So when I received the baton pass, I just ran and ran until I couldn't run anymore. We took second behind East Germany.

"Getting up on the victory stand with my teammates, I realized that I was going home from my first Olympics with a silver medal. Of course, I wish we had won, but

that doesn't mean I wasn't thrilled by being up there. And, anyway, there was Montreal in 1976 to look forward to."

After the '72 Olympics, Cheryl came home and kept working at school and track. She graduated from college in 1974 and got a job with the Federal Reserve Bank. And, at the same time, she started working toward the 1976 Olympics.

Cheryl collected many trophies and prizes in her running career, but the greatest reward track gave to the skinny girl from Brooklyn was a chance at a whole new life. For Cheryl, being one of the Atoms made the difference between being nobody and being somebody very special.

Fred Thompson might have known it all along, but Cheryl didn't realize just how special she was until February 5, 1970, when she set the first of her several world records. "It was in Toronto, Canada," she recalled. "I had never run the 600-yard event before in my life, but I felt prepared because I had been training well.

"There were so many girls in the event that it was split into two heats, both to count as finals. That meant you could win your heat and still lose the race — if the girls in the other section had faster times. I was in the second section, and my goal was to beat the time of the winner in the first heat.

"There were three and three-quarter laps to run in all. With about two laps left, I heard Freddy yelling, 'Go! Go! What are you waiting for?' and I went!

"I won my heat, then walked around the track to where Freddy and my teammates were waiting. It was funny — everybody was jumping up and down and smiling and reaching out to me. I asked, 'Did I win?' What I meant was, did I beat the fastest time of the first heat? They just kept smiling. Then Freddy said, 'Look up at the clock.' So I looked, and the clock read 1:22.2. I said, 'That's nice, I won.' Freddy just kept looking at me and said, 'I think it's a new world record.'

"I thought he was kidding, until they announced it over the loudspeaker. Then the tears came. I was so excited, and I couldn't believe it. I just could never imagine that *I* had really broken a world record — me, who'd never run a 600 before, and had never, never thought of myself as a world-recordholder. It was too much for me to understand. Freddy was overjoyed, and I was, too.

"They told me to jog a victory lap, and I went around the track crying, with my mind in a total fog. At that moment, I felt as if I'd never be tired, as if I could run forever.

"That night, after I'd calmed down a little, I thought about it. Lots of people break world records, but *me* — wow! I thought about how lucky I was to be an Atom, and of all the things it had given me, and it was so wonderful."

Note: Cheryl Toussaint did not go on to the 1976 Olympics. Her job at the bank did not leave her time enough to train. But she did have time to help other kids. She joined Fred Thompson in a new sports program for girls. She wanted to give them the same kind of coaching she had been lucky enough to have herself.

READING COMPREHENSION

Summarizing. Choose the best phrase to complete each sentence. Then write the complete statements on your paper.

1. To be a member of the Atoms, you had to _____ (win races regularly, do well in school, have a nice personality).

2. Cheryl's greatest interests as a teen were in _____ (school and track, school and dating, track and dating).

3. What Cheryl needed most as a teen was _____ (a better place to live, money, a belief in her abilities).

4. Cheryl's greatest reward from track was _____ (realizing she was special, the gold medal she won, the money she earned).

Interpreting. Write the answer to each question on your paper.

1. What did Cheryl do that proved she was not a "slow learner" in school?

2. Why didn't Fred Thompson praise new members of the Atoms at first?

3. In what ways did Fred Thompson influence Cheryl?

For Thinking and Discussing

1. Success in sports often helps people to succeed in other areas. Can you explain why?

2. Cheryl said that if she had made the Olympic track team on her first try, it might have been her "ruination." What did she mean? Do you agree?

UNDERSTANDING LITERATURE

Conflict. When people or feelings fight each other, there is a *conflict*. Conflict makes a story exciting. Sometimes there is a conflict between different feelings within one person. For example, if you want to play ball but know that you should do your homework, you have a conflict.

Another kind of conflict is between two people. A third kind of conflict is caused by a difficult situation. If two friends have an argument and then meet by accident at a party, the conflict may be caused by the situation.

Read the statements below. Then decide which kind or kinds of conflict best describe each statement.

1. Cheryl's shoe came off in the race. If she stopped, she would lose.

2. Cheryl wanted to give up running, but she'd miss the excitement if she did.

3. Cheryl wanted to run in the 1976 Olympics, but she did not have time to train.

4. Cheryl wanted praise but her coach did not praise his new runners.

WRITING

Do you have a special goal? Maybe it is not as ambitious as being in the Olympics. But, to you, it's probably just as important. Describe your goal in a few sentences. Now think of five activities that you could do each day to help you reach this goal. List them.

There Must Be a Losing Coach

by Samuel W. Taylor

Swede Jones had to win, for his team and for his own self-respect. But if he did, what would that do to his father?

When the girl came into the lobby, the State football team was sitting around waiting until it was time to go to sleep. They had traveled halfway across the country to play tomorrow's game. They were nervous but trying not to show it. Everyone thought they'd win easily — but you never could tell. And the Wildcats would be ready for them. In fact, everyone knew that the job of the Wildcat coach rested on winning this game. He'd use all he had against State.

But when the girl came into the lobby, the 34 State players forgot about the game. Coach Happy Hough, in the middle of speaking to a reporter, looked up. So did the reporter. The girl slowly searched the faces of the team.

Then she said, "Swede." All eyes turned to the tall, blond end who got to his feet.

"Hello, Marta," he said, and walked over to her.

"I know you've been busy," Marta said. "But I thought you might give us a call." She lowered her voice. "Andy wants to see you."

He glanced over his shoulder. "It's almost time to turn in," he said.

"You could be nice about it," she said. "Or do you think he'll try to bribe you?"

"Let's not go into things."

"Swede, you've hurt him a lot. He's still your father, you know. And you haven't even called him."

"I'll ask Coach." Swede crossed to where Happy Hough was talking with the reporter.

"I'd like to go out for an hour, Coach."

Happy Hough looked at the clock. Four minutes to nine. "Be in by 10," he said.

"You're really generous," the reporter said. He began to laugh, until he saw Happy Hough's icy stare. The coach had gotten his nickname for the same reason fat men are called Tiny.

"Just like old times," the girl said, as she drove Swede down the winding road. "A moon and a car and — us."

Swede said nothing. It hurt to think about the past. He didn't like to do it.

"How are you making out, Swede?"

"Okay."

"You're first-string end, I hear."

"Yes."

"That's nice going for a sophomore."

He said nothing, and she gave up trying to make small talk. Marta pulled up before a diner, and Swede followed her in. It was empty, except for the heavyset man in the back booth.

He was Andy Jones, coach of the team Swede was going to play against tomorrow.

"Hello, Swede."

"Hello, Dad."

Both men felt uneasy, although each of them tried not to show it.

Swede saw that his father had changed in the year and a half since he'd seen him. That had been in Texas, before Andy Jones got the head coaching spot out here. He looked as if he was beginning to bend under the pressure of more than 20 years as a coach. Twenty years can be a long time — mostly high school coaching, here and there. He was always hoping and waiting for the big chance.

And then last spring he'd finally got his bid for head coach — on a one-year contract. He had to produce a winning team in one season. This season his Wildcats had won two, tied one, and lost four. It was no secret that unless the Wildcats won tomorrow, he'd be out of a job.

"You're looking fine, Swede," Andy Jones said. Swede said that he felt all right. Marta talked about the weather. It was a stiff meeting. Swede hadn't wanted it to take place. There was nothing he could say anymore to his girl or his father, without bringing up the past. And that was settled long ago.

The door of the diner opened and slammed shut. Swede turned to see the reporter who'd been talking with Coach Happy Hough back at the lodge. The reporter was looking from Andy Jones to Swede and trying not to seem surprised.

"Hello," Andy Jones said. He nodded at Swede. "This is my boy."

"*Your* boy?"

"No, I'm not buying off the State players. Swede's my son."

"Oh, your *son*. Say! That's a story! Father against son. And if the son's team wins — you don't mind if I use it, Andy?"

"Yes, I do mind."

"Well, after all, Andy — somebody else would pick it up, if I didn't. And where would my job be?"

Andy didn't answer. He might have argued a year ago, but not now. It was too late.

"Say, Andy, how come your boy's not playing for us, instead of State?" the reporter asked.

"You've got your story," Swede said, rising. "Now get out of here."

"Well, sure, Swede," the reporter said. "Sure. I was just leaving anyhow."

"I'm sorry this happened," Andy Jones said.

"It'll sell more tickets," Swede answered. "I've got to go, Dad. It was nice seeing you again."

Driving back to the hotel, the girl said, "You see how he's changed?"

"Yeah."

"Football did it to him. Do you understand why he wanted to keep you out of the game?"

"Dad's getting old, is all," Swede said.

"He's 44. If they'd only given him a two-year contract. What can a man do in one year? And if he fails now, how long will it be before he gets another chance as head coach?"

Swede didn't say anything. They pulled up in front of the hotel. "Maybe I'll see you again before we go," he said.

As he walked inside, she called his name. It took all his strength not to turn back to her.

The next morning, Coach Happy Hough spoke to Swede. "You read the *Telegram* this morning?" he asked.

"No. But I know what it said," Swede answered.

Coach Hough waited for him to go on.

When Swede didn't speak, the coach said, "I might have been told about it."

"I hoped it wouldn't come out." Swede took a deep breath. "Dad and I never got along. That's all. He didn't want me to play football. So I left home."

"He didn't want you to get hurt?"

It was hard for Swede to put this into words. "It's because I want to follow it up and be a coach myself. Dad wanted me to be a doctor. He said that — well, you know what the coaching game is, Coach."

Happy Hough nodded. "I know."

He turned to three reporters coming in. One of them was the *Telegram* reporter, who asked, "Any change in the lineup, Coach?"

"Yes, Warbuck at right end."

"Instead of Jones?" He knew Swede played right end. There was no need to say it. Happy Hough ignored the question.

Late in the fourth quarter of the game, State was losing by three points.

"Swede!" Coach Hough barked. "Warm up!"

It was the first time the coach had called him by his nickname. "I don't want to put you in there today, but you know how to hang onto Flint's passes. Do you want to go in?"

"Yes," Swede said. He had no choice.

"It's only a game — but the game's like that. You understand?"

"Yes."

State ran several yards with the ball. The Wildcats prepared for a pass. When they closed in, Flint called the 71 play. This was the Flint-to-Jones play, already becoming famous.

Swede dropped into position. At the count of nine, the ball snapped from center. Swede put on all the steam he had for 30 steps. Then he looked back over his shoulder. The pass was leading him, and still high. The ball was too far in front of him.

And then, somehow, everything seemed to freeze. In this frozen moment, Swede wondered if he could call on his reserve strength. It always came to him in a pinch. It made him sure, deep inside, that he'd be All-American. But now his father's future was in his hands. Should he catch that pass or let it go?

His father was praying for Swede to miss that pass. Coach Hough had put Swede in the game to catch it. Swede hadn't known there would be this moment.

He was still running. The ball was spinning. It was out of his reach!

Then he took an extra step, faster than he could possibly run. He jumped higher than he could possibly jump. When his fingers felt the sting of the ball, the Wildcats were a full step behind. The single step made the difference, and Swede went over the line for six points and the game.

Andy Jones got up from the bench and walked over to shake hands with the winning coach.

"Congratulations, Happy," he said. "Your boys played a great game."

"Thanks, Andy. I was just lucky."

With this done, Andy Jones turned away to face the wolves alone.

Swede came out of the field house. Marta was waiting. She'd been crying. She'd been against him in the old argument with his father. She was hurt now. It hurt her to see Andy Jones beaten.

"That was a great catch, Swede," she said.

"Thanks." There was nothing more to say. "Well, good-bye."

"I'll drive you home," she said.

He didn't know how to refuse the ride.

"Your mother will have dinner ready. Steak for you," Marta said, when they reached the car. "Let's sit here awhile until the parking lot empties."

Swede knew he couldn't face his father. He said. "There's a dinner for the team tonight. Please drop me at the hotel."

She took his big hand, looking up at him. Her eyes were still red from crying. "It's all right, Swede. We want you to come home for dinner. We all understand."

Swede said nothing. He didn't understand.

"There's a teaching job open for Andy in Texas. He's going to take it."

Swede's throat was tight. It was hard for him to see his father beaten.

She said, "I really think he's glad, in a way."

"If he'd had another year here to build a team — "

"No. He doesn't feel that way, now. He knows that he just isn't cut out to be a big-time coach. But you see he couldn't give up until he'd had his chance — until he *did* know. Now he'll be happy as a teacher. If he'd taken the job last year, he'd always have thought he could have been a great coach.

"It's the toughest game of all," Marta went on. "One coach always has to lose, and every coach must always win. That's why you like it. It's a challenge. You're like Andy was 20 years ago. You've got to meet the challenge. You've got to know."

That was it, Swede realized. He'd never thought about it that way.

"You see," Marta said, "I'm trying to think things out for myself. There was a moment when you were after that pass, when things seemed to stand still. I realized then what I'm trying to say now. Swede, if you hadn't made that last try for that pass, I wouldn't have been waiting for you. Shall we go?"

"Yes," Swede said. "Let's go." He realized he was hungry, and happy at the idea of having dinner at home again.

READING COMPREHENSION

Summarizing. Choose the best phrase to complete each sentence. Then write the complete statements on your paper.

1. The big football game was between the team Swede played for and _____ (the State team, a team from Texas, the team his father coached).

2. Swede left home because his father _____ (asked him to leave, didn't want him to become a coach, wanted him to play for the Wildcats).

3. For Andy Jones, losing the game against State meant losing _____ (Swede's respect, his job, a bet).

4. After the game, Swede and Andy probably _____ (wouldn't face each other, had a fight, understood each other better).

Interpreting. Write the answer to each question on your paper.

1. What was Marta's relationship to Swede?

2. Why do you think Andy Jones wanted Swede to be a doctor, not a coach?

3. Why, according to Marta, was coaching "the toughest game of all"?

For Thinking and Discussing.

1. Did Swede do the right thing by catching the final pass?

2. Would Swede make a good coach? Why or why not?

UNDERSTANDING LITERATURE

Conflict. In "There Must Be a Losing Coach," Swede's conflict is caused by a difficult situation. Whatever Swede does will be good in some ways and bad in others.

The following are some decisions Swede could make in order to solve a difficult problem. Write one reason why the decision would have been good or bad.

1. Call his father when he came into town.
   a. This would have been a good decision because _____.
   b. This would have been a bad decision because _____.

2. Try to win the game.
   a. This would have been a good decision because _____.
   b. This would have been a bad decision because _____.

3. Let his father's team win the game.
   a. This would have been a good decision because _____.
   b. This would have been a bad decision because _____.

WRITING

Imagine that you are the reporter in the story. The big game has been played. Andy Jones and his team have lost. What questions would you ask Andy, Happy Hough, Swede, and Marta? Write four questions. After each question, write the name of the person you would ask.

Muhammad Ali's African Battle

by Larry Bortstein

Two black Americans were to battle for the heavyweight championship of the world. The eyes of people everywhere were on them — as they fought in Africa.

It was a most unlikely spot for a world heavyweight championship fight. But the city of Kinshasa, in Zaire, Africa, was where Muhammad Ali would try to get back his title from George Foreman.

It was October 29, 1974. Ali and Foreman had come to this far-off place to fight for the big prize. There was no bigger prize in sports.

Many other countries had tried to stage this important match. Zaire was a young nation. A black American named Don King had gone to its leaders. He had told them he could put on the most colorful event in their history. He turned out to be right.

Zaire (pronounced zy-ear) had a long history of fighting. But it wasn't the kind done in the ring. Zaire's fighting history had more to do with war and revolution.

The nation was once known as the Belgian Congo. It was ruled by Belgium. For 50 years, the people of the Congo had hated Belgian rule. Then they broke away and gained their freedom in 1960. A few years later, the country took a new name, Zaire. For many years, its beautiful capital city had been called Leopoldville. That was in honor of a Belgian king. Now they named it Kinshasa.

Zaire is known for its rich diamond and copper mines. It is the third largest country in Africa. In the last few years, it has made gains in business, and its people are better off. Most of the people are of the Bantu nation. The chief language is French.

But the thing that put Kinshasa on the map was the fight. The world watched two black Americans travel more than 10,000 miles to trade punches.

The fight was to be held in the huge Twentieth of May Stadium, which was usually used for soccer. Foreman was the world champion. He had knocked out Joe Frazier in January, 1973.

Ali had won the championship, as Cassius Clay, in 1964. Now he was trying to get back the crown that had been stripped from him in 1967. That was when he refused to go into the U.S. Army during the Vietnam War. Ali and Foreman were to receive $5,000,000 each for this first heavyweight title fight ever held in Africa.

The fight had a wild build-up. Well-known people from all over the world found their way to Kinshasa. There were actors, politicians, and rich sports fans. It was an adventure for them.

Hundreds of sports writers from big papers everywhere went to Zaire. Then, a few days before the fight was to take place, there was an accident. Foreman got a cut over his left eye during training. He asked to have the fight put off for a while. There was talk that he needed the extra time to get in shape. Talk flew fast and thick. The fight was set for a new date, October 30, Zaire time.

There was another worry. The new date was in the African rainy season. A heavy downpour was very possible.

Things were wild enough because of the time difference. The fight would start at 4 a.m., Zaire time. Don King wanted to make sure the fight would go on at 10 p.m., New York time, the night before. That was for theater TV audiences.

The fight wound up with the largest audience of any fight in history. With trees and mountains in the background, over 100,000 fans watched. Most of them were Zairians in bright costumes. Many millions more saw it on television, and on theater TV, all over the world. Luckily, it didn't rain.

And what a fight they saw! Like most title fights, it was supposed to go 15 rounds. But this fight was different from most others. A puncher was matched against a boxer.

From its beginning, in the far past, boxing has had two kinds of fighters. One is the hitter who goes in for the knockout. The other is the "boxer," who uses speed and smartness. He keeps away from the heavy hitter. He piles up points by beating him to the punch. Quick hands and quick feet are his best tools.

Ali is a boxer. The ring's great strong men — champs like Joe Louis, Jack Dempsey, and Rocky Marciano — have mostly been "punchers."

Foreman was thought to be every inch a "puncher." In fact, the champion from Houston, Texas, was one of the most powerful punchers of all time. He had won all 46 of his fights as a full-time fighter. Forty-four of his wins had been by knockout — like the win over Frazier that gave him the crown. Mostly, Foreman used hard right-hand shots for his knockouts.

Because of that right hand, everything seemed to be in Foreman's favor. He weighed more than Ali — 220 pounds, to Ali's 216½. At 26, Foreman was six years younger than Muhammad. Even if Ali could stay away from Foreman's hardest punches — could he land his own often and hard enough?

The audience didn't have to wait long for its answer. Ali took over almost from the start. The crowd in Kinshasa roared for Ali, whom they thought a great black leader. During a few days in Zaire, Muhammad had become a great public favorite. He went into the ring to the tune of the Zairian national anthem. He held his right hand up over his head.

A lot of people thought Ali would dance around the ring on his toes to stay away from Foreman. He had done that in many

of his early fights. Muhammad had made the style famous. It had never before been used by a heavyweight. Most of them are too big and heavy for such dancing.

"I float like a butterfly and sting like a bee," Ali often said. But his floating and stinging days were over. He and his trainer,

Angelo Dundee, had new ideas. They were meant to save Ali's strength. If it worked, the plan would tire Foreman out, too.

The new plan was hardly noticed in the first few rounds. But in the third round, it began to pay off. Foreman was trying to pound Ali with his powerful right hand. But instead of stepping to the side, or dancing, Ali backed into the ropes. Then he slid along the ropes. Foreman followed him, still throwing punches.

Some of Foreman's punches landed on Ali's body and head. But Muhammad kept moving along the ropes. He used them to keep from falling. Sometimes he leaned back. That way he did not feel the full force of Foreman's punches. The more blows Foreman landed, the less they counted. And he got more tired. That is what Ali and Dundee had hoped.

Muhammad knew it meant getting hit more than he liked. "He could have kept hitting me with the good right or with a left jab," he said later. "But as it turned out, I was able to take his punches very well."

Ali's pro career had begun in 1960. He was almost unmarked. Almost no one could hit him in the face. But in his fight with Foreman, Ali was hit often and hard on his head and body.

He was able to take Foreman's punishment. He was thrown off balance by some of Foreman's hard shots, but he quickly shook them off. "They're not that bad," he told Dundee between rounds.

During rounds five, six, and seven, Muhammad seemed to be gathering steam. Foreman, six years younger, seemed to be breathing heavily. Ali's face and eyes were puffy, but he was holding up well. The men came out for the eighth round. It was clear that Foreman was almost dead on his feet.

Muhammad tore after Foreman with a series of stinging lefts and rights. Foreman held on bravely. He wasn't going to give up his championship without a struggle.

But by the third minute of the round, he could no longer defend himself. Muhammad drove two rights into George's middle. Then came two lefts, then another right. Foreman later said he couldn't remember Ali's last few punches. He fell to the canvas.

Foreman did not try to get up. The count went all the way to 10. Only then did he lift himself a little. It was much too late, of course. He was now an ex-champion of the heavyweights. The "boxer" had beaten the "puncher" to the punch.

Reporters, photographers, and fans milled around Ali. For the first time they could remember, he looked like he had been beaten up. "Yeah, he hit me good a few times," Ali said. "But I'm the champ, right? That's all I care about."

Muhammad was right. Getting the title back was good reason to howl. For a long time, Ali and his friends had felt that he was the real champ. To them, he was taking a vacation. Now he was back on top again. It felt good.

But even if he had lost in Zaire, Muhammad would still have been champ to millions. Ali has always been one of the great sports heroes for people around the world. Most of them have never seen him fight. For that matter, they care little about boxing.

To these millions, Muhammad Ali doesn't have to lay a glove on a man to be a champion. He just has to be himself.

READING COMPREHENSION

Summarizing. Choose the best phrase to complete each sentence. Then write the complete statements on your paper.

1. The 1974 heavyweight championship fight drew attention _____ (almost entirely in Africa, almost entirely in the U.S., all over the world).

2. Before the fight, Muhammad Ali was _____ (heavyweight champ of the world, trying to get the title back, aiming for the title for the first time).

3. Compared to Ali, Foreman was _____ (older and more experienced, smarter and faster, younger and heavier).

4. Ali won the fight mainly by _____ (landing a lot of punches, dodging Foreman's punches, tiring Foreman out).

Interpreting. Write the answer to each question on your paper.

1. Which fighter — Foreman or Ali — became the public favorite in Zaire?

2. Why was the fight held so early in the morning (4 a.m.) in Zaire?

3. What did Ali mean by, "I float like a butterfly and sting like a bee"?

4. Why didn't Ali dance around the ring to keep away from Foreman?

For Thinking and Discussing. What do you think was more important to Ali — the money he got from the fight or being the champ? Explain your answer.

UNDERSTANDING LITERATURE

Conflict. The conflict in "Muhammad Ali's African Battle" is between two people: Ali and Foreman.

Think about the differences between the two fighters. Then answer the questions about the conflict between Ali and Foreman.

1. What were the differences in fighting style? Who was a boxer? Who was a puncher?

2. What was the difference in age? Who was younger?

3. What was the difference in weight? Who weighed more?

4. What did each fighter expect? Who expected to win? Who was the world champion before the fight? Who had lost the championship and wanted it back?

WRITING

Larry Bornstein wrote: "But even if he had lost in Zaire, Muhammad would still have been champ to millions. Ali has always been one of the great sports heroes for people around the world." What made Ali such a hero? On your paper, list two reasons why you think people felt this way about him.

Think of someone else who is a hero to you. It may be someone famous or just someone that you know. Give reasons why this person is a hero. List the reasons on your paper.

Winning . . . and Losing!

by Sarah Thonney

Your father is obsessed with turning you into an Olympic swimmer, but you've begun to hate the sport. Should you lose an important race on purpose, or would that hurt your father too much?

Here I am, writing this down so you'll know what it is like for me to be pushed and pushed until I can't go anymore.

I have been swimming for seven years in competition, having swimming meets every weekend in the summer and one or more a month in the winter. The only thing that keeps me swimming is my father. If it weren't for the way he looks every time I talk about quitting, I wouldn't be where I am now, at the Nationals, a meet large enough to scare anybody.

I'm so scared right now that I'd like to run. I never used to be scared. Everything was so much fun — the lights and the people in their bright clothes with their cameras. Now it seems like a nightmare. The more Dad pushes me, the more afraid I get.

You see, Dad's afraid, too. He's afraid of the water. To appease his own fear, he started me on swimming lessons when I could barely walk, and he's been pushing me ever since. I'm 16 years old now. That's a long time to have been pushed.

Yesterday I swam in the prelims, and I was so scared that I thought I was going to be sick. I made the finals, just from the joy of swimming fast. When Dad found out I had won, he called home and told Mom. Everyone in this city knows who I am from Dad's bragging, but I'll bet Mom hasn't told a soul at home. She just doesn't care.

I don't think I'm exactly ugly for a boy, but I have the prettiest little sister that ever was. That's all Mom cares about. Oh, she loves me, I suppose, in her own way. She feeds me and keeps my clothes clean, but she doesn't really care what I do. You know how people say a father falls over his daughter and a mother falls over her son? Well, it's the opposite in our family. Dad won't leave me alone, and Mom doesn't give me much thought. I'd like to talk to her about my career, and

what I do in school, and my girl. If I did, though, she'd say, "That's nice, Johnny," and go on with whatever she was doing. I know. I tried it once.

I see Dad coming this way now, so I'll have to stop writing. I like to write. In fact, I want to major in English in college, but Dad roars like thunder and finally gets that hurt look if I mention it.

Right now Dad is acting different. I think that, for once, he is doubting my ability. I kind of hope so, because I think I'm going to lose.

All he did while he was here was pace up and down, up and down. He kept telling me to eat something. Then, when I did, he told me not to eat too much. It's getting so I can hardly go to the bathroom without him.

There are some kids my age here, so I wandered over to talk and get acquainted. All of a sudden Dad runs up, grabs me, and stands there telling me I should get my rest and plenty of the right kind of food. Then he makes me come back and lie down. I feel like such a fool!

I said a while back that swimming used to be fun. It still is for some people. Of course you have to get up extra early so there's time for your breakfast to digest, but after that it's fun. The meets are crowded with all kinds of people. I always have a sleeping bag and plenty of comic books. There are all sorts of card games,

excitement, and noise.

Meets are still like that, I guess, but no longer for me. I don't get near the excitement anymore.

I want to lose, but if I do, it will just kill Dad. And if I win, he'll brag all over the whole country, and I'll never be able to run my own life. I have to lose without hurting Dad. I wish I could talk to him, but he won't listen. Once I tried to talk to him about writing, and he nearly blew his top. He likes to write, too, but he wants me to be something he never was. He wants me to be something I don't want to be, and don't think I ever will be.

I can see him over by the edge of the pool, pacing. He's the one who needs food and rest. He's scared. He is afraid I am going to lose. Maybe I will, just to see him suffer the way he has made me suffer all

these years. I know I can't, though. For all his dominating ways, I love him.

I've got to do my best, but I'm not going to let him run my life anymore. I'm going to tell him . . . .

I told him. It didn't do any good. He didn't even listen. I'm going to keep on talking, though, and someday he is going to listen to me.

I'm not scared anymore, just numb. I can feel some of the excitement, but it doesn't really penetrate. I'm going to lose. I feel like a mechanical doll.

I can feel the way it will be — like a hundred times before, except for the end. They'll call my name in the first call, then in the final call. All of us will be in our proper lanes, and out of the corner of my eye I'll see Dad. We'll dive in and swim a few strokes to loosen up. Then we'll go

back to the starting point and get into our positions.

"Timers and judges ready?" the starter will shout. The judges and timers will nod as they raise their watches.

"Swimmers up!" the starter will yell, and we'll get ready.

Bang! The noise will make me jump. It always does, but that's fine, for I start well with a push from my legs.

Sometimes there are false starts. There won't be one today, though, not in a big race like the Nationals . . . .

After the race I came back to my sleeping bag and saw this paper I've been writing, and I laughed and laughed. It seemed as if my whole purpose in writing this was gone. I almost threw it in the trash.

You see, I won. I don't know whether I'm glad or not.

Dad is thrilled. He called Mom and she said to me, "That's nice, dear." Dad is bragging, of course. He won't leave me alone.

I had almost lost on purpose, but once I was out there, I couldn't. I'd have had to live with knowing I had deliberately hurt him, just for myself. I'd have had to live with knowing that every time I looked at him, he would have that hurt look in his eyes. At least there won't be that to worry about for a few more weeks.

But here I am worrying again, for Dad says the Olympics are next. I wish he'd sit down and listen just for a moment. I want to be a teacher. I don't want to be a champion.

Dad . . . listen, please, Dad.

Mom . . . Mom, please.

Listen to me . . . somebody!

READING COMPREHENSION

Summarizing. Choose the best pnrase to complete each sentence. Then write the complete statements on your paper.

1. The narrator, Johnny, wants to lose his next race in order to _____ (embarrass his father, shock his friends, quit swimming in competitions).

2. At the same time, Johnny doesn't want to lose, because that would _____ (hurt his father, embarrass both his parents, hurt his swimming career).

3. The way Johnny sees his dilemma, there is _____ (a simple solution, no solution, no easy solution).

Interpreting. Write the answer to each question on your paper.

1. How do Johnny's parents feel about his success in swimming?

2. Why is it hard for Johnny to discuss his goals with his parents?

3. Why is Johnny's father so concerned about swimming?

4. What does the title of the story mean? Using the words *winning* and *losing*, turn the title into a complete sentence.

For Thinking and Discussing

1. What should Johnny do?

2. Suppose Johnny asked a counselor to speak to his parents about his dilemma. If you were the counselor, what would you say to them?

UNDERSTANDING LITERATURE

Conflict. In "Winning. . .and Losing!" Johnny's conflict is partly between his father and himself. It is also between different feelings inside himself.

Decide which kind or kinds of conflicts each of the numbered sentences below reflects. On your paper, write the kind(s) of conflict next to the number of each sentence. If there is no conflict, write "No conflict."

1. The more Dad pushes me, the more afraid I get.

2. Yesterday I made the finals, just from the joy of swimming fast.

3. I want to major in English, but Dad roars like thunder if I mention it.

4. I want to lose, but I don't want to hurt Dad.

5. Dad likes to write, too, but he wants me to be something he never was.

6. I've got to do my best, but I can't let him run my life anymore.

7. I told him that he can't run my life anymore, but he didn't even listen.

WRITING

Swede in "There Must Be a Losing Coach" and Johnny in "Winning. . .and Losing!" face similar dilemmas. List the reasons why each dilemma is tough. Then write a paragraph stating which dilemma seems tougher to you — and why.

Section Review

VOCABULARY

Words in Context. Some words have more than one meaning. For example:

We took the 4 o'clock *train* to Houston. The team had to *train* for the Olympics.

In the first sentence, *train* means "a set of railroad cars." In the second sentence, *train* means "practice." You have to understand the *context*, or the rest of the sentence in which the word is used, to know which meaning is called for.

Number your paper from 1 to 8. Then read each sentence below. Use the context to find the correct meaning of the word in italics. choose the meaning from the list of definitions.

Definitions

part of a race	competition
trainer	drink
squeeze	emergency
come face-to- face	carriage

1. She ran the last *lap* of the race quickly.

2. Did the cat *lap* up all the milk?

3. Energy comes to him in a *pinch*.

4. Tight shoes can *pinch* your toes.

5. Who is the *coach* of the team?

6. Have you ever ridden in a *coach*?

7. He is at a swimming *meet*.

8. Did you *meet* his father?

READING

Cause and Effect. A *cause* is something that makes another thing happen. For example, Cheryl became a good student because Fred encouraged her. Fred's encouragement was the cause. The *effect* is the result — *Cheryl became a good student.* Words and phrases such as *because, since, so that, as a result,* and *for this reason,* often tell you that there is a *cause-and-effect* relationship in a sentence.

Write each of the numbered sentences below on your paper. Then underline the cause once, and the effect twice. Example: Cheryl became a good student because Fred encouraged her.

1. Cheryl was excited because she had set a world's record in the 600-yard race.

2. As a result of Cheryl's studying, she won a scholarship to college.

3. Swede's dad didn't want him to play football, so Swede left home.

4. Since he had done his best, Andy Jones was content to take the new job.

5. Ali kept letting Foreman hit him so that Foreman would get tired out.

6. Ali was the champ again, and for this reason he was happy.

7. The more Johnny's dad pushes him, the more afraid Johnny gets.

8. I see Dad coming this way now, so I'll have to stop writing.

WRITING

Description. When you write a description, your aim is to help readers see and feel the subject clearly. In order to achieve this, you need to be specific. You should try to use words that appeal to the five senses: sight, hearing, touch, taste, smell.

Step 1: Set Your Goal

Choose one of the following topics for a description:

a. In "There Must Be a Losing Coach," the author never tells you what Swede looks like. Write a description of Swede as you imagine him.

b. Write a description of a sports event. The event could be one that you saw or one that you participated in as a player.

Step 2: Make a Plan

Begin planning your description by picturing your subject. List all the details you "see." Suppose, for example, that the author of "Winning . . . and Losing!" wanted to describe the race. She might list details about how the water looked and felt, what other racers were doing, and how the narrator felt physically and emotionally.

Also decide what idea about your subject you want to get across. Then choose the details that help communicate this idea to include in your description. If the author of "Winning . . . and Losing!" wanted to get across an idea of how it actually felt to swim in the race, she would select details about what the narrator saw and felt.

Once you have listed the details you want to include, you should decide how you want to organize them. If you are describing an event, you will probably want to organize your description in time order. If you are describing a person, place, or thing, you will probably want to use spatial order. When you use spatial order, you guide the reader from one place to another. For example, when describing a room, you might start with the shelves and move on to the windows, and then go to the couch along the wall.

Now make a list of the details you want to include in your description and decide how you want to organize them.

Step 3: Write the First Draft

When you write your first draft, keep in mind the impression you want readers to get. Try to follow the organization you planned and use your list of details. But feel free to make changes as you go along. Try to make your details clear and vivid. A draft of a description of the swimming race might begin like this:

As I pushed off I heard the crowd cheer. I moved through the water. I could feel my arms cut into it. Water splashed up each time I slapped or kicked it. I pulled toward the far end of the pool, which no longer was so far away.

Step 4. Revise Your Description

When you revise your draft, think about how to make the description more vivid.

151

Remember you want to appeal to your readers' senses. Ask yourself if you can see, hear, touch, taste, or smell each detail.

One way to make the description clear is by using specific nouns and verbs. For example, *cottage* is more specific than *house*, and *whispered* is more specific than *said*. The author of the description above might decide to replace *moved* with *sped* or *slid*. When you are finished revising your description, proofread it for mistakes in spelling, grammar, and punctuation.

QUIZ

The following is a quiz for Section 4. Write the answers in complete sentences on your paper.

Reading Comprehension

1. In "Cheryl Toussaint," why did Coach Thompson think good grades were so important? How did this affect Cheryl?

2. In "There Must Be a Losing Coach," why did Happy Hough decide to put Swede into the game?

3. Why do you think Swede was happy to go home for dinner after the game?

4. In "Muhammad Ali's African Battle," why did Ali change his fighting style?

5. In "Winning. . .and Losing!," why doesn't Johnny lose the race he plans to lose on purpose?

Understanding Literature

6. Cheryl wanted to train for the 1976 Olympics but didn't have time. How did she resolve this conflict?

7. Swede resolved his conflict by doing his best in the game. Do you think he made the best decision? Why?

8. In one sentence, explain why Swede and his father did not get along.

9. State three ways in which George Foreman and Muhammad Ali were different from each other.

10. Johnny has not resolved his conflict by the end of the story. How do you think he should resolve it? Why?

ACTIVITIES

Word Attack. Puns depend on the double meaning of a word. They often make people sigh and moan and groan. Occasionally, they make people laugh. The words below are found in the stories in this section. Each of them has at least two meanings. Make up puns with the words. Try out the puns on your friends. Hear the groans!

pinch	lap	track
card	season	fan
revolution	Box	

Speaking and Listening. Pretend you are a radio sportscaster covering the Ali-Foreman fight or another sports event. Give a play-by-play description of the event.

Researching

1. Write a biography of a sports figure you like. Find information about the person's life and his or her career in the library. Articles in magazines such as *Sports Illustrated* may be a good source of information.

2. Write a report about your favorite sport. Include information about the history of the sport, how it is played, the rules, and famous players. Use the encyclopedia to find information.

Creating. Invent a new sport. Write instructions for playing the sport and make up a list of rules. Give your instructions and rules to some friends and have them try to play the game.

PEARL BUCK

*Pearl Buck wrote
books about ordinary people whose
lives were changed by history. Some
of the people were Chinese. Some
were American. Pearl Buck
understood both cultures — because
she had been part of each of them.*

Biography

Pearl S. Buck

Pearl S. Buck was a famous American writer who grew up in China. Her parents, Absalom and Caroline Sydenstricker, were Presbyterian missionaries.

In 1892, when Pearl was born, they were on leave in West Virginia. Five months later, they returned to China.

Absalom believed that since he was teaching the Chinese, he should live like them. At that time, Chinese men wore their hair in a long braid, so Absalom let his hair grow long and braided it. The Sydenstricker family dressed and ate like the Chinese. Pearl learned to speak Chinese before she could speak English. She played with Chinese children and did not consider herself "different."

In 1900, however, a secret society called the Boxers tried to drive all foreigners out of China. Many people were killed. Pearl's family had to hide in another city until the trouble was finally over.

When Pearl was 17, she came to the United States to attend college. In 1914, when she graduated, she was asked to teach at the college. But after a year, she went back to China because her mother was very sick.

When her mother got well, Pearl took a teaching job. She met and married John Buck, an American missionary who was teaching the Chinese new ways of farming.

In 1927, a revolution broke out in China. Once more, foreigners were being killed. Pearl Buck was now teaching

In 1949, Pearl Buck founded Welcome House. Asian-American children lived here while they waited for adoption.

English literature at the University of Nanking. She and her two children were in danger, but an old Chinese farm woman whom she knew let them hide in her tiny house.

Pearl Buck wrote later, "I have had that strange and terrible experience of facing death because of my color. The only reason I was not killed was that my Chinese friends knew me under my skin and risked their lives for me."

The Bucks managed to escape to Japan. Everything they owned, however, was lost. To help support the family, Pearl Buck began to write.

Her second book, *The Good Earth*, describes the life of Wang Lung, a poor Chinese farmer whose love of the land helps him to live through years of hardship. The book became a bestseller, and then it was made into a fine film. Because of the great success of *The Good Earth*, Pearl Buck was rich and famous at the age of 39.

From then on, Pearl Buck never stopped writing. She wrote more than 65 books, plus hundreds of short stories and essays. Some of them are about Americans. But she is most remembered for her stories about the Chinese. In 1938, she won the Nobel Prize for Literature, the highest honor an author can get.

Pearl Buck felt that she belonged to both China and the United States. She believed that she had been chosen to build a bridge between the East and West. After World War II, she set up the Pearl S. Buck Foundation to help people adopt children who were half-American and half-Asian. She gave it almost $7,000,000 of her own money. She and her second husband, Richard J. Walsh, adopted nine children themselves.

Pearl Buck died in Vermont in 1973. She was 80 years old, and she was still working. On her desk was an unfinished novel called *The Red Earth*. It was about the grandchildren of Wang Lung in *The Good Earth*.

On the following pages, you will find two stories that take place on Christmas Day. "Once Upon a Christmas" is a true story. It will show you how natural it was for Pearl Buck to welcome into her home the first of many homeless children.

"Christmas Day in the Morning" is not a true story, but it could be. It shows the binding strength of love between members of a family and the power of love to waken love.

In "Begin to Live," a young man goes home to his family and girlfriend after losing an arm in World War II. He feels as if he's lost his heart, as well, after seeing so much death. He is surprised when his father understands . . . and gives him some good advice. This story shows how wars can wound the human spirit, as well as the body, and how understanding can heal the wounded spirit.

A selection from *The Good Earth* will give you a taste of Pearl Buck's well-known novel. You will see how close a land they cultivate — and to each other — even though they speak few words.

Once Upon a Christmas

by Pearl S. Buck

"Once Upon a Christmas" is a true story. The young woman living in North China is Pearl Buck herself. And the little boy who becomes her "Christmas present" was the first of many children she brought up. But even true stores often leave questions.

It is Christmas Eve. The house is still. I have put the last gift under the Christmas tree.

I treasure these last few minutes. My home is warm. It is alive with past memories and present life.

Strange and wonderful things have happened to me at Christmas. I have come to expect the unexpected. I wonder what will happen this year.

While I wonder, I remember another Christmas. That Christmas was a long time ago. And I was very far from here.

I was very young then, and newly married. My husband and I lived in a small, ancient city in North China. We were the only Americans. I was trying hard not to be lonely.

My parents were coming to spend Christmas. How I looked forward to that! I had been preparing for days.

We would have a wild goose instead of a turkey. There would be a special pudding made of dried fruits. And I had decorated with bamboo instead of holly.

Then, on the morning of Christmas Eve, I got a telegram. My mother was not well enough to visit. And my father must stay with her!

Suddenly, Christmas was empty. I tried to hide my disappointment. But the day dragged. I was glad when evening came.

I lit the kerosene lamps — there was no electricity in our city. I played Christmas carols. My husband and I talked about happier Christmases. At last, the day ended.

It was midnight, and I could not sleep. I got up and looked out the living room window. I saw a star shining above the city wall.

At that moment, I heard a knock on the front door. Who could be there at such an hour? Bandits? Thieves? Perhaps I should not open the door.

But I did open it. A small Chinese boy stood there. He later told me he was ten. But he looked five or six. He was very thin and dressed in rags. What I remember are his eyes. He had huge, dark eyes.

He did not speak. He just stood there, looking up at me.

"Who are you?" I asked in Chinese.

"I am no one," he said.

"But what is your name?" I asked.

"I have no name," he said.

"Where are your parents?"

"I have no parents."

I stared at him. "But where did you come from?"

"I came from nowhere," he said.

"And you are going nowhere?"

"Nowhere," he said.

"Then why come to me?"

He shook his head, not able to answer. He kept looking at me with those huge eyes.

Who was this lovely, lonely child? A beggar? But why here at our door? And why here tonight at midnight?

"Come in," I said. "You must be hungry."

He came in quietly. I then saw how thin he was. He was trying not to shiver. His hair was brown with dust.

Then I went back to bed. For some reason, I, too, was able to sleep.

In the morning, I returned to the living room. He was already awake. He was sitting on the floor, looking at the Christmas tree.

"Do you remember who you are this morning?" I asked.

He gave me a shy smile and shook his head. Then he said, "I have come to live with you."

And that was the way it was. He shared our Christmas Day. I did not miss anyone.

I took him out and bought him clothes. He acted as if he had always lived with us.

We named him Noel. Our friends and neighbors did not know where Noel came from. They did not know who he was. Or, if they did, they did not tell us.

Noel never remembered any of his life before that Christmas Eve.

I do not remember that he was ever any trouble. He liked to study. People liked him. But he made no close friends.

Noel grew into a tall, brilliant young man. He wanted to be a doctor. He became a good one. He was kind to the poor and the helpless. He seemed completely devoted to the sick.

Then the war came. China was split in two. Everywhere the Communists were fighting the Nationalists.

In our city, both sides were angry with Noel. This was because he treated all the wounded men the same. Noel did not care which side they were on.

The Communists won. All the Ameri-cans were asked to leave China. I begged Noel to go with us.

But he refused, smiling and gentle. "I must stay with my people," he said. "They will need me more than ever."

"But will the Communists let you be yourself?" I asked.

"I am only a doctor," he said. "How can they complain about that? They need doctors."

So we parted. I felt that I was leaving a younger brother.

At first, we wrote letters. But, later, it seemed better if we did not write. Noel was under suspicion because he got letters from America. And I was under suspicion because I got letters from China.

Then I heard how he had died. A friend escaped from China and told me.

Noel was the only doctor within hundreds of miles. People came to him from everywhere. Wounded soldiers from both sides asked for his help.

The Communists warned Noel not to treat their enemies. He smiled and said nothing. He went on treating anyone who came to him.

One night, he was called out of his sleep. Going to the door, he saw three men. They seemed ordinary enough. They asked him to visit a very sick man.

Noel went with them at once. After turning the first corner, they shot him. Noel died instantly.

This is all I know. But it is not of his death that I think tonight. I think of Noel as I saw him that Christmas Eve, long ago. I think of that little child from nowhere who knocked at my door.

READING COMPREHENSION

Summarizing. Choose the best phrase to complete each sentence. Then write the complete statements on your paper.

1. When Pearl Buck heard a knock on her door at midnight, she wondered if she would find _____ (a lost child, bandits, a Christmas gift).

2. According to the boy, he was _____ (a beggar, a runaway, an orphan).

3. When Noel became a doctor, he treated soldiers on both sides of the war in China because he was _____ (given no choice, devoted to the sick and injured, paid well to do so).

Interpreting. Write the answer to each question on your paper.

1. Why was Pearl Buck lonely on this particular Christmas Eve?

2. Why do you think she was going to serve wild goose instead of turkey?

3. Why did she name the boy Noel?

4. Why do you think the boy became such a good doctor when he grew up?

For Thinking and Discussing

1. What events in Noel's life might have led him to Pearl Buck's door?

2. Why do you think Pearl Buck took the boy in and became a mother to him? If someone in your neighborhood found a child at the door one night, what would that person probably do?

UNDERSTANDING LITERATURE

Setting. The setting of a story is the time and place of the events. Authors usually describe the setting by giving details about *when* and *where* the events take place.

Answer the following questions about the setting in "Once Upon a Christmas."

1. Where did Pearl Buck and her husband live when they were first married?

2. What details do you know about their home? What did they use for lights instead of electricity? How did Pearl Buck decorate her home at Christmas?

3. Decide whether each statement below tells you the *where*, or the *when* part of the setting. Write *where* or *when* on your paper.

   a. "That Christmas was a long time ago."
   b. "I fixed him a bed on the couch in the living room."
   c. "Then the war came."
   d. "In our city, both sides were angry with Noel."
   e. "At first, we wrote letters."
   f. "I think of Noel as I saw him that Christmas Eve, long ago."

WRITING

Imagine that you are Pearl Buck. Write a letter to Noel explaining why he must leave China and come to America. Or imagine that you are Noel. Write a letter to Pearl Buck explaining why you feel you must stay in China.

Begin to Live

by Pearl S. Buck

Tim comes back from World War II changed in body and mind. His family and his girl friend can see the outside change. But they seem to expect him to think and feel as he did before the war. He feels lost and alone. Then understanding comes — from the last place he had thought to look for it.

The train went swinging around the curve. Out of the window, Tim saw the town. The wild grin on his face froze.

"What's the matter?" Bob asked him.

Tim stood up. He pulled his baggage from the rack. "I'm home," he said.

He kept grinning to hide the way he felt. The other men were staring at him. Soon he'd tell them all good-bye. He'd probably never see them again.

He had not thought of this until now. He had only been thinking of seeing his family and the town.

"Well, Tim. . . . Don't forget to write," Bob said.

"Sure," Tim said. He couldn't stop grinning. He hoped his mother wouldn't cry when she saw him.

He was so much luckier than some of the other wounded soldiers. He was already used to doing without his arm. Now if he could only begin where he had left off two years ago.

The train stopped at the station. Tim leaped up. The men yelled at him. They crowded around the windows.

Bob whistled. "Hey, look at the blonde!" That was Kit. She was surrounded by his family.

Tim leaped to the railroad platform. He dropped his bags. He put his arm around Kit and held her tight.

He felt her tremble. She laughed and pushed him a little. Her eyes were wet. "Tim," Kit said, "here's your mother — your dad — and Mary — "

But Tim could hardly pull himself together. He felt dizzy. It was not because of Kit. It was because he was still alive.

Now he really knew it was all over. He would never have to feel the bomber lift him into the night. He was back to stay.

"Tim, son — " He felt his mother's soft cheek.

"Well, Tim," his father said, and coughed.

Mary put her arms around his neck.

"Grown, haven't you, kid?" Tim asked.

"Oh, Tim," she said. "I want you to meet Frank. We're going to get married."

"You aren't old enough — " He tried to tease his sister.

"I hope to fly a plane myself," said Frank. His bony young hand was strong.

Everybody was trying to get to Tim at once. More than half the town was there. It was all as he had imagined it.

Somehow, he would forget the past two years.

They went back to the house where Tim had lived with his family. It seemed both familiar and strange.

"It sure is good to be home," Tim said.

They all sat down and looked at him. And he looked at them. He wanted to tell them. . . . What did he want to tell them?

Tim laughed. "I feel the way I used to feel. You know . . . after I got off the roller coaster at the fair."

They laughed, too. Here they were. This was the moment they had all looked forward to. And none of them knew what to do with it.

His mother got up. "I'll go and see about dinner. I have everything you like, Tim."

She went over to him. She put her hand on his shoulder. "It's you—you're real—"

The tears came into her eyes. He knew she was thinking about the arm. He could not speak.

"Now, Mother," Tim's father said.

"Oh, I know," she said. "But I can't get used to him — after everything — "

They made excuses so he could be alone with Kit. She walked over to where he was standing. She put her arms around him.

He ran his hand through her hair. He had dreamed of doing this. "This is when I'd like my hand back," Tim said.

"I'm thankful you're here at all," she said. "Much more than thankful."

Then he wanted to tell her everything. But how could he describe what he had been through?

He bent and kissed her. Better not to talk.

"Dinner's ready," his mother called.

"Sit down everybody," Tim's mother said. "Now, Father, put the gravy on the mashed potatoes. Tim, butter that roll while it's still hot. Mary, pass the olive oil — "

His mother tossed the salad. "Goodness, Tim. I was so relieved when we beat Italy. Then I could get olive oil again!"

Italy! His best friend had been killed there. He decided not to say anything.

"This roast is in your honor, Tim," his mother said.

His father carved the roast.

"Tim likes it rare, Father," his mother said. Tim started to speak but could not. He liked his roast well-done now. He had to forget the way raw, red flesh looked — bombed flesh.

"Thanks, Dad," he said. Tim took his plate. He covered his slice of roast with mustard.

They were good to him after dinner. His mother told him to take a nap. Tim went upstairs to his old room. Everything was the same. He found an old pair of pajamas and put them on.

He remembered the last time he had slept here. Everything was so different then. He had been a boy.

He was not a boy now. He knew everything — life and death. He especially knew death. He did not know how to begin living again. Even with Kit. . . .

They had to begin to live. But how? In the army, somebody always told you. He sighed and fell asleep.

When Tim woke, he heard laughter and voices. The house was full of people. He lay still, listening.

I don't want to get up again, ever, Tim thought. But in a moment, he saw his mother's face.

"What's going on downstairs?" he asked her.

"Some people have come over," she said. "Do you feel like coming down?"

"Sure," Tim said.

He got up slowly and put his uniform back on. He looked just the way he always did before he took off.

Only there were no more missions! No more fights!

Tim hurried down. They were all waiting for him in the big living room.

"Hi, everybody!" Tim shouted. He made himself go on. It was like taking a nose dive.

In a minute, they were around him. They patted his back. They shook his hand. He knew they did not know what to say.

He knew they had all been told not to ask questions. But he could feel them wanting to know.

They were the same, and he was not. He knew now that this was the trouble. He would never be the same again.

It was not his arm. It was everything he had been through — good and bad.

Tim went over to Kit's house that evening. They sat together in a big armchair. Kit was very quiet.

"Asleep?" he asked. She shook her head. Her eyes were full of tears.

"What is it?" Tim asked. He was frightened. Did she feel the change in him?

"I'm crying because I'm happy," Kit said.

Why couldn't he say it? Why couldn't he tell her they would be married right away? She was waiting to hear him say it.

But the words would not come.

"I guess getting a job is the first thing I should do," Tim told his father.

They were alone, eating breakfast.

"Hoping to get your old job back?" his father asked.

Tim and his father had never been very close. His father was a quiet man, a hard-working lawyer. Tim had never thought much about his father.

"You don't want to go on with flying?" his father asked.

"No!" Tim said.

"I can understand that," his father said. "But why don't you go and see your old boss, Mr. Gedsoe?"

Tim was still wearing his uniform when he entered Mr. Gedsoe's office.

"Been expecting you," Mr. Gedsoe said. "I thought you'd be wanting your old job back."

"Is my job still here?" Tim asked.

"You can begin whenever you like," Mr. Gedsoe said. "We're glad to have you home, Tim. You've got a good future here."

"Thank you, sir," Tim said.

But did he want to sit in this office? He did not know. He felt he had to mention his arm.

"I don't think my arm will hold me up on the job," Tim said.

"Of course not," Mr. Gedsoe said quickly.

"Lucky I still have my left arm," Tim said.

Mr. Gedsoe looked away. There was guilt in his face.

Tim walked home slowly. He heard running footsteps behind him. It was Frank.

"You passed right by our house," Frank said. "I was just on my way to get Mary. We're going to look at furniture."

"Already?" Tim smiled.

"We're not getting married just yet," Frank said. "I wanted to ask your advice about it. My mom and dad want us to wait. Mother says—"

"I'd say, don't wait. Get married before you go overseas," Tim said.

"I'm — I'm really glad to hear you say that."

"It'll be easier for you when you come back," Tim said. "It will give you something to go on. You'll have your orders, so to speak."

Tim longed to tell Frank some of the things he had learned. But what had he learned? You didn't really learn anything in war. It got worse, not better.

That's why so many of the fellows took to drinking. But you couldn't drink if you were going up in the air. You had to face death cold sober.

It wasn't his own death he had found the hardest to face. It was having to let death loose on a lot of other human beings.

Of course, you couldn't think. Some of them were able not to think. But he had not been one of those.

Tim was surprised when his father asked him to drop by the law office. The office was as it had always been.

Tim sat down and waited to hear what his father had to say.

"Tim," his father began, "do you remember when you wanted to make a new model of an electric typewriter? I thought it was a good idea."

"I haven't thought about it lately," Tim said.

"Gedsoe is interested in the project. But I don't think you should be satisfied with his terms. He wants complete rights to your idea.

"I'd like to have our firm represent you. No reason why you should let Gedsoe — Tim, you aren't listening," his father said.

"How did you know?" Tim asked.

"You feel stopped. Don't you? Nothing is real to you."

"How did you know?" he whispered. Tim had never thought his father understood him.

"You don't know if you want to go back to your job. You don't know if you want to marry Kit. You can't go backward. And yet you don't know how to take the next step."

"That's about it," Tim said. "But how did you know?"

"War makes a man forget what is real," his father said.

"It seemed horribly real," Tim said.

"Only life is real. You have to get back into life."

"I can't seem to feel anything."

"When I came back from war, I didn't want to marry your mother," his father said.

"How did you tell her?" Tim asked. "I haven't been able to tell Kit."

"Good. You must not tell her. That is — if you still want to marry her."

"I don't know if I ever want to get married."

"I had to go through that, too," his father said.

"How did you get yourself going again?" Tim asked.

"My father put me on a legal case. A man's life was in question. Even that didn't seem real."

"You didn't tell Mother how you felt?"

His father leaned across the desk. "I found out that you can't tell anybody. It is only the people who have been through war that know. You can't tell people, Tim. You have to keep it to yourself. You have to begin to live."

"Begin to live?" Tim said.

"Just begin. Begin to work. Begin to love. It doesn't matter how you feel. You begin to act. And then feeling comes. And things are real again."

"I think you're right," Tim said. "I know you're right. I . . . thanks, Dad."

His father opened a drawer and took out some papers. He began to read. He became, again, the same man that Tim had always remembered.

Tim went out into the sunny street. It was still too early to meet Kit. But never mind. Why shouldn't he go and find her? She'd be at home.

Tim walked into Kit's house, as he used to do.

"Kit!" he called.

He heard her coming down the stairs.

"I look terrible, Tim," Kit said. "I've been helping Mother, and I haven't changed. . . ."

She had on blue slacks and an old sweater. There was a smudge around her eyes.

"You've been crying," he said.

She shook her head. "I rubbed my eyes. That's all. They got full of dust. We cleaned the attic."

But he knew she had been crying. He knew it, and he felt nothing. He had seen so many women cry over their dead children.

What were the orders? "Begin to live," his father had said.

"Kit, I don't want to wait any longer." His lips were dry as he spoke. "Kit, when are we going to get married?"

"Oh — I thought you were never going to ask me."

That was what she had been crying about.

"Let's get married right away, Kit."

"When, Tim?"

"Today — tomorrow — you set the day and the hour."

"Tim, you're sure?"

"Sure," he said.

"Today, a week? Tim, I can get ready. I want to begin to live. I've waited so long."

"Today, a week, we'll begin," he said.
She put her head against his shoulder.
But he did not speak. He stood holding
her hand. In the silence, he felt something
begin to beat in his chest. Was it his heart?

READING COMPREHENSION

Summarizing. Choose the best phrase to
complete each sentence. Then write the
complete statements on your paper.

1. When Tim went home, he noticed a
   big change in _____ (his family, Kit,
   the way he felt about life).

2. With Kit at first, he _____ (tried to
   explain what the war was like, pretended he hadn't lost an arm, didn't
   express his real feelings).

3. Tim's father advised Tim to _____
   (act normal, tell people what he's been
   through, take a vacation).

Interpreting. Write the answer to each
question on your paper.

1. What did Kit hope Tim would say?

2. Why did the war seem "horribly real"
   to Tim? What haunted him about it?

3. What did Tim's father mean when he
   said, "War makes a man forget what
   is real"? What was real to him?

For Thinking and Discussing. What advice did Tim's father give him? Was it
good advice? Explain your answer.

UNDERSTANDING LITERATURE

Setting. In "Begin to Live," time is very
important. The story is about Tim's past
(the war), present (life at home), and future (getting a job and getting married).

Read the following statements. Then
answer the questions on your paper.

1. In the past, Tim worked for Mr. Gedsoe. How did this affect Tim's future?

2. Tim had to face the death of other human beings during the war. How did
   this affect Tim when he came home?

3. During the war, Tim was wounded
   and lost an arm. Do you think this
   would affect Tim in the future?

4. Tim's father also had gone to war.
   Which of his father's war experiences
   were similar to Tim's own experiences?

5. In "Begin to Live," Tim's feelings are
   very important to the plot. What if
   Tim had come home feeling happy and
   full of life? How would the plot of the
   story have been different?

WRITING

In "Begin to Live," Tim wished that he
could begin where he had left off two
years ago. Do you think this was possible?
List two reasons why you think it was
possible for Tim to go back in time. Then
list two reasons why he couldn't. Look
back in the story if you need to.

From

The Good Earth

by Pearl S. Buck

The Good Earth *is Pearl Buck's most famous novel. It is about people who owned small farms in China many years ago. They lived as their parents and grandparents had lived for thousands of years. Women were little more than slaves. But men, too, worked hard and had few comforts.*

This brief selection from The Good Earth *shows how important the land is to Wang, the farmer, and O-lan, his wife. The land takes their time and their work — and it provides for new life.*

Wang Lung was working hard with the growing wheat. He worked with his hoe, day after day. His back throbbed with weariness.

One day, her shadow fell across the ground over which he bent himself. There she stood, with a hoe across her shoulder.

"There is nothing to do in the house until nightfall," she said. Without speech, she took the piece of ground to the left of him. She fell into steady hoeing.

The sun beat down upon them, for it was early summer. Her face was soon dripping with sweat. Wang Lung had his coat off. His back was bare. But she worked with her thin coat covering her shoulders. It grew wet and clung to her like skin.

They moved in time with each other, hour after hour. They did not say a word. He felt close to her, and it took the pain from his labor. He did not think, in words, of anything. There was only movement, and turning this earth of theirs over and over to the sun. This earth formed their home and fed their bodies. The earth lay rich and dark. It fell apart lightly under the points of their hoes.

Sometimes they turned up a bit of brick, a splinter of wood. It was nothing. Some

time, in some age, bodies of men and women had been buried there. Houses had stood there. They had fallen and gone back into the earth. So also would their house, some time, return into the earth. So would their bodies also. Each had his turn at this earth.

They worked on, moving together. They were making this earth give fruit. They did not speak in their movement together.

When the sun had set, he straightened his back slowly and looked at the woman. Her face was wet and streaked with the earth. She was as brown as the very soil itself. Her wet, dark clothes stuck to her square body.

She smoothed a last patch of earth.

Then in her usual plain way, she spoke, straight out. Her voice was flat and very plain in the silent evening air.

"I am with child."

Wang Lung stood still. What was there to say about this thing, then? She stooped to pick up a bit of broken brick. It was as though she had said, "I have brought you tea," or as though she had said, "We can eat." It seemed as ordinary as that to her!

But to him — he could not say what it was to him. His heart swelled. It stopped, as though there was no room for it to beat. Well, it was their turn at this earth!

He took the hoe suddenly from her hand. He said, his voice thick in his throat, "Let be for now. It is a day's end."

READING COMPREHENSION

Summarizing. Choose the best phrase to complete each sentence. Then write the complete statements on your paper.

1. Wang Lung's wife, O-lan, was _____ (a hard worker, lazy, privileged).

2. When O-lan said she was going to have a child, Wang Lung _____ (was too tired to care, told her he loved her, felt very happy).

3. To Wang Lung and O-lan, the earth was _____ (hateful because it meant hard work, frightening because bodies were buried there, important because it was the source of life).

Interpreting. Write the answer to each question on your paper.

1. What reason did O-lan give for helping Wang Lung to hoe the land?

2. Were Wang Lung and O-lan used to working hard? Why?

3. When Wang Lung and O-lan expected a child, the author observed, "Well, it was their turn at this earth!" What did the author mean?

For Thinking and Discussing

1. Why do you think Wang Lung and O-lan said so little to each other while hoeing and sharing the news that they were going to have a child?

2. What can you tell about the characters from their actions? From the author's descriptions?

UNDERSTANDING LITERATURE

Setting. In "Once Upon a Christmas," the title tells you *when* the events take place. The spirit of the holiday probably helped Pearl Buck decide to take in Noel. Think about the title *The Good Earth*.

1. Why do you think Pearl Buck chose the title *The Good Earth*? What is good about the earth in the selection?

2. Write three sentences that describe the earth where Wang Lung and O-lan were farming.

An author often describes the setting by using words that appeal to the senses: sight, hearing, touch, smell, or taste. Which senses do you think are important in each description below?

"One day, her shadow fell across the ground. . . ."

"The sun beat down upon them, for it was early summer."

"The earth lay rich and dark."

"When the sun had set, he straightened his back slowly. . . ."

"Her voice was flat and very plain in the silent evening."

WRITING

Think of a place outdoors that you know well. Write a paragraph describing that place. Tell what it looks like, and what it feels like to be there. Try to use words that appeal to the senses.

Christmas Day in the Morning

by Pearl S. Buck

Robert wonders where the magic of Christmas is—now that his children are grown and gone. He finds the answer in a memory of a Christmas morning years ago when he was a boy.

He awoke suddenly and completely. It was four o'clock, the hour at which his father had always called him to get up and help with the milking. Strange how the habits of his youth clung to him still! His father had been dead for 30 years, and yet he awoke at four o'clock in the morning. He had trained himself to turn over and go to sleep, but this morning, because it was Christmas, he did not try. Yet what was the magic of Christmas now? His own children had grown up and gone. He was left alone with his wife. Yesterday she had said, "Let's not trim the tree until tomorrow, Robert. I'm tired." He had agreed, and so the tree remained out in the back entry.

Why did he feel so awake tonight? For it was still night, clear and starry. No moon, of course, but the stars were extraordinary! Now that he thought of it, the stars seemed always large and clear before the dawn of Christmas Day. There was one star now that was certainly larger and brighter than any of the others. He could even imagine it moving, as it had seemed to him to move one night long ago.

He was 15 years old and still on his father's farm. He loved his father. He had not known it until one day a few days before Christmas, when he had overheard what his father was saying to his mother.

"Mary, I hate to call Rob in the mornings. He's growing so fast and he needs his sleep. If you could see how he sleeps when I go in to wake him up! I wish I could manage alone."

"Well, you can't, Adam." His mother's voice was brisk. "Besides, he isn't a child anymore. It's time for him to take his turn."

"Yes," his father said slowly, "But I sure do hate to wake him."

When he heard these words, something in him awoke: his father loved him! There would be no more loitering in the mornings and having to be called again. He got up after that, stumbling blind with sleep,

174

and pulled on his clothes, his eyes tight shut, but he got up.

And then on the night before Christmas, that year when he was 15, he lay thinking about the next day.

He wished he had a better present for his father. As usual, he had gone to the ten-cent store and bought a tie for his father. It had seemed nice enough until he lay thinking, and then he wished that he had heard his father and mother talking in time for him to save for something better.

He lay on his side, his head supported by his elbow, and looked out of his attic window. The stars were bright, much brighter than he ever remembered seeing them, and one star in particular was so bright that he wondered if it were really the Star of Bethlehem.

"Dad," he had once asked when he was a little boy, "what is a stable?"

"It's just a barn," his father had replied, "like ours."

Then Jesus had been born in a barn, and to a barn the shepherds and the Wise Men had come, bringing their Christmas gifts!

The thought struck him. Why should he not give his father a special gift, too, out there in the barn? He could get up early, earlier than four o'clock, and creep into the barn and get all the milking done. He'd do it alone, milk and clean up, and then when his father went in to start the milking, he'd see it all done. And he would know who had done it.

He laughed to himself as he gazed at the stars. It was what he would do, and he mustn't sleep too soundly.

He must have awakened 20 times, scratching a match each time to look at his old watch — midnight, and half-past one, and then two o'clock.

At a quarter to three he got up and put on his clothes. He crept downstairs, careful of the creaky boards, and let himself out. The big star hung lower over the barn roof, a reddish gold. The cows looked at him, sleepy and surprised. It was early for them, too.

He fetched some hay for each cow and then got the milking pail and the big milk cans.

He smiled, thinking about his father, and milked steadily, two strong streams rushing into the pail, frothing and fragrant. The task went more easily than he had ever known it to before. Milking for once was not a chore. It was something else, a gift to his father, who loved him. He finished, the two milk cans were full, and he covered them and closed the milk-house door carefully, making sure of the latch. He put the stool in its place by the door and hung up the clean milk pail. Then he went out of the barn and barred the door behind him.

Back in his room he had only a minute to pull off his clothes in the darkness and jump into bed, for he heard his father up. He put the covers over his head to silence his quick breathing. The door opened and he lay still.

"Rob!" his father called. "We have to get up, son, even if it is Christmas."

"Aw-right," he said sleepily.

"I'll go on out," his father said. "I'll get things started."

The door closed and he lay still, laughing to himself. In just a few minutes his father would know.

The minutes were endless — ten, fifteen, he did not know how many — and

he heard his father's footsteps again. The door opened and he lay still.

"Rob!"

"Yes, Dad —"

"You son of a gun." His father was laughing, a queer sobbing sort of a laugh. "Thought you'd fool me, did you?" His father was standing beside his bed, feeling for him, pulling away the cover.

"It's for Christmas, Dad."

He found his father and clutched him in a great hug. He felt his father's arms go around him. It was dark and they could not see each other's faces.

"Son, I thank you. Nobody ever did a nicer thing."

"Oh, Dad, I want you to know . . . ." He did not know what to say. His heart was bursting with love.

"Well, I reckon I can go back to bed and sleep," his father said after a moment. "No — the little ones are awake. Come to think of it, I've never seen you children when you first saw the Christmas tree. I was always in the barn. Come on!"

He got up and pulled on his clothes again and they went down to the Christmas tree, and soon the sun was creeping up to where the star had been. Oh, what a Christmas, and how his heart had nearly burst again with shyness and pride as his father told his mother and made the younger children listen about how he, Rob, had got up all by himself.

"The best Christmas gift I ever had, and I'll remember it, son, every year on Christmas Morning, so long as I live."

Outside the window now the great star slowly sank. He got up, put on his slippers and bathrobe, went softly upstairs to the attic and found the box of Christmas-tree decorations. He took them downstairs into the living room. Then he brought in the tree. It was a little one — they had not had a big tree since the children went away — but he set it in the holder. Then carefully he began to trim it. It was done very soon, the time passing as quickly as it had that morning long ago in the barn.

He went to his library and fetched the little box that contained his gift to his wife, a star of diamonds, not large but dainty in design. He tied the gift on the tree and then stood back. It was pretty, very pretty, and she would be surprised.

But he was not satisfied. He wanted to tell her — to tell her how much he loved her. It had been a long time since he had really told her, although he loved her in a special way, much more than he ever had when they were young. That was the true joy of life, the ability to love! He was quite sure that some people were genuinely unable to love anyone. But love was alive in him; it still was.

It occurred to him suddenly that it was alive because long ago it had been born in him when he knew his father loved him. That was it: love alone could waken love.

And he could give the gift again and again. This morning, this blessed Christmas Morning, he would give it to his beloved wife. He could write it down in a letter for her to read and keep forever. He went to his desk and began his love letter to his wife: *My dearest love . . . .*

READING COMPREHENSION

Summarizing. Choose the best phrase to complete each sentence. Then write the complete statements on your paper.

1. Robert, the narrator, recalls the Christmas when he was 15 and the gift _____ (his parents gave him, he gave his father, he didn't get).

2. He milked the cows before his father got up to _____ (prove he was a man, have more time to open his gifts, show his father he loved him).

3. He wanted to do this because he _____ (was treated like a child, was usually too busy to enjoy Christmas, had discovered that his father loved him).

4. As a result of this memory, Robert feels _____ (sad, old, loving).

Interpreting. Write the answer to each question on your paper.

1. What sight makes Robert recall the Christmas when he was 15?

2. When he was 15, why did he think that milking the cows for his father would be a better gift than a tie?

3. When the narrator gets up and trims the tree, why do you think the time passes "as quickly as it had that morning long ago in the barn"?

For Thinking and Discussing. The narrator thinks that some people are unable to love anyone, and that love alone can waken love. What is your opinion?

UNDERSTANDING LITERATURE

Setting. In "Christmas Day in the Morning," time is important. The story begins on Christmas morning in the present. Then it goes back in time to describe a Christmas morning in the past. Then it returns to Christmas morning in the present. The middle section, the memory of a long-ago Christmas, is called a "flashback." And in this case, the memory has an effect upon the narrator in the present time.

Read the following questions. Then write the answers on your paper.

1. As the story begins, is the narrator young or old? How do you know?

2. Is he excited about Christmas? How can you tell?

3. In the flashback, is the narrator young or old? How do you know?

4. In the flashback, is he excited about Christmas? How can you tell?

5. When he gets up — after the flashback — and puts on his bathrobe, is he looking forward to Christmas? What makes you think so?

6. He has a gift for his wife. What else does he decide to give her and why?

WRITING

Suppose Robert had not recalled the Christmas when he was 15. What kind of Christmas would he have in the present? Describe it briefly in writing.

Section Review

VOCABULARY

Synonyms. Choose the correct synonym to complete each sentence and write the synonym on your paper.

1. At the beginning of "Once Upon a Christmas," the setting is *festive*. It is Christmas Eve, and Pearl Buck has decorated her home and made a special dinner. Another word that could describe a festive setting is _____ (joyful, lonely, old-fashioned).

2. In "Begin to Live," certain things are *familiar* to Tim when he returns home after being away for two years. They are just the way they used to be. Another word that could describe a familiar setting is _____ (new, well-known, strange).

3. In the selection from *The Good Earth,* the setting is *harsh*. Farming the land is hard work and it makes Wang Lung and O-lan very tired. Another word that could describe a harsh setting is _____ (frightening, friendly, difficult).

4. In "Christmas Day in the Morning," the flashback has a *rural* setting. When Robert was a boy, he lived on a farm that had cows and a barn. Another word that could be used to describe a rural setting is _____ (country, urban, uncivilized).

READING

Drawing Conclusions. To understand a story, you sometimes have to *draw conclusions*. This means that you use facts to conclude, or decide about, something. For example, in "Once Upon a Christmas," the boy told Pearl Buck, "I have come to live with you." He also said, "I have no parents." From these facts, you can draw the conclusion that the boy needed a home.

Choose the best phrase to complete each sentence. Then write the phrases as complete statements on your paper.

1. In "Once Upon a Christmas," Pearl Buck wrote, "Strange and wonderful things have happened to me at Christmas. I have come to expect the unexpected. I wonder what will happen this year." From this paragraph, you can draw this conclusion:
   a. Her life was filled with surprises.
   b. Her life was dull and boring.

2. At the end of "Begin to Live," Tim and Kit are together. "But he did not speak. He stood holding her hand. In the silence, he felt something begin to beat in his chest. Was it his heart?" From this paragraph, you can draw this conclusion:
   a. Tim could not feel any emotions.
   b. Tim began to feel emotions again.

3. In the selection from *The Good Earth,* "Wang Lung was working hard with the growing wheat. He worked with his hoe, day after day. His back throbbed with weariness." From this

paragraph, you can draw this conclusion:

a. Wang Lung was not strong.

b. Wang Lung worked even when he was tired.

4. In "Christmas Day in the Morning," the narrator recalled that his wife had said to him, "Let's not trim the tree until tomorrow, Robert. I'm tired." From her statements, you can draw this conclusion:

a. She was feeling the spirit of Christmas.

b. She was not excited about Christmas.

WRITING

A Composition. A composition is made up of several paragraphs on a single topic. It begins with an introductory paragraph and ends with a conclusion. Each of the other paragraphs covers a single aspect of the topic.

Step 1: Set Your Goal

When you are given a composition assignment, your first task is to narrow the topic. To do this, you should think about what aspects of the topic interest you most. You should also think about how long your composition will be.

You will be writing a composition at least five paragraphs long on this topic: living in a foreign country. If you have moved from one country to another, you may use your own experiences. If not, you will write about what you think the experience would be like.

Narrow the topic by choosing certain aspects of it to write about. If the topic were life on a farm, for example, you might decide to limit your composition to the work a farm family does.

Step 2: Make a Plan

Once you have a narrow topic, jot down ideas and information you want to include. Next, organize the points into groups of similar ideas. Each group will make up one paragraph in the composition.

For a composition about life on a farm, you might end up with three groups of ideas: (1) Farm families work together, (2) farming is hard work, and (3) making things grow is very satisfying.

Step 3. Write the First Draft

Write the body of the composition before you write the introduction and conclusion. Write one paragraph to cover each group of ideas. For each paragraph, write a topic sentence that states the main idea of the paragraph.

When you have finished drafting the body of the composition, it is time to write the introduction and the conclusion. The introduction serves two purposes: It gives the readers an idea of what the composition is about, and it arouses their interest. The conclusion usually serves to sum up what you have written.

Step 4. Revise Your Composition

When you revise your composition, ask yourself these questions:

☐ Does the introduction tell what the composition is about? Does it grab the readers' attention?

☐ Do all the details relate to the purpose of the composition?

☐ Are the paragraphs arranged in the best order? Do they flow smoothly from one to the other?

☐ Does the conclusion sum up what you have to say about the topic?

When you have finished revising your composition, proofread it, and copy it over neatly.

QUIZ

The following is a quiz for Section 5. Write the answers in complete sentences on your paper.

Reading Comprehension

1. How did Pearl Buck survive in China after the revolution in 1927?

2. In "Once Upon a Christmas," why did Noel and Pearl Buck stop writing to each other after she returned to America?

3. In "Begin to Live," what can you tell about Kit's love for Tim?

4. In the selection from *The Good Earth*, how did O-lan seem to feel about having a child?

5. In "Christmas Day in the Morning," how did Robert feel about his wife?

Understanding Literature

6. Why did Pearl Buck feel she belonged to both America and China?

7. How would Noel's life have been different if he had not lived during a war?

8. Explain the importance of the title of the story "Begin to Live."

9. Why was the earth so important to Wang Lung and O-lan?

10. In "Christmas Day in the Morning," why did the narrator's present attitude toward Christmas change?

ACTIVITIES

Word Attack. In "Christmas Day in the Morning," Buck says the stars were "extraordinary." In this word, the prefix *extra-* means "outside a boundary or scope." So *extraordinary* means beyond what is ordinary.

1. Try to think of other words with the prefix *extra-*. Explain how each one tells how something is outside a boundary or scope. You may use the dictionary if you need help

2. Make up at least five *extra-* words of your own, *extrasilly*, for example. Write a definition of each word you create and use it in a sentence.

Speaking and Listening. Find a partner and act out one of these scenes:

1. Tim's mother and father on the day before he arrives home, discussing what to expect and how to behave.

2. Kit and her mother shortly before Tim arrives at Kit's house, discussing why Tim hasn't proposed.

Be prepared to perform the scene for the class.

Researching. Do library research about China. You may explore any of the topics below or one of your own. Be prepared to report your finding to the class.

☐ Chinese art

☐ China's revolutions

☐ farming in China

☐ education in China

☐ Confucious

Creating. In "Christmas Day in the Morning," Rob gives his father a gift that cannot be found in a store and bought with money. Think of some things you could give as gifts that cannot be bought. Write listings for a catalogue describing the gifts and giving "prices." (The price of Rob's gift was a number of hour's sleep and some hard work.) You might also include an illustration of each item. Use your entries and those of your classmates to make a "Priceless Gifts" catalogue.

OUTLOOKS

*Is each of us
alone? Is life a game of luck and
wishes? Do you follow the leader or
think for yourself? Can you be just
like someone else? It all depends on
your outlook.*

Outlooks

A person who sees the dark side of life and expects the worst to happen is known as a *pessimist*. And a person who sees the bright side of life and expects the best to happen is known as an *optimist*.

Suppose a pessimist and an optimist are each handed a glass partly filled with milk. It is said that the pessimist will see the glass as half-*empty*, while the optimist will see it as half-*full*.

Your outlook on life has a lot to do with what you "see" and expect from life. It affects the way you treat other people — and yourself.

Does luck or fate seem to run your life? Or do you have some control over the way your life goes?

When things go wrong because of a mistake you made, do you blame someone else? Do you quickly try to correct the situation?

When you meet someone who is new at school, do you want to find out what that person is like? Or do you steer clear of the newcomer, thinking that he or she should earn the right to be your friend?

When you can't do something you want to do, do you lose your temper? Do you sulk? Do you find something else to do — maybe something even *better*.

Questions like these can get you thinking about the different kinds of outlooks that people have. You can also learn about different outlooks on life by reading the three short stories, two poems, and book selection in this section.

In the selection from the novel *Carlota*, a teenaged girl suddenly finds herself in a life-or-death situation. Will she panic? Or will she use her wits and her skills to save herself?

In "The Antique Sale," Kelly does something that goes against her conscience. Why? To keep a friendship which, to her, seems more important than anything else. Is it worth it? Read this story to find out.

The narrator of "Me," a poem, describes a self who is changed, bit by bit, by everyday experiences. The narrator of another poem, "Alone," is sure that nobody can make it through life alone. What do these two poems tell you about human outlooks?

In "The Open Window," two people speak briefly with each other. One of them flees in terror, while the other finds their encounter amusing. As you will see, their outlooks are quite different.

In "Antaeus," a country boy gets a city gang to turn an almost unbelievable dream into something real . . . for a while, at least. This story will show you how powerful a person's dream can be.

The following selection is from Carlota, *a novel written by Scott O'Dell. The novel is based on the life of a real person, Luisa Montero. It takes place in southern California during the 1800's, at the time of the Mexican-American War. California was still a part of Mexico.*

Carlota de Zubarán lives with her father, Don Saturnino, her grandmother, Doña Dolores, and her sister Yris. Their ranch is called Dos Hermanos, or Two Brothers. They are a proud family.

Carlota's brother has died and Don Saturnino has raised Carlota like a son. She can ride a horse, throw a lasso, and beat the best male riders.

The de Zubarán family is drawn into fighting the American army during the war. At the battle of San Pasqual, Carlota finds out that she is more than brave. She learns to trust her own feelings of tenderness and compassion.

In the selection you are about to read, Carlota and her father, Don Saturnino, are going to a secret lagoon they have named the Blue Beach. There they have discovered an old, sunken Spanish ship. In the ship there are two chests of gold coins. Carlota must swim into the sunken ship to collect coins for the ranch and her sister's wedding.

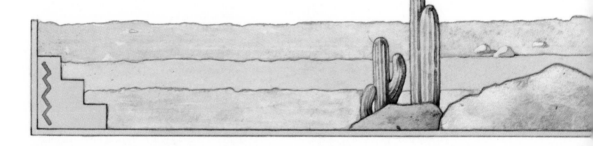

My father wore his thickest pants, his thickest jacket, and a pair of high boots. These clothes were for the wild country that lay between the Ranch of the Two Brothers and the Blue Beach. He carried his best musket, his tinderbox, and his powder horn. I dressed similarly, but carried no weapon except a knife.

I rode my stallion, Tiburón, and my father rode a horse called Santana.

The river would be running very fast.

We chose the north bank and followed it through heavy brush and patches of cactus until we had ridden for two hours.

We crossed the river where it widened and ran knee-deep. It was still a good hour's ride to the Blue Beach, but it was here we made our first check.

My father and I had been coming to Blue Beach for two years. On the three trips we had made, we had been followed, sometimes by one or two Indians. But to

this day, no one had followed us farther than where we had crossed the river. Here we had managed to lose them.

From this spot, the river ran down between two high cliffs. At the bottom of these cliffs were two beaches, one facing the other.

The beaches were strips of fine sand. Someone might call the beaches green or the color of turquoise, but to us they were blue and this is what we called them — the Blue Beaches.

We tied our horses and climbed up to the top of one of the cliffs. From there, we made our second check. We could watch the trails, one coming along the river, and one from the sea.

"What do you see?" my father said. He liked to test my eyesight. "Are we followed?"

"I see nothing on the trail," I said, "either from the river or from the sea."

"What is the brown spot among the oaks?"

"Where?"

"Up the river about three hundred yards."

"I see nothing."

"Look once more."

I looked hard and at last made out the brown spot among the oaks. "It is a cow grazing," I said.

"There are two, and one is not a cow but a calf," my father said.

"You have good eyes," I said.

"And you will have them someday," my father said.

"Never so good as yours."

"Better. *Mucho más.*"*

* *Mucho más:* much more

My father was silent for a while. Then he said. "Tomorrow is Carlos's birthday. He would have been eighteen had he lived."

"He would have liked these journeys," I answered.

"Perhaps. Who knows? It is enough that you like them. You do like them, Carlota?"

"Everything, Father," I said. "Everything."

After awhile, we crawled down from the cliff. We reached the Blue Beach and took off our boots and stepped into the water. The water was cold, both the sea water that met the river and the river water itself.

Stripped to my underclothes, I splashed water on myself. I found that this was the best way to approach cold water.

I took in a great gulp of air, and held my breath for a minute. Then I let out all the air in a quick whoosh. Then I took in a greater gulp. This air I held for two minutes. I repeated this three times. The third time I counted up to four minutes.

It had taken me two years to build up to where I could hold my breath for this length of time. My father had heard of pearl divers in La Paz who could hold their breath for five minutes. I had tried this but had fainted.

We stepped further into the lagoon, careful not to stir the sand.

As my foot touched a smooth slab of stone, I bent down and lifted it carefully. I set it to one side. Beneath it was a rock-lined hole filled with water. The hole was about the size of my body.

At the bottom of this hole was something that looked like the trunk of a tree. But it was the mainmast of a ship, which my father said was some 70 feet in length. It was the kind of ship that two centuries before had sailed the seas between China and the coast of California and Mexico.

My father said that these ships often carried great treasures, and so became the prey of American and English pirates.

Some of these treasure ships had been captured. Others had run into reefs. Still others had tried to escape from pirates by hiding in lagoons such as the one at Blue Beach.

"This must have been a large lagoon at one time," my father said when we had first discovered the ship. "A good place to hide a ship. But when it was inside, something happened and it never returned to the sea."

Hidden in the ship's hold, near the stump of the mainmast, were two chests filled with coins. The coins were of pure gold.

The two chests were well beneath the surface of the water. This was fortunate, for had the chests been exposed, some passing Indian or cowboy would have found them.

There were many things to do before the chests could be reached. Usually it took me half a day to bring up a pouch of coins.

The place where I had to dive was too narrow for my father. He had tried to squeeze through when we first found the ship, but halfway down he got stuck and I had to pull him back. So it was my job to go into the cave-like hole. My father stood beside it and helped me to go down and to come up.

I buckled a strong belt around my waist. To it I tied a *riata** that was 50 feet long and strong enough to hold a stallion. I tied my knife to my wrist — to protect myself against rays and big eels.

Taking three deep breaths, I prepared to let myself down into the hole. Then I started down.

It took me about a minute to reach the hold where the chests lay. I now had two minutes to get the coins loose and carry them to the surface. We had tried putting the coins in a sack and pulling them up. But we had trouble with this because of the underwater currents.

The coins lay in the chests stuck together. I always expected to find them gone, but they were still there. No one had come upon them during the seven months since our last visit.

The first time I had dived and brought up a handful of coins, I said to my father that we should empty both the chests and take the coins home.

"Then everyone will talk," my father said. "As soon as they saw the gold coins, the news would spread the length of California."

"We don't need to tell anyone. I can hide them in my chest at home," I said.

"The news would fly out before the sun set. At the ranch there are many eyes."

I still thought it was a better idea to empty the chests before someone else did. But I could see that my father enjoyed

* *riata*: lasso

192

these trips to the Blue Beach, so I said no more.

The sun was overhead and its rays came down through the narrow hole. With my knife I pried loose a handful of coins. They were a dark green color and covered here and there with a few barnacles. I set the coins aside.

My lungs were beginning to hurt, but I had not felt the tug of the riata yet. That would be my signal from my father that I had been down three minutes. I pried loose a second handful and put my knife away. Finally, I felt the tug of the riata, so I gathered the coins. They were heavy.

Fish were swimming around me as I went up through the hole, but I saw no sting rays or eels. I did see a shark lying back on a ledge, but it was a sandshark, which is not dangerous.

On my third trip down, I brought up about the same number of coins as the other times. The pouch we had brought was now full. I asked my father if we had enough.

"Are you tired?" he said.

"Yes, a little."

"Can you go down again?"

"Yes."

"Then go."

I dived twice more. It was on the last dive that I had trouble. The tug of the riata had not come, but I was tired. So I started away from the chests with one handful of coins. Close to the chests, I had noticed what seemed to be two pieces of wood covered with barnacles. They looked as if they might be part of a third and larger chest.

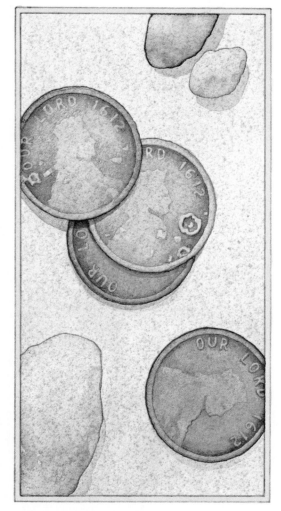

I stuck my knife at a place where the two pieces of wood seemed to join. It was possible that I had found another chest filled with coins.

As the knife touched, the two pieces of wood moved a little. Suddenly, I felt something on my wrist. I drew back the hand that held the knife. Rather, I tried to pull it back. But it would not move. I was caught by the wood, or so I thought.

I felt a tug upon the riata. It was the signal from my father to come to the

surface. I answered him with two quick tugs of the riata.

Now I felt a hot pain run up my arm. I tried to open my fingers to drop the knife, but my hand was numb. I could not move my fingers. Then I looked down into the water and saw a slight movement where my hand was caught. At the same moment I saw a long fleshy tongue sliding along my wrist.

I had never seen a burro clam, but I had heard tales about them. Stuck to rocks or timbers, they grow to half the size of a man. Many unfortunate fishermen had lost their lives in the burro's jaws.

I gave a long, hard tug on the riata to let my father know that I was in trouble. Again I saw the burro's tongue as it opened its lips a little.

I dropped the coins I held in my other hand. The burro had closed once more on my wrist. But then it began to open again.

As the burro's jaws began to open and close, I put my knees against the shell and pushed with all my strength. I fell backward upon the ship's deck. My hand was free. With what breath I had left I moved toward the hole. I saw the sun shining above and climbed toward it. The next thing I saw was my father's face and I was lying on the beach. He took my knife in his hand.

I told him what had happened. My father said, "The knife saved your life. See the mark here. The steel blade kept the burro's jaws open. Enough to let you pull yourself free."

He pulled me to my feet and I put on my clothes.

"Here," he said, passing me the reins of his horse. "Ride Santana, he goes easier than Tiburón."

"I'll ride my own horse," I said.

"Good, if you wish it."

"I wish it," I said. I knew he didn't want me to say that my hand was numb.

"Does the hand hurt?"

"No."

"Some?"

"No."

"You were very brave," he said.

My father wanted me to be braver than I was. I wanted to say I was scared. But I didn't because he expected me to be as brave as Carlos. It was at times like this that I was angry at my father and at my dead brother, too.

"It was good luck," I said.

"Luck and bravery often go together," my father said. "If you do not hurt, let us go."

I got on the stallion and settled myself in the saddle. "Yes," I said, "let us go."

READING COMPREHENSION

Summarizing. Choose the best phrase to complete each sentence. Then write the complete statements on your paper.

1. Carlota and her father went to Blue Beach to _____ (go swimming, hunt for seafood, collect gold coins).

2. It had taken Carlota two years to get to the point where she could _____ (handle a knife like an expert, hold her breath for four minutes, stay in very cold water for half an hour).

3. On her last dive for the day, Carlota barely escaped from a _____ (sandshark, burro clam, sting ray).

4. Carlota was sometimes angry at her father because she felt that he _____ (treated her like a child, expected her to be as brave as Carlos, wanted her to act more like a lady).

5. After Carlota escaped death by drowning, her father told her that she was _____ (easily frightened, careless, brave).

Interpreting. Write the answer to each question on your paper.

1. What did Carlota carry underwater to protect herself from sting rays and big eels?

2. Why did Carlota, not her father, dive for the coins?

3. What special skills did Carlota need to do this?

4. Why did Carlota's father tell her to ride his horse home?

5. Why did Carlota say she'd ride her own horse home?

For Thinking and Discussing

1. Carlota tells the reader that she was scared when she was caught by the burro clam, but her father says that she was brave. Can a person be both scared and brave in the same situation?

2. Should parents raise daughters and sons the same way? Why or why not?

UNDERSTANDING LITERATURE

Point of View. Think about what the words *point of view* really mean: the *point*, or spot, from which a person *views*, or sees, something. Point of view is important because it can change the way you see things.

For example, if you saw a city from an airplane, the buildings would look very small. But if you walked on the street, the buildings would tower above you.

The way you experience an event also depends on your point of view. Your past experiences and plans for the future can change the way you see things.

In the selection from *Carlota*, the story is told from Carlota's point of view. You don't know the story from her father's point of view. Try to imagine how Carlota's father might have felt about some of the events in the selection.

Read the following sentences. Write each sentence on your paper. After the sentence, write the name of the person speaking — Carlota or Don Saturnino. Ask yourself if the sentence is written from Carlota's or Don Saturnino's point of view.

1. I felt that I had to be as brave as my brother Carlos.

2. My daughter Carlota is a brave girl — just as brave as my son Carlos was before he died.

3. I was getting tired, but I made two more dives.

4. I was afraid that the burro clam would kill me.

5. I felt a tug on the rope and knew my daughter was in trouble.

6. I never should have let her make that dive. I knew she was getting tired.

Now think about the setting in this selection, and answer this question:

7. Where did the events take place? When did the events take place?

WRITING

Put yourself in the place of Don Saturnino, Carlota's father. Write a paragraph describing what happened at the beach and how you felt when Carlota made her last dive. Tell how you pulled her up, and how you felt afterward. Describe the events from Don Saturnino's point of view.

The Antique Sale

by Cyndy Hecht

Most of us have known someone like Roseanne. Someone whose friendship we didn't want to lose — until the price of keeping it turned out to be too high. This story by a student tells about a day when everything changed.

Whenever I hear the "William Tell Overture," I remember the fall of my seventh-grade year. I had a good friend named Roseanne who could whistle the whole "Overture." She rode her brother's bike, and she could spit farther than anyone else I knew.

I'll never forget the day Roseanne and I went to Mrs. Weissburg's antique sale. It was after school. We were sitting outside the bakery, eating doughnuts. Roseanne was telling me gossip about movie stars. I was interested because my mother never let me buy gossip magazines.

"Ready to ride home?" I asked when we had finished our doughnuts.

"Let's take the long way," she said.

As I got on my bike, I tried to imagine what Roseanne wanted to do. I should have told her that I had to go home. But I didn't want to make her angry. Being able to call Roseanne my friend meant everything to me.

"Follow me," Roseanne shouted as she rode off. "You have to do whatever I do."

She rode her bike over the curb. Then she laughed as she bounced on her seat.

"That's not good for your bike," I warned.

"You're just chicken," said Roseanne.

"I am not," I said.

I put on the brakes as my bike rolled over the curb. I wondered what Roseanne had in mind. One time, she pushed her next-door neighbor, Dougie, off his scooter. Then she threatened to make him eat a worm if he told.

Now Roseanne moved into the middle of the street. She took her hands off the handlebars.

"No hands," she said. Then she looked back at me.

"But, Roseanne . . . " I said.

"No hands," she said.

The car behind us honked. Roseanne moved to the side of the road. Then she yelled after the car, "You old bag!"

"Where are we going?" I asked.

"You want that I tell?" she said with a heavy German accent.

Then I knew we were going to Mrs. Weissburg's. She was a woman who lived four blocks from my house. During winter

198

vacation, she always invited the neighborhood kids over for Christmas cookies.

The year before, Roseanne had broken one of her little glass animals. Mrs. Weissburg said not to worry about it. But I know Roseanne hadn't been worried. Since then, she had been making fun of Mrs. Weissburg's accent.

"Here we are," said Roseanne, pointing to Mrs. Weissburg's house. A sign saying "Antique Sale" was nailed to a tree.

Roseanne rode her bike up the driveway. She had no trouble pedaling up the steep hill. I got off my bike and walked it up the hill. I locked the bikes together. Then I followed Roseanne to the back of the house.

She walked over to a card table set up in front of a wooden shed. On the table was a shoe box with an opening cut out of the top.

"Look in there," Roseanne said.

I looked through the opening. Inside were a few dollar bills.

"This is going to be fun," Roseanne said. "Come on."

I followed her to the back door. She knocked. There was still time to tell her that I had to leave. But I didn't say anything.

Mrs. Weissburg opened the door. "Roseanne and Kelly, come in," she said. "How nice you come and see me. I don't have cookies today, but we make some. You want?"

"Well, we'd really like to see your antiques," Roseanne said. "We're so interested in the past."

I looked at Roseanne in surprise.

"Of course you can see the antiques," Mrs. Weissburg said. "You liked them yesterday, Roseanne, no? I get my sweater."

When she had gone, I turned to Roseanne. "You were here to see her yester — " I began.

"Shut up and listen," Roseanne said. "She'll take us into the shed. I'll tell her we forgot to lock our bikes."

"Then what?" I asked weakly.

Roseanne began to whistle the "William Tell Overture." "Then we split it 50-50, no?" she said laughing.

I thought about trying to talk Roseanne out of it. But I knew she wouldn't listen.

Mrs. Weissburg came back. "I don't know why you girls want to see my old things. But you want to see, I show you." She led us to the shed.

"We love to see things from the past, don't we, Kelly?" Roseanne said. Then she jabbed me in the ribs.

"Yes, we do," I said. "The past is so interesting."

"Let me see what I have that you would like," said Mrs. Weissburg. She took us inside the shed. "You want to see a doll?" she asked. "She's real china."

"Oh, we love dolls, don't we, Kelly?"

"Yes," I said. I wanted to get on my bike and ride away.

"I think I saved a dress or two," Mrs. Weissburg said. "In the old country, I had one doll. I used to dress her up and pretend she was going to a party."

I was staring at Roseanne. She turned to me and grinned.

"Here it comes," I thought. I swallowed hard.

"Did you lock the bikes, Kelly?" Roseanne asked. I looked at Mrs. Weissburg and then at Roseanne.

"Kelly," Roseanne said, "did you lock the bikes?"

"No," I said, looking down. "I forgot."

"I'd better go and lock them," Roseanne said. She smiled sweetly. "You stay here, Kelly. I'll be right back." And she left the shed.

"Such a nice girl," Mrs. Weissburg said. "I had a best friend. We used to play dolls. . . ." I hardly listened as she talked about their dolls.

"See this tea set?" she asked, pointing.

"It's very nice," I told her.

"It was my grandmother's. She used it on Sundays to serve company."

She handed me one of the cups. I traced one of the pale pink roses with my finger. I didn't know how to begin to tell her about Roseanne.

Then Roseanne came back into the shed. "Mrs. Weissburg," she said, "it's later than I'd thought. We really should be going, don't you think so, Kelly?"

"Yes, we'd better go," I said.

"You girls come visit again soon," Mrs. Weissburg said. "Next time, I have cookies for you. You like?"

"Oh, yes," Roseanne said. "But we really have to leave now."

"You girls stay longer next time," said Mrs. Weissburg.

As we walked to our bikes, Roseanne whispered to me, "We get $2.50 each."

"I don't want it," I whispered back.

"Of course you do."

I unlocked the bikes. As we rode off, Mrs. Weissburg waved from the top of the driveway.

"Come again!" she called. "Good-bye!"

The wind blew dried leaves across the street as we rode home. Hands in the air, Roseanne whistled the "William Tell Overture" and laughed.

After that, I stopped riding past Mrs. Weissburg's house. I didn't go to her house for Christmas cookies ever again.

Roseanne and I were put in different classes. I tried to avoid her as much as possible.

I wanted to tell Mrs. Weissburg what happened. I wanted to pay her back. But she died a year later. Six months after that, Roseanne moved to the West Coast. I never saw her again.

READING COMPREHENSION

Summarizing. Choose the best phrase to complete each sentence. Then write the complete statements on your paper.

1. After Kelly was led to Mrs. Weissburg's house, she realized that Roseanne planned to steal _____ (money, antiques, glass animals).

2. Kelly went along with the plan because she _____ (thought it would be fun, figured Roseanne would succeed, wanted Roseanne to be her friend).

3. At Mrs. Weissburg's house, Roseanne pretended that she _____ (wanted some cookies, collected glass animals, was interested in antiques).

4. After what happened at Mrs. Weissburg's house, Kelly _____ (felt relieved, became friendly with Mrs. Weissburg, avoided Roseanne).

Interpreting. Write the answer to each question on your paper.

1. Where did Mrs. Weissburg keep the money from the sale of her antiques?

2. How did Roseanne know where it was?

3. How can you tell that Mrs. Weissburg liked young people?

4. Why did Kelly stop riding past Mrs. Weissburg's house?

For Thinking and Discussing. Was Kelly as much at fault as Roseanne? Why or why not?

UNDERSTANDING LITERATURE

Point of View. In "The Antique Sale," Kelly tells the story from her own point of view. She uses the words *I* and *me* to tell about herself. The story is told in the *first person.*

Here is a sentence written in the first person: "I'll never forget the day Roseanne and I went to Mrs. Weissburg's antique sale." Here is the same sentence written as if the narrator were *not* a character in the story: "Kelly would never forget the day she and Roseanne went to Mrs. Weissburg's antique sale."

On your paper, rewrite the following paragraphs in the first person.

1. The thought struck her after the bus pulled away. She was at the wrong stop. Everything looked different to the girl. In fact, she had no idea where she was.

2. He ran until his feet were numb. For a moment, he forgot where he was. Then the crowd roared. He thought something was wrong. Instead, they were cheering him as he crossed the finish line.

WRITING

Write a paragraph about an experience you have had with a friend. Tell about the experience from your own point of view. You might be the narrator. Write in the first person. Use the words *I* and *me* when you are writing about yourself.

Me

by Linda Sue Estes (student)

I am the sum
Of all the people I have ever met,
All the things I have ever done,
All the places I have ever seen.
Bits, pieces, and fragments.
You thought it was me you saw
Yesterday,
But you were wrong.
Excuse me,
I am not myself today,
Or yesterday,
Or tomorrow.
Are you who you think you are?

1. In this poem, the writer says that she is all of her experiences. She is not just one of them. Do you ever feel like a different person at different times? When does that happen? Do you think those different selves are all you?

2. What makes you feel that you know who you are? Is it when you are with someone? Is it when you are alone? Is it something that you do?

3. Do you think the writer is asking a serious question at the end of the poem? Or is she trying to be funny?

4. How do you think the writer would answer her own question? How would you answer it for yourself?

The Open Window

by Saki

Vera was so worried about her poor, dear aunt. It was such a sad story. Vera simply had to tell it to the man who came visiting. But what did he see through the open window that made him run away?

"**M**y aunt will be down soon," said the very cool young lady of 15. "While you wait, you must try to put up with me."

Framton Nuttel tried to find the right thing to say. He should please the niece, of course. Still, he should seem to want to meet the aunt very much.

Framton was in the country as part of a cure for his nerves. His sister had given him letters to people she knew there. "If you don't speak to a soul, your nerves will be worse than ever," she had said. "Some of these people are quite nice." Framton did not think that visits to strangers would help much. He hoped that Mrs. Sappleton, the aunt, was one of the "nice" ones.

"Do you know many people around here?" asked the niece.

"Hardly a soul," said Framton. "My sister stayed with friends here about four years ago. She gave me letters to some of them — so they would know who I was."

"Then you know almost nothing about my aunt," said the cool young lady.

"Only her name and address," said Framton. He wondered if Mrs. Sappleton was married, or a widow. Something about the room made him think a man lived there.

"The terrible thing happened to her just three years ago," said the girl. "That would be since your sister was here."

"The terrible thing?" asked Framton. Terrible things seemed out of place in this quiet country spot.

"You may wonder why we keep that window wide open on an October afternoon," said the niece. She pointed to a large French window that opened onto a lawn.

"It *is* warm for the time of year," said Framton. "But does that window have anything to do with the terrible thing?"

"It started when they went out through that window, three years ago today. Her husband and her two young brothers — they were going hunting. They never came back. They slipped into a swamp and drowned. Their bodies were never found.

That was the terrible part of it." Here the girl's voice lost its coolness. "My poor aunt! She thinks they will come back some day! They and the little brown dog that was with them. She believes that they will walk in through the window, just as they used to do. That is why the window is kept open every evening.

"My poor, dear aunt. She has often told me how they went out. Her husband had his red coat over his arm. Ronnie, her younger brother, was singing an old song:

'My Bonnie Lies Over the Ocean.' He did that to tease her — she said it got on her nerves. You know, sometimes, on a still, quiet evening like this, I get a creepy feeling. I almost think they will all walk in through that window. . . ."

She broke off, shaking her head. Framton was glad when the aunt came into the room, saying how sorry she was to be so late.

"I hope you have enjoyed talking to Vera," she said.

"She has been very interesting," said Framton.

"I hope you don't mind the open window," said Mrs. Sappleton brightly. "My husband and brothers will be home soon. They've been hunting, and they always come in this way. They'll have shot some birds, so they'll make a mess of my poor carpets. But that's the way you men are, isn't it?"

She rattled on cheerfully. She talked about hunting, and how it might be better next winter. To Framton, it was awful. He tried to change the subject. He saw that Vera's aunt was not paying him much attention. Her eyes were on the open window and the lawn. He was sorry that he had come to visit on this, of all days.

"The doctors say I should do nothing exciting, and get lots of rest," Framton explained. He had not yet learned that few people are interested in the health of others. "Now, as to what I should eat, they don't agree."

"No?" said Mrs. Sappleton. Then her face grew brighter. But it was not because of what Framton was saying.

"Here they are at last!" she cried. "Just in time for tea. And they look as if they were muddy up to their eyes!"

Framton turned toward the niece, to give her an understanding look. The girl was staring out through the open window. Her eyes were wide with fear.

In the gray light, three figures were walking across the lawn toward the window. They carried guns under their arms. One of them had a red coat over his shoulders. A tired brown dog kept close to their heels. Without making a sound, they drew near the house. Then a young voice began to sing, "My bonnie lies over the ocean. . . ."

Framton jumped to his feet and made a mad dash for the door. Out in the road, a man on a bicycle had to run into a hedge to keep from hitting him.

"Here we are, my dear," said the man with the red coat, coming in through the window. "We're muddy, but most of it's dry. Who was that who rushed out as we came up?"

"A very strange man, a Mr. Nuttel," said Mrs. Sappleton. "He could only talk about being ill, and then dashed off without a word of good-bye. You would think he had seen a ghost."

"I think it was the dog," said Vera. "He told me he was awfully afraid of dogs. He was once chased into a graveyard in India by a pack of wild dogs. He had to spend the night in a grave that had just been dug. The dogs barked and howled and snapped just above him all night. It was enough to make anyone lose their nerve."

Making up exciting stories at short notice was Vera's specialty.

READING COMPREHENSION

Summarizing. Choose the best phrase to complete each sentence. Then write the complete statements on your paper.

1. The story Vera told Framton was ——

   (the awful truth, a lie, a secret).

2. Vera told the story after she made sure Framton ————————
   (was a friend of her aunt, knew little about her aunt, enjoyed jokes).

3. Framton ran off because he was —— (afraid he had just seen ghosts, afraid of dogs, embarrassed).

4. Vera explained to the others that Framton ran off because he was —— (afraid he had just seen ghosts, afraid of dogs, embarrassed).

Interpreting. Write the answer to each question on your paper.

1. Why was Framton in the country?

2. Why did Vera tell Framton about "the terrible thing" that happened three years ago?

3. Why did Framton try to change the subject when Mrs. Sappleton kept talking about her husband and brothers and their hunting?

4. What details did Vera include in her story to make it seem real to Framton?

For Thinking and Discussing. Do you think Vera's joke on Framton Nuttel was harmful or harmless? Why?

UNDERSTANDING LITERATURE

Point of View. In "The Open Window," the narrator is not a character in the story. You learn what happens from the point of view of the narrator, not from the point of view of any one character. This is called *third-person narration*. Here is an example: "Framton Nuttel tried to find the right thing to say." Later, the narrator says, "Making up exciting stories at short notice was Vera's specialty." In "The Open Window," the narrator seems to know what each character is thinking or feeling.

Read the following two passages. They are written in the *first person*. Rewrite each passage in the *third person*.

1. My name is Vera. I am 15 years old. I live with my aunt. Life can be boring here sometimes, so I amuse myself by making up exciting stories.

2. My name is Framton Nuttel. One day I went to visit a friend of my sister. On that day, I had the most frightening experience of my life!

WRITING

In "The Open Window," Vera liked to make up exciting stories. Imagine Vera in the following situation: A man arrives at the door selling leashes, food, and flea collars for dogs. Vera tells him about her dog, and suddenly the salesman wants to leave. What exciting story could she make up? Write one or two paragraphs. Start by writing "Vera said."

Antaeus

by Borden Deal

In Greek mythology, Antaeus (an-TAY-us) was a giant wrestler who could not be harmed as long as he touched earth. That's where his strength came from. He was finally defeated by Hercules, who lifted him off the ground and crushed him. This story is about a modern Antaeus. He's a country kid who has moved to the city — away from the earth and crops he loves.

This was during the wartime, when lots of people were coming North for jobs in factories and war industries, when people moved around a lot more than they do now and sometimes kids were thrown into new groups and new lives that were completely different from anything they had ever known before. I remember this one kid, T.J. his name was, from somewhere down South, whose family moved into our building during that time. They'd come North with everything they owned piled into the back seat of an old-model sedan that you wouldn't expect could make the trip, with T.J. and his three younger sisters riding shakily on top of the load of junk.

Our building was just like all the others there, with families crowded into a few rooms, and I guess there were twenty-five or thirty kids about my age in that one building. Of course, there were a few of us who formed a gang and ran together all the time after school, and I was the one who brought T.J. in and started the whole thing.

The building right next door to us was a factory where they made walking dolls. It was a low building with a flat, tarred roof that had a parapet all around it about head high and we'd found out a long time before that no one, not even the watchman, paid any attention to the roof because it was higher than any of the other buildings around. So my gang used the roof as a headquarters. We could get up there by crossing over to the fire escape from our own roof on a plank and then going on up. It was a secret place for us, where nobody else could go without our permission.

I remember the day I first took T.J. up there to meet the gang. He was a stocky, robust kid with a shock of white hair, nothing sissy about him except his voice — he talked in this slow, gentle voice like you never heard before. He talked different from any of us and you

noticed it right away. But I liked him anyway, so I told him to come on up.

We climbed up over the parapet and dropped down on the roof. The rest of the gang were already there.

"Hi," I said. I jerked my thumb at T.J. "He just moved into the building yesterday."

He just stood there, not scared or anything, just looking, like the first time you see somebody you're not sure you're going to like.

"Hi," Blackie said. "Where are you from?"

"Marion County," T.J. said.

We laughed. "Marion County?" I said. "Where's that?"

He looked at me for a moment like I was a stranger, too. "It's in Alabama," he said. He made me feel like I ought to know where it was.

"What's your name?" Charley said.

"T.J.," he said, looking back at him. He had pale blue eyes that looked washed-out but he looked directly at Charley, waiting for his reaction. He'll be all right, I thought. No sissy in him . . . except that voice. Who ever talked like that?

"T.J.," Blackie said. "That's just initials. What's your real name? Nobody in the world has just initials."

"I do," he said. "And they're T.J. That's all the name I got."

His voice was resolute with the knowledge of his rightness and for a moment no one had anything to say. T.J. looked around at the rooftop and down at the black tar under his feet. "Down yonder where I come from," he said, "we played

211

out in the woods. Don't you-all have no woods around here?"

"Naw," Blackie said. "There's the park a few blocks over, but it's full of kids and cops and old women. You can't do a thing."

T.J. kept looking at the tar under his feet. "You mean you ain't got no fields to raise no watermelons or nothing in?"

"Naw," I said scornfully. "What do you want to grow something for? The folks can buy everything they need at the store."

He looked at me again with that strange, unknowing look. "In Marion County," he said, "I had my own acre of cotton and my own acre of corn. It was mine to plant and make ever' year."

He sounded like it was something to be proud of, and in some obscure way it made the rest of us angry. "Huh!" Blackie said. "Who'd want to have their own acre of cotton and corn? That's just work. What can you do with an acre of cotton and corn?"

T.J. looked at him. "Well, you get part of the bale offen your acre," he said seriously. "And I fed my acre of corn to my calf."

We didn't really know what he was talking about, so we were more puzzled than angry; otherwise, I guess, we'd have chased him off the roof and wouldn't let him be part of our gang. But he was strange and different and we were all attracted by his stolid sense of rightness and belonging, maybe by the strange softness of his voice contrasting our own tones of speech into harshness.

He moved his foot against the black tar. "We could make our own field right here," he said softly, thoughtfully. "Come spring, we could raise us what we want to . . . watermelons and garden truck and no telling what all."

"You have to be a good farmer to make these tar roofs grow any watermelons," I said. We all laughed.

But T.J. looked serious. "We could haul us some dirt up here," he said. "And spread it out even and water it and before you know it we'd have us a crop in here." He looked at us intently. "Wouldn't that be fun?"

"They wouldn't let us," Blackie said quickly.

"I thought you said this was you-all's roof," T.J. said to me. "That you-all could do anything you wanted to up here."

"They've never bothered us," I said. I felt the idea beginning to catch fire in me. It was a big idea and it took a while for it to sink in, but the more I thought about it, the better I liked it. "Say," I said to the gang. "He might have something there. Just make us a regular roof garden, with flowers and grass and trees and everything. And all ours, too," I said. "We wouldn't let anybody up here except the ones we wanted to."

"It'd take a while to grow trees," T.J. said quickly, but we weren't paying any attention to him. They were all talking about it suddenly, all excited with the idea after I'd put it in a way they could catch hold of it. Only rich people had roof gardens, we knew, and the idea of our own private domain excited them.

"We could bring it up in sacks and boxes," Blackie said. "We'd have to do it while the folks weren't paying any attention to us, for we'd have to come up to the roof of our building and then cross over with it."

"Where could we get the dirt?" somebody said worriedly.

"Out of those vacant lots over close to school," Blackie said. "Nobody'd notice if we scraped it up."

I slapped T.J. on the shoulder. "Man, you had a wonderful idea," I said, and everybody grinned at him, remembering that he had started it. "Our own private roof garden."

He grinned back. "It'll be ourn," he said. "All ourn." Then he looked thoughtful again. "Maybe I can lay my hands on some cotton seed, too. You think we could raise us some cotton?"

We'd started big projects before at one time or another, like any gang of kids, but they'd always petered out for lack of organization and direction. But this one didn't . . . somehow or other T.J. kept it going all through the winter months. He kept talking about the watermelons and the cotton we'd raise, come spring, and when even that wouldn't work he'd switch around to my idea of flowers and grass and trees, though he was always honest enough to add that it'd take a while to get any trees started. He always had it on his mind and he'd mention it in school, getting them lined up to carry dirt that afternoon, saying in a casual way that he reckoned a few more weeks ought to see the job through.

Our little area of private earth grew slowly. T.J. was smart enough to start in one corner of the building, heaping up the carried earth two or three feet thick, so that we had an immediate result to look at, to contemplate with awe. Some of the evenings T.J. alone was carrying earth up to the building, the rest of the gang distracted by other enterprises or interests, but T.J. kept plugging along on his own, and eventually we'd all come back to him again and then our own little acre would grow more rapidly.

He was careful about the kind of dirt he'd let us carry up there and more than once he dumped a sandy load over the parapet into the areaway below because it wasn't good enough. He found out the kinds of earth in all the vacant lots for blocks around. He'd pick it up and feel it and smell it, frozen though it was sometimes, and then he'd say it was good and growing soil or it wasn't worth anything and we'd have to go on somewhere else.

Thinking about it now, I don't see how he kept us at it. It was hard work, lugging paper sacks and boxes of dirt all the way up the stairs of our own building, keeping out of the way of the grownups so they wouldn't catch on to what we were doing. They probably wouldn't have cared, for they didn't pay much attention to us, but we wanted to keep it secret anyway. Then we had to go through the trap door to our roof, teeter over a plank to the fire escape, then climb two or three stories to the parapet and drop down onto the roof. All that for a small pile of earth that sometimes didn't seem worth the effort. But T.J. kept the vision bright within us, his words shrewd and calculated toward the fulfillment of his dream; and he worked harder than any of us. He seemed driven toward a goal that we couldn't see, a particular point in time that would be definitely marked by signs and wonders that only he could see.

The laborious earth just lay there during the cold months, inert and lifeless, the clods lumpy and cold under our feet when we walked over it. But one day it rained and afterward there was a softness in the air and the earth was live and giving again with moisture and warmth. That evening T.J. smelled the air, his nostrils dilating with the odor of the earth under his feet.

"It's spring," he said, and there was a gladness rising in his voice that filled us all with the same feeling. "It's mighty late for it, but it's spring. I'd just about decided it wasn't never gonna get here at all."

We were all sniffing at the air, too, trying to smell it the way that T.J. did, and I can still remember the sweet odor of the earth under our feet. It was the first time in my life that spring and spring earth had meant anything to me. I looked at T.J. then, knowing in a faint way the hunger within him through the toilsome winter months, knowing the dream that lay behind his plan. He was a new Antaeus, preparing his own bed of strength.

"Planting time," he said. "We'll have to find us some seed."

"What do we do?" Blackie said. "How do we do it?"

"First we'll have to break up the clods," T.J. said. "That won't be hard to do. Then we plant the seed and after a while they come up. Then you got you a crop." He frowned. "But you ain't got it raised yet. You got to tend it and hoe it

and take care of it and all the time it's growing and growing, while you're awake and while you're asleep. Then you lay it by when it's growed and let it ripen and then you got you a crop."

"There's those wholesale seed houses over on Sixth," I said.

T.J. looked at the earth. "You-all seem mighty set on raising some grass," he said. "I ain't never put no effort into that. I spent all my life trying not to raise grass."

"But it's pretty," Blackie said. "We could play on it and take sunbaths on it. Like having our own lawn. Lots of people got lawns."

"Well," T.J. said. He looked at the rest of us, hesitant for the first time. He kept on looking at us for a moment. "I did have it in mind to raise some corn and vegetables. But we'll plant grass."

He was smart. He knew where to give in. And I don't suppose it made any difference to him, really. He just wanted to grow something, even if it was grass.

"Of course," he said, "I do think we ought to plant a row of watermelons. They'd be mighty nice to eat while we was a-laying on that grass."

We all laughed. "All right," I said. "We'll plant us a row of watermelons."

Things went very quickly then. Perhaps half the roof was covered with the earth, the half that wasn't broken by ventilators. T.J. showed us how to prepare the earth, breaking up the clods and smoothing it and sowing the grass seed. It looked rich and black now with moisture, receiving of the seed, and it seemed that the grass sprang up overnight, pale green in the early spring.

We couldn't keep from looking at it, unable to believe that we had created this delicate growth. We looked at T.J. with understanding now, knowing the fulfillment of the plan he had carried alone within his mind. We had worked without full understanding of the task but he had known all the time.

We found that we couldn't walk or play on the delicate blades, as we had expected to, but we didn't mind. It was enough just to look at it, to realize that it was the work of our own hands, and each evening the whole gang was there, trying to measure the growth that had been achieved that day.

One time a foot was placed on the plot of ground . . . one time only, Blackie stepping onto it with sudden bravado. Then he looked at the crushed blades and there was shame in his face. He did not do it again. This was his grass, too, and not to be desecrated. No one said anything, for it was not necessary.

T.J. had reserved a small section for watermelons and he was still trying to find some seed for it. The wholesale house didn't have any watermelon seed and we didn't know where we could lay our hands on them. T.J. shaped the earth into mounds, ready to receive them, three mounds lying in a straight line along the edge of the grass plot.

Somewhere or other, T.J. got his hands on a seed catalogue and brought it one evening to our roof garden. "We can order them now," he said, showing us the catalogue. "Look!"

We all crowded around, looking at the fat, green watermelons pictured in full color on the pages. Some of them were split open, showing the red, tempting meat, making our mouths water.

"Now we got to scrape up some more seed money," T.J. said, looking at us. "I got a quarter. How much you-all got?"

We made up a couple of dollars between us and T.J. nodded his head. "That'll be more than enough. Now we got to decide what kind to get. I think them Kleckley Sweets. What do you-all think?"

He was going into esoteric matters beyond our reach. We hadn't even known there were different kinds of melons. So we just nodded our heads and agreed that Yes, we thought the Kleckley Sweets, too.

"I'll order them tonight," T.J. said. "We ought to have them in a few days."

"What are you boys doing up here?" an adult voice said behind us.

It startled us, for no one had ever come up here before, in all the time we had been using the roof of the factory. We jerked around and saw three men standing near the trap door at the other end of the roof. They weren't policemen, or night watchmen, but three men in plump business suits, looking at us. They walked toward us.

"What are you boys doing up here?" the one in the middle said again.

We stood still, guilt heavy among us, levied by the tone of voice, and looked at the three strangers.

The men stared at the grass flourishing behind us. "What's this?" the man said. "How did this get up here?"

"Sure is growing good, ain't it?" T.J. said conversationally. "We planted it."

216

The men kept looking at the grass as if they didn't believe it. It was a thick carpet over the earth now, a patch of deep greenness startling in the sterile industrial surroundings.

"Yes sir," T.J. said proudly. "We toted that earth up here and planted that grass." He fluttered the seed catalogue. "And we're just fixing to plant us some watermelon."

The man looked at him then, his eyes strange and far-away. "What do you

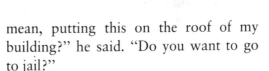

mean, putting this on the roof of my building?" he said. "Do you want to go to jail?"

T.J. looked shaken. The rest of us were silent, frightened by the authority of his voice. We had grown up aware of adult authority, of policemen and night watchmen and teachers, and this man sounded like all the others. But it was a new thing to T.J.

"Well, you wan't using the roof," T.J. said. He paused a moment and added shrewdly, "So we just thought to pretty it up a little bit."

"And sag it so I'd have to rebuild it," the man said sharply. He started turning

217

away, saying to another man beside him, "See that all that junk is shoveled off by tomorrow."

"Yes, sir," the man said.

T.J. started forward. "You can't do that," he said. "We toted it up here and it's our earth. We planted it and raised it and toted it up here."

The man stared at him coldly. "But it's my building," he said. "It's to be shoveled off tomorrow."

"It's our earth," T.J. said desperately. "You ain't got no right!"

The men walked on without listening and descended clumsily through the trap door. T.J. stood looking after them, his body tense with anger, until they had disappeared. They wouldn't even argue with him, wouldn't let him defend his earth-rights.

He turned to us. "We won't let 'em do it," he said fiercely. "We'll stay up here all day tomorrow and the day after that and we won't let 'em do it."

We just looked at him. We knew that there was no stopping it. He saw it in our faces and his face wavered for a moment before he gripped it into determination.

"They ain't got no right," he said. "It's our earth. It's our land. Can't nobody touch a man's own land."

We kept on looking at him, listening to the words but knowing that it was no use. The adult world had descended on us even in our richest dream and we knew there was no calculating the adult world, no fighting it, no winning against it.

We started moving slowly toward the parapet and the fire escape, avoiding a last look at the green beauty of the earth that

T.J. had planted for us . . . had planted deeply in our minds as well as in our experience. We filed slowly over the edge and down the steps to the plank, T.J. coming last, and all of us could feel the weight of his grief behind us.

"Wait a minute," he said suddenly, his voice harsh with the effort of calling. We stopped and turned, held by the tone of his voice, and looked up at him standing above us on the fire escape.

"We can't stop them?" he said, looking down at us, his face strange in the dusky light. "There ain't no way to stop 'em?"

"No," Blackie said with finality. "They own the building."

We stood still for a moment, looking up at T.J., caught into inaction by the decision working in his face. He stared back at us and his face was pale in the poor light.

"They ain't gonna touch my earth," he said fiercely. "They ain't gonna lay a hand on it! Come on."

He turned around and started up the fire escape again, almost running against the effort of climbing. We followed more slowly, not knowing what he intended. By the time we reached him, he had seized a board and thrust it into the soil, scooping it up and flinging it over the parapet into the areaway below. He straightened and looked at us.

"They can't touch it," he said. "I won't let 'em lay a dirty hand on it!"

We saw it then. He stooped to his labor again and we followed, the gusts of his anger moving in frenzied labor among us as we scattered along the edge of earth, scooping it and throwing it over the par-

apet, destroying with anger the growth we had nurtured with such tender care. The soil carried so laboriously upward to the light and the sun cascaded swiftly into the dark areaway, the green blades of grass crumpled and twisted in the falling.

It took less time than you would think . . . the task of destruction is infinitely easier than that of creation. We stopped at the end, leaving only a scattering of loose soil, and when it was finally over, a stillness stood among the group and over the factory building. We looked down at the bare sterility of black tar, felt the harsh texture of it under the soles of our shoes, and the anger had gone out of us, leaving only a sore aching in our minds like over-stretched muscles.

T.J. stood for a moment, his breathing slowing from anger and effort, caught into the same contemplation of destruction as all of us. He stooped slowly, finally, and picked up a lonely blade of grass left trampled under our feet and put it between his teeth, tasting it, sucking the greenness out of it into his mouth. Then he started walking toward the fire escape, moving before any of us were ready to move, and disappeared over the edge.

We followed him but he was already halfway down to the ground, going on past the board where we crossed over, climbing down into the areaway. We saw the last section swing down with his weight and then he stood on the concrete below us, looking at the small pile of anonymous earth scattered by our throwing. Then he walked across the place where we could see him and disappeared toward the street without glancing back,

without looking up to see us watching him.

They did not find him for two weeks. Then the Nashville police caught him just outside the Nashville freight yards. He was walking along the railroad track; still heading south, still heading home.

As for us, who had no remembered home to call us . . . none of us ever again climbed the escape-way to the roof.

READING COMPREHENSION

Summarizing. Choose the best phrase to complete each sentence. Then write the complete statements on your paper.

1. T.J. convinced the gang that it would be fun to _____ (play a joke on the owner of the factory next door, have a garden, travel to the South).

2. During the winter, T.J. got the gang to _____ (clean off the roof, carry dirt up to the roof, buy seeds).

3. After the factory owner said the garden would be destroyed, T.J. _____ (destroyed it himself, said he'd go to court, threatened to fight the man).

4. Later, T.J. was found _____ (planting another garden, destroying the roof next door, heading for his old home in the south).

Interpreting. Write the answer to each question on your paper.

1. What did members of the gang find different about T.J.?

2. Why were they impressed with him?

3. In what way was T.J. like Antaeus of the Greek myth?

4. What was T.J. seeking at the end?

For Thinking and Discussing. The narrator says that T.J. planted something in the boys' minds as well as in their experience. What did he plant in their minds? Did this affect their lives?

UNDERSTANDING LITERATURE

Point of View. In "Antaeus," the narrator is a character in the story. He is a member of the gang. He tells us what the characters say and do, and what he thinks about the action. He is a *first-person* narrator, but he is not the main character. The main character is T.J..

Suppose T.J. had been the narrator. Write the number of each statement below that T.J. would *not* have made if he had told the story. Then write a sentence explaining why.

1. "He talked different from any of us and you noticed it right away."

2. "You mean you ain't got no fields to raise nothin' in?"

3. "But he was strange and different and we were all attracted by his stolid sense of rightness and belonging."

4. "'Well. I did have it in mind to raise some corn and vegetables.'"

5. "He worked harder than any of us. He seemed driven toward a goal that we couldn't see."

6. "He was a new Antaeus, preparing his own bed of strength."

WRITING

Suppose you were the factory owner who feared that the weight of the garden would damage the roof. Could you get the boys to appreciate your concern? Write what you would say to them.

Alone

by Maya Angelou

Lying, thinking
Last night
How to find my soul a home
Where water is not thirsty
and bread loaf is not stone
I came up with one thing
And I don't believe I'm wrong
That nobody,
But nobody
Can make it out here alone.

Alone, all alone
Nobody, but nobody
Can make it out here alone.

There are some millionaires
With money they can't use
Their wives run round like banshees
Their children sing the blues

they've got expensive doctors
To cure their hearts of stone.
But nobody
No nobody
Can make it out here alone.

Alone, all alone
Nobody, but nobody
Can make it out here alone.

Now if you listen closely
I'll tell you what I know
Storm clouds are gathering
The wind is gonna blow
The race of man is suffering
And I can hear the moan,
Cause nobody,
But nobody
Can make it out here alone.

Alone, all alone
Nobody, but nobody
Can make it out here alone.

1. The writer of this poem seems sure of what she is saying. Which lines state the point of the poem very strongly?

2. A "banshee" is a kind of female ghost that is known for its wailing cry. Why do you think "banshees" is used to describe some millionaires' wives? Does the poet think that millionaires need other people?

3. What things or experiences might make someone say, "Nobody can make it out here alone"? Have you known someone who didn't need other people?

Section Review

VOCABULARY

Figurative Language. To make stories more lively, authors sometimes use *figurative language*. Instead of writing, "I began to like the idea," an author might write, "I felt the idea beginning to catch fire in me." The idea does not *actually* burst into flames. It does not *actually* burn inside someone. But someone might suddenly like an idea so much that it might *feel* as if it were catching fire inside.

Here are some examples of figurative language taken from the stories and poems in this section. On your paper, write what each sentence means in your own words.

1. "The news would fly out before the sun set."

2. "I am the sum/Of all the people I have ever met,/All the things I have ever done,/All the places I have ever seen."

3. "They were . . . all excited with the idea after I'd put it in a way they could catch hold of it."

4. "It [the grass] was a thick carpet over the earth now, . . ."

5. "The adult world had descended on us . . ."

6. "We stood still, guilt heavy among us, . . ."

7. ". . . when it was finally over, a stillness stood among the group and over the factory building."

8. ". . . the anger had gone out of us, leaving only a sore aching in our minds like overstretched muscles."

READING

Facts and Opinion. Some sentences state *facts*. Facts are either true or false. There is always a way of checking whether they are true or not. For example:

Two plus two equals four.
Scott O'Dell wrote Carlota.

But *opinions* are statements that cannot be proved true or false. They say what someone believes or feels about something. For example:

Summer is better than winter.
Math is the hardest subject.

Someone might disagree with these opinions. The person who disagrees has a different opinion.

Number your paper from 1 to 8. Next to the number of each sentence, write whether the sentence states a fact or an opinion.

1. "The past is so interesting."

2. "Roseanne and I were put in different classes."

3. "The people there are quite nice."

4. "Framton did not think that visits to strangers would help much."

5. "My father and I had been coming to Blue Beach for two years."

6. "The building right next door to us was a factory."

7. ". . . .nothing sissy about him except his voice. . . ."

8. "Then the Nashville police caught him outside the Nashville freight yards."

WRITING

Comparisons. When you compare two things, you tell how they are alike and how they are different. In order to write a comparison of two things, you have to observe them carefully. When you do this, you can find similarities and differences between almost any two things.

Step 1: Set Your Goal
Choose one of these topics for a comparison:

a. Write a comparison of the two girls, Roseanne and Kelly, in "The Antique Sale." Include similarities and differences in any of the following characteristics: their ages, interests, backgrounds, behavior, and character traits.

b. Suppose you were T. J. in "Antaeus." You want to help your new friends understand what life in the country was like. Write a comparison of your old home and your new one. Include similarities and differences in any of the following aspects of your life: your homes, your schools, your activities, and the physical appearances of the places.

Step 2: Make a Plan
Make two lists of ideas for your comparison: one of similarities, the other of differences. You may want to divide the list into sections for different topics. For example, suppose you were writing a comparison of what Framton Nuttel in, "The Open Window," thought was happening and what really was happening. The lists of similarities and differences might be divided into these categories: what Vera, Mrs. Sappleton's niece, was like; what Mrs. Sappleton was thinking and feeling; and what Mr. Nuttel saw out the window.

Once you have made the lists, you need to decide how to organize the ideas. You can use any one of these three methods:

1. Tell all the ways the two things are similar in one paragraph. Tell all the ways they are different in another. In a comparison about "The Open Window," you would write one paragraph telling all the ways in which what Nuttel thinks is happening are like what is really happening. You would write a second paragraph telling how what he thinks is happening is different from reality.

2. Tell about one of your subjects in one paragraph. Tell about the other subject in a separate paragraph. In a comparison about "The Open Window," you would write a paragraph about the way Nuttel perceives things and a paragraph about the way things really are.

3. Discuss each point of comparison, one at a time, with a separate paragraph on each point. In a comparison about "The Open Window," you would write a paragraph on each point used in your lists of ideas. Each paragraph would include both similarities and differences.

Step 3. Write Your First Draft

Write a first draft, following the method of organization you selected. The order in which you use your ideas will depend on the method. Remember, if the method doesn't seem to work well, you can change your mind and try another.

After you have written the draft of the comparison, write a theme statement for it. A theme statement is like the topic sentence of a paragraph: It tells the main idea. A theme statement, however, is used for a longer piece of writing. The theme statement for a comparison about "The Open Window" might say, "With a little help from Vera, Framton Nuttel's imagination turned an ordinary family into an eerie collection of ghosts."

Step 4. Revise Your Comparison

When you revise your comparison, ask yourself these questions:

☐ Have you followed one method of organization throughout?

☐ Is your theme statement clear?

☐ Do you clearly state the important similarities and differences?

Also try to make your statements more specific. You might add examples to illustrate the similarities and differences. For example, in a comparison about "The Open Window," you might say, "When Mr. Sappleton and his bothers appear, they look muddy to Mrs. Sappleton and ghostly to Mr. Nuttel."

After you have revised your comparison, proofread it and copy it over neatly.

QUIZ

The following is a quiz for Section 6. Write the answers in complete sentences on your paper.

Reading Comprehension

1. The main character in *Carlota* is a brave girl. What facts in the selection support this statement?

2. In "The Antique Sale," why did Kelly go along with Roseanne's plan to steal money from Mrs. Weissburg?

3. List three details that were true in the story that Vera made up in "The Open Window."

4. In the story "Antaeus," how do the boys feel when the grass sprouts? What have they learned from T.J.?

5. In the poem "Alone," why does the poet think the race of man is suffering? Is this an example of a fact or an opinion?

Understanding Literature

6. Write a sentence describing the nar-

rator of *Carlota*.

7. From which character's point of view is "The Antique Sale" written?

8. Which selection is an example of third-person narration?

9. Is "Alone" written in the first person or the third person?

10. From whose point of view is "Antaeus" written?

ACTIVITIES

Word Attack

1. The following words from the stories is this section all imitate sounds:

whoosh	howled
shhh	creaky

Write down a word for each sound described below. You can use sound words you know or make up your own.

a. A book drops on the floor.

b. A drinking glass drops on the floor.

c. Heavy rain pounds down on the roof.

d. A faucet is leaky.

e. A fire alarm goes off.

Use all your sound words in a scary or funny story about a haunted house.

2. The words below are from stories in this section. Use your dictionary to find out what language each word came from and what it meant in that language.

lasso	lagoon
robust	bravado

Speaking and Listening. "The Open Window" is a ghost story. Do you know any others? Have you ever told one? Try telling a ghost story to your classmates. Turn off the lights, pull down the shades, and see if you can scare them.

Researching. Find a book of myths in the library and read the whole story of Antaeus and his fight with Hercules. Be prepared to tell the story in class. Decide if you think "Antaeus" is a good name for the story by Borden Deal.

Creating. In the poem "Me" the author says she is made up of all her experiences and everyone she knows. Write a poem of your own that describes who you are. Tell about the people and places you know and the experiences you have had.

LANGSTON HUGHES

DREAMS

Hold fast to dreams
For if dreams die
Life is a broken-winged bird
That cannot fly.

Hold fast to dreams
For when dreams go
Life is a barren field
Frozen with snow.

— Langston Hughes

Biography

Langston Hughes

One summer day in 1920, a black teenager got on a train in Cleveland, Ohio. He had just graduated from high school. He had been class poet. Now he was on his way to Mexico, where his wealthy father lived. He planned to ask him for money to go to college.

As the train went through the South, a poem came to him. He scribbled it down on an envelope. When he got to Mexico, he sent it to a magazine in New York. It was published. A brilliant career had begun.

Today the poetry of Langston Hughes has been printed in more languages than the work of any other modern American poet. Before he died in 1967, he had also written plays, stories, TV scripts, newspaper articles, and words for songs. Most of his writing had the same theme: what it was like to be black in America.

Langston Hughes was born in Joplin, Missouri, in 1902. His mother, Carrie Langston Hughes, had been a school teacher. His father, James Hughes, kept a store. The marriage broke up while Langston was a baby. James Hughes went to Mexico, where he made a fortune as a rancher and real estate man.

Carrie Hughes did not find life easy. She had to find work, wherever it was.

She left her son with his grandmother in Kansas.

Mary Langston told her grandson stories about his grandfather. He had been active in the Underground Railroad, which had brought slaves out of the South to freedom. Later, Langston was to draw on those stories when he wrote about Harriet Tubman, the brave "conductor" on the Underground Railroad. Langston probably had women like his mother and grandmother in mind when he wrote "Mother to Son."

Langston was 12 when his grandmother died. He went to live with his mother in the Middle West. In school there, he began to write poetry. He decided to become a writer.

But James Hughes had other ideas. Langston spent his first year out of high school in Mexico. He learned that money was the most important thing in his father's life. James wanted his son to be an engineer, because of the money they made. Even so, he gave Langston money for a year at Columbia University.

But the young man found the New York college stuffy and too big. When the year was up, he got a job on a freighter. He threw his books overboard, so he could see things with fresh eyes. "With that trip," he wrote, "I began to live."

When the ship docked at an African port, Langston left it. He traveled in the continent of his ancestors. Then he moved to Europe for a while.

Back in Washington, D.C., he had trouble finding steady jobs. He took one in a restaurant while he went on writing.

One day Vachel Lindsay, a famous poet, ate at the restaurant. Langston stuck three of his poems under Lindsay's plate. Lindsay read them to an audience that night. Because of the publicity he got, Langston won a scholarship to Lincoln University in Pennsylvania. By the time he graduated, he had two books published.

He wrote on many subjects in many forms. But he had a special talent for poems and stories that told how black people felt, in their own language. He was one of the first black writers to write for his own people, not to explain them to whites.

"Thank You, M'am," and "Harriet Tubman: The Moses of Her People" are examples of this kind of writing. The first is a short story about a black woman who understands why a boy has grabbed her pocketbook, but wants to make sure he'll never try it again. The second is a biography of an amazing black leader who had some very human qualities.

"Early Autumn," another short story, is a bit different. It shows two people who were once in love running into each other many years later. They may or may not be black. What is important is the sense of loss, which can be felt by any person.

Langston Hughes's poems, like his stories, express joy, sorrow, and determination. When he wrote, "Hold fast to dreams," he knew that for many people life *was* "a broken-winged bird that cannot fly" or "a barren field frozen with snow." He knew what it meant to feel that life is "sometimes goin' in the dark/ Where there ain't been no light." And he gave people the courage to continue on.

Thank You, M'am

by Langston Hughes

The young purse-snatcher said he was sorry. But that wasn't enough for the woman with the large purse. She said he'd remember her, and she was right. But how could he find the words to thank her?

She was a large woman with a large purse that had everything in it but a hammer and nails. It had a long strap, and she carried it slung across her shoulder.

It was about 11 o'clock at night, and she was walking alone, when a boy ran up behind her and tried to snatch her purse. The strap broke with the tug the boy gave it from behind. But the boy's weight and the weight of the purse caused him to lose his balance. Instead of taking off full blast, the boy fell on his back on the sidewalk, and his legs flew up.

The large woman simply turned around and kicked him right square in his blue-jeaned sitter. Then she reached down and picked the boy up by his shirt. She shook him until his teeth rattled.

After that the woman said, "Pick up my pocketbook, boy, and give it here."

She still held him tightly. But she bent down enough to let him pick up her purse. Then she said, "Now ain't you ashamed of yourself?"

Firmly gripped by his shirt front, the boy said, "Yes'm."

The woman said, "What did you want to do it for?"

The boy said, "I didn't aim to."

She said, "You lie!"

By that time, two or three people passed, turned to look, and some stood watching.

"If I turn you loose, will you run?" asked the woman.

"Yes'm," said the boy.

"Then I won't turn you loose," said the woman.

"Lady, I'm sorry," whispered the boy.

"Um-hum! Your face is dirty. I got a great mind to wash your face for you. Ain't you got nobody home to tell you to wash your face?"

"No'm," said the boy.

"Then it will get washed this evening," said the woman, starting up the street, dragging the frightened boy behind her.

He looked about 14 or 15, thin and wild, in tennis shoes and blue jeans.

The woman said, "You ought to be my son. I would teach you right from wrong. Least I can do right now is to wash your face. Are you hungry?"

"No'm," said the boy. "I just want you to turn me loose."

"Was I bothering you when I turned that corner?" asked the woman.

"No'm."

"But you put yourself in contact with me," said the woman. "If you think that contact is not going to last a while, you got another thought coming. When I get through with you, sir, you are going to remember Mrs. Luella Bates Washington Jones."

Sweat popped out on the boy's face, and he began to struggle. Mrs. Jones stopped, put an arm about his neck, and continued to drag him up the street.

When she got to her door, she dragged the boy inside, down a hall, and into a large furnished room at the rear of the house. She switched on the light and left the door open.

The boy could hear other roomers laughing and talking. Some of their doors were open, too, so he knew he and the woman were not alone. The woman still had him by the neck in the middle of her room.

She said, "What is your name?"

"Roger," answered the boy.

"Then, Roger, you go to the sink and wash your face," said the woman. She turned him loose — at last. Roger looked at the door — looked at the woman — looked at the door — and went to the sink.

"Let the water run until it gets warm," she said. "Here's a clean towel."

"You gonna take me to jail?" asked the boy, bending over the sink.

"Not with that face. I would not take you nowhere," said the woman. "Here I am trying to get home to cook me a bite to eat, and you snatch my pocketbook! Maybe you ain't been to your supper, either, late as it be. Have you?"

"There's nobody home at my house," he said.

"Then we'll eat," said the woman. "I believe you're hungry — or been hungry — to try to snatch my pocketbook!"

"I want a pair of new shoes," said the boy.

"Well, you didn't have to snatch my pocketbook to get some shoes," said Mrs. Luella Bates Washington Jones. "You could of asked me."

"M'am?"

The water dripping from his face, the boy looked at her. There was a long pause. After drying his face and not knowing what else to do, he dried it again. Then he turned around. The door was open. He would make a dash for it down the hall. He would run, run, run!

The woman was sitting on the day bed. After a while she said, "I were young once, and I wanted things I could not get."

There was another long pause. The boy's mouth opened. Then he frowned, not knowing he frowned.

The woman said, "Um-hum! You thought I was going to say *but*, didn't you? You thought I was going to say, *but I didn't snatch people's pocketbooks!*

Well, I wasn't going to say that." Pause. Silence. "I have done things, too, which I would not tell you, son — neither tell God, if He didn't already know. Everybody's got something in common. Sit down while I fix us something to eat. You might run that comb through your hair so you will look presentable."

In another corner of the room behind a screen was a gas plate and an icebox. Mrs. Jones got up and went behind the screen. The woman did not watch the boy to see if he was going to run now. She didn't even watch her purse, which she left behind her on the day bed. But the boy took care to sit on the far side of the room, away from the purse, where he thought she could easily see him out of the corner of her eye if she wanted to. He did not trust the woman not to trust him. And he wanted to be trusted now.

"Do you need somebody to go to the store," asked the boy, "to get some milk or something?"

"Don't believe I do," said the woman, "unless you want sweet milk yourself. I was going to make cocoa out of this canned milk I got here."

"That will be fine," said the boy.

She heated some lima beans and ham, made the cocoa, and set the table. The woman did not ask the boy anything about where he lived, or his folks, or anything else that would embarrass him. Instead, as they ate, she told him about her job in a hotel beauty shop, what the work was like, and how all kinds of women came in and out, blondes, redheads, and brunettes. Then she cut him half of her 10-cent cake.

"Eat some more, son," she said.

When they finished eating, she got up and said, "Now here, take this $10 and buy yourself some shoes. And, next time, do not make the mistake of latching onto my pocketbook or nobody else's — because shoes got by devilish ways will burn

your feet. I got to get my rest now. But from here on in, son, I hope you will behave yourself."

She led the way down the hall to the front door and opened it. "Good night! Behave yourself, boy!" she said, as he went down the steps.

The boy wanted to say something other than "Thank you, m'am," to Mrs. Luella Bates Washington Jones. But although his lips moved, he couldn't even say that, as he turned at the foot of the stoop and looked up at the large woman in the door. Then she shut the door.

READING COMPREHENSION

Summarizing. Choose the best phrase to complete each sentence. Then write the complete statements on your paper.

1. When Roger grabbed Mrs. Jones's pocketbook, she _____ (threatened to tell his folks, said he belonged in jail, showed him that she would not be pushed around).

2. After that, Mrs. Jones treated Roger like a _____ (criminal, kid who can't be trusted, son who can make mistakes).

3. Roger probably _____ (soon forgot Mrs. Jones, did not forget Mrs. Jones, for a long time, grabbed the next purse he could).

Interpreting. Write the answer to each question on your paper.

1. What did Roger want to buy with the money he tried to steal?

2. Why didn't Mrs. Jones close the door and hide her purse while Roger was in the room?

3. Why did Mrs. Jones tell Roger that she had done things which she didn't like to talk about?

For Thinking and Discussing

1. Did Mrs. Jones do the right thing when she gave Roger $10 to buy shoes? Why or why not?

2. Why do you think Mrs. Jones wanted to help Roger?

UNDERSTANDING LITERATURE

Theme. The theme of a story is the author's message. It is the most important idea in a piece of literature. Stories, play, and poems can all have a theme.

Suppose you read a story about love. You could discover the theme by asking, "What does the author mean to say about love? Does the author think falling in love is wonderful, funny, or sad?"

Sometimes, the author *tells* you the theme. But sometimes the message is not stated. In "Thank You, M'am," what the characters say — and don't say — can help you discover the theme.

1. What does Mrs. Jones say that shows she wants to teach Roger something he'll never forget?

2. What does Mrs. Jones tell Roger to let him know she understands how badly he wanted the shoes?

3. Mrs. Jones says, "I have done things, too, that I would not tell. . . ." What do you think this means?

4. When he leaves, Roger can't even say, "Thank you, m'am." What does this tell you about the story's message?

WRITING

Roger learned that trust and self-respect are more important than anything money can buy. After he left Mrs. Jones's apartment, do you think he felt trusted and cared for? Write a paragraph telling how you think Roger felt about his experience with Mrs. Jones.

Harriet Tubman: The Moses of Her People

by Langston Hughes

Harriet Tubman was not afraid. She could not read or write. Her only map was the stars. But she had faith, courage, and intelligence. Because of her, hundreds reached Canada to become free men and women. This is the true story of her life and work.

"Then we saw the lightning, and that was the guns. And then we heard the thunder, and that was the big guns. And then we heard the rain falling, and that was the drops of blood falling. And when we came to get in the crops, it was dead men that we reaped."

So the escaped slave, Harriet Tubman, described one of the battles of the war between the North and the South. She took part in the war, for she was in the thick of the fighting. Before the war, Harriet Tubman worked for the cause of freedom. After the war, she spent her life helping her people get ahead.

She was born in Maryland, a slave. She was one of 11 sons and daughters. No one kept a record of her birth, so the exact year is not known. But most of the other facts about her life have been set down. She was a plain child, unhappy, strong-willed, wild. She always hated slavery.

Harriet had no teaching of any sort, except the whip. As a little girl, she was sent to work in the Big House. On the first day, her mistress whipped her four times. Once, she ran away. She hid in a pig sty for five days. She ate the scraps thrown to the pigs.

"There were good masters and mistresses, so I've heard tell," she once said, "but I didn't happen to come across any of them."

Harriet never liked to work as a servant in the house. She showed her feelings, and was soon ordered to the fields. One day, when she was in her early teens, something happened. It changed her whole life.

A young slave, without asking, went to a country store. The overseer followed him, to whip him. He ordered Harriet to help tie him up. As Harriet refused, the slave ran. The overseer picked up a heavy iron weight from the scales. He threw it. But he did not hit the man. He struck Harriet's head, almost crushing it. It left a deep scar forever.

The girl lay between life and death for days. When, at last, she was able to work again, she had blackouts. These lasted all her life. They would come upon her at any time, any place. It would seem as if she had suddenly fallen asleep.

Sometimes in the fields, sometimes in church, she would "go to sleep." No one could wake her until the fit had passed. When she was awake, this did not affect her thinking. But her master thought the blow had made her half-witted. Harriet let him go on believing this. And she went on praying to God to free her from slavery.

When she was about 24, she married a cheerful fellow named Tubman. He did not care about leaving slave country. A few years later, Harriet's old master died.

She heard that she and two of her brothers were to be sold. They decided to run away together.

It was dangerous to tell anyone. Harriet had no chance to let even her mother know directly. But on the evening she was leaving, she went around singing:

> When that old chariot comes
> I'm going to leave you
> I'm bound for the Promised Land. . .

The way she sang that song let Harriet's friends and family know that the Promised Land meant the North. That night she left

the Brodas Plantation, on the Big Buckwater River, never to return.

Before dawn, her brothers were frightened. They went back to the slave huts before they were missed.

But Harriet went on alone through the woods by night. She hid by day. She had no map, and could not read or write. But she trusted God and her own sense of direction. She used the North Star to guide her. Somehow, she got to Philadelphia and found work. She was never again a slave.

But Harriet could not be happy. All her family were still slaves. She kept thinking about them. Some months later, she went back to Maryland.

She hoped that her husband would come north with her. He said he did not wish to go. She led others north, however. Within two years of her own escape, she had secretly returned to the South three times. She had rescued two brothers, a sister and her children, and a dozen more slaves.

The Fugitive Slave Law of 1850 now made it dangerous for runaways to stop anywhere in the United States. So Harriet led her followers to Canada, where they would be safe and free. There she spent

a winter begging, cooking, and praying for them. Then she returned to Maryland to rescue nine more slaves.

Harriet's fame as a fearless leader of "freedom bands" spread fast. Large rewards were offered by slaveholders for her. But she was never caught, and she never lost any of her followers to the slave catchers.

One reason for this was that Harriet did not allow any slave to turn back. She knew that a weak or frightened runaway who returned to slavery might be whipped into betraying the others.

Her method was simple. Harriet Tubman carried a pistol. When anyone said he could not, or would not, go on, Harriet pulled out her gun. She said, "You *will* go on — or you'll die." The strength or courage to go on was always found after a look into the muzzle of Harriet's gun. Everyone who started out with Harriet Tubman lived to thank her for freedom.

Long before the war between the States, many slaves were escaping. Many white people in the North were helping them. The routes to freedom became known as the "Underground Railroad." Secret "stations" were set up. There escaping slaves might be hidden, warmed, and fed — in homes, barns, and sometimes even churches.

Slave-owners were losing thousands of dollars' worth of slaves by escape every year. Harriet Tubman became known as a "conductor" on the Underground Railroad. She was not the only conductor, but she was the most famous. She was also one of the most daring. Once she brought 25 slaves to freedom at once.

Harriet had a great sense of humor. She liked telling one story about herself. Not being able to read, she once went to sleep on a park bench — under a sign that offered a big reward for catching her.

She might have been a great actress, people said. Without makeup, she could hollow out her cheeks and wrinkle her forehead, to look like a very old woman. She would make her body smaller and act as if her legs were weak when she wanted to look different.

Once, she made a trip to Maryland to rescue some of her family. She had to pass through a village where she was known. She bought two hens. She tied them by their feet and hung them around her neck. Then she went slowly along.

Sure enough, a slave catcher came up the street. He might know her, she thought. So she let go of the noisy chickens in the middle of the street. Then she ran after them. She tried not to catch them, so she could run down the road after them. She ran out of the slave catcher's sight, while everyone on the street laughed.

Sometimes, when angry masters were after their slaves, Harriet would get on a train headed south. Nobody thought runaway slaves would be going south. Sometimes she would dress the women, and herself, as men. Babies would be given sleeping medicine to keep them quiet. Then they would be wrapped up like bundles.

Sometimes she would wade for hours up a stream to throw the hounds off the track. In the dark, when there was no North Star, she would feel the trees for the moss that grows on the north side.

That would serve as a guide toward freedom.

Harriet's looks were ordinary, but she was a great leader. Among the slaves, she began to be known as Moses. She asked for nothing. Between rescue trips or speeches, she would work as a cook or scrub floors. She might borrow, but she never begged money for herself. Anything given to her went toward the cause of freedom. So did most of what she earned.

The war between the States began. Harriet became a nurse for the Union armies. Then she was a scout and a secret agent behind the Rebel lines.

She was not really a trained nurse, and, as a woman, could not be a soldier. Yet she did dangerous war work on the Confederate land. She was never paid for this, although she had been promised $1,800.

After the war, she needed money to care for her aged parents. Friends tried to get the War Department and Congress to pay her the $1,800. But it was never paid.

One of the things Harriet did during the war was to lead a raid. She got together nine black scouts and river pilots. Then, with a Union colonel, she led about 150 black soldiers up the Combahee River. The Boston *Commonwealth* for July 10, 1863, reported:

> Guided by a black woman, they dashed into the enemy's country, destroying millions of dollars' worth of supplies, striking terror into the hearts of the rebels. They brought off nearly 800 slaves and thousands of dollars' worth of property.

The report went on to say that Harriet Tubman had gone behind the enemy lines many times, finding out important facts.

Harriet Tubman was over 40 years old when Abraham Lincoln signed the Emancipation Proclamation. It made the freedom she had worked for into law.

She lived for almost 50 years after the war was over. Some people thought she was 100 years old when she died in 1913. She was surely over 90.

In her old age, a reporter came to see her one afternoon at her home in Auburn, New York. As he was leaving, Harriet looked toward an orchard near her house. "Do you like apples?" she said.

He said that he liked them. She asked, "Did you ever plant any apples?"

The writer said that he had not.

"No," said the old woman, "but somebody else planted them. I liked apples when I was young. And I said, 'Some day I'll plant apples for other young folks to eat.' And I guess I did."

Her apples were the apples of freedom. Harriet Tubman lived to see the harvest.

READING COMPREHENSION

Summarizing. Choose the best phrase to complete each sentence. Then write the complete statements on your paper.

1. After Harriet Tubman escaped from slavery to the North, she went back to Maryland in order to _____ (visit her family, rescue her family, kill her former owners).

2. Every slave who traveled with Harriet Tubman _____ (was allowed to turn back, reached freedom safely, had to wear a disguise).

3. Harriet Tubman was a "conductor" on the "Underground Railroad," which was _____ (a train that ran between the South and North, a tunnel running between the South and North, the name for the routes people used for escaping slavery).

4. Harriet Tubman is best known for _____ (leading military raids during the Civil War, leading so many slaves to freedom, urging Abraham Lincoln to sign the Emancipation Proclamation).

Interpreting. Write the answer to each question on your paper.

1. When Harriet went north on foot, how could she tell which way to go at night?

2. When Harriet led a group of slaves to freedom, why wouldn't she let anyone turn back?

3. What did young Harriet Tubman mean when she said she would plant apples for other young folks to eat? What was the "harvest" that she lived to see?

For Thinking and Discussing. Why was Harriet Tubman such a great leader? What qualities of leadership did she have? Do you think that great leaders usually have a great sense of humor? Why or why not?

UNDERSTANDING LITERATURE

Theme. Sometimes the *title* of a story helps you discover the theme. The title of this story is "Harriet Tubman: The Moses of Her People." In the Bible, Moses led his people out of Egypt, where they worked as slaves. So Harriet Tubman was called the Moses of her people. Her actions show how she helped her people.

1. Harriet Tubman would not let anyone else be hurt. What action did she take in her early teens that showed she was against hurting anyone?

2. Because of the deep love she had for her people, Harriet Tubman did more than lead them to freedom. What did she do for her freedom bands?

3. The great courage of single individuals has changed many wrongs in the world. What courageous things did Harriet do to abolish slavery during the Civil War?

4. What risks did she take for her people?

WRITING

Newspaper articles usually stick to the facts. An article about Harriet Tubman might not *explain* what kind of person she was, or what she believed. It might only tell what she *did*. Still, her actions would show a theme.

Write a short newspaper article about Harriet Tubman. Make sure the things you write about her get the theme across to the reader. Make up a title for your article.

Dream Deferred

by Langston Hughes

What happens to a dream deferred?

Does it dry up
like a raisin in the sun?
Or fester like a sore —
And then run?
Does it stink like rotten meat?
Or crust and sugar over —
like a syrupy sweet?

Maybe it just sags
like a heavy load.

Or does it explode?

1. To *defer* means to put off until another time. Can a dream be deferred by the dreamer? Can it be deferred by someone else?

2. A sore that *festers* has become infected. It hurts, and takes some time to heal. Does it also take time for something to dry up in the sun, or to sag like a heavy load? How do these things compare with the time it takes for an explosion?

3. Is this poem about the same kind of dream as the poem "Dreams"?

Mother to Son

by Langston Hughes

Well, son, I'll tell you:
Life for me ain't been no crystal stair.
It's had tacks in it,
And splinters,
And boards torn up,
And places with no carpet on the floor —
Bare.
But all the time
I'se been a-climbin' on,
And reachin' landin's,
And turnin' corners,
And sometimes goin' in the dark
Where there ain't been no light.
So boy, don't you turn back.
Don't you set down on the steps
'Cause you finds it's kinder hard.
Don't you fall now —
For I'se still goin', honey,
I'se still climbin',
And life for me ain't been no crystal stair.

---

1. Describe in your own words what the speaker in this poem means by a "crystal stair."

2. What have the stairs been like that she has known?

3. Why is this woman telling her son about the hardships of her life? Does she just want to complain? If not, what is her purpose?

Early Autumn

by Langston Hughes

Bill and Mary were in love when they were young. They separated over something unimportant. Now, years later, they meet unexpectedly. How do you suppose they feel?

When Bill was very young, they had been in love. Many nights they had spent walking, talking together. Then something not very important had come between them, and they didn't speak. Impulsively, she had married a man she thought she loved. Bill went away, bitter about women.

Yesterday, walking across Washington Square, she saw him for the first time in years.

"Bill Walker," she said.

He stopped. At first he did not recognize her, to him she looked so old.

"Mary! Where did you come from?"

Unconsciously, she lifted her face as though wanting a kiss, but he held out his hand. She took it.

"I live in New York now," she said.

"Oh"— smiling politely. Then a little frown came quickly between his eyes.

"Always wondered what happened to you, Bill."

"I'm a lawyer. Nice firm, way downtown."

"Married yet?"

"Sure. Two kids."

"Oh," she said.

A great many people went past them through the park. People they didn't know. It was late afternoon. Nearly sunset. Cold.

"And your husband?" he asked her.

"We have three children. I work in the bursar's office at Columbia."

"You're looking very . . . " (he wanted to say old) . . . well," he said.

She understood. Under the trees in Washington Square, she found herself desperately reaching back into the past. She had been older than he then in Ohio. Now she was not young at all. Bill was still young.

"We live on Central Park West," she said. "Come and see us sometime."

"Sure," he replied. "You and your husband must have dinner with my family some night. Any night. Lucille and I'd love to have you."

The leaves fell slowly from the trees in the Square. Fell without wind. Autumn dusk. She felt a little sick.

"We'd love it," she answered.

"You ought to see my kids." He grinned.

Suddenly the lights came on up the whole length of Fifth Avenue, chains of misty brilliance on the blue air.

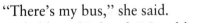

"There's my bus," she said.

He held out his hand. "Good-bye."

"When . . ." she wanted to say, but the bus was ready to pull off. The lights on the avenue blurred, twinkled, blurred. And she was afraid to open her mouth as she entered the bus. Afraid it would be impossible to utter a word.

Suddenly she shrieked very loudly. "Good-bye!" But the bus door had closed.

The bus started. People came between them outside, people crossing the street, people they didn't know. Space and people. She lost sight of Bill. Then she remembered she had forgotten to give him her address — or to ask him for his — or tell him that her youngest boy was named Bill, too.

READING COMPREHENSION

Summarizing. Choose the best phrase to complete each sentence. Then write the complete statements on your paper.

1. Bill and Mary had once been _____ (in love, married, engaged).

2. When they met for the first time in years, Bill didn't recognize Mary at first because she _____ (had dyed her hair, looked so old, wore such expensive clothes).

3. They spoke of visiting each other's families, but they probably didn't because they _____ (were afraid they would fall in love again, hated each other now, felt too much had come between them).

Interpreting. Write the answer to each question on your paper.

1. What time of year did Mary and Bill meet after so many years?

2. Who seemed more interested in seeing the other — Mary or Bill? Why?

3. Why didn't Mary say good-bye when Bill did?

4. What clues are you given that Mary probably still loved Bill after they broke up?

For Thinking and Discussing. When two friends, or two people in love, break up, is it usually over something important — or not? Should they try to patch things up?

UNDERSTANDING LITERATURE

Theme. The *theme* of a story is the most important idea in the story. Sometimes the *title* of a story will help you discover its *theme*.

The title of this story is "Early Autumn." Autumn is often thought of as an "aging" or "dying" time of year. Grass and flowers die. Leaves fall off trees. The days get shorter and colder.

In "Early Autumn," the things that the characters say — and do not say — can help you discover the theme. So can the author's description of the setting. The setting includes when and where the action takes place.

1. Bill said, "You're looking very. . . ." What did he almost say?

2. After they spoke of their children, Mary wanted to say, "When . . . ?" What might she have wanted to say?

3. After Mary got on the bus, the bus started. "People came between them outside . . . people they didn't know. Space and people." What does this suggest has happened to the relationship between Mary and Bill?

WRITING

As Mary rode home on the bus, what was she probably thinking about? Meanwhile, what was Bill thinking about?

Put yourself in the shoes of one of these two characters. Write a paragraph telling how you feel about this brief meeting after so many years.

Section
Review

VOCABULARY

Dialect. In a story or play, the characters often speak the way they would in person. Spoken language is often different from standard written language. It is informal. It may contain expressions, slang, or pronunciations that are casual.

In different parts of the country, people pronounce words differently. They may also use different words to mean the same thing. (In "Antaeus," a story in Section 6, that's why T.J., who came from the South, sounded strange to the narrator, who was from the North. The narrator must have sounded strange to T.J., too.)

Langston Hughes was good at using dialect to make his characters seem real. In "Thank You, M'am," Roger says "Yes'm" and "No'm." People often drop a part of the word when they speak.

Here are some examples of dialect from this section. Number your paper from 1 to 5. Rewrite the words that appear in italics in standard written English.

1. "You *gonna* take me to jail?"

2. "You *could of* asked me."

3. "I *were* young once. . . ."

4. "Life for me *ain't been no* crystal stair."

5. "And *reachin' landin's*/And *turnin'* corners."

READING

Inference. Suppose you read a paragraph in which the author talks about Fourth of July celebrations, tasty barbecues, fun-filled days at the beach, and softball in the park. You can *infer,* or tell from the facts, that the author is saying that summer is wonderful. When you read, you can often make inferences.

1. Langston Hughes's father didn't want him to be a writer, yet he gave Langston money for a year at Columbia University. What does this tell you about Langston's father?

2. When Roger grabbed Mrs. Jones's pocketbook, she kicked him, held him by the collar, and shook him. What does this tell you about Mrs. Jones?

3. Harriet Tubman said, "There were good masters and mistresses, so I've heard tell, but I didn't happen to come across any of them." What does this tell you about the way the slaves that Harriet Tubman knew were treated?

4. In "Mother to Son," the mother told her son not to "set down on the steps" because "I'se still climbin'/And life for me ain't been no crystal stair." What do you know about the woman from this?

5. When Bill and Mary saw each other in "Early Autumn," she "lifted her face as though wanting a kiss, but he held out his hand." What does this tell you about Mary and Bill?

WRITING

A Persuasive Letter. There are many times when it is important to convince someone to do something for you or to allow you to do something. You may also seek to persuade someone to share your opinions. One way to convince someone to share your opinions and act on them, is to write the person a persuasive letter.

Step 1: Set Your Goal
Choose one of the following topics for a persuasive letter.

a. Pretend that you are Roger in "Thank You, M'am." Many years have gone by and you are now living on your own in a different city. You find out that your parents caught your younger brother or sister with a stolen radio. Write a letter to the brother or sister to persuade him or her to give up stealing.

b. Pretend you are Langston Hughes when he was a young man. You know your father wants you to become an engineer. Write a letter to your father to persuade him to pay for you to go to college — where you plan to study to become a writer.

Step 2: Make a Plan
Begin by making a list of reasons why the person you're writing to should do what you want. One of the people helping Harriet Tubman, by writing a rich friend to ask for money, might list these reasons:

☐ Nobody should be forced to be a slave.

☐ Tubman has shown she can get slaves safely to freedom.

☐ The money will be used to help her travel back and forth to Canada.

☐ Many people are already helping Tubman.

☐ Most slaves are treated cruelly.

Notice that some of the reasons appeal to the emotions ("Most slaves are treated cruelly"). Others are cool statements of facts ("The money will be used to help her travel back and forth to Canada"). It is good to have a balance of both kinds of reasons in your letter.

Once you have your list, arrange it in order — either from least important to most important or from most important to least important.

Now think of possible objections your reader might have. Try to answer each objection. For example, the reader of the letter about Harriet Tubman might say that Tubman doesn't have enough education to be the leader of such a difficult enterprise. You could respond with examples of how she has demonstrated her leadership abilities.

Step 3: Write Your First Draft
Begin your persuasive letter with a paragraph stating your opinion and telling what you want the person to do. Next write one or two paragraphs giving the facts and examples you listed and answering objections the reader might have. Conclude with a paragraph that restates

your opinion, but leaves the matter open for further discussion. For example, the writer of the letter about Harriet Tubman might conclude this way:

I believe the work Harriet Tubman is doing is most important and deserves our full support. I would be happy to tell you more about her and to answer any questions you have when we meet next Friday.

Step 4. Revise Your Persuasive Letter

When you revise a persuasive letter, think about it from your reader's point of view. Will he or she be convinced by your arguments? Have you avoided saying anything or using a tone that the person might find insulting? Have you provided facts and appealed to the reader's emotions? Have you answered any objections the reader might have?

Proofread the letter carefully and copy it over neatly. If you want to convince someone to do something, it is most important to show yourself at your best.

QUIZ

The following is a quiz for Section 7. Write the answers in complete sentences on your paper.

Reading Comprehension

1. How did Langston Hughes learn about the Underground Railroad?

2. In "Thank You, M'am," what can you tell about Mrs. Jones from the facts in the story?

3. What can you infer about Harriet Tubman from her statement to the reporter?

4. According to Langston Hughes, what happens to a dream deferred?

5. In "Early Autumn," what can you infer about Mary from the fact that her youngest boy was named Bill?

Understanding Literature

6. Explain what Langston Hughes tried to do in most of his writing.

7. In "Thank You, M'am," what did Roger probably learn from his experience with Mrs. Jones?

8. When Harriet Tubman kept the young slave from being whipped, how did this mark a change in her life?

9. In "Mother to Son," find the lines that state the message of the poem. Then write the message in your words.

10. In one sentence, state the theme of "Early Autumn."

ACTIVITIES

Word Attack

1. The words below are from the stories and poems in this section. Some words have no prefixes or suffixes. Others may have as many as three. Find the root word in each word. (If a word has

no prefixes or suffixes, list the whole word.) You may use the dictionary if you need help.

unconsciously	separated
latching	freighter
embarrass	devilish
deferred	fester
betraying	unimportant
unexpectedly	impulsively
rescue	desperately
	proclamation

Write an adventure story about a spy. Try to use as many of the words you listed as you can in your story.

2. Below are some of the many compound words found in this section. List a compound word that has the opposite meaning of the one in the story. The words can be real ones or ones you make up (*lightup* for *blackout*, for example.) Use your new words in sentences that show their meanings.

icebox	runaways
overseer	underground
makeup	overboard

Speaking and Listening. Team up with one of your classmates to act out this scene: One of you will be Harriet Tubman, the other will be her husband. Harriet should try to persuade her husband to escape. Her husband should try to convince Harriet not to. Be prepared to present your scene in class.

Researching. Do research to find the answers to these questions, based on "Harriet Tubman: The Moses of Her People":

1. Why does moss only grow on the north side of trees?

2. What was the Fugitive Slave Law of 1850?

3. Where is the Combahee River?

4. What states did Harriet Tubman have to pass through to get from Maryland to Canada?

5. How far did she have to travel?

Creating. Find a book of poems by Langston Hughes in the library. Pick a poem that is not included in this section. Copy it. Then draw or paint an illustration to go with it, or create some music for it.

ANIMALS

THE FLOWER-FED BUFFALOES

The flower-fed buffaloes of the spring
In the days of long ago,
Ranged where the locomotives sing
And the prairie flowers lie low: —
The tossing, blooming, perfumed
grass
Is swept away by the wheat,
Wheels and wheels and wheels spin
by
In the spring that still is sweet.

But the flower-fed buffaloes o
spring
Left us, long ago.
They gore no more, they bello
more,
They trundle around the hill:
more: —
With the Blackfeet, lying lo
With the Pawnees, lying lo
Lying low.

— Vachel Lindsay (1879-1931)

Animals

People have always needed animals.

In early times, people hunted animals for food. Later, when they raised their own food and built their own homes, they found that animals could help them perform tasks. Oxen and mules could be trained to pull plows and wagons. Horses and dogs could be trained to herd cattle and sheep. And a variety of animals were found to be useful at guarding homes.

In recent times, animals continue to perform valuable tasks for people — often tasks which we cannot do as well. Think of dogs, for example. Guide dogs help blind people find their way to schools, stores, jobs, theaters, and many other places. Dogs with a keen sense of smell can track down children who have gotten lost. They can help police find drugs which have been smuggled into the country. And they can find bombs which have been planted in buildings.

Animals also entertain people. They perform tricks in circuses. They play roles in movies and TV programs. People enter them in horse shows, dog shows, and country fairs to see which ones are best bred or best trained. They are also entered in races to see which are the fastest.

For many people, though, animals are most important as pets. Pets can be fun, loyal, and loving. Some pets have even risked their lives to save their owners from death.

The stories in this section will show you people relating to animals in different ways. In "No Hero," a poor farmer is willing to wrestle with a bear because he is desperate for the money he'll win if he lasts long enough. Can a tall, thin man possibly hold out against a 386-pound mass of strength? Read this to find out.

Then enjoy four short poems about four different animals by a humorist. And don't be surprised if you smile. The poems show one man's unusual way of viewing a panther, a canary, a termite, and a shrew.

In "Zlateh the Goat," a farm animal must be sold to a butcher because she is growing old and her owners need money. But will they sell her after she saves one of their lives?

In "Weep No More, My Lady," a boy finds a very unusual dog in the swamp where he lives. The dog can laugh and even cry. But she cannot bark. After the boy trains the dog to hunt birds, he must make a very tough decision.

Besides stories and poems, this section includes an article, "Hitchhikers in the Sky." Do some birds "hitchhike" on other birds when they migrate? Scientists aren't sure of the answer to this question. But after reading the article, you may come up with a theory of your own.

No Hero

by Jesse Stuart

Everybody at the fair thought the thin man was crazy. How could he wrestle with a 386-pound bear? But a man with hungry children will try almost anything for money — especially when he has a secret up his sleeve. (In the story, people call Hester "Ichabod Crane," who is a famous character with a tall, thin body.)

I had been walking for seven miles. I stopped to catch my breath and do some thinking.

The bright lights of Landsburg were in front of me. Behind me were the dark hills where my crops had failed.

Mollie and our three children were in a shack among these hills.

"Hester, we can't go another day without bread," Mollie had said. She couldn't understand why I was going to Landsburg. And I couldn't tell her what I had in mind.

Nature had been against me. It wasn't that I wouldn't work. I was willing to work.

But the bad weather had killed my crops. I couldn't make it rain. There wasn't anything I could do. All I'd worked for was lost.

Nature was against me in another way that I couldn't help. I'd grown up tall as a beanpole. And I was thin as a young tree. So they wouldn't hire me at the iron works.

I was near Landsburg now. I could see bright lights along the streets. There was one really bright spot in the town. And in a few minutes, I had reached it.

People filled the fairground. They were almost running over each other. They were standing in line to buy rings to throw over pegs. They were waiting to ride the merry-go-round and the merry-mixup.

Money was flowing like water. And everybody was happy. I wished for a little of the money. But my time was coming.

An announcer stepped out on a platform.

"We are looking for a man to stay with old Bruin five minutes tonight," he said. "Is there a man who will wrestle this 386-pound bear?"

The crowd was silent.

"Stay in the cage with old Bruin for five minutes, and earn $25," the announcer said. "Earn $25 for every extra five minutes. And there will be $100 extra if you wrestle him."

258

"I'll try it, sir," I said.

"That bear will kill you, man," someone said. "Ain't you afraid of him, Slim?"

"Yes, I am," I said.

"Come up here, Slim," the announcer said. "Let the crowd have a look at you!"

When I climbed up on the platform, everybody laughed.

"Ever do any wrestling, Slim?" the announcer asked.

"Never did," I said.

More people gathered in to have a look at me.

"Nobody's stayed with that bear three minutes," said a big man.

"Hogg Morton stayed the longest," someone said. "He stayed two minutes! Had the bear down once! But that bear almost killed Hogg!"

"Buddie Walker didn't stay 10 seconds," another man said. "Bear just knocked him against the cage once. And that was it!"

"How long do you think you can last?" the announcer asked.

"Five minutes," I said. "Maybe longer."

"Mr. Hester King says he'll stay with the bear five minutes or longer. And you say he won't. Let's see who is telling the truth!" the announcer said.

"Old Ichabod, the beanpole, will soon find out," someone shouted.

"Wait until you see this man in wrestling trunks," the announcer said. "Worth the price of admission, folks!"

I followed the announcer into the tent. The crowd rushed to buy tickets.

I went into a dressing room to change. I thought about my children. Then I thought about big Bruin. I wondered just what would happen.

I was ready. The manager warned me not to be too scared. He said the referee — Johnnie Norris — would make sure Bruin didn't hurt me.

The manager pushed back a flap of the tent. We walked into the arena. People were crowded close to the cage.

The big black bear was inside the cage. He walked around, looking at the people.

I walked among the crowd. Everybody screamed with laughter. I was now getting near the cage door.

"Timekeeper here?" the referee asked.

"Yep," the timekeeper said.

"All right. Start your watch," Johnnie said. He unlocked the cage door. "Shake hands with Bruin," he told me.

I shook Bruin's paw gently. Everybody in the tent became very quiet. Bruin backed away.

Then he moved clumsily toward me. He pushed me against the side of the cage. He acted like he wanted to finish me in a hurry.

"Won't be long," someone said.

I got back on my feet. I ran in between old Bruin's outstretched paws. Old Bruin tried squeezing on me.

I hugged close to Bruin. I put my hands gently on his back. Then he shoved me back. He slapped me again. He knocked me against the side of the cage.

But it didn't hurt me. And I didn't stay long. I ran back into his arms.

"Three minutes," said the timekeeper. "Longest anybody has stayed yet!"

Old Bruin slapped me hard. I hit the bars of the cage, and saw stars.

I was clinched with old Bruin again. I let my hands fall gently up and down his back. Bruin was settling down. My chin rested on his head.

"Five minutes," the timekeeper called.

We stood there paw-locked and arm-locked. Time was flying. Once Johnnie Norris passed us. He had a worried look on his face.

"Ten minutes," the timekeeper said.

Then Bruin put his red tongue out like

a tired dog. I felt his hot breath sizzle past my ear. The sweat was pouring from my face. Holding up big Bruin wasn't easy.

"Has he hypnotized that bear?" someone shouted.

About that time, Bruin pushed me to the floor. But he didn't come after me. He looked like a very tired wrestler.

I got back on my feet. Bruin came to meet me. He slapped me gently with his paws. I did a little footwork around the cage.

Bruin's front paws were spread apart. I rushed in and clinched him.

"Fifteen minutes," the timekeeper said. There were shouts from the crowd.

"Seventy-five dollars," I thought.

Then I put my chin back on Bruin's head. I put my big hands on Bruin's back. This time Bruin went down. And I fell down beside him.

Johnnie Norris ran up to check our shoulders. The crowd screamed loud enough to raise the tent.

My right arm was around Bruin's neck. We lay there, side by side.

"What's wrong here?" Johnnie asked.

"Nineteen minutes," the timekeeper said. Shouts went up again.

"Who said old Ichabod Crane couldn't wrestle?" someone said.

They didn't know it. But I knew Bruin was ready for a rest on the floor.

"Twenty minutes!" the timekeeper said.

"Old Ichabod Crane is some wrestler!" a man shouted.

"Twenty-four minutes," the timekeeper announced.

Then big Bruin rolled over on his back. The crowd went wild. There were

screams, shouts, and whistles.

"Let's have a count. Bruin's down! He's down!" someone shouted.

Bruin didn't offer to get up. His big mouth was open.

"You must have played my bear foul," Johnnie Norris said.

"I did not," I said. "You'll see Bruin's not hurt. He's tired, but happy."

"First time that bear was ever down," Johnnie said.

Johnnie Norris started to get big Bruin

up. But the bear gave him a hit on the top of his head. It sent Johnnie flying towards the other side of the cage.

"Two hundred and twenty-five dollars!" someone said. "Think of it! Ichabod Crane beat old Bruin!"

The manager let me through the cage door. He then dragged Johnnie outside. The men lifted me onto their shoulders.

They carried me out of the tent and all over the fairgrounds. They shouted, "Here's Ichabod Crane! He beat the bear!"

Everybody laughed and screamed and shouted. The manager paid me the money. I was a hero for the night. But they didn't know how I did it.

I didn't tell them or anybody what a friend I'd made of Bruin. I didn't tell them that I'd once owned a pet bear.

You see . . . a bear likes to be rubbed between the ears and on the tummy. I suppose it wasn't exactly fair.

But Mollie and the kids had to eat. Gentling old Bruin was an easy dollar.

263

READING COMPREHENSION

Summarizing. Choose the best phrase to complete each sentence. Then write the complete statements on your paper.

1. Hester King agreed to get in a cage with old Bruin because he _____ (hoped to win some money, wanted to show how brave he was, thought it would be a good joke).

2. People at the fair thought Hester didn't have a chance against Bruin because he was _____ (a coward, not very smart, so tall and thin).

3. He won the contest because he _____ (hypnotized Bruin, knew something about bears, was a pro wrestler).

Interpreting. Write the answer to each question on your paper.

1. What did Hester need when he went to the fair?

2. Why did the crowd laugh when Hester was about to enter Bruin's cage?

3. Why did Johnnie Norris accuse Hester of not playing by the rules when old Bruin rolled over on his back?

4. How did Hester "beat" old Bruin?

For Thinking and Discussing

1. If a person's family is hungry, does the person have a right to do anything to feed them?

2. Why do you think this story is called "No Hero"? Is the title right?

UNDERSTANDING LITERATURE

Mood. Suspense, fear, joy, and sorrow are all feelings. Most problems have feelings, or moods. When one feeling in a story is stronger than all the others, that feeling is called the *mood* of the story. Authors often use description to create a mood. Here is an example: "The water rolled softly, rocking the boats like cradles. A warm summer breeze hummed a lazy tune." In this passage, the mood is one of peacefulness. The author makes you feel peaceful by describing peaceful sights and sounds.

1. At the beginning of "No Hero," there is a mood of excitement. How does the author's descritption of the fairgrounds create this mood?

2. What does the timekeeper do that helps build suspense and excitement?

3. How does the author describe the crowd after 24 minutes have passed? What kind of mood does that create?

4. The author describes how people talk to Hester before the wrestling match. What do they say that creates a feeling of danger?

5. What does the bear do during the match that creates a mood of danger in the story?

WRITING

Suppose the author had wanted to create a mood of boredom. Write two paragraphs describing a boring fair, a tired crowd, and a dull bear.

Animal Poems

by Ogden Nash

The Panther

The panther is like a leopard,
Except it hasn't been peppered.
Should you behold a panther crouch,
Prepare to say Ouch.
Better yet, if called by a panther,
Don't anther.

The Canary

The song of canaries
Never varies,
And when they're moulting
They're pretty revolting.

The Shrew

Strange as it seems, the smallest
    mammal
Is the shrew, and not the camel.
And that is all I ever knew,
Or wish to know, about the shrew.

266

The Termite

Some primal termite knocked on wood
And tasted it, and found it good,
And that is why your Cousin May
Fell through the parlor floor today.

1. Ogden Nash was a well-known writer of funny short poems. Would these poems be as funny if they didn't rhyme? Which pair of rhyming lines do you think is the funniest?

2. Look again at "The Panther." In what way is a leopard *peppered*? When a panther crouches, what will it probably do next? What does "anther" really mean?

3. Do you think the shrew is a familiar animal to many people? Do you think Ogden Nash would agree with you?

4. The word *moulting* is used to describe a bird losing its feathers. Why would a moulting canary be revolting?

5. The word *primal* suggests that termites have been around for a long time. Who got the last laugh in this poem — the insects or the people?

Zlateh the Goat

by Isaac Bashevis Singer

Isaac Bashevis Singer writes in the Yiddish language. Many of his stories are about poor Jews who lived in villages in Russia and Poland many years ago.

In the winter, people celebrated Hanukkah, the Feast of Lights. A Hanukkah without gifts was a sad holiday. But, in this story, Reuven the fur trapper had no money for gifts. He decided to send his son Aaron to sell Zlateh, the family's aging goat. As it turned out, Zlateh helped — in another way — to make this Hanukkah happy.

At Hanukkah time, the road from the village to the town is usually covered with snow. But this year the winter had been a mild one.

The farmers complained. There would be a poor crop of winter grain.

For Reuven, the fur trapper, it was also a bad year. After thinking about it for a long time, he decided to sell Zlateh the goat.

She was old, and gave little milk. The town butcher had offered eight gulden for her. Reuven would use the money to buy Hanukkah gifts for his children.

Reuven told his son, Aaron, to take the goat to town. No one in Aaron's family was happy about this. His mother wiped tears from her eyes. His younger sisters cried loudly.

Aaron put on his warmest jacket. He placed a rope around Zlateh's neck. He took two slices of bread and cheese to eat on the road.

The family said good-bye to Zlateh. The goat stood patiently. She licked Reuven's hand. Zlateh trusted human beings. She knew they always fed her. They never did her any harm.

Aaron led Zlateh along the road to town. The goat seemed surprised. She'd never come this way before.

The road was different. They passed new fields and pastures. A dog barked and ran after them. Aaron chased it away with his stick.

The sun was shining when Aaron left the village. Suddenly, the weather changed. A large black cloud appeared in the east.

It quickly spread across the sky. A cold wind blew in with it.

At first, it looked like rain. But it began to hail. The hail turned to snow.

In his 12 years, Aaron had seen all kinds of weather. But he had never seen a snow like this one. It was so thick, it shut out the light of the day.

In a short time, their path was completely covered. The wind became as cold as ice. The road to town was narrow and winding.

Aaron no longer knew where he was. He could not see through the snow. The cold went through his jacket.

At first, Zlateh didn't seem to mind the snow. She was also 12 years old. The goat knew what winter was like.

But her legs sank deeper and deeper into the snow. She looked at Aaron in amazement. Her eyes seemed to ask: "Why are we here?"

Aaron hoped a farmer would come along. But no one passed by.

The snow grew thicker. It fell in large, spinning flakes. Aaron saw that he was no longer on the road. He was lost.

The wind howled. It blew the snow around. Zlateh stopped. She could no longer walk. She made a bleating noise. It was as if she begged to be taken home.

Icicles hung from her white beard. Her horns were covered with frost.

Aaron knew they must find shelter, or they would freeze to death. This was no ordinary storm. It was a mighty blizzard.

The snow had reached Aaron's knees. His hands were numb. He could no longer feel his toes. He choked when he breathed. Zlateh's bleating began to sound like crying.

Suddenly, Aaron made out the shape of a hill. He wondered what it could be. Who had piled snow into such a huge heap?

He moved toward it. He dragged Zlateh after him. It was a large haystack, covered with snow. Aaron knew that they were saved.

With great effort, he dug his way through the snow. He was a village boy and knew what to do.

Aaron finally reached the hay. He scooped out a nest for himself and the goat.

It was cold outside. But it stayed warm in the hay. And the hay was food for Zlateh. She began to eat.

Outside, the snow kept falling. It quickly covered the tunnel Aaron had dug.

There was very little air in their hideout. Aaron made a kind of window through the hay.

Zlateh finished eating. She seemed to trust people again. Aaron ate his two slices of bread and cheese. But he was still hungry.

He looked at Zlateh. Her udders were full of milk. He lay down next to her. He squirted her sweet milk into his mouth.

Zlateh had never been milked that way. But she did not mind. It was her way to reward Aaron for finding her a shelter made out of food.

Outside, it had grown dark. The dried hay reminded Aaron of the warm summer sun. He moved closer to Zlateh. She was warm and soft. He had always loved her. But now she was like a sister.

Aaron was alone, away from his family. He wanted to talk. He began to talk to Zlateh.

"Zlateh," he said. "What do you think has happened to us?"

"Maaaa," Zlateh said.

"If the snow keeps falling, we will have to stay here for days."

"Maaaa," Zlateh bleated.

"You can't speak. But I know you understand. I need you. And you need me. Isn't that right?"

"Maaaa."

Aaron became sleepy. He made a pillow out of hay and fell asleep.

When Aaron woke up, he didn't know if it was morning or night. It was still dark outside. The snow kept falling. The wind howled.

Aaron woke up hungry. He had eaten all his food. But Zlateh had plenty of milk.

For three days, Aaron and Zlateh stayed in the haystack.

The snow kept falling. Sometimes, Aaron felt that there had never been a summer. It was as if the snow had always fallen.

He was a snow child. He was born of the snow. And so was Zlateh. Aaron and Zlateh slept all night. They slept a good part of the day.

Aaron dreamed about warm weather. He dreamed of green fields and singing birds.

By the third night, the snow had stopped. But Aaron was afraid to go home in the darkness.

The sky was clear. The moon shone. Aaron dug his way out and looked at the world.

The next morning, he heard sleigh bells.

The haystack was not far from the road. The farmer who drove the sleigh showed him the way home.

Aaron had decided in the haystack that he would never part with Zlateh.

Aaron's family and neighbors had searched for him. But they could not find him during the storm.

They were afraid he and Zlateh were lost. Aaron's mother and sisters cried for him. His father was sad and silent.

Suddenly, one of the neighbors came running to their house. He told Reuven

that Aaron and Zlateh were coming up the road.

There was great joy in the family. Aaron told them how he had found the stack of hay. He told them how Zlateh had fed him with her milk.

Aaron's sisters kissed and hugged Zlateh. They gave her a special treat of chopped carrots and potato peels.

Nobody ever again thought of selling Zlateh.

The cold weather continued. The farmers needed to buy furs from the fur trapper once more.

When Hanukkah came, Aaron's mother fried pancakes every evening. Zlateh got some, too. She often visited the kitchen. She was never turned away.

Sometimes Aaron would ask her about the time in the snow. "Zlateh, do you remember the three days we spent together?"

And Zlateh would scratch her neck with a horn. She would shake her white, bearded head.

"Maaaa," she would say. That sound expressed all her thoughts, and all her love.

READING COMPREHENSION

Summarizing. Choose the best phrase to complete each sentence. Then write the complete statements on your paper.

1. Reuven decided to sell Zlateh in order to buy _____ (a younger goat, Hanukkah gifts for his children, firewood).

2. Aaron and Zlateh had to find shelter or they would _____ (be lost, be lonely, freeze to death).

3. Aaron and Zlateh _____ (kept each other alive, did not trust each other, could not help each other).

4. After the blizzard, Zlateh was _____ (sold to the butcher, stolen, given special treatment).

Interpreting. Write the answer to each question on your paper.

1. At the beginning of the story, what was there about Zlateh that made Reuven decide to sell *her*, instead of another farm animal or possession?

2. Why did the blizzard take Aaron by surprise?

3. How did Aaron and the haystack help Zlateh survive?

4. How did Zlateh help Aaron survive?

For Thinking and Discussing. In many lands, people celebrate holidays in the winter by lighting lights and giving gifts. What do lights and gifts do for people during a long, hard winter?

UNDERSTANDING LITERATURE

Mood. The setting and the action in a story help create the mood. Think about the mood in "Zlateh the Goat." Read the paragraphs below. Then answer the questions on your paper.

> Reuven told his son, Aaron, to take the goat to town. No one in Aaron's family was happy about it. His mother wiped tears from her eyes. His younger sisters cried loudly.

1. How did Aaron's sisters *act* when they heard Zlateh must be sold?

2. What mood, or feeling, does this create in the story?

> The sun was shining when Aaron left the village. Suddenly, the weather changed. A large black cloud appeared in the east. It quickly spread across the sky. A cold wind blew in with it.

3. Weather almost always creates strong feelings. Which words in the passage build a mood of fear and danger?

> Aaron dreamed about warm weather. He dreamed of green fields and singing birds.

4. What feeling or mood does Aaron's dream create?

5. What was it like inside the haystack? Did Aaron feel safe there?

WRITING

Do you think animals feel love, fear, trust, or other human emotions? Write a paragraph that includes at least three reasons for your opinion.

Hitchhikers in the Sky

by John K. Terres

Every spring millions of birds migrate north to their summer homes, and every fall they fly south again. When the trip is too long and hard, do small birds sometimes hitch a ride on the backs of large birds? Folklore says they do. Science says they probably don't.

I first heard the story from my mother. She got it from her mother, who grew up in the mid-1800's near the great salt marshes[1] of southern New Jersey.

In those times, the small towns by the marshes were peopled mostly by retired seamen, called baymen. Each day these baymen went out in their boats to fish or to rake clams and oysters from the bottom of the bay. They also went out to hunt, and Grandmother's story told about what happened on one hunting trip.

One fall day, the story went, a bayman shot a large migrating bird. It was either a wild goose or a swan, and he shot it as it flew over the marsh. There's nothing unusual in that, of course. But when the hunter picked up the bird, a small one of a different species fell out of its feathers.

I thought the story was just a piece of South Jersey folklore,[2] left over from a time when people would believe almost anything. But then, in November 1936, a newspaper in St. Louis printed a similar tale. The story claimed that a hummingbird had been found in the feathers of a Canada goose shot in British Columbia. But I was still doubtful.

In the years that followed, I forgot all about those stories. But then in 1972, I discovered another "goose-carries-small-bird" tale. I found it in a book by Al Martin, an Englishman who lived in a cabin deep in the Maine woods.

Do Hummingbirds Ride Geese?

One fall evening, a friend of Martin's visited him. The man laid a Canada goose, which he had shot that morning, on Martin's table. Then he took a ruby-throated

---

[1]salt marshes — low, flat areas flooded with sea water
[2]folklore — stories, customs, and beliefs based on experiences of ordinary people

275

hummingbird out of his tobacco pouch and placed it on the goose.

"Al," the man said, "when I picked up the goose, this little fellow rolled out of its feathers. He was still alive, but he died in my hands."

Stories about hitchhiking birds have been told for hundreds of years, in many different parts of the world.

Martin was impressed. He wrote: "I am just as sure that ruby-throated hummingbirds will ride a goose as I am that aviators ride planes."

Although I believed Martin, I couldn't help wondering if his friend had played a joke on him. Yet I also wondered how the friend (if he was joking) could have killed a goose and a hummingbird at the same time.

I still doubted that a large bird would let a smaller one ride on its back, especially for a long distance. I had no scientific evidence that such a relationship could exist. When I began reading up on the subject, however, I found many tales of hitchhiking birds; and these tales were not limited to Maine and New Jersey.

Free Riders Around the World

For centuries, I learned, hunters along the east coast of England had held a deep-

rooted belief about the goldcrest.[3] They were convinced that this tiny bird made overwater trips on the back of some larger bird. Egyptian peasants had arrived at the same basic idea. They maintained that small birds could not fly across the Mediterranean Sea. They said that when these birds migrated between Europe and Africa, they crossed the water on the backs of storks and cranes.

In the eighteenth century the Tartars of south-central Russia had a similar belief. When fall comes, they said, each migrating crane takes on its back a little corncrake[4] and carries it to warmer lands.

In the early 1920's, the American naturalist Ernest Ingersoll published a record of bird hitchhiking stories. "This popular notion is almost world-wide," he wrote. It is based on observations made by many people in many different places. And the theory "continues to be held by competent observers." Therefore, Ingersoll concluded, "one cannot well dismiss it with disdain."

Among the "competent observers" that Ingersoll mentioned was Theodor von Heuglin, an expert on African birds.

---

[3]goldcrest — Europe's smallest bird, only three and a half inches long
[4]corncrake — a weak-flying bird of the rail family

When told of the Egyptian belief that small birds travel across the Mediterranean Sea on the backs of bigger birds, Heuglin showed no surprise. "I do not laugh," he said, "for the thing is known to me."

In November of 1880, the *New York Evening Post* published a letter about migrant birds. The writer claimed to have seen small birds flying up from the backs of larger ones on the island of Crete. According to Ingersoll, the letter was later printed in *Nature*.[5]

Soon afterwards, *Nature* printed a second letter. This one came from John Rae, a Scotsman who was an early explorer of northwestern Canada. Rae said the Cree Indians believed that "a small bird, one of the Fringillidae,"[6] migrates north on the back of the Canada goose. "These geese," wrote Rae, "reach Hudson Bay about the last of April . . . The Indians state that when they are fired at, little birds are seen flying away from them."

In the same year, Dr. James Cushing Merrill published a similar report. Dr. Merrill was an Assistant Surgeon in the U.S. Army Medical Corps and a well-known naturalist. While stationed at Fort Custer, Montana, Merrill learned of a Crow Indian belief. The Indians said that sandhill cranes and whooping cranes ferried small birds during migration. The Indians called the hitchhikers *napite-shu-utl*, or "crane's back.". From their description, Merrill concluded that the small birds were grebes.

The Piggyback Question

The piggyback question was discussed again in 1944, in an article in *The Scientific Monthly*. The author, W. L. McAtee, was a distinguished biologist. He was also an editor of books for the U.S. Fish and Wildlife Service. We know, he wrote, "that the young of certain birds ride their parents, . . . but the question remains whether any birds are carried by their fellows in full flight. Folklore says they are; science, however, does not know."

McAtee presented several hitchhiking reports, including one from an English sea captain in the Strait of Gibraltar. Watching a flock of geese through field glasses, the captain noticed small birds rising from the backs of the geese and then returning. Some of the passengers on the ship said they saw the same thing.

"Are we . . . to believe these tales or reject them?" asked McAtee. He answered by repeating an old saying: "Where there is so much smoke, there must be fire." He also pointed out that tired birds sometimes light on moving ships to rest. Therefore, he said, "we should not doubt too strongly" that they also light on larger birds.

Because these tales about birds riding on birds have been told so often, many people believe there must be some truth in them.

Some thirty years after McAtee's article, naturalist Roy Bedichek took up the

---

[5]*Nature* — a respected scientific journal published in Great Britain
[6]Fringillidae | frĭn jĭl′ ĭ dē | — a bird family that includes finches, sparrows, and buntings

that albatrosses are capable of this.]

" 'I don't believe that any birds hibernate.' [The poor-will does.]

" 'I don't believe that any birds are sensitive to the Earth's magnetism.' [Birds in general use magnetic lines as guides when they migrate.]

" 'I don't believe that any birds can carry water in their plumage.' [The Old World sand-grouse can do this.]

" 'And finally, I don't believe that small birds hitchhike on larger birds when migrating.'

"Now," Amadon concludes, "all of these phenomena have been proved except the last. I still doubt it, but my scientific skepticism has been overcome before, and it may be again."

Waiting for Proof

As for myself, I'm still wondering about that South Jersey bayman. I don't know whether he really found a small rider on a bird he shot, or just told a tall tale. I need more proof before I can fully accept such stories. But I do believe that small birds are smart enough to take advantage of a free ride. I also know that the wise watcher of birds is always ready to abandon a cherished disbelief.

Illustrations by Dave Allen

Naturalist and author John K. Terres is the former editor of Audubon *Magazine and author of* The Audubon Society Encyclopedia of North American Birds *(Alfred A. Knopf, Inc., 1980).*

question in *Adventures With a Texas Naturalist.* Almost every year, Bedichek wrote, some newspaper prints a story about a hitchhiking hummingbird as if it were fact. Science has no use for such stories, he said.

But even Bedichek admitted that folklore might sometimes contain a grain of truth. He wrote: "Any widespread belief, though in itself absurd, still has some reason for its existence."

From Folklore to Fact

Dean Amadon, former chairman of the bird department at the American Museum of Natural History, does not believe that birds hitchhike. However, he says that birds have made him change his mind before, and they might do it again. He explains: "Had I been asked some years ago to list statements about birds that were considered . . . folklore, I would have written [the following]:

" 'I don't believe that any birds are capable of staying in flight for days or even weeks at a time.' [It has since been proved

READING COMPREHENSION

Summarizing. Choose the best phrase to complete each sentence. Then write the complete statement on your paper.

1. There are many folktales about hitchhiking birds, but _____ (no one believes them, the tales are false, there is no scientific proof).

2. People have been interested in migrating birds for _____ (about ten years, hundreds of years, a century).

3. The theory of feathered hitchhikers explains how some small birds can _____ (migrate long distances, learn to fly, find food).

Interpreting. Write the answer to each question on your paper.

1. Why didn't the author believe his mother's story about hitchhiking birds when he first heard it?

2. Why did he later decide there might be some truth to the story?

3. Dean Amadon doesn't believe that birds hitchhike. However, he does believe that birds may make him change his mind. Explain why.

For Thinking and Discussing. "Where there is so much smoke, there must be fire," W. L. McAtee said about the tales of hitchhiking birds. What did he mean?

Suppose you wanted to convince scientists that birds really do hitchhike. What kind of proof would you have to give them?

UNDERSTANDING LITERATURE

Author's Purpose. Every author has a purpose for writing. The purpose may be to persuade, inform, or entertain.

The author of "Hitchhikers in the Sky" wanted to inform his readers. To achieve his purpose, he organized his information in a clear and interesting way.

1. The italic blurb below the title on page 275 tells you what the article is about. Sum up the main idea.

2. Think about the information each subheading gives you. Then add a subheading of your own. Tell where in the article it belongs.

3. Important points are restated to make sure they are clear. The blurb on page 278 explains an old saying that is quoted on the same page. Read the blurb. Then find the quotation it explains.

4. Quotations from experts show that the author has researched his subject thoroughly. Which expert opinion did you find most convincing? Why?

WRITING

"Any widespread belief . . . has some reason for its existence," wrote naturalist Roy Bedichek.

Choose a common folk belief or superstition, such as the idea that opening an umbrella indoors is unlucky. Use the encyclopedia to find out how the idea got started. Then explain, in writing, the reason for the existence of the belief.

Dance of the Animals

from the Pygmies (Africa)

The bird flies,
Flies, flies, flies,
Goes, comes back, passes,
Mounts, hovers, and drops down.
I am the bird.
Everything lives, everything dances,
everything sings.

The monkey, from bough to bough,
Runs, leaps, and jumps,
With his wife, with his little one,
His mouth full, his tail in the air:
This is the monkey, this is the monkey.
Everything lives, everything dances,
everything sings.

I throw myself to the left,
I turn myself to the right,
I am the fish
Who glides in the water, who glides,
Who twists himself, who leaps.
Everything lives, everything dances,
everything sings.

1. This poem is a song of celebration. It comes from the Pygmy people of Africa. What do you think is being celebrated? Is it only the animals that are named in the song?

2. There is movement going on all through this poem. Find the words that suggest motion.

3. The Pygmies dance while they sing this song. Picture how the dancing might look. Would just one person dance, or the whole village? Would the dance be like the animals' movements in the poem?

4. What does this poem suggest to you about how the Pygmies feel about animals? Do they feel close to them, or far away and different? Do the animals seem like enemies or friends?

Weep No More, My Lady

by James Street

There had never been a dog like My Lady in the part of Mississippi where Skeeter lived. My Lady could fight anything. But she was lost until Skeeter found her. She couldn't bark. But she could laugh, and she could even cry. The last time Skeeter saw her cry, it was the end of his boyhood.

The moonlight symphony of swamp creatures stopped abruptly. The dismal bog was as peaceful as unborn time. The thin man glanced back at the boy and motioned for him to be quiet.

But it was too late. A jumbo frog rumbled a warning. The swamp squirmed into life as its inhabitants rushed to safety.

Suddenly, a haunting laugh echoed through the wilderness. It was like a chuckling yodel, ending in a weird "gro-o-o."

The boy's eyes were wide and staring. "That's it, Uncle Jess. Come on! Let's catch it!"

"Uh, oh." Jesse Tolliver gripped his shotgun. "That ain't no animal. That's a thing."

They hurried in the direction of the sound that Skeeter had been hearing for several nights. Swamp-born and reared, they feared nothing they could shoot or outwit. They slipped out of the swamp and to the side of a ridge.

Suddenly, Jesse put out his hand and stopped the child, then pointed up the slope. The animal, clearly visible in the moonlight, was sitting on its haunches. Its head was cocked sideways as it chuckled. It was a merry little chuckle.

Skeeter grinned, then said, "Sh-h-h. It'll smell us."

Jesse said, "Can't nothing smell that far. Wonder what the darn thing is?"

The animal, however, did smell them. She was about 16 inches high and weighed 22 pounds. Her coat was red and silky. There was a blaze of white down her chest and a circle of white around her throat. Her face was wrinkled and sad.

Jesse shook his head. "Looks something like a mixture of bloodhound and terrier."

"It's a dog, all right," Skeeter said.

"Can't no dog laugh."

"That dog can." The boy began walking toward the animal. "Here. Here. I ain't gonna hurt you."

The dog turned her head from one side to the other and watched Skeeter. She was trembling, but she didn't run. When Skeeter knelt by her, she stopped trembling.

He petted her. She looked up at him and blinked her big eyes. Then she turned over, and Skeeter scratched her. She closed her eyes, stretched, and chuckled. Jesse walked up. The dog leaped to her feet and sprang between the boy and the man.

Skeeter calmed her. "That's just Uncle Jess."

Jesse shook his head again. "I still say that ain't no dog. She don't smell, and she don't bark. And look at her! Licking herself like a cat."

"Well, I'll be," Skeeter said. "Never saw a dog do that before. She's a lady, and I'm gonna name her that. She's mine, because I found her."

"Lady, huh?"

"No, sir. My Lady. If I name her just plain Lady, how folks gonna know she's mine?" He began stroking his dog again. "Gee, Uncle Jess, I ain't never had nothing like this before."

"It still don't make sense to me," Jesse said. But he didn't care. He was happy because the child was happy.

Like most mysteries, there was no mystery at all about My Lady. She was a lady — a Basenji, one of those strange, barkless dogs of Africa. Her ancestors were pets of the Pharaohs.

A bundle of nerves and muscles, she would fight anything. My Lady could scent game up to 80 yards. She ran like an antelope and was odorless, washing herself before and after meals.

The only noises she could make were a piercing cry that sounded almost human, and that chuckling little yodel. She could chuckle only when happy, and she had been happy in the woods. Now she was happy again.

My Lady was worth more than all the possessions of Jesse and his nephew. Several dogs had been shipped to New Orleans. While crossing Mississippi, My Lady had escaped from the station wagon. Her keeper had advertised in several newspapers. But Jesse and Skeeter never saw newspapers.

Skeeter said, "Come on, M'Lady. Let's go home."

The dog walked proudly at the boy's side to a cabin on the bank of the bayou. Skeeter crumbled corn bread and put it before her. She sniffed the food at first, then ate it only when she saw the boy fix a bowl for his uncle.

She licked herself clean and explored the cabin. Satisfied at last, she jumped on Skeeter's bed and went to sleep.

"Acts like she owns the place," Jesse said.

"Where you reckon she came from?" the boy asked.

"Circus, maybe." Jesse looked at M'Lady quickly. "Say, maybe she's a freak, and run off from some show. Bet they'd give us two dollars for her."

"You don't aim to get rid of her?"

The old man lit his pipe. "Skeets, if you want that thing, I wouldn't get rid of her for anything."

"I thought you wouldn't, because you like me so much. And I know how you like dogs, because I saw you cry when yours got killed. But you can share M'Lady with me."

Jesse sat down, blowing smoke into the air to drive away mosquitoes. The boy got a hammer and began cracking nuts. He pounded the meat to pulp, so his uncle could chew it.

Skeeter's yellow hair hadn't been cut for months and was tangled. He had freckles, too. His real name was Jonathan. His mother was Jesse's only sister, and died when the child was born.

No one ever knew what happened to his father. Jesse, a toothless old man with faded blue eyes, took him to bring up. He called him Skeeter because he was so little.

In the village, people wondered if Jesse

was fit to raise a little boy. They considered him lazy. Jesse had lived all his 60 years in the swamp. He earned a few dollars selling jumbo frogs and pelts. But mostly, he just paddled around the swamp, watching things and teaching Skeeter about life.

The villagers might have tried to send Skeeter to an orphanage, but for Joe (Cash) Watson, the storekeeper. Cash was a hard man, but fair. He often hunted with Jesse, and the old man had trained Cash's dogs.

Jesse never wanted much, just a 20-gauge shotgun for Skeeter and a set of false teeth for himself.

"Someday I'm gonna get them false teeth," he often told Skeeter. "Then I'm gonna eat me enough corn on the cob to kill a goat."

The boy cracked as many nuts as his uncle wanted, then put the hammer away. He glanced over at his dog. "Gosh, Uncle Jess. I'm scared somebody will come get her."

"I ain't heard of nobody losing no things around here."

"That's so," Skeeter said. "But you don't reckon she belonged to somebody like me, do you? I know how I'd feel if I had a dog like her, and she got lost."

Jesse said, "She didn't belong to another fellow like you. If she had, she wouldn't be so happy here."

Skeeter fed M'Lady biscuits and molasses for breakfast. Although the Basenji ate it, she was still hungry when she went into the swamp with the boy. He was hoping he could find a bee tree or signs of wild hogs.

They were at the edge of a clearing when M'Lady's nose suddenly tilted. She froze to a flash point, pausing only long enough to get set. Then she darted to the bayou, at least 60 yards away. She dove into a clump of reeds and snatched a water rat. My Lady was eating it when Skeeter ran up.

"Don't do that," he scolded. "Ain't you got more sense than to run into the water after things? A snake or a 'gator might snatch you."

The Basenji dropped the rat and tucked her head. She knew the boy was unhappy with her.

Skeeter tried to explain. "I didn't mean to hurt your feelings. Don't cry." He stared at the tears in her eyes. "She is crying!"

Skeeter called her and ran toward the cabin.

"Uncle Jess! Guess what else my dog can do!"

"Whistle?" the old man laughed.

"She can cry!"

"What made her cry?" Jesse asked.

"Well, sir, we were walking along. All of a sudden she got a scent and flash pointed and then . . ."

"Then what?"

"Uncle Jess, we must have been 50 or 60 yards from that rat when she smelled it."

"What rat?"

The child told him the story, and Jesse couldn't believe it.

"Come on, Uncle Jess," Skeeter said. "I'll show you." He whistled for M'Lady.

The dog came up. "Hey," Jesse said. "That thing knows what a whistle means. Shows she's been around folks." He caught the dog's eye and commanded, "Heel!"

M'Lady turned toward Skeeter and chuckled softly. She'd never heard the order before.

Her curved tail suddenly was still, and her head was poised.

"Flash pointing," Jesse said. "Well, I'll be a monkey's uncle!"

M'Lady held the strange point only for a second. She then dashed toward a corn patch about 80 yards from the cabin.

Halfway to the patch, she broke her run and began creeping. A whir of feathered lightning sounded in the corn. A group of quail exploded almost under her nose. She sprang and snatched a bird.

"Partridges!" Jesse's jaw dropped.

The child was as motionless as stone. Finally, he found his voice. "She was right here when she smelled them birds. A good 80 yards."

"I know she ain't no dog now," Jesse said. "Can't no dog do that."

"She's a hunting dog from way back," Skeeter said.

Jesse walked toward M'Lady, and told her to fetch the bird. But the dog didn't understand. Instead, she pawed it. "Well," Jesse said. "She ain't no bird hunter."

"She can do anything," Skeeter said. "Even hunt birds. Maybe I can make a bird dog out'n her."

"Maybe a coon dog, but not a bird dog. I know about dogs."

"Me, too," said Skeeter. And he did. He'd seen Jesse train many dogs, even pointers. He'd helped him train Big Boy, Cash Watson's prize gun dog.

Jesse eyed Skeeter and read his mind.

"It can't be done, Skeets."

"Maybe not, but I aim to try."

"But she'll flush birds," Jesse said.

"I'll learn her not to."

"She won't hold no point. Any dog will flash point. And she'll hunt rats."

"I'm gonna learn her just to hunt birds. And I'm starting right now," Skeeter said.

"Want to bet?" Jesse challenged.

"Yes, sir. If I don't train my dog, then I'll cut all the wood for a year. If I do, you cut it."

"It's a deal," Jesse said.

Skeeter ran to the bayou and recovered the rat the M'Lady had killed. He tied it around the dog's neck. The Basenji tried to claw it off. Failing, she ran into the house and under a bed. But Skeeter made her come out.

M'Lady looked sad. The boy tapped M'Lady's nose with the rat and left it around her neck.

"You've got yourself a real job," Jesse said. "Even if you get her trained, you'll lose her in the brush. She's too fast and too little to keep up with."

"I'm gonna learn her everything. I got us a gun dog, Uncle Jess."

It takes judgment and patience to train a bird dog properly. But to train a Basenji to hunt only quail took something more than patience. It never could have been done except for that strange bond between a boy and a dog.

M'Lady's devotion to Skeeter was so complete that she would do anything to earn a pat. It wasn't difficult to teach her to heel and follow at Skeeter's feet.

The dog learned that when she chased

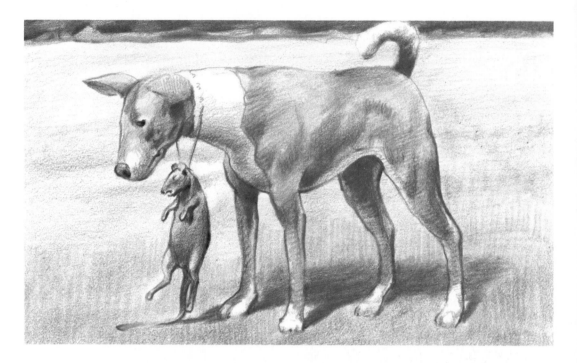

and killed a rat or rabbit, it would be tied around her neck. The only things she could hunt without being punished were quail. Skeeter punished her by scolding. He never hit his dog.

Jesse watched the dog's progress and pretended not to be impressed. He never gave suggestions. M'Lady learned quickly. But the job of teaching her to point birds seemed hopeless.

Skeeter knew she'd never point as pointers do, so he worked out his own system. He taught her to stand motionless when he shouted "Hup!"

The lessons continued for days and weeks, and slowly M'Lady learned her chores.

She learned that the second she smelled birds, she must stop and stand still until Skeeter flushed them. She learned that she must not quiver when he shot.

Teaching her to fetch was easy. Teaching her to retrieve dead birds without hurting them was difficult. But soon M'Lady's education was complete.

Skeeter led Jesse into a field one day and turned his dog loose. M'Lady flashed to a point almost immediately. She stayed steady until the boy flushed and shot. Then she leaped away, seeking and fetching dead birds.

Jesse was proud. "Well, Skeets, looks like you got yourself a bird hunter."

"Yes, sir," Skeeter said. "And you've got yourself a job." He pointed to the woodpile.

The swamp was dressing for winter when Cash Watson drove down that day to give his dog a workout.

He brought Jesse a couple of cans of smoking tobacco and Skeeter a bag of peppermint jawbreakers. Cash locked his fine dog in the corncrib for the night. He was warming himself in the cabin when he noticed M'Lady for the first time. She was sleeping in front of the fire.

"What's that?" he asked.

"My dog," said Skeeter. "Ain't she a beauty?"

"She sure is." Cash grinned at Jesse. Skeeter went out to the well.

Cash asked his old friend, "What kind of mutt is that, Jesse?"

"Search me," Jesse said. "Skeets found her in the swamp."

M'Lady cocked one ear, got up, and stretched. She then turned her tail toward Cash and walked out, looking for Skeeter.

The men laughed. "Something's wrong with her throat," Jesse said. "She can't bark. When she tries, she makes a funny sound."

"Well," Cash said, "trust a young one to love the ugliest dog he can find."

"Wait a minute," Jesse said. "She's a bird-hunting fool."

Just then Skeeter entered. Cash said, "Hear you got yourself a bird dog, son."

"Well, now, I'll tell you, Mr. Cash. M'Lady does everything except tote the gun."

"She must be good. Why not take her out with Big Boy tomorrow?"

"Me and my dog don't want to show Big Boy up."

"Whoa! Any old boiler can pop off steam." Cash winked at Jesse.

"Well, now, sir, I'll just double-dog dare you to run your dog against mine."

Cash admired the boy's confidence. "All right, son. It's a deal. What are the stakes?"

Skeeter started to mention the 20-gauge shotgun he wanted, but changed his mind. He reached down and patted M'Lady, then looked up. "If my dog beats yours, then you get them false teeth for Uncle Jess."

Jesse's chest was tight. Cash glanced from the boy to the man. He, too, was proud of Skeeter. "I wasn't aiming to go that high. But all right. What do I get if I win?"

"I'll cut you ten big bundles of stovewood."

Cash offered his hand, and Skeeter took it. "It's a race," Cash said. "Jesse will be the judge."

The wind was rustling the sage. There was a nip in the early morning air, when they took the dogs to a clearing and set them down. Skeeter snapped a bell around M'Lady's neck. At a word from Jesse, the dogs were released.

Big Boy bounded away and began circling around the brush. M'Lady tilted her nose into the wind and ripped away toward the sage.

Cash said, "She sure covers ground."

Skeeter didn't try to keep up with her, but waited until he couldn't hear the bell.

He then ran to the clearing where he had last heard it. And there was M'Lady on a point.

Cash laughed. "That ain't no point, son. That's a squat,"

"She's got birds," Skeeter said.

"Where?"

Jesse leaned against a tree and watched.

"She's pointing birds in that sage."

"Boy, now that's what I call some pointing. Why, Skeeter, it's 60 or 70 yards to that sage."

Just then Big Boy flashed by M'Lady, his head high. He raced to the edge of the sage, caught the wind, and whipped around. He froze to a point. Cash directed Jesse's attention to the point.

"That's M'Lady's point," Skeeter said. "She's got the same birds Big Boy has."

Jesse joined them. "The boy's right, Cash. M'Lady is pointing them birds. She can catch scents up to 80 yards."

Cash said, "Aw, go on. You're crazy." He walked over and flushed the birds.

Skeeter picked one off and ordered M'Lady to fetch. When she returned with the bird, the boy patted her. She began chuckling.

Cash really studied her then. "Hey!" he said. "A Basenji! That's a Basenji!"

"A what?" Jesse asked.

"I should have known." Cash was very excited. "That's the dog that was lost by the rich Yankees. I saw about it in the paper." He happened to look at Skeeter then, and wished he had cut out his tongue.

Cash quickly tried to change the subject. "Just because it was in the paper don't make it so. I don't believe it's the same dog, come to think of it."

"Do you mean to tell them where the dog is?" Skeeter asked.

Cash looked at Jesse, then at the ground. "It ain't none of my business."

"How about you, Uncle Jess?"

"I ain't telling nobody nothing."

"I know she's the same dog," Skeeter said. "On account of I just know it. But she's mine now. And ain't nobody gonna take her away from me." He ran into the swamp. M'Lady was at his heels.

Cash said, "I'm sorry, Jesse. If I'd kept my big mouth shut, he'd never known the difference."

"It can't be helped now," Jesse said.

"Of course she beat Big Boy. Them's the best hunting dogs in the world. And she's worth a mint of money."

They didn't feel up to hunting, and returned to the cabin to sit on the porch. Neither had much to say. They kept looking toward the swamp where Skeeter and M'Lady were walking along the bayou.

"Don't you worry," Skeeter told his dog. "Ain't nobody gonna bother you."

He sat on a stump, and M'Lady put her head on his knee. She wasn't worrying. Nothing could have been more contented than she was.

"I don't care if the sheriff comes down." Skeeter pulled her onto his lap and held her. "I don't give a whoop if the governor comes down. Even the President of the United States! Ain't nobody gonna take you."

His words gave him courage, and he felt better — but only for a minute. Then the tug-of-war between him and his conscience started.

"Once I found a knife and kept it, and it was all right," he mumbled.

But this is different, his conscience told him.

"Finders, keepers; losers, weepers."

No, Skeeter.

"Well, I don't care. She's mine."

Remember what your Uncle Jess said.
"He said a heap of things."

Yes, but you remember one thing more than the rest. He said, "Certain things are right, and certain things are wrong. And nothing ain't gonna ever change that. When you learn that, then you're fit to be a man."

Skeeter fought off the tears as long as he could, but finally gave in. His sobs caused M'Lady to look into his face and wonder why he was acting that way when she was so happy. He put his arms around her neck and pulled her to him. "My little old puppy dog. Poor little old puppy dog. But I got to do it."

He sniffed back his tears, and got up and walked to the cabin. M'Lady curled up by the fire. The boy sat down, watching the logs sputter for several minutes.

Then he said, "Uncle Jess, if you keep something that ain't yours, it's the same as stealing, ain't it?"

Cash stared into the fire.

Jesse puffed his pipe slowly. "Son, that's something you got to settle with yourself."

Skeeter stood and turned his back to the flames, warming his hands.

"Mr. Cash," he said slowly. "When you get back to your store, please let them folks know their dog is here."

"If that's how it is. . . ."

"That's how it is," Skeeter said. "It's best for M'Lady. She's too good for the swamp. They'll give her a good home."

Jesse looked hurt. Cash said, "Your dog outhunted mine, Skeets. You win them false teeth for your uncle."

"I don't want them," Jesse said. "I don't care if I never eat no corn on the cob." He

got up and hurried outside the cabin.

Cash said he'd better be going. He left Skeeter by the fire, petting his dog.

Jesse came back in and pulled up a chair. Skeeter started to speak, but Jesse spoke first. "I been doing a lot of thinking lately. You're growing up. The swamp ain't no place for you."

Skeeter forgot about his dog and faced his uncle, surprised.

"I reckon you're too good for the swamp, too," Jesse said. "I'm going to send you into town for a spell." He didn't look at the boy.

"Uncle Jess!" Skeeter said. "You don't mean that. You're just saying that on account of what I said about M'Lady. I said it just to keep you from feeling so bad about our dog going away. Uncle Jess, I ain't ever gonna leave you." He buried his face in his uncle's shoulder. M'Lady put her head on Jesse's knee.

"Reckon I'll take them false teeth," Jesse said, at last. "I been wanting some for a long, long time."

Several days later, Cash drove down and told them the man from the kennels was at his store. Skeeter didn't say a word, but called M'Lady. They got in Cash's car. All the way to town, the boy was silent. He held his dog's head in his lap.

The keeper took one look at M'Lady and said, "That's her, all right. Miss Congo III." He turned to speak to Skeeter, but the boy was walking away. He got a glance at Skeeter's face, however. "I wish you fellows hadn't told me. I hate to take a dog away from a kid."

"He wanted you to know," Cash said.

"Mister," Jesse said, "I'd like to swap you for that hound. Now, she ain't good for much. . . ."

The keeper smiled. "If she was mine, I'd give her to the kid. But she's not for sale. The owner wants to breed her and establish her line in this country. And if she was for sale, she'd cost more money than any of us will ever see." He called Skeeter and offered his hand. Skeeter shook it.

"You're a good kid. There's a reward for this dog."

"I don't want no reward. I don't want nothing, except to be left alone." M'Lady crouched, showing her fangs. The keeper shrugged.

"Wild elephants couldn't pull that dog away from that boy," he said.

"That's all right, mister." Skeeter un-

snapped the leash and tossed it to the keeper. Then he walked to the station wagon. He opened the door of a cage and called, "Here, M'Lady!"

She ran to him. "Up!" he ordered. She didn't hesitate, but leaped into the cage. The keeper locked the door.

M'Lady poked her nose between the bars, expecting a pat. The boy rubbed her head. She tried to move closer to him, but the bars held her. She looked at the bars, then tried to push them aside. Then she clawed them.

A look of fear suddenly came to her eyes. She fastened them on Skeeter. She couldn't make a sound, for unhappiness had closed her throat. Slowly, her eyes filled up.

"Don't cry no more, M'Lady. Everything's gonna be all right." Skeeter reached out to pat her. But the station wagon moved off, leaving him standing there in the dust.

Back on the porch, Jesse lit his pipe. He said, "Cash, the boy has lost his dog, and I've lost a boy."

"Aw, Jesse, Skeeter wouldn't leave you."

"That ain't what I mean. He's growed up, Cash. He don't look no older, but he is. He growed up that day in the swamp."

Skeeter walked into the store, and Cash followed him. "I've got that reward waiting for you, Jonathan."

It was the first time anyone ever had called him that. It sounded like man talk.

"And that 20-gauge shotgun is waiting for you," Cash said. "I'm gonna give it to you."

"Thank you, Mr. Cash." The boy bit

his lower lip. "But I don't aim to do no more hunting. I don't never want no more dogs."

"Know how you feel. But if you change your mind, the gun's here for you."

Skeeter looked back toward the porch where Jesse was waiting. He said, "Tell you what, though. When you get them false teeth, get some with a couple of gold teeth in them. Take it out of the reward money."

"Sure, Jonathan."

Jesse joined them. Skeeter said, "We better be getting back toward the house."

"I'll drive you down," Cash said. "But first I aim to treat you to some lemon soda and sardines."

"That's mighty nice of you," Jesse said. "But we better be getting on."

"What's the hurry?" Cash opened the soda.

"It's my time to cut wood," Jesse said. "That's what I get for betting with a good man."

READING COMPREHENSION

Summarizing. Choose the best phrase to complete each sentence. Then write the complete statements on your paper.

1. Jesse knew the dog had been around people because she _____ (had been trained to hunt birds, knew what a whistle meant, knew how to heel).

2. While Skeeter trained My Lady, Jesse never gave suggestions because he _____ (did not want to be bothered, did not want Skeeter to win the bet, wanted Skeeter to find his own ways to teach her).

3. When My Lady outhunted Cash Watson's dog, Cash owed Skeeter _____ (a pile of stovewood, another dog, some false teeth for Jesse).

4. According to Jesse, Skeeter became a man when he _____ (trained his first bird dog, figured out what was right and wrong, owned his first shotgun).

5. When Skeeter returned My Lady to her owner, he was very _____ (angry, proud, sad).

6. At the end of the story, Jesse was _____ (angry at Skeeter, proud of Skeeter, disappointed in Skeeter).

Interpreting. Write the answer to each question on your paper.

1. What did Skeeter and Jesse find strange about My Lady at first?

2. Has Jesse done a good job of bringing up Skeeter? Give examples to support your opinion.

3. What did Jesse mean when he told Cash Watson, "the boy has lost his dog, and I've lost a boy"?

4. Why do you think Skeeter did not take the reward money from Cash?

For Thinking and Discussing. Do you believe in the saying "Finders, keepers; losers, weepers"? If you find something, should you be able to keep it? Why or why not?

UNDERSTANDING LITERATURE

Mood. In "Weep No More, My Lady," There are several different moods. The mood changes as different parts of the story are told. Read the passages taken from the story. Then choose the mood that best describes each passage. Write the mood on your paper next ot the number for each passage.

1. "The moonlight symphony of swamp creatures stopped abruptly. The dismal bog was as peaceful as unborn time. The thin man glanced back at the boy and motioned for him to be quiet."
   a. angry
   b. peaceful
   c. sad

2. "The Basenji dropped the rat and tucked her head. She knew the boy was unhappy with her.
   "Skeeter tried to explain. 'I didn't mean to hurt your feeling. Don't cry.' He stared at the tears in her eyes. 'She is crying!' "
   a. surprised
   b. humorous
   c. fearful

3. " 'Well, now, I'll tell you, Mr. Cash. M'Lady does everything except tote the gun.'
   " 'She must be good. Why not take her out with Big Boy tomorrow?'
   " 'Me and my dog don't want to show Big Boy up.'
   " 'Whoa! Any old boiler can pop off steam.' Cash winked at Jesse.

   " 'Well, now sir, I'll just double-dog dare you to run your dog against mine.' "
   a. serious
   b. sorrowful
   c. humorous

4. " 'Uncle Jesse!' Skeeter said. 'You don't mean that. You're just saying that on account of what I said about M'Lady. I said it just to keep you from feeling so bad about our dog going away. Uncle Jess, I ain't ever gonna leave you.' He buried his face in his uncle's shoulder. M'Lady put her head on Jesse's knee."
   a. joyful
   b. sorrowful
   c. peaceful

5. "M'Lady poked her nose between the bars, expecting a pat. The boy rubbed her head. She tried to move closer to him, but the bars held her. She looked at the bars, then tried to push them aside. Then she clawed them.
   "A look of fear suddenly came to her eyes. She fastened them on Skeeter. She couldn't make a sound, for unhappiness had closed her throat. Slowly, her eyes filled up."
   a. angry
   b. unhappy
   c. humorous

WRITING

Imagine that you are Skeeter. A year has pased since you last saw Jesse. Write a letter to Jesse about your experience with My Lady. Try to use words in your letter that show how you feel.

VOCABULARY

Using Context Clues. Most people know only a fraction of the words in a dictionary. No one knows all of them. But you can learn the meanings of many new words in a story by using *context clues*. Context clues are the other words in a story, or a sentence, that help you learn the meaning of a word you do not know.

Do you know the meaning of the word *scorcher* in the sentence: "The sun beat down on the city; it was such a *scorcher*, you could fry an egg on the sidewalk"?

There are clues in the sentence that tell you what *scorcher* means. The words *sun beat down*, and *you could fry an egg on the sidewalk* help you learn that a *scorcher* is a very hot day.

Use the context clues in the following sentences to learn the meaning of each word in italics. Number your paper from 1 to 15. Write the meaning of each word written in italics.

1. When Hester walked into the *arena*, it was filled with people who wanted to see the show.

2. Someone thought that Hester had *hypnotized* the bear because it looked very sleepy.

3. When Hester hugged Bruin close to him, he was *clinched* with the old bear.

4. Aaron's family needed money, so they decided to sell Zlateh the goat for eight *gulden*.

5. When Zlateh looked at Aaron in *amazement*, her eyes were filled with wonder.

6. "Aaron knew they must find *shelter*, or they would freeze to death."

7. "This was no ordinary storm. It was a mighty *blizzard*."

8. Aaron's hands and feet were *numb*. His fingers and toes had no feeling.

9. Every spring birds *migrate* north, and every fall they fly south.

10. Some bird experts and many other *competent* observers believe that birds hitchhike.

11. My Lady didn't bark. She was a *Basenji*, one of those barkless dogs of Africa.

12. My Lady dove into the *bayou*. The water there was dangerous, but she didn't know that.

13. A group of *quail* exploded almost under her nose. She sprang and snatched a bird.

14. The swamp came to life as its *inhabitants* — frogs, snakes, and insects — rushed to safety.

15. Skeeter's *conscience* bothered him. Something inside told him that it was not right to keep My Lady.

READING

Making Judgments. When you make a *judgment*, you form an opinion based on facts. Your own knowledge and experience help to make good judgments.

For example, suppose you read, "Gary saw people running down the street. He knew that something terrible had happened." You might ask, "Was Gary right to think something bad had happened? Are there other reasons people could be running down the street?" Suppose a big fair or circus had come to town. Then you might think that Gary was very quick to jump to a conclusion. Suppose you happen to know that Gary often thinks the worst will happen. Then you might make a *judgment* about the kind of person Gary is and what he thought about the people running down the street.

Read the following passages taken from the stories in Section 8. Then use your best judgment to answer the questions.

> Everybody at the fair thought the thin man was crazy. How could he wrestle with a 386-pound bear?

1. Why did people think Hester couldn't wrestle old Bruin? Was it reasonable for the crowd to think he would fail?

> I was ready. The manager warned me not to be too scared. He said the referee — Johnnie Norris — would make sure Bruin didn't hurt me.

2. What had people told Hester about other men who tried to wrestle old Bruin? Why did the manager tell Hester he would be safe?

> Aaron knew they must find shelter, or they would freeze to death.

3. Do you think Aaron was right? Why or why not?

> "The wise watcher of birds is always ready to abandon a cherished disbelief."

4. Do you think this is a reasonable statement for a scientist to make? Why or why not?

> "Where you reckon she came from?" the boy asked.
>
> "Circus maybe . . . maybe she's a freak, and run off from the show."

5. Was it reasonable for Jesse to think My Lady was from the circus? Why or why not?

> My Lady's devotion to Skeeter was so complete that she would do *anything* to earn a pat.

6. Is the word *anything* used to mean *absolutely everything*? Would she jump off a tall building or stand still in the snow for hours? Why or why not?

> But to train a Basenji to hunt only quail took something more than patience. It *never* could have been done except for that strange bond between a boy and a dog.

7. Is this a fair thing to say? What do you already know about My Lady to support your answer?

> "I don't *never* want no more dogs."

8. What are Skeeter's feelings at the time? Do you think he will always feel this way?

WRITING

A Review. Reviews give opinions of such things as plays, movies, books, restaurants, and so forth. When you write a review, you base your opinions on your personal standards about what is good and bad. Your standards are not exactly the same as anyone else's. And you do not use the same standards all the time. You might, for example, use one set of standards for a TV show and another set for a book.

Step 1: Set Your Goal

Think about the stories you have read in this unit. Decide which one you would most like to write a review of. It could be the one you liked best, the one you liked least, or one you found especially interesting for some reason.

You will write a review of the story for people who have not read it and who do not know you.

Step 2: Make a Plan

First, decide what your standards are. Think about stories you have read that you really liked. What did they have in common? What about the ones you did not like? Why didn't you like them? You might discover that you like stories with a lot of action in them. You might find you prefer funny stories to sad ones. You might discover that the characters are more important to you than the plot. Or you might find that completely different things matter to you.

Next apply your standards to the story you decided to review. Suppose that your standards include the following:

☐ You like stories about people who are like you.

☐ You like stories that deal with real problems.

☐ You like stories that have clear resolutions, with no loose ends.

If you were writing a review of "The Antique Sale" in Section 6, you would find it met the first two standards, but not the third. You would probably end up writing a "mixed review" of the story. Once you have identified your standards and decided how the story meets (or doesn't meet) them, look for specific details and examples from the story to help your reader understand your opinion of it. In a review of "The Antique Sale," you might list activities, such as riding bicycles and eating doughnuts, to show that the characters are very like other teenagers.

Write the examples you find in your story under the standards you identified.

Step 3. Write the First Draft

When you write your first draft, keep in mind that it will be read by strangers. You must let them know what your standards are. Also, remember that they have not read the story; they want you to tell them what it is like.

First, write an opening statement that gives your overall opinion. The opening statement in a review of "The Antique

299

Sale" might say, "Although the ending is somewhat disappointing, I found the story to be worth reading."

Next, write a paragraph for each standard you listed. The paragraph should identify the standard and tell how the story met (or did not meet) it. It should use specific examples from the story. A review of "The Antique Sale" might include this paragraph:

Unfortunately, the ending does not live up to the rest of the story. It just fades out without any clear resolution. Kelly lists all the things she would have liked to do, but she does nothing. I would have liked to see her take action — any action.

Conclude your review with a sentence that tells whether or not you recommend the story to your readers. The review of "The Antique Sale" might end like this:

If you like real stories about real people with real problems, you will probably enjoy "The Antique Sale."

Step 4. Revise Your Review

When you revise your review, try to put yourself in the place of your readers. Will the review give the readers a sense of what the story is like? (If not, you should include more details and examples from the story.) Will it help readers to decide whether or not they want to read the story? Will they know what your standards are?

After you have revised your review, proofread it and copy it over neatly.

QUIZ

The following is a quiz for Section 8. Write the answers in complete sentences.

Reading Comprehension

1. In "No Hero," does Bruin's manager have any reason to believe that Hester might have hypnotized the bear?

2. In one sentence, explain why Cousin May in "Animal Poems," fell through the parlor floor.

3. In "Zlateh the Goat," why did Aaron say to Zlateh: I need you. And you need me?

4. In "Hitchhikers in the Sky," we learn that the young of certain birds ride their parents. Does this prove that the theory of hitchhiking birds is true? Why or why not?

5. In "Weep No More, My Lady," why is Skeeter "growed up" after he returns My Lady to her owner?

Understanding Literature

6. What mood, or feeling, is very strong throughout most of "No Hero"?

7. In "Zlateh the Goat," what setting helps create a mood of fear? Of safety?

8. "Dance of the Animals" is a song of celebration. What words would you use to describe the mood?

9. How do you think Ogden Nash

wants you to feel as you read his animal poems?

10. What event in "Weep No More, My Lady" creates a feeling of suspense? Of sadness?

ACTIVITIES

Word Attack

1. The name of the bear in "No Hero" is Bruin. Use your dictionary to find out why this is a very good name for a bear. Also find out what language *bruin* comes from and what the word means in that language.

 Then look up the following animal names from this section to learn what languages they come from and their meanings in the original language:

alligator	canary	termite

2. Homophones are words that sound alike but are spelled differently. Think of an animal name that is a homophone for each of the following words. Use each pair of words in a sentence. Example: "Isn't that a dear deer, dear?" Jenny asked her husband.

bare	dough	bore
muscle	yew	hoarse

Speaking and Listening. Suppose animals could talk. What would the ones in the stories in this unit want to tell us? Hold a panel discussion in which each panelist is an animal from one of the stories: Bruin (the bear from "No Hero"), Zlateh the goat, My Lady (the dog from "Weep No More, My Lady"), and a Canada goose from "Hitchhikers in the Sky." The topic of the panel is "People: What's Wrong With Them — and What's Right."

Researching. In this section, you read about how Basenjis are bred to hunt. Other breeds of dogs also work for people. With your classmates, make a book entitled "Working Dogs." Use books in the library to find out about at least three breeds of dogs and the work they do. Write one paragraph about each breed. When you are finished, put your paragraphs into the book. You may illustrate your paragraphs if you like.

Creating. Some animal names also have other meanings. What other meanings do the ones below have? How do the meanings relate to the animal? Use a dictionary to find the answers. Then make a chart that lists the animal name in one column, the other meaning or meanings in the next, and an explanation in the third. Include illustrations in the third column that help show the meaning of the word. You could, for example, draw a goat dressed as a teenager to show the two meanings of *kid*. Add other animal names to your chart if you like.

ape	tiger	crane
shrew	sheep	butterfly

MYTH AND LEGEND

*Myths and
legends are some of the oldest stories
in the world — stories of great deeds,
fantastic battles, and perfect love.
Let your imagination take you
through the ages . . . .*

Myth and Legend

The ancient Greeks believed that the world was ruled by many different gods and goddesses. These gods and goddesses could make magical things happen. At the same time, they were very human. Like mortals, they could become angry or jealous. If you were favored by a god, you were in luck. But if you made a god angry, you were in trouble.

Myths were invented by the ancient Greeks to try to give meaning to a world that was hard to understand and harder yet to control. In many of their myths, heroes, and heroines must face a series of dangers if they are to overcome the forces of evil. But sometimes they are aided by a sympathetic god or goddess.

"The Golden Fleece" is such a myth. Its hero is Jason, whose father was King of Thessaly before he died. Jason's rightful place on the throne has been taken over by Pelias, his uncle. As Jason tries to win his kingdom from his evil uncle, he must prove his strength and courage in a series of tests.

Can he tame the fire-breathing bulls in the kingdom of Colchis? Can he defend himself against an army of one thousand soldiers? Can he capture the magical Golden Fleece while it is guarded by a fierce dragon? Read this myth to find the answers.

Legends are stories that have been handed down from early times. They were not written down for many years, so the details were often changed. Like myths, many legends show heroes and heroines fighting against evil forces, sometimes with the aid of magic. But legends are usually based on real heroes and real events.

"The Legend of King Arthur" is filled with magical objects and events. But the Arthur of the legend was probably based on an *actual* military leader named Arthur. And about 1500 years ago, when this legend takes place, Britain really *did* need a leader to unite the country and drive out the Saxons.

As you read about Jason and King Arthur, keep these two questions in mind:

1. What qualities should a leader have?
2. Is it harder to fight a war or to keep peace?

The Golden Fleece

Myths are stories that show what people believed long ago. The ancient Greeks believed the world was ruled by many different gods. They believed that most events were caused by these gods.

"The Golden Fleece" is a Greek myth. It shows that the ancient Greeks believed in magical events. They believed that people called oracles could see into the future.

In "The Golden Fleece," an oracle predicts the future for a young hero named Jason. This is the kind of myth we would call an adventure story today. Jason faces many dangers as he tries to win his kingdom from his evil uncle, Pelias.

Jason's hardest task is to capture the golden wool of a magic sheep. This wool is called the Golden Fleece. It is guarded by a dragon in a distant land.

Can Jason fight the dragon and win? Can he prove his strength, courage, and wisdom?

Old King Aeson of Thessaly was worn and weary with the heavy cares of governing his people. He longed to have his handsome son, Jason, take his place on the throne. But Jason was young, much too young to rule over a kingdom. Yet the king was too old and too tired to go on.

So Aeson called his brother, Pelias, before him and said: "My brother, I can no longer rule. While my little son, Jason, is still a child, I would have you take the throne in my place. But you must agree that when Jason reaches manhood, he, the rightful ruler, shall be king."

Pelias agreed. But secretly he made up his mind that Jason would never be seated upon the throne of Thessaly. To find out just how he might keep the kingdom for himself, Pelias went to an oracle. The oracles were fortune-tellers. In those days, people believed that an oracle had the power to see into the future.

After mumbling a few charms and burning some magic powders, the oracle told Pelias, "Don't fear anyone who doesn't come with and without a shoe!"

This strange reply satisfied Pelias that he had nothing to fear from Jason. But he wanted to make sure that Jason would

never cause him trouble. After the old King Aeson died, Pelias had Jason banished to a faraway land, many weeks' journey from Thessaly.

There in that far-off country, Jason was reared. He grew from babyhood into boyhood; and when it came time for Jason to go to school, he was sent to study with the centaurs. A centaur was a strange creature, half man and half horse. Below the waist, the centaur had the four legs and body of a horse, which gave him the

Young Jason's special teacher was Chiron, the chief of the centaurs. Chiron was delighted with Jason's wit and quickness. Chiron taught so well, and Jason learned so readily, that soon the youth was a master of the manly arts and had a goodly store of the world's wisdom.

Jason did not know that he was a king's son. But when the young prince reached manhood, Chiron the centaur was satisfied that Jason was fit to be a king. He told Jason the story of his royal birth. Jason decided to win his throne back from his wicked uncle, Pelias.

So Chiron asked an oracle for advice on how Jason should overcome his uncle. Again came a strange reply:

"Who seeks the crown shall wear a leopard's hide!" said the oracle.

Following the oracle's words, Jason went deep into the forest and killed a leopard. Then Jason dressed himself in the leopard's skin. He said farewell to Chiron and set forth on his way to Thessaly.

Soon Jason came to a rushing river. The stream was wide and rough. Its current was so strong that the people who stood on the river bank warned Jason not to try to cross. Many had tried, the people said, but no one had been able to cross the river alive.

But Jason stepped into the raging current. The swirling waters pulled angrily at the young man who dared its power. The trunks of huge trees being carried down the stream rushed at Jason like mad things. One slip — one moment of carelessness — and Jason would go down, never to be seen again. Step by step he made his way across. Those who watched from the riv-

speed and strength of that animal. From the waist up, the centaur was a man, gifted with intelligence. The centaurs were famous for being very learned. In addition, they were known for their tremendous bravery and skill as fighters and archers.

er's banks held their breaths. There were only three steps, two steps, one step more to go — when suddenly the watchers saw Jason swept off his feet!

A groan went up from many lips. The young man who had braved the current was lost! But no! One powerful arm reached up and grasped a large branch of a tree that hung over the river. Slowly Jason pulled himself to safety on the far bank. He had won his first great test!

Jason rested for a moment. Then he stood up. Suddenly he realized that one of his feet was bare. He had lost one of his sandals in the rushing river. But Jason wanted to reach Thessaly, so he strode forward.

It was not long before Jason came to his own city. As he walked through the streets of Thessaly dressed in a leopard skin and one sandal, there was a great commotion. Seeing this handsome youth, people remembered the old prophecy that a young man would appear wearing only one sandal, and that he would be their rightful king.

The false king pretended that he was glad to see Jason. Pelias said he had only been holding Jason's kingdom for him until his return and that he would be glad now to turn the throne over to the returning prince.

Then Pelias tried to trick Jason with a royal feast of welcome. With his nephew in fine humor, Pelias craftily told Jason of a glorious adventure. It would make the youth famous all over the world. "Far away, in the land of Colchis, there is a Golden Fleece," he said. "This fleece is the wool of a golden sheep that is the rightful property of your family. But the Golden Fleece is held by the king of Colchis. It is guarded by a dragon that never sleeps. If I were a young man, nothing would stop me from winning the Golden Fleece."

When Jason heard this story, he was determined to win fame and glory by capturing the Golden Fleece. This was just as Pelias had planned. He was sure that Jason would be killed.

Jason called for brave men to accompany him on his adventure. From all parts of Greece they came. Jason chose only the bravest and the best. Soon there were 50 of the greatest heroes of Greece together in Thessaly.

Jason asked Argus, a famous boatbuilder, to build him a ship large enough to hold 50 men. So Argus built a vessel, the likes of which had never been seen before. It was strong and large.

When their ship was finished, the heroes called it the *Argo,* after Argus, the builder; and they themselves were called the Argonauts. The 50 heroes set forth from Thessaly with Jason at their head. Good fortune seemed to favor them. For when the Argonauts came to Thrace, they were warned by Phineus, the sage, of a great danger that lay before them.

In the sea ahead, there were two rocky islands between which they must pass. But whenever anything tried to pass, these islands would come crashing together with great speed. Anything caught between the two islands was crushed to splinters.

"To avoid this terrible catastrophe," said Phineus, "when you approach the islands, let loose a dove. The dove, flying between the islands will cause them to rush together. But the dove can fly through swiftly enough to escape destruction. Then, at the moment when the islands start returning to their former places, you and your men row with all your might. With the help of the gods you may be fast enough to get through before the islands rush together again."

Jason and his companions thanked Phineus and continued on their way. Soon they came to the islands. The Argonauts drew as near to the fearful passage as possible. Then they released the dove. Straight as an arrow the bird flew between the islands. A roaring sound filled their ears as the islands came rushing together

with a crash. But the dove was safe; only her tail feathers were caught between the rocky walls of the islands.

Jason's men sat at the oars, ready at Jason's signal to row with all their strength. The moment the islands had separated enough for the *Argo* to fit through, Jason gave the signal. Then, as one man, the Argonauts pulled their oars. The sweat stood out on every brow as they pulled. Swift as a bird the *Argo*, with its crew of heroes, sped between the islands. The islands separated their full distance, and then with fearful speed came crashing together again. By just the breadth of a hair, the *Argo* slipped through. Actually, the tip of the dreadful islands grazed the stern of the boat.

At last the heroes came to the kingdom of Colchis. Jason made known to the king his determination to get the Golden Fleece. The king laughed.

"O ho, you think that all you have to do is come here and demand the Golden Fleece and it is yours! Not so fast, my young fellow. The first thing you must do is to harness the fire-breathing bulls. Then you must plow the stony field that lies next to the temple of Mars. After that, you must sow the dragon's teeth in the field. Then we shall see what happens."

But Jason was not frightened or discouraged. "Let us not delay a moment," he cried. "Lead us to our tasks!"

So the king led Jason and his companions to the field of the bulls. The fierce red eyes of the bulls glared angrily at Jason and his bold crew. As the bulls pawed the ground, the fiery breath curled from their nostrils and scorched the ground for many yards around them. No one could get close to the ferocious beasts without being burned to a crisp by the flames they breathed. The Argonauts were forced to withdraw from the field.

That night, in the Argonauts' camp, Jason was in despair. Suddenly a maiden stood before him. It was the king's daughter, Medea. She had fallen in love with Jason.

"Do not be downhearted," she said. "No mortal man could have overcome those enchanted bulls without help. But I can help you. If you promise to marry me, I will help you to win the Golden Fleece."

Jason agreed. Then she gave him a magic herb. "This will tame the bulls," she said.

Next, she gave him a heavy black stone, saying, "Use this when the need arises."

At dawn the next morning, Jason went into the field alone. When the bulls came stamping toward him, he held out the magic herb and lo! the bulls became tame! They permitted Jason to yoke them to the plow.

When the king and his court awoke, there was Jason, quietly plowing the field of Mars with the now-gentle bulls.

The king was furious. He suspected treachery, but he never suspected his own daughter.

"Here," he said, "in this warrior's helmet are the dragon's teeth. Sow them in the field you have plowed."

Jason took the helmet and did as he was told. No sooner had he dropped the seeds than little shiny points began to appear. As Jason watched, the points grew.

Soon, to his horror, he saw a most remarkable thing. Each of the teeth was becoming an armed warrior. First their spears appeared, then their helmets and, right under his eyes, Jason saw an army of soldiers come up out of the ground. No sooner had they sprouted than the soldiers and their spears rushed upon him. Jason drew his sword to fight, but how could one man hope to win against so many?

Then he remembered the weapon Medea had given him. The stone. That was it! Now must be the time to use it!

Quick as a flash, Jason threw the stone right into the middle of the army. The man who was hit, sure that his neighbor had struck him, turned angrily and struck him back. In a matter of moments, the thousand soldiers who had sprung from the dragon's teeth were fighting each other. They fought each other, instead of Jason, until not one of the army was left alive.

Now the king's daughter quickly drew near to Jason.

"Quick!" whispered Medea. "To the fleece!"

She handed Jason a magic potion.

Jason rushed to the garden where the fleece, guarded by the dragon who never slept, was hanging on a tree.

Jason sprinkled a few drops of the potion before the dragon. Its hideous head rolled from side to side as it fell into a deep sleep. Then Jason drew his sword and cut off the dragon's head. He looked about him, and there hanging on the limb of a tree was the Golden Fleece. It gleamed like the sun. Jason captured the precious prize and shouted to his companions to follow him to their ship. Medea ran for the ship, too, for she knew what her fate would be when her father discovered her part in helping Jason — as he surely would.

In a rage, the king gathered his men together. He chased his daughter and the Argonauts, hoping to catch them before they reached their ship. But the Argonauts were too swift and too strong for the king's men, and they made their escape.

The *Argo,* with its brave crew, had many dangerous moments on the return voyage. But with the help of the gods, who applauded their bravery, they at last reached Thessaly again.

Now, with the help of Medea and the 50 heroes, Jason forced the evil King Pelias to yield the kingdom to him, its rightful ruler.

READING COMPREHENSION

Summarizing. Choose the best phrase to complete each sentence. Then write the complete statements on your paper.

1. Pelias wanted to rule Thessaly, so he _____ (killed Aeson, put Jason in prison, sent Jason far away).

2. When Jason first returned to Thessaly, he was wearing only one sandal, a sign that he was _____ (unlucky, the son of Pelias, the rightful king).

3. Pelias thought that if Jason went in search of the Golden Fleece, he would _____ become famous, become rich, be killed).

4. The Argonauts were _____ (the bravest heroes of Greece, guards of the Golden Fleece, friends of Pelias).

5. Jason captured the Golden Fleece with the help of _____ (Pelias, the king of Colchis, Medea).

Interpreting. Write the answer to each question on your paper.

1. Why was Jason determined to win the throne of Thessaly from Pelias?

2. Why did Jason dress himself in a leopard's skin?

3. How did a dove help Jason and the Argonauts?

4. Why did Medea want to help Jason, even though her father was trying to get rid of him?

5. How did Jason manage to harness the fire-breathing bulls and plow the stony field? How did he deal with the army of one thousand soldiers that sprouted from the dragon's teeth that he planted?

For Thinking and Discussing

1. The oracle said to Pelias: "Don't fear anyone who doesn't come with and without a shoe!" What did the oracle mean? Can you restate this in your own words?

2. Have you ever heard someone make a prophecy? If so, what was it? Did it come true? How is a modern-day fortune-teller similar to an oracle? How is it different?

UNDERSTANDING LITERATURE

Theme. In many myths, the forces of good fight against evil. The hero or heroine stands for goodness and is brave, clever, and kind. Like Jason, the hero is usually a king or a leader loved by the people.

In "The Golden Fleece" goodness wins over evil. Jason comes into his rightful place because he is a true hero. He is brave enough to kill a dragon and clever enough to conquer an army. He is also handsome and loved by Medea.

But Pelias lies to his brother, King Aeson, cheats Jason, and even tries to get him killed. Pelias is evil. He is defeated because he does not deserve to be king.

1. Explain why Chiron the centaur thought Jason fit to be a king. Why did he tell Jason the story of his royal birth?

2. Would you think of Jason as a hero even if he weren't a king? Why?

3. If Pelias had kept his promise to his brother, Jason would have become king without a struggle. How would that change the theme of "The Golden Fleece"?

WRITING

When you read a myth, you can always tell who is bad and who is good. But in real life, you can't always tell. No human being is all good or all bad. Choose one character from this myth. Make a list of that person's characteristics. Are they all good, all bad, or a combination of both?

The Legend of King Arthur

Legends are stories handed down from earlier times. They are often based on events in history or real heroes from the past. No one is sure whether King Arthur really lived or not. But there probably was a strong military leader named Arthur who lived in Wales between the years 400 and 600 A.D. At the same time, a character named Arthur was the hero of magical legends.

The first stories about King Arthur were written over a thousand years ago. During the Middle Ages, Arthur was the most popular hero in English and French literature.

As new legends were written, the story changed. Characters from other legends were brought into the King Arthur legend. And stories about other kings were changed to make Arthur the hero.

What made people admire King Arthur so much? At first, writers saw him as a strong leader. This was something the people may have needed but didn't have. During the Middle Ages, writers saw King Arthur as a sensitive, civilized man. And the Round Table, where Arthur met with his knights, became an example of a wonderful past—a time when life was simple and noble.

In "The Legend of King Arthur," which you are about to read, you can see the importance of justice in King Arthur's court. You can understand Sir Lancelot's sense of honor. And you can feel the sadness of the love between Arthur and Guinevere.

It was Christmas Eve of the year 500. All the knights, lords, and kings of Britain were at a church in London. They had gathered to pray for help.

King Lot of Orkney stood up to speak. "Even now, Saxon soldiers are crossing the sea from Germany," he said. "They plan to take over Britain. They must be stopped!"

King Mark of Cornwall spoke up. "The Saxons are skilled in war. If they invade Cornwall, how can I stop them? My army is small."

The other kings and lords and knights nodded in agreement.

Then the Bishop of London spoke. "This is a dark age for Britain. The country is divided into too many small kingdoms. We need a leader who can lead us all against the Saxons. Can't we agree to fight together under a single leader?"

Then the kings, lords, and knights began to argue among themselves. Different nobles wanted different leaders. No single person seemed strong enough or wise enough to bring them all together.

Finally the Bishop of London said, "Let us pray that a new king will rise. We must keep our eyes open for a sign."

When the nobles left the church, their eyes opened in wonder. A huge stone was in the churchyard where nothing had been before. A powerful sword had been driven into the stone, halfway to the handle.

These words were carved on the stone: *Whoever pulls this sword from this stone is the true King of Britain.*

The nobles crowded around the stone.

One by one, they tried to pull the sword out. None of them could move it at all.

"This must be very strong magic," King Mark said.

A thin, bearded man in a long brown cloak stood at the edge of the churchyard. It was Merlin, the court wizard of the late King Uther. Merlin had great magical powers and could see into the future. He knew who would finally pull the sword from the stone. And he knew that this person was miles and miles away on that Christmas Eve.

Young Arthur

Spring came, and still Britain had no king. But young Squire Arthur wasn't worried about this. He was too busy learning how to be a squire for his brother, Sir Kay.

At Easter, there was a big tournament in London. It would be Sir Kay's first chance to prove himself as a knight. He was nervous, but he tried to cover this up by bragging a lot. He also bossed Arthur around more than usual. Arthur tried to be helpful, but it wasn't easy to please Kay.

Many people went to London for the tournament. The air was filled with brightly colored flags. The streets were crowded with people, both rich and poor, all in their finest clothes.

Before his first jousting match, Sir Kay rode to the jousting field. Arthur ran along behind his horse.

Kay suddenly realized that he had left

his sword back at the inn. He blamed it on Arthur.

"You idiot!" he cried. "You forgot to hand me my sword this morning. Run back and get it."

Arthur knew it was his duty to follow Kay's orders, so he ran back to the inn. When he got there, it was locked, for the innkeeper had gone to the jousting matches for the day.

Arthur glanced at the church across the street. He saw a sword sticking out of a huge stone in the yard. He didn't know why it was there. All he knew was that he had to borrow it for a while.

When Arthur grabbed the sword, it slid out of the stone. He carried it swiftly to Sir Kay and explained, "I couldn't get your sword. But I found this one."

Sir Kay recognized the sword. His mind worked quickly.

He went over to his father and cried, "Look! Here is the sword from the stone! I must be the true King of Britain!"

The crowd around them fell silent. But Kay's father, Sir Ector, was suspicious. He knew that Kay sometimes told lies.

"Did you pull this sword out of the stone?" he asked.

"It's here, isn't it?" said Sir Kay.

"I want to see you pull it out again," Sir Ector said.

Sir Ector and Sir Kay rode to the church. Arthur ran behind them, and the crowd followed.

Sir Ector pushed the sword back into the stone. Sir Kay tried to pull it out again, but failed.

Kay hung his head. "I didn't pull the sword out, Father," he said. "I don't know

who did. All I know is that Arthur brought it to me."

Everyone turned to look at the young squire. Arthur explained, "Kay needed a sword, so I borrowed this one. I am sorry if I did something wrong."

Sir Ector said, "Try to pull it out, Arthur."

Arthur grasped the handle of the sword. He hardly had to pull at all. The sword slipped smoothly out of the stone.

The people in the crowd fell to their knees. Arthur stood with the sword in his hand, confused.

"What does this mean, Father?" he asked.

Sir Ector sighed and said, "I am not your real father, Arthur. I adopted you when you were a baby. You were brought to me by a stranger in a long brown cloak. He told me to love you like a son, and I have. But now we must learn who you really are."

Just then, the stranger in the brown cloak entered the yard. People in the crowd whispered, "It's Merlin! It's Merlin!"

Merlin walked up to Arthur and said, "Arthur, you are the true King of Britain. You are the only son to the late King Uther Pendragon. Your father was killed in a battle when you were a baby. I took you to Avalon, the Land of Mystery, where a spell was placed upon you. You shall be the greatest king this land shall ever know."

The crowd stared at young Arthur. He stood straight and held his head high. The people felt they were at the beginning of a great age.

"Hail to King Arthur!" they shouted.

EXCALIBUR

The New King

It wasn't easy to be accepted as King of Britain. Many of the other kings didn't want to be ruled by a teenager. So Arthur had to prove himself in battle.

First, he had to fight the Saxons who were attacking southern England. Arthur formed an army of loyal knights and led them. Soon they drove the Saxons out of that part of the land.

Next, Arthur struggled to gain control of the rest of Britain. Some kings fought hard against Arthur and his knights. But others were willing to join Arthur's army. They were glad to be protected by a strong king.

Arthur's army grew larger and more powerful. Soon all the British forces were under his leadership.

The Saxons were still attacking parts of Britain. But now the British forces were united. Arthur had become a skilled general. The Saxons finally gave up and sailed back to Germany.

All of this took 10 years. After so many

water near the boat. It was the arm of a woman, and she held a golden sword.

Arthur took the sword. Then the hand disappeared into the water.

"This sword is called Excalibur," Merlin said. "It is a gift from the Lady of the Lake. Your first sword was a sword of war. Excalibur is a sword of peace."

"But this sword looks stronger than my other one," said Arthur.

"It is more difficult to keep peace than it is to fight a war," said Merlin. "You must be very strong to rule in peace."

Arthur felt it was time to form a royal court at Camelot. At Easter, he invited all his knights to a great feast at the castle. They came from all over Britain.

The knights who gathered in the courtyard were rude and rough. They bragged about their skills in battle. They argued about who would get to sit at the head of the dining table. Arthur watched them from a window and sighed. It would take a lot to civilize these men.

When Arthur opened the door to the dining hall, the knights pushed their way in. Then they stopped and stared at the hall. It had a high ceiling and stained-glass windows. In the center was a huge round table with 150 chairs around it.

Arthur sat in a chair which was like everyone else's. "Merlin made this table for me," he said. "When we sit here, no knight will be more important than any other. Each one will be judged by how well he behaves as a knight."

The knights hurried to the table. Each chair had a name written on it in gold.

Arthur explained, "When a man becomes worthy of joining us, his name will

years of war, Arthur was eager to have peace. He was glad to go home to his beautiful castle, Camelot.

One day, shortly after Arthur returned to Camelot, he and Merlin walked to a lake near the castle. Arthur said, "Merlin, you must help me plan for the future."

Merlin nodded, but said nothing. He walked to a small boat at the edge of the lake. He stepped into it, waving for Arthur to follow, and Arthur followed him.

The boat glided to the middle of the lake. Suddenly, an arm rose out of the appear on an empty chair. When a knight loses his honor, his name will disappear from his chair. That way, we will know who has behaved well. No one shall stain the honor of the Round Table."

Sir Gawain spoke up. "How do we know how a knight should behave? All we know is how to fight in battle."

Arthur said, "In a peaceful society, people live by laws. In the next few years, I will try to make good laws for my people."

Then Sir Gareth spoke up. "But this is wild country, my lord. Outlaws make the roads dangerous. Beasts and dragons fill the woods. There is also a great deal of evil magic loose."

"This is true," said Arthur. "But it is time to bring peace to Britain. All of you knights must help me. I depend upon you to set a good example. That's why I have some special rules for you.

"Never commit murder. Never be a traitor. Never be cruel. Always help the weak. Always keep your word. Always fight on the side of right and justice."

The knights repeated this vow. They agreed to repeat the vow together every year at Easter. Each man sat tall, proud to be a knight at the Round Table.

Merlin's Warning

Soon all of Britain heard about the Round Table and Arthur's court at Camelot. Poets, musicians, and artists went to live in Arthur's castle. It became a center of culture.

Arthur knew he needed a queen to help him hold court, and he knew who this queen should be. Her name was Guinevere. She was the beautiful daughter of King Leograunce. The first time Arthur saw her, he had fallen in love.

Guinevere gladly agreed to marry King Arthur. The wedding was held at Camelot. The court celebrated with a three-day feast. Everyone admired the new Queen, except for Merlin.

At the feast, Merlin sat beside Arthur's half-sister, Morgana LeFay. Morgana wanted to be a wizard like Merlin. He had been teaching her about magic.

"Guinevere is certainly beautiful," Morgana said to Merlin.

Merlin frowned. "She is lovely," he said. "But her beauty will bring about the ruin of this court. Arthur wouldn't listen to me, though. He's too much in love."

Morgana watched her half-brother closely. It was true: Arthur looked madly in love. Morgana's lips curled in a sneer. She secretly hated him and was jealous of his power. Now Merlin had given her a clue that would help her cause trouble.

Suddenly Merlin stood up. Everyone in the hall became quiet to hear the wizard's words.

"I must leave you now," he announced. "I must go away with the Lady of the Lake, the great magician of Avalon. I know that she will put me to sleep for hundreds of years. I have seen this in my future. I can do nothing to change it. Besides, I love the Lady of the Lake — as much as Arthur loves Guinevere."

Arthur jumped up. "You cannot leave

us now!" he cried. "The hardest part is just beginning. It was easy to win battles. But now we are creating a new way of life. I need your help."

"You don't need my help to be a good king," Merlin said. "To be a good king, you must be a good man. You already are that."

"But we must teach people to live by right, not by might," said Arthur.

"My magic cannot help you there," said Merlin, "Just remember one thing, all of you. You will all die someday. But the story of the Round Table will be told forever. Now, farewell."

"Don't go, Merlin!" Arthur cried. "I don't want to lose you!"

"It is my fate," Merlin said, going out the door. "Now you must prove that you can stand on your own." Then he was gone.

While the feast went on, Arthur sat quietly. Guinevere tried to cheer him up. He smiled when he looked into her beautiful eyes. But he felt lost and lonely without Merlin.

From across the hall, Morgana LeFay watched her half-brother. As long as Merlin had been around, Morgana had behaved herself. But now maybe she could make Arthur suffer.

Two New Knights

There were still a few empty chairs at the Round Table. Young men came from all over Britain, hoping to win a chair.

One year at the Easter feast, Lady Nimue walked into the hall. She was a magician and an old friend of Merlin's. She led in a handsome young squire, who was dressed in white. Queen Guinevere felt her heart skip a beat as she watched the young man kneel before Arthur.

"I bring a new knight to you, my lord," Lady Nimue said to King Arthur. "His name is Lancelot. He is the son of King Ban, but he was raised by the Lady of the Lake. She brought him up to be the greatest knight of the Round Table."

Lady Nimue pointed to one of the empty chairs at the Round Table. The name Lancelot appeared there in gold. Arthur smiled and raised his sword, Excalibur. He touched Lancelot on each shoulder with the sword.

"Rise, Sir Lancelot," he said. "You are now a knight of the Round Table."

As Lancelot rose, he saw Queen Guinevere. She was staring at him and blushing. He could not take his eyes away from her.

"This is my wife, Queen Guinevere," Arthur said proudly.

"I knew she must be the Queen," Lancelot said. "I heard that she is the most beautiful woman in Britain. Now that I have seen you, my lady, I must agree."

Queen Guinevere tried to appear calm. "Welcome to Camelot, Sir Lancelot," she said. Inside she was trembling.

Just then, Morgana LeFay entered the hall. She was leading a young squire, too. This one looked mean. Instead of wearing white, he was dressed in blood red. This was Mordred, Morgana's son.

"Brother Arthur," Morgana said, "I bring you a new knight. This is Mordred,

your nephew. Surely you won't refuse to make him a knight."

Arthur felt uneasy. He had a feeling that some great evil had entered his court. But he felt he must be loyal to his half-sister's son. So he made Mordred a knight, too.

Mordred's name appeared in gold on a chair. He and Lancelot both took their places at the Round Table.

A Rumor

Even without a war, the knights were busy. There were robbers, monsters, cruel landlords, and evil magicians all over the land. There were many poor people who needed help from Camelot. So the knights were often away, fighting against evil.

The knights became heroes to the British people. Sir Gawain, Sir Tristram, Sir Percival, and Sir Galahad were famous. But the most famous knight of all was Sir Lancelot.

Of all the knights, Lancelot was away from Camelot the most. Whenever he stopped at the castle, he did not stay long.

This hurt Arthur's feelings. He thought that Lancelot was his best friend. He did not know that Lancelot had a good reason for staying away from Camelot.

Lancelot had fallen in love with Queen Guinevere the moment he first saw her. He could tell from her eyes that she loved him, too. But they both loved King Arthur, and they did not want to hurt him.

They never talked to each other about this powerful love. In fact, they avoided each other as much as they could.

Seven years passed. There was little crime left in Britain, thanks to the members of the Round Table. People had learned to settle disagreements through law rather than violence.

There wasn't much for the knights to do anymore. They began to spend most of their time at Camelot. Even Lancelot had a hard time finding reasons to stay away.

Now the knights had more time to gossip and to be jealous of one another. It was a perfect situation for a trouble-maker like Mordred, whose mother had taught him to hate Arthur.

One day, Mordred sat drinking with Sir Agravain, Gawain's brother. Agravain was a weak knight, and he was jealous of the heroic knights like Gawain and Lancelot. Mordred knew this.

"Have you noticed Lancelot and Guinevere lately?" Mordred asked.

Agravain shrugged. "No. What is there to notice?"

"They keep looking at each other when Arthur's back is turned," Mordred said. "Something is going on between them."

"I wouldn't be surprised," Agravain said. "It would be just like Lancelot to flirt with Arthur's wife. He thinks he's better than the rest of us."

Mordred smiled. He knew that Agravain had a big mouth. Soon the rumor would be all over Camelot.

When Gawain heard the rumor, he spoke to Arthur. "You and I know that Guinevere is loyal to you," Gawain said. "We also trust Lancelot completely. But these rumors could become dangerous. The knights are getting restless."

Arthur frowned, remembering Merlin's warning to him about Guinevere. "I wish that Merlin were here," he said. "I need his advice."

"That reminds me," Gawain said. "A strange thing happened to me yesterday, while I was out riding. I stopped to give my horse a drink of water. Then I saw a puff of smoke, and I heard Merlin's voice. It told me to tell you that your knights should search for the Holy Grail."

"The Holy Grail is a very magical cup," Arthur said. "It has been lost for years. Only someone with a perfectly pure heart can see the Holy Grail. If one of our knights could see it, that would bring great honor to the Round Table."

"It would be a very difficult search," Gawain said.

"Good," said Arthur. "Our knights need a new challenge. I hope that Merlin sends us a sign."

The Holy Grail

The sign came at the next Easter feast.

Arthur and his knights were seated at the Round Table. Arthur looked around proudly.

"This is the finest group of men who ever sat at one table," he told them. "This is Britain's brightest hour."

Suddenly, a great wind shook the castle. There was a mighty crash of thunder. Then a brilliant sunbeam shone through a window.

The knights saw a shining cup floating through the air. It was a vision of the Holy Grail, covered with a veil of white silk. It passed down the length of the hall and then disappeared.

Sir Gawain jumped to his feet. "This is a sign from Merlin," he said. He put his hand upon his sword. "I swear by my sword that I will search for the Holy Grail. I will go anywhere and face any danger to find it."

Many other knights stood up, too. They also promised to search for the Grail.

King Arthur sat still and sighed. "I will be proud if one of you finds the Holy Grail. Yet I am sad to see you leave on this search. Many of you will die far from Camelot. We will never be together like this again."

For seven years, King Arthur's knights searched for the Holy Grail. A strong magic kept the Grail hidden. Many knights died while trying to find it. Others finally gave up the search.

Sir Lancelot and Sir Gawain learned that the Grail was at Castle Carbonek. They rode for months until they found the castle, hidden deep in a dark forest.

They went inside to the secret chapel where the Grail was kept. The door to the chapel opened by itself. A brilliant light streamed out and made Lancelot faint.

A voice from the air said, "Sir Lancelot, you are not worthy to see the Holy Grail."

Sir Gawain thought he saw the Holy Grail for a second through the doorway. He started toward it. But the chapel door swung shut, and he could not open it.

Sir Lancelot and Sir Gawain rode sadly away from Castle Carbonek. They had no choice but to return to Camelot.

Later, word reached Camelot that Sir

HOLY
GRAIL

329

Galahad had found the Holy Grail. Galahad was the purest of all the knights. He had never done a bad deed or had a bad thought. That was why he was able to see the Grail. But after seeing it, he died. It was as though he had no more reason to live.

Trouble

King Arthur's knights slowly returned to Camelot. Things were different now. There were many empty seats around the Round Table. And Mordred was stirring up more trouble than ever.

Late one night, Morgana LeFay visited her son. "I have a plan for getting Arthur," she told him. "You must catch Lancelot and Guinevere together," she said. "Then you can accuse them of being traitors to the King. Arthur could not ignore that because he has to uphold his laws. He would have to punish them, and that would break his heart."

Mordred grinned and said, "I'll get Agravain to help."

A few days later, Queen Guinevere was walking in the garden. She saw Lancelot sitting by a rose bush, deep in thought. Usually she would have walked the other way. But Lancelot looked so sad that she couldn't help speaking to him.

"What is the matter?" she asked. "You've been so quiet lately."

"I am very tired," he said. "For years I've been trying to be a good knight. But when I searched for the Grail, I was not able to see it. A voice told me I was not worthy."

"Not worthy?" Guinevere asked.

"It's true. I have one wrong feeling in my heart. I haven't been strong enough to get rid of it. I am in love with you, my lady. I have loved you since the day we met."

Guinevere turned pale. She whispered, "And I love you. I have fought against it for years."

They stared at each other, trembling. "But we cannot hurt Arthur," Lancelot said. "Maybe I should go away for good."

Just then, Mordred and Agravain jumped out from some bushes. They were followed by four other knights.

"We heard everything!" Mordred shouted. "You were plotting against the King! You are traitors, and you must die!"

Lancelot pulled out his sword. The six knights were no match for him. He killed Sir Agravain and wounded two others. Then he climbed over the garden wall and left Camelot. "I'll get him yet," muttered Mordred. Then he pointed his sword at Guinevere and ordered her inside.

Mordred took Guinevere to King Arthur. He told the King what he had heard. Arthur tried not to listen, but his knights began to argue with him.

"The laws must apply to everyone," said Sir Gawain. "You say traitors must die. Guinevere is a traitor, so she must die."

Arthur looked sadly at his wife. She turned her face away, ashamed. Arthur felt his heart sink.

"I cannot change the law," he said.

"Law is the basis of our peace and civilization. Not even the King can go against it."

"She must die at the stake!" shouted Mordred.

War

The next morning, firewood was piled high in the courtyard. Guinevere was led out and tied to a stake at the center of the pile. The firewood was lit, and the flames crept toward her.

Suddenly the crowd heard hoofbeats approaching. Lancelot, riding a white horse, burst into the courtyard. He swept Guinevere away from the flames and rode off with her.

Sir Gawain ran to Arthur, his face red with anger. "Lancelot has broken your law again!" he said.

"But a knight should save his Queen from danger," Arthur said. "Lancelot had to do this."

"Lancelot killed my brother Agravain," Gawain said. "He has betrayed you, and he has broken the law. He must be punished, my lord."

Arthur sighed and said, "You are right. We must declare war against Lancelot."

Half of the knights of the Round Table fought with Arthur and Gawain. But the others left to join Sir Lancelot. Knights who had been friends were now enemies.

Arthur's army followed Lancelot over to France. While he was gone, he left his nephew, Mordred, in charge of the kingdom. Arthur thought he would not be gone for long. But the war dragged on for months and months.

One day Arthur and Gawain were fighting side by side. Suddenly, Lancelot appeared with his sword raised. He began to swing it at Arthur. When he recognized who it was, he dropped his sword.

Gawain shouted, "Why don't you fight, you traitor?"

Lancelot shook his head. "I could not hurt my King," Then he knelt before Arthur. "I have never been a traitor to you, my lord. Can't you forgive me and end this foolish war?"

"Let us go to my tent," Arthur said.

Arthur, Gawain, and Lancelot sat up all night talking. By dawn, they had made peace.

"I must get back to Britain," Arthur said. "Mordred has been causing trouble. He raised everyone's taxes, just to make himself rich. He tried to put Guinevere in prison. He says he will fight me if I go back. I must not lose my kingdom."

Lancelot said, "Mordred has been behind all of this. He was the one who made you think I was a traitor."

Arthur looked closely at his friend. "But you still love Guinevere, don't you?" he asked.

Lancelot sighed. "I cannot help that, my lord. But that does not mean I cannot be your loyal friend. You will need help in fighting Mordred. I will follow you to Britain soon and help you win back your kingdom."

So Arthur and his army sailed back to Britain. Mordred heard they were coming and sent out an army to fight them.

The Final Battle

The night before the battle, Arthur dreamed he saw Merlin. Merlin said, "Do not fight Mordred tomorrow. Make a truce with him for one month. By then, Lancelot will be here to help you."

The next morning, Arthur's army was ready to enter battle. But Arthur rode out first, to make a truce with Mordred.

As he set out, Gawain said, "Be careful, my lord."

"I cannot trust Mordred," Arthur said. "Watch us as we talk. If you see any of his men pull a sword, give the order to fight."

Arthur and Mordred met each other in the middle of a plain. They agreed to sign a truce.

As they were signing, a snake slid out of some bushes. It bit one of Mordred's men on the heel. The man pulled out his sword to kill the snake.

Gawain saw the flash of the sword. He shouted to Arthur's men to attack. Mordred's men eagerly started fighting, too.

By evening, the plain was covered with bodies. The grass was stained with blood. All of the best knights of the Round Table lay dead. Mordred's army had met the same fate.

King Arthur looked around him sadly. He said to the young knight beside him, "The end has truly come."

Then he saw Mordred leaning on his sword among the dead men. "There is the traitor who brought this about," Arthur said. "Give me my spear quickly, Sir Bedivere."

THE
TRUCE

Sir Bedivere said, "Leave him alone, my lord. His mother's magic may be protecting him. Besides, he has lost. There are two of us left and only one of him."

"I must kill him," Arthur said. "He destroyed my kingdom."

Arthur took his spear. He ran toward Mordred shouting, "Death to you, you traitor!"

Arthur's spear ran through Mordred's body. But with his last breath, Mordred struck Arthur's head with his sword.

Arthur fell to the ground. Sir Bedivere ran to him and picked him up. He carried Arthur to a nearby lake. The water was red in the setting sun.

Arthur whispered, "Take Excalibur. Throw it into the water."

Sir Bedivere took the sword to the edge of the lake. It was a beautiful sword. He hated to throw it away. But the King had told him to do this. So he hurled the sword into the lake.

As the sword flashed in the sunset, a hand and an arm rose out of the lake. It was the arm of a woman, and her hand caught the sword by the handle. Then it disappeared into the water.

Then the boat drifted into the evening mist and disappeared with the setting sun.

A month after the final battle, Lancelot returned to Britain. He went to speak to Guinevere, who was now living in a convent.

She told Lancelot about Arthur's end. Then she said, "That is why I am living in this convent. None of this would have happened if it hadn't been for me."

Lancelot shook his head and took her hand. "Arthur had forgiven us," he told her. "He knew we loved him. It was Mordred's fault."

He paused, then added, "The age of Camelot is over. But Britain must go on, even without Arthur. Maybe we have learned something about how to live in a civilized world. I believe that much of Camelot will always be with us."

READING COMPREHENSION

Summarizing. Choose the best phrase to complete each sentence. Then write the complete statements on your paper.

1. In the year 500, Britain needed a leader to _____ (invade Germany, drive magic out of the land, unite the country and drive out the Saxons).

2. King Arthur's first task was to prove that he was a good _____ (lawmaker, military leader, magician).

3. When peace came, Arthur knew he must teach his people to live by _____ (right, might, magic).

Sir Bedivere ran to tell King Arthur what had happened. But he couldn't find the King.

Sir Bedivere looked back at the water. Then he saw King Arthur lying on a white boat, floating slowly away on the lake.

"My lord!" shouted Sir Bedivere. "Please don't leave!"

He heard the King's voice floating to him over the water. "I must go now to Avalon. Merlin is waiting for me there. You shall go back to tell our story. Tell everyone about Camelot, the Round Table, and the peace we brought to Britain."

4. Arthur's ruin was plotted by _____ (Morgana and Mordred, Lancelot and Guinevere, Merlin and Morgana).

5. Lancelot and Guinevere were in love with each other, but _____ (denied it, both loved Arthur, never said a word about it).

Interpreting. Write the answer to each question on your paper.

1. Arthur's first sword was a sword of war. What kind of sword was Excalibar, his second sword?

2. Why did Arthur have his knights sit at a round table, not a long table?

3. Why was Merlin sorry when Arthur married Guinevere?

4. Why did Mordred start the rumor about Lancelot and Guinevere?

5. Why couldn't Lancelot see the Holy Grail?

6. Why did the knights of the Round Table divide into two armies?

7. Why did Arthur forgive Lancelot and Guinivere?

For Thinking and Discussing

1. Why did Merlin say Arthur would need a stronger sword for peace than for war?

2. Why do you think Merlin's magic could not help people to live by just laws?

3. Do you blame Lancelot and Guinevere for being in love?

UNDERSTANDING LITERATURE

Theme. A legend is a story that started by being told. Each time it was told, it changed a little. People left out parts or added parts of their own. Finally, someone wrote down the legend to be read by generation after generation.

Most legends have strong themes. The King Arthur legend shows the importance of justice and peace. And it shows that good can win over evil. The key to the theme of a legend is often a *symbol*.

In literature, a symbol is an object that stands for an idea. For example, a crown may be a symbol of power or royalty. There are many symbols in the King Arthur legend.

Look at the list of symbols below. Then match each symbol with the idea it stands for in this legend. On your paper, write each symbol next to the idea it stands for.

Symbols
sword
the Round Table
Holy Grail
Camelot
Lancelot's white clothing
Mordred's blood-red clothing

Ideas
holiness
peace and happiness
power
goodness
evil
equality

Section Review

VOCABULARY

Using Context Clues. In each statement below the context clues help you learn the meaning of the word written in italics. Read each statement. Then write the best definition.

1. People believed that an *oracle* had the power to see into the future.
   a. king
   b. fortune-teller
   c. teacher

2. Jason asked Argus, the famous boat-builder, to build him a *vessel*.
   a. boat
   b. house
   c. castle

3. Sir Kay missed his chance to compete in the *tournament*.
   a. party
   b. election
   c. contest

4. Before his first *jousting match*, Sir Kay forgot his sword.
   a. fight
   b. feast
   c. race

5. As Sir Kay's *squire*, Arthur knew it was his duty to follow Kay's orders.
   a. enemy
   b. helper
   c. teacher

6. Morgana's lips curled in a *sneer*. She secretly hated Arthur.
   a. sad expression
   b. hateful expression
   c. curious expression

7. Because Lancelot's heart was not perfectly pure, he was not *worthy* to see the Grail.
   a. strong enough
   b. smart enough
   c. good enough

8. "You were plotting against the King!" Mordred shouted. "You are *traitors*, and you must die!"
   a. robbers
   b. important people
   c. disloyal people

9. Lancelot was a faithful friend to Arthur and never *betrayed* him.
   a. honored
   b. acted against
   c. liked

10. Arthur declared a *truce* with Lancelot, and the fighting stopped.
    a. contest
    b. argument
    c. peace

READING

Inference. When you make an inference, you use clues in the story plus what you know about life to draw a conclusion. For example, in "The Legend of King Arthur," Mordred told Agravain that something was going on between Lancelot and Guinevere. Mordred "knew that Agravain had a big mouth. Soon the rumor would be all over Camelot." The legend does not say that Agravain spread the rumor. But from the clues and what you know about life, you can *infer* that he did. The clue is that Agravain had a big mouth.

Read each paragraph. Then use the clues in the paragraph and your own knowledge to answer the questions. Write the answers in complete sentences on your paper.

At last the heroes came to the kingdom of Colchis. Jason made known to the king his determination to get the Golden Fleece. The king laughed.

1. Why did the king laugh? What did he think of Jason's determination to get the Golden Fleece?

Jason sprinkled a few drops of the potion before the dragon. Its hideous head rolled from side to side as it fell into a deep sleep.

2. What kind of potion did Jason sprinkle before the dragon?

These words were carved on the stone: *Whoever pulls this sword from this stone is the true King of Britain.*
The nobles crowded around the stone. One by one, they tried to pull the sword out. None of them could move it at all.

3. Why did the nobles try to pull the sword from the stone? Why didn't any of them succeed?

As Lancelot rose, he saw Queen Guinevere. She was staring at him and blushing.
Queen Guinevere tried to appear calm. "Welcome to Camelot, Sir Lancelot," she said. Inside she was trembling.

4. How did Guinevere feel when she first met Lancelot?

"The Holy Grail is a very magical cup," Arthur said. "It has been lost for years. Only someone with a perfectly pure heart can see the Holy Grail. If one of our knights could see it, that would bring great honor to the Round Table."

5. If one knight could see the Holy Grail, how would this bring honor to all the knights of the Round Table?

Arthur looked sadly at his wife. She turned her face away, ashamed. Arthur felt his heart sink. "I cannot change the law," he said. "Law is the basis of our peace and civilization. Not even the King can go against it."

6. How did Arthur feel about having to sentence Guinevere to death? Why was it so difficult to make this decision?

"The age of Camelot is over," said Lancelot. "But Britain must go on, even without Arthur. Maybe we have learned something about how to live in a civilized world. I believe that much of Camelot will always be with us."

7. What did Lancelot think Camelot had taught people?

QUIZ

The following is a quiz for Section 9. Write the answers in complete sentences on your paper.

Reading Comprehension

1. Who were the Argonauts in the myth of "The Golden Fleece"? What did they call their ship?

2. In what ways did Medea help Jason to capture the Golden Fleece?

3. In "The Legend of King Arthur," how did Arthur become King?

4. How did Arthur want the people of Britain to change their way of life?

5. When Arthur and Mordred signed the truce, a final battle broke out. What event in the legend shows that the final battle was really started by accident?

Understanding Literature

6. What magical things did Jason do in the myth of "The Golden Fleece"?

7. Which character stands for evil deeds in this myth?

8. In "The Legend of King Arthur," what was the importance of the Round Table in Arthur's court?

9. Arthur said, ". . . we must teach people to live by right, not by might." What did he mean?

10. Merlin said, "Just remember one thing all of you. You will all die someday. But the story of the Round Table will be told forever." How was this a warning to King Arthur and the knights?

WRITING

A Speech. Many people become very nervous when they have to speak in front of a group. One way to make public speaking less scary is to plan ahead.

Step 1. Set Your Goal

a. Imagine you are Jason in "The Golden Fleece." You have returned home to claim your throne. You will make a speech to your people explaining who you are and why you are the rightful king and telling them what they can expect from your government.

b. You are Sir Bedivere in "The Legend of King Arthur." You are traveling throughout England telling people about Camelot, the Round Table, and the peace you brought to Britain.

Think about who your audience is. How much do your listeners know about the subject of your speech?

Step 2: Make a Plan

Most speeches have three parts: the introduction, body and conclusion. Begin by planning the body. Make a list of all the points you can think of that should be covered. Then organize your ideas in a logical way. If King Arthur were writing the speech in which he first explained the Round Table and the new order to the knights, he might have made these notes:

Round Table

round — no head or foot (all equal)

worthy — name on chair

unworthy — name removed

New Order

knights to set good example

knights to follow rules: never murder, never be traitors, never be cruel, always help the weak, always keep word

knights to fight for right and justice

Step 3: Write Your First Draft

First write a draft of the body of your speech, following the plan you made in Step 2. Then write an introduction. In the introduction you should do two things: (1) tell the audience what the subject is, and (2) capture the audience's attention. King Arthur might have written this introduction:

> I'm sure you've all noticed the new table. Well, that's not all that's new around here. Today is the beginning of a new order, and the table is at the center of it.

Finally, draft the conclusion. It should summarize your main points and give the audience something to think about. King Arthur might have concluded this way:

> From today forward all knights are to be equal. All knights are to serve the cause of right and justice. All knights are to be good examples, not only for people living today but for all those down through the centuries who will hear the story of the Round Table.

Step 4: Revise Your Speech

Set aside your speech for a few days. Then revise it. Remember, your speech will be heard by your audience, not read.

ACTIVITIES

Word Attack

1. The heroes who sailed with Jason on the *Argo* are called the *Argonauts*. The word *astronaut* also contains the word part *naut*. Use your dictionary to answer these questions:

   a. What language does *naut* come from?

   b. What does it mean?

   c. What does *nautical* mean?

   d. What is a *nautilus*?

2. Three words that appear in "The Golden Fleece" — *manhood, babyhood,* and *boyhood* — end with the suffix *-hood*. Figure out the meaning of *-hood* in these words. Then list four other words in which *-hood* has the same meaning.

Speaking and Listening. Rehearse the speech you wrote for the writing activity on page 340 and prepare to present it in class.

Researching. Did Jason live a completely happy life after he returned home and claimed his kingdom? Do library research to find out. Write a few paragraphs telling what you learned.

Creating. Write an entry on jousting for a sports encyclopedia. First do research to find out how knights of the Middle Ages jousted. Use the information you find to write your entry.

ADVENTURE AND SUSPENSE

*Imagine a new,
unusual experience. Add some
excitement, danger, and courage.
That's an* adventure. *What happens
next? That's* suspense.

Adventure and Suspense

When you read stories of adventure and suspense, you can look danger in the face — without getting hurt. You can be transported to the wilderness of Alaska or to a steamboat going down the Mississippi River — without moving from your chair. You can imagine the excitement or terror that characters feel — without actually going through their experiences.

As you read this section, you can join an Eskimo boy and his dog on a floating island of ice. They have been trapped there for three days without food. Will the boy have to kill the dog, which he loves, in order to survive? Find out by reading "Two Were Left."

Then you can listen to the tale of a man who has committed murder. What kind of man is this? Why does he keep telling you how calm and wise he is? Learn why the story is called "The Tell-Tale Heart"— and be glad it's just a story.

Next, you can experience the terror of being trapped underwater in a pond — without getting wet. After Priscilla makes several attempts to stay alive, she is sure she is going to die. After you experience her struggles, you will probably be able to appreciate the new way she views her life.

After that, join Huck Finn and two con artists in a wild adventure from Mark Twain's famous book, *The Adventures of Huckleberry Finn*. You will see how greed can turn some people into frauds. And you will see how easily other people can be cheated by these frauds.

Finally, put yourself in the place of a reporter who is out of work. To earn some money, you plan to spend the night in a museum of waxworks, surrounded by wax figures of well-known murderers. Then you will write about the experience and sell the story to a newspaper. But when you find yourself alone in the museum's Murderers' Den, you become very uneasy. Are your eyes playing tricks on you? Or is one of those "wax" murderers really alive? Enjoy reading "The Waxwork" — from the safety of your chair.

Two Were Left

by Hugh B. Cave

The Eskimo boy and his dog were alone on an island of ice.
Would one of them have to die so the other could live?

On the third night of hunger, Noni thought of the dog. Nothing lived on the floating ice island but those two.

When the ice broke up, Noni had lost his sled, his food, his furs, even his knife. He had saved only Nimuk, his great devoted husky. And now the two, marooned on the ice, watched each other cautiously. Each one kept his distance.

Noni's love for Nimuk was real, very real. It was as real as hunger and cold nights. It was as real as the pain of his injured leg in its homemade brace.

But the men of his village killed their dogs when they needed food, didn't they? And without thinking twice about it.

And Nimuk, he told himself, would soon be looking for food. "One of us will soon be eating the other," Noni thought.

He could not kill the dog with his bare hands. Nimuk was powerful, and less tired than he. A weapon, then, was necessary.

Noni took off his mittens. He unstrapped the brace from his leg. He had made the brace from bits of harness and two thin strips of iron.

Noni pushed one of the iron strips into a crack in the ice. He began to rub the other against it with slow strokes.

Nimuk watched him. The dog's eyes glowed brightly. Noni worked on, trying not to remember why.

The slab of iron had an edge now. It had begun to take shape. By daylight, Noni had finished the knife.

Noni pulled the knife from the ice. The sun's glare reflected from the knife. It blinded him for a moment. Noni forced himself to call the husky.

"Here, Nimuk!" he called softly.

The dog watched him suspiciously.

"Come here," Noni called.

Nimuk came closer. Noni saw fear in the animal's eyes. He saw hunger and suffering in the dog's heavy breathing and dragging movements.

His heart wept. He hated himself and fought against it.

Nimuk came closer. Now Noni felt a thickening in his throat. He saw the dog's eyes. Nimuk was suffering.

Now! Now was the time to strike!

A great sob shook Noni's body. He cursed the knife. He swayed blindly. He threw the knife far away from him. He stumbled toward the dog and fell.

The dog growled as he circled the boy's body. And now Noni was sick with fear.

In throwing away the knife, he had left himself defenseless. He was too weak to

crawl after it now. He was at Nimuk's mercy, and Nimuk was hungry.

The dog had circled him. Nimuk was creeping up from behind. Noni heard the rattle of saliva in the savage throat.

He shut his eyes, praying that the attack might be quick. He felt the dog's feet against his leg. He felt Nimuk's hot breath against his neck. A scream gathered in the boy's throat.

Then he felt the dog's hot tongue licking his face. Noni's eyes opened. He couldn't believe it. Crying softly, he pulled the dog's head down against his own. . . .

The plane came out of the south an hour later. Its pilot was a young man from the coast patrol. He looked down and saw the large floating island. And he saw something flashing.

It was the sun gleaming on something shiny, which moved. The pilot was curious. He flew lower, circling the island. Now he saw a dark, still shape that looked human. Or were there two shapes?

He set his plane down on the water and investigated. There were two shapes, boy and dog. The boy was unconscious but alive. The dog whined but was too weak to move.

The shining object was a homemade knife, stuck point first into the ice, and quivering in the wind.

READING COMPREHENSION

Summarizing. Choose the best phrase to complete each sentence. Then write the complete statements on your paper.

1. Noni and Nimuk were helpless because they _____ (had lost their way in a storm, were injured, were stranded on a floating ice island without food).

2. When he had the chance, Noni did not kill Nimuk because he _____ (was blinded by the sun's glare, was afraid of the dog, loved him too much).

3. The knife _____ (hurt both the boy and the dog, hurt only the dog, helped save the boy and the dog).

Interpreting. Write the answer to each question on your paper.

1. Why didn't Noni have any food with him?

2. Why did Noni decide he must kill Nimuk? Give three reasons.

3. How did the pilot happen to spot the boy and the dog? Would he have seen them otherwise?

For Thinking and Discussing. If Noni had killed Nimuk, what do you think would have happened later? How did the boy and the dog help each other?

UNDERSTANDING LITERATURE

Theme. A character often learns something from an experience or event in a story. In "Two Were Left," thinking about what Noni learned can help you discover the theme. Answer these questions about what he learned.

1. What had Noni already learned about the men of his village?

2. What did Noni learn when he saw Nimuk's eyes?

3. What did he learn about his dog after he threw the knife away?

4. From this experience, what did Noni learn about himself?

5. How did Noni's kindness help save his life?

WRITING

Imagine that a month has passed since Noni and Nimuk were rescued. If someone asked Noni what he had learned from his experience, what do you think he would say?

Write three paragraphs. In the first, tell what Noni *thought* was going to happen. In the second paragraph, tell what really *did* happen. In the third paragraph, tell what Noni's experience might have *meant* to him.

The Tell-Tale Heart

by Edgar Allan Poe

A mind can imagine a reason for murder. But when the murder is done . . . what else will that mind imagine?

It is true that I am nervous. Very nervous. But I don't think that means that I am crazy. Listen. See how calmly I can tell you the whole story.

I can't say how the idea first entered my brain. But once there, it haunted me day and night. There wasn't any reason for it. I liked the old man. He never did anything to me. I had no desire for his money.

I think it was his eye! Yes, it was that! One of his eyes looked like the eye of a vulture. It was a pale blue eye, with a film over it. Whenever it looked at me, my blood ran cold. Slowly, very slowly, I made up my mind to take the life of the old man. I would rid myself of that eye forever.

I was never kinder to the old man than during the week before I killed him. I made my move slowly and carefully. Every night at midnight, I opened his door. I opened it very gently. When I had made an opening large enough for my head, I put in a dark lantern. The lantern was closed so that no light showed. Then I pushed my head into the room. It took me an hour to place my whole head so that I could see the man lying on his bed. Ha! Would a madman have been so wise as this? Then, when my head was well in the room, I opened the lantern carefully. I opened it just enough for a single ray of light to fall upon the vulture eye.

This I did for seven long nights — every night just at midnight. But the eye was always closed. This made it impossible for me to do what I had to do. It was not the old man who bothered me. It was his Evil Eye.

I boldly went into his room every morning and asked him if he had slept well. So you see, he would have been very clever to suspect that every night, just at 12:00, I looked in on him as he slept.

On the eighth night, I was more careful than usual in opening the door. Never before had I felt how smart I was. I felt the power that I had. To think that I was opening the door and he was not even dreaming of my secret thoughts. I laughed to myself at the idea.

Perhaps he heard me. He moved suddenly. Now you may think I drew back. No. His room was dark as pitch, so I knew he could not see the opening of the door. I pushed it slowly.

I had my head in and was about to open the lantern. My thumb slipped on the tin fastening. The old man sat up in bed. "Who's there?" he cried out.

I kept quite still. I did not move an inch. Finally I heard a slight groan. I knew it was a groan of terror — terror in the face of death. It was not a groan of pain or grief. Oh, no. It was the low, choking sound that comes from the bottom of the soul. I knew the sound well. Many a night, when all the world slept, it had come from my own being.

I knew the terror the old man felt. I pitied him, although I laughed inside. I knew he had been lying awake ever since

the first slight noise. His fears had grown ever since. He tried to tell himself, "It is nothing but the wind in the chimney.... It is only a mouse crossing the floor.... It is just a cricket."

Yes, he was trying to comfort himself. But death was approaching with its black shadow before him. It was the shadow that caused the old man to feel my presence in the room.

I waited a long time. Then I opened the lantern a very, very little bit. I opened it carefully — until a single ray shot out and fell upon the vulture eye.

It was wide open! I grew angry as I looked at it. I could see it perfectly. That dull blue with an ugly film over it. It chilled my bones.

Then I heard it — a low, dull, quick sound. It was like the sound a watch makes when wrapped in cotton. It was the beating of the old man's heart. It made my anger grow.

But even then I kept still. I hardly breathed at all. I kept the ray of light shining upon the eye. The beat of the heart grew quicker and quicker, and louder and louder.

I told you already that I am nervous. I am. In the dead hour of the night, in the awful silence of that old house, that noise terrified me. But, for some minutes longer, I stood still.

The beating grew louder, louder! Then a new fear seized me. The sound might be heard by a neighbor! The old man's hour had come!

With a loud yell, I threw open the lantern and leaped into the room. He screamed once — only once. I dragged him to the floor and pulled the heavy bed over him.

Then I smiled. The deed was almost done. For many minutes the heart beat on with a muffled sound. This, though, did not bother me. It would not be heard through the wall.

Finally it stopped. The old man was dead. I removed the bed and looked at the body. Yes, he was stone dead. I put my hand on his heart and held it there many minutes. No heartbeat. His eye would trouble me no more.

If you think I am crazy, you will think so no longer when I tell you the wise way in which I hid the body. I worked quickly but silently. I took up three planks from the floor and put the body in the space below. Then I replaced the planks

so well that no human eye — not even his — could have found anything wrong. There was no blood to wash out. A tub had caught it all. Ha ha!

Soon after I'd finished, someone knocked at the door. I went to open it with a light heart. What had I to fear?

Three policemen came in. A neighbor had heard a scream and had gone to the police station.

I smiled and invited them in. The scream, I said, was my own. I had been dreaming. I told them that the old man was away in the country. I took them all over the house and told them to search — search *well*.

Finally I took them into his room. I asked them to sit down. I placed my own chair upon the very spot that covered his body.

The policemen were satisfied. My manner had shown them that I was very much at ease. We talked about all sorts of things.

Before long, though, I felt myself getting pale. I wanted them to leave. My head hurt and I imagined a pounding in my ears. Still they sat and talked. The pounding in my ears became louder. I talked faster to get rid of it, but it kept getting louder. Finally, I found that the noise was not within my ears.

I became very pale. I kept talking more quickly and in a louder voice. Yet the sound got louder, too. What could I do? *It was a low, dull, quick sound — like the sound a watch makes when it is wrapped in cotton.*

I gasped for breath. Yet the police officers did not seem to hear the sound.

I talked more quickly. The noise got louder. What could I do? I raved. I swore. I swung the chair on which I had been sitting and scraped it over the planks. Still the noise grew louder — *louder*!

The men kept talking and smiling. Was it possible that they did not hear? No. They heard. They *knew*! They were making fun of my terror.

Anything was better than this. I could no longer stand their smiles. I felt that I must scream — or die. The noise was louder — louder — *louder*!

"Enough!" I screamed. "I admit the deed! Tear up the planks! Here, here! It is the beating of his hideous heart!"

READING COMPREHENSION

Summarizing. Choose the best phrase and write the complete sentence on your paper.

1. The narrator of this story is _____ (insane, wise, brave).

2. The narrator was very kind to the old man the week before he killed him because he _____ (felt sorry for him, was actually a nice man, didn't want the old man to suspect anything terrible was going to happen).

3. For seven nights in a row, he could not kill the old man because _____ (he lost his nerve, his conscience hurt him,

the man's eye was closed).

4. The police may not have thought the narrator was guilty at first because he _____ (let them search all over, placed his chair over the place where the body was hidden, was known to be kind and wise).

5. What the narrator really heard at the end of the story was _____(a watch tickling, the heartbeat of the old man, the sound of his own nervous heart or guilty mind).

Interpreting. Write the answer to each question on your paper.

1. Why did the narrator want to kill the old man?

2. Why does the narrator keep telling the reader how calm and wise he is?

3. Why did the narrator finally admit his crime to the police?

4. Did the narrator really hear the beating of the old man's heart at the end?

For Thinking and Discussing. Discuss the following questions as thoughtfully as you can.

1. Why do you think the narrator invited the police to stay after they had searched the house? Why do you think he placed his own chair over the hidden body? Why did he confess to the murder?

2. Some criminals return to the scenes of their crimes. Why do you think they would.

UNDERSTANDING LITERATURE

Theme. In "The Tell-Tale Heart," thinking about the title can help you understand the theme. Ask yourself, "What did Edgar Allan Poe want to show about a person's conscience?" Then answer the questions below.

1. When did the narrator first hear the old man's heart? How did this make him feel?

2. When the police came, the narrator heard the heart beating again. How does the title of the story explain what happened next? What does *tell-tale* mean in the title?

3. Could the young man really have been hearing his *own* heart? What could his heart have been saying?

4. What does Edgar Allan Poe show about the narrator's reaction to his own crime?

5. Can you think of a connection between the title "The Tell-Tale Heart" and the feeling of suspense in the story?

WRITING

Imagine that you are the old man. You have seen the young man acting very strangely. You suspect that something terrible might happen. What could you do? Who could help you? Write what you could have done. Would you decide to help yourself? Or would you try to help the young man? How?

House Fear

by Robert Frost

Always — I tell you this they learned —
Always at night when they returned
To the lonely house from far away
To the lamps unlighted and fire gone
    gray,
They learned to rattle the lock and key
To give whatever might chance to be
Warning and time to be off in flight;
And preferring the out- to the in-door
    night,
They learned to leave the house-door
    wide
Until they had lit the lamp inside.

1. In this poem, Robert Frost tells you about what some people learned. What did the people in this poem do when they came home to a lonely house?

2. What did the people think needed warning "to be off in flight"? Did they fear something in the house, or did they fear the emptiness of the house?

3. The people did not close the door until they had lit the lamp. How is the feeling in a dark room different from the feeling in a room with a light on?

4. What words in the poem create an *eerie* feeling?

Priscilla in the Pond

by John Savage

Priscilla was trapped. She felt the icy grip of death.
Was there a way to escape?

Priscilla was always ready for anything. She did very well in love and business. This was because she knew that nothing could last forever. She felt strong and lucky. She knew that nothing could surprise her completely. She felt like this until the day she fell into the pond.

She fell off a long bridge near the restaurant. If it had been June or July, someone would have been there. With the year nearly over, the restaurant was empty. The pond was covered with ice. So were the boards of the bridge. That was why she slipped.

It was really silly. Her hip hit the weak railing of the bridge. The railing broke, and she fell through. She fell several feet. Then her shoulder and the side of her head hit the ice.

She was almost knocked out, but she began to try to swim. Her fur coat was clumsy, but it helped her to float. Before she knew it, she had risen to the ice. Sadly, the hole she had made in the ice was somewhere else. There wasn't any air.

She was afraid for a second or two. Then she got control of herself. She was a good swimmer. The pond wasn't Lake Superior. All she had to do was find the hole in the ice and get out.

Her coat was bunched under her arms. Her head ached. There was a loud roaring in her ears. Maybe the roaring was from hitting the ice. Maybe it was from holding her breath too long. She would have to be quick.

She took off her shoes and let them go. She pulled off her coat and pushed it away. Then she realized that her eyes had been shut tight since she fell in.

She opened them. Blue light was coming from above. She raised both hands and

356

pushed against the ice. This forced her lower into the water. The ice *did* look thin. She knew skaters didn't trust it. If only she could get her feet on something solid! Then maybe she could break out.

She pointed her feet downward, feeling for the bottom. She only felt more water. She swam a few yards and tried again. Still no bottom. Her best chance was to search for the hole she fell into. She couldn't do much without air.

She kept her eyes open and turned slowly in a circle. She hoped the water near the hole would be brighter. Instead, she saw something dark. Was it part of the bridge? If it was, it was a good direction to try.

She swam toward the dark thing. As

she did so, it began to seem the only hope she had. Then she saw what it was. Stupid fur coat! It looked like a walrus or an angel of death, watching her. It wasn't fair.

The roaring in her ears grew louder. Her chest muscles jerked, trying to breathe. There wasn't much more time.

Beyond the coat was more darkness. This time it must be the bridge. She swam toward it. Now she couldn't stop the terrible pains in her chest.

Soon she saw a post straight ahead. It was brownish-green. She ran her hand up the post, expecting the ice to stop her. Instead, her hand touched something like packed snow. She forced her fingers up into the slush. They went right through, into the air above.

She clawed a larger hole, using both hands. It was very narrow. The sun's heat had warmed the post, but not enough. The space between the hard ice and the wood was too narrow. Her body would not fit through. If it was too narrow for her head too, she would die.

She grabbed the post and forced her head up beside it. One cheek scraped on the ice. The other cheek scraped on the wood. A moment later, her face was above water. The hole in the ice held her head tightly. She was free to escape, but only downward.

Priscilla shouted for help. She did it again and again. No one came.

She pushed her shoulders against the ice around the post. She could not break it. She held tight to the post. She pushed her head as high as it would go and looked

out. She was facing the restaurant. There was no sign of a break in the ice beside the bridge.

She gritted her teeth and lowered herself into the water. She turned her head. Then she came up, facing the other way. This time she saw something. It was the part of the railing she fell through, 20 yards away.

She took three big breaths, and held the last one. Then she lowered her head and let go of the post. She pushed off toward the bridge. She would use the bridge as a guide. Then she would have no trouble finding the hole in the ice.

She turned out to be wrong about that. Following the line of the bridge was easy enough. But it was impossible to guess how far she had swum. A few seconds passed.

Priscilla was very confused. Ten yards to go? Five? She swam a little farther. She stopped to search the underside of the ice. She turned in a small circle, then a large one. All she could see was the shadow of the bridge. Its direction seemed to keep changing.

She wasn't going to find the hole. The truth came to her very slowly. As soon as she was sure, she swam to the nearest post. She touched it, and pushed her hand upward. This time, the ice wasn't so soft. Hard ice came within two inches of the wood. She wasn't going to be able to get her head through.

Slowly, she lowered her hand. Now she was going to die.

But the idea of dying was more scary than she had thought. She had planned to be strong during her final moments. But to be strong, she must be able to breathe. Her locked throat was almost too tired to keep the water out. She saw how she would spend the last minutes of her life. She would be jerking like a fish on the bank of a river. She could not stand it.

Her mind grew clear. Somehow she must find a way to live. She must earn her way to a better death.

Priscilla held her breath and pushed away from the post. She swam along the bridge shadow. The bridge was long, but it had to lead to shallow water. She kept going.

She swam for longer than she thought she could stay alive. She kept going until the bottom of the pond was within a few feet of the ice. Then she stopped. She planted her feet in the mud. With her

back, she pushed upward against the ice.

At first, the ice held. It only creaked a bit, like a heavy gate. Then it gave way with a crash. She stood up, throwing off big slabs of ice. It was like being born.

Priscilla stumbled to the shore. She sat down against a tree. Then she began to feel very cold. She stood up and started for home. It would be terrible to freeze to death now, right at the beginning.

READING COMPREHENSION

Summarizing. Choose the best phrase and write the complete sentence on your paper.

1. Priscilla's ability to survive depended on _____ (using her fur coat to help her stay afloat, finding a way to get air, yelling loudly enough for help).

2. Each time she became afraid, she would _____ (call for help, give up, gain control of herself).

3. Priscilla wanted to _____ (live forever, have someone with her when she died, be strong and calm in the face of death).

4. Right after she escaped from the pond, Priscilla was concerned about _____ (freezing to death, the condition of her clothes, her job).

Interpreting. Write the answer to each question on your paper.

1. What caused Priscilla's fall into the pond?

2. When Priscilla thought she was going to die, she saw how she would spend the last minutes of her life. How did she picture herself, and why couldn't she stand it?

3. At that point, she felt she "must earn her way to a better death." What did she mean?

4. When Priscilla finally reached shallow water and broke through the ice, why was it "like being born"?

For Thinking and Discussing.

1. Will Priscilla's experience change her view of life? Her behavior? Explain.

2. Have you ever been in a very dangerous situation? What happened? When people are in danger, are they able to find more strength or courage than they thought they had?

UNDERSTANDING LITERATURE

Theme. In "Priscilla in the Pond," Priscilla had to solve many problems. But she had a strong will to live and a great belief in her ability to take care of herself. Priscilla never gave up, even though her situation seemed hopeless.

1. Here are some problems that Priscilla had to face. Explain how she solved each problem.
   a. "The railing broke, and she fell through. . . . All she had to do was find the hole in the ice and get out."
   b. "Soon she saw a post straight ahead. . . . The sun's heat had warmed the post, but not enough. The space between the hard ice and the wood was too narrow."
   c. "Priscilla stumbled to the shore. She sat down against a tree. Then she began to feel very cold."

2. How many times did Priscilla try to find her way out of the pond?

3. "Priscilla in the Pond" is an exciting story. Do you think the author also wanted to show something about human nature? In your own words, write the important idea, or message, of the story.

WRITING

Imagine that a newspaper reporter wanted to interview Priscilla. Write five questions the reporter might ask. Then write an answer Priscilla might give for each question.

The Dead Man and His Gold

From The Adventures of Huckleberry Finn *by Mark Twain*

Mark Twain was the name Samuel Clemens used when he became a writer. He was born in 1835 and grew up in Missouri at the time when steamboats and big lumber rafts traveled the Mississippi River. In his twenties he became a steamboat pilot on the Mississippi. But he longed for travel and adventure. Many of the exciting books and stories he wrote were based on his own experiences.

Mark Twain is best known for his humorous adventures, especially The Adventures of Tom Sawyer *and* The Adventures of Huckleberry Finn. *These, along with other works made him one of America's most famous authors.*

The Adventures of Huckleberry Finn *takes place in the 1840's. Slavery was still legal then in some parts of the U.S. Huck Finn lives in a small town in Missouri, near the Mississippi River. Early in the story, Huck runs away. He paddles a canoe to a nearby island. He hides there until it's safe to travel down the river.*

On the island, he meets Jim, who is also running away. Jim, a slave, wants to live where slavery is not allowed. Huck and Jim travel along the river on a large raft that they find. At one of their stops, they let two men come aboard. The men pretend to be a duke and a king. Huck and Jim know they are really con artists who trick people out of their money. But they play along with them to avoid trouble.

Huck and Jim visit towns along the river. When they do this, Jim has to stay on the raft. That's because people in the area are on the lookout for a runaway slave. What happens when the "duke" and the "king" join the boys? That story follows.

When it got towards night, we tied the raft to a tree near a village. The king and the duke figured we were safe. We'd traveled a full day from Bricksville, where they had cheated the people out of their money.

They judged it wouldn't be safe to try the same trick here. The news might have worked its way down the river faster than we did.

So they worked their brains for a while, but they couldn't come up with a plan. Finally, the king said he'd go into the village anyway. He'd just trust in Providence — meaning the devil, I reckon.

We had bought store clothes at our last stop. The king put on his new suit, and he got me to put mine on.

In his store clothes, that liar looked about as honest as anybody. He wanted me to paddle him back up the river in our canoe. There was a steamboat taking on freight back there.

"We'll get on that steamboat," the king says. "We'll come back here on it. Then we'll tell the villagers we came down from St. Louis."

So I started paddling the king up the river. Soon we saw a country boy carrying some baggage on the shore. The king told me to paddle over to him, which I did.

"Where are you bound for, young man?" the king calls out.

"The steamboat," the boy answers. "I'm going to New Orleans."

"Get aboard," says the king.

"My servant will help you with those bags." Then he says to me, "Adolphus, jump out and help the gentleman."

I did, and we all three started on again. The country boy was mighty thankful for the ride.

"At first," he says, "I thought you were Reverend Harvey Wilks, getting here too late."

"No," the king says, "I'm Reverend Alexander Blodgett. I hope Mr. Wilks didn't miss anything by being late."

"He didn't miss any property," the feller says. "That's still there. But he missed seeing his brother Peter die last night. Peter would have given anything to see Harvey before he died. He talked about his brothers Harvey and William all the time. William's the deaf and dumb brother."

"Did anybody send word to the brothers?" the king asks.

"They sent word a month or two ago. That's when Peter Wilks first took sick."

The King Hatches a Plan

He went on, giving the king more and more details. The king kept asking questions, pretending to be friendly. Little by little, he got the whole story. Here's what he learned:

Peter Wilks had taken care of his three nieces. They were the daughters of a brother who had died. When Peter got sick, he wanted to see his other two brothers, who lived in England.

Before they could get here, Peter died. He had left a letter for them, though. It would tell them where his money was hidden. It would also tell how the property should be divided up for the three girls.

The country boy described Peter's nieces

and friends. He said Harvey would know them because Peter had written to him about them.

The king pretended to be sad about Peter's death. But he was really memorizing every detail.

When we got to the steamboat, the country boy went aboard. We didn't, though. Instead, the king went ashore.

Then he tells me, "Go back and get the duke and our new baggage."

Well, I saw what he was up to. When I got back with the duke, the king told him the whole story. While he told it, he tried to sound like an Englishman. He did it pretty well, too, for a liar.

"That's the whole story," the king says. "How are you on the deaf and dumb?"

"Don't worry," the duke says. "I've played deaf and dumb."

We waited for the next steamboat, and went aboard. Steamboats usually don't

stop at small villages. But we got this one to let us off at Peter Wilks's village.

A group of men appeared. The king says to them, "Can you gentlemen tell me where Peter Wilks lives?"

One of them says, "I'm sorry, sir. The best we can do is tell you where he did live. He died last night."

Then the king, the old fraud, started crying. "Our poor brother!" he cries. "He's gone, and we never got to see him!"

Then he turned and made a lot of strange signs with his hands. The duke watched the signs and busted out crying himself.

The men gathered around and said all sorts of kind things to them. Those two acted as if they'd die of sorrow. It was enough to make a body ashamed of the human race.

More Tears and Hogwash

The news was all over town in two minutes. Pretty soon, we were in the middle of a crowd marching to Peter Wilks's house.

When we got there, the three girls were standing at the door. I recognized Mary Jane, Susan, and Joanna from the way the country boy had described them.

Mary Jane was the oldest and very beautiful. Her eyes were all lit up at the sight of her uncles.

The girls led the king and the duke to Peter's coffin. Everybody got quiet, so you could have heard a pin drop. Then those two rascals busted out crying again. Every-

body else started in crying, too. That place got mighty damp.

Then the king made a speech about how he'd miss his dear, dead brother. He named his brother's closest friends, then invited them to dinner. He told them his brother had written to him about them. That's how he knew their names.

Mary Jane fetched the letter that Peter had left behind. The king read it out loud and cried some more.

It said the house and $3,000 would go

"If anybody up there suspects us now, they won't after this!"

When we got upstairs, everybody gathered around the table. The king counted the money — all $6,000 of it.

Then he says, "My poor, dead brother was generous to these three girls. He would have done more if he hadn't feared hurting William and me. I think I know what my brother here would like to do about that."

He turned to the duke and made some signs with his hands. The duke pretended to understand the signs, and he hugged the king.

Then the king says, "Mary Jane, Susan, and Joanna, take this money. It's a gift from him that died yesterday."

The girls hugged the king and the duke. The brothers crowded around with tears in their eyes.

"You dear, good souls," somebody says.

The Doctor Warns the Girls

Then I noticed a big man I hadn't noticed before. He stood listening and looking, not saying anything. When he started laughing, the other people looked shocked.

One man says to him, "Dr. Robinson, what are you laughing at? Ain't you heard the news? This is Harvey Wilks."

The king smiled and held out his hand to Dr. Robinson. "Is this my poor brother's good friend and doctor?" he says.

"Keep your hands off me!" the doctor says. "You don't sound like an Englishman. It's the worst imitation I've ever heard. You're a fraud!"

to Harvey and William. Then it told where the $6,000 of gold was hidden in the cellar.

The king and the duke went down to the cellar. They had me lead the way with a candle. When they found the bag of gold, they poured the coins on the floor. My, did their eyes shine!

Then the duke says, "I've got an idea. Let's go upstairs and give this money to the girls."

"That's a clever idea," the king says.

Well, the others were shocked by that. They all tried to quiet the doctor down. But it wasn't any use.

The doctor tells the girls, "I'm your friend. I warn you that these two liars are not your uncles. Mary Jane, turn these rascals out. I beg you to do it!"

Mary Jane says, "Here's my answer to you." Then she gave the bag of gold to the king. "Take this $6,000, Uncle," says she. "Invest it for us any way you want."

"All right," says the doctor. "I tried. But someday you'll feel sick whenever you think of this moment."

The king says, "When that happens, we'll be sure to send for you."

That made the others laugh. The doctor left the house.

I Get Trapped Telling Lies

That evening after supper, Joanna got to asking me about England.

"Did you ever see the king?" she says.

"Of course I have. He goes to our church."

"I thought he lived in London."

"He does."

"But you live in Sheffield."

I saw that I was in trouble. So I let on that I was choking on a chicken bone, while I thought up an answer.

Then I says, "I meant he goes to our church when he's in Sheffield. He comes there for the sea baths."

"How you talk," she says. "Sheffield isn't on the sea."

"Who said it was?"

"You did."

"I never did. I said he comes to take the sea baths."

"Well," says she, "how can he take sea baths if it isn't on the sea?"

"Looky here," I says. "Did you ever see Congress water?"*

"Sure," she says.

"Did you have to go to Congress to get it?"

"Why, no."

"Well, neither does the king have to go to the sea to get a sea bath. He wants his sea baths hot. So sea water is sent to the palace in Sheffield, where it's heated. He gets the water the way we get Congress water — in barrels."

Well, she kept asking me questions, and I kept thinking up answers. Finally, she

---

* Congress water was mineral water from Congress Springs in Saratoga, New York.

says, "Honest, now, haven't you been telling me a lot of lies?"

Just then Mary Jane came in. "Joanna," she says, "it isn't right for you to say that to him. How would you like to be talked to like that? You shouldn't say anything that will make a person feel ashamed."

I says to myself, "What a girl this is! I can't let those two old reptiles rob her of her money!"

Then Susan came in and heard what was going on. She made Joanna apologize. Joanna did it right away.

They made me feel so low down and mean. I says to myself, "I'll steal that money back for them or bust!"

I Steal the King's Loot

I told the girls I was going to bed — but I meant some time or another. I couldn't tell anybody about those two thieves without getting myself in trouble. I had to steal that money in a way that nobody would suspect me.

I figured it would be in the king's room. I started to search his room — when I heard footsteps. So I hid in the closet.

The king and the duke came in.

The duke says, "That doctor bothers me. I think we should take the money and get out of here."

"What?" the king says. "We still have the property to sell. It's worth about $9,000."

"Well," the duke says, "I don't see why we have to rob the orphans of everything."

"We're only robbing them of this money," the king says. "The people that buy the property are the ones that will

suffer. When it comes out we didn't own it, the sale won't be any good. The property will go back to the girls."

The king talked him blind. Finally, the duke agreed to stay on.

They decided that the money wasn't safe where it was now hidden. So they hid it in another place in the room. Now I knew where it was.

Before they were down the stairs, I had that bag of gold in my hands. Then I went up to my room and stayed in bed until I couldn't hear any sounds.

I carried the money downstairs. I still didn't know where to hide it for the girls to find. It had to look as if I didn't have anything to do with it.

I went around looking for a hiding spot. I came into the room where Peter's body was. The coffin was open over his head, but closed over the rest of him.

Suddenly, I heard footsteps. I had to get rid of the gold. The only place I could see to hide it was in the coffin. So I slid the bag under the coffin lid, onto Peter's chest. Then I hid behind the door.

Mary Jane came in and kneeled down by the coffin. I didn't dare tell her about the king's plan. It would be better if she found the money after we left.

I slipped out of the room and up to bed, feeling blue. If the money could stay where it is, I thought, all right. After we get down the river 100 miles, I could write to Mary Jane and tell her about it.

But suppose the money is found when the coffin is closed up. Then the king will get it again. After that, nobody will be able to steal it from him again.

I Up and Tell the Truth

Well, they had the funeral, and they buried Peter. I couldn't tell from the king's face if he had gotten the money back. That put me in a fix. Now I didn't know if I should write to Mary Jane.

The next morning, I saw her crying. "Miss Mary Jane," I says, "tell me about it."

She said she'd thought she'd be happy going to England after the property was sold. But now the trip was spoiled for her. Her uncles had just sold one of Peter's slaves to a buyer down the river. Then they sold the slave's children to another buyer up the river.

"Oh, dear" she cries. "The mother and her children aren't going to see each other anymore!"

"But they will!" I says. "I know that!"

This slipped out before I could think. Of course, Mary Jane wanted to know how I could be sure. Then I had a decision to make. The truth seemed strange, but there it was.

"All right," I says, "brace up, Miss Mary Jane. I've got to tell you the truth. Those two uncles of yours aren't uncles, after all. They're a couple of frauds."

I Leave a Message for Mary Jane

When I told her the whole story, it jolted her. She jumped up with her face burning like sunset.

"The brutes!" she says. "Let's not waste a second. We'll have them tarred and feathered and thrown in the river!"

"Wait," I says. I was thinking about Jim, back there on the raft. More than anything else, I had to get back and help him get away.

"I have to stay with those frauds awhile longer," I says. "If you told on them now, I might be safe. But there's another person you don't know about. He'd be in big trouble."

I knew I could get away with him if we rode the raft at night. So I asked Mary Jane to wait till it got dark. She agreed.

"Wait in your room till 11:00," I says. "If I don't show up by then, it means I'm gone and safe. Then you can get those rascals jailed."

"Good," she says. "I'll do it."

"If I get away, I won't be here to prove those frauds aren't your uncles. But you just tell the judge to send word to Bricksville. Let the people there know you've got the men who cheated them. That will bring witnesses to tell who those frauds really are."

Then I told her to let them sell the property. The sales would not hold up — once the truth got out.

Finally, I says, "There's one more thing — the gold."

"They've got that," she says. "And it makes me feel pretty silly to think how they got it."

"You're wrong there," I says. "They ain't got it. I mean I think they ain't got it."

I told her about swiping the bag and hiding it for her. I said I was sorry for not hiding it in a good place.

"Where did you hide it?" she asks.

I couldn't tell her. I didn't want her thinking again about the coffin and her dead uncle. Besides, I didn't know if the gold was still in the coffin.

"I'd rather not tell you where I put it," I says. "But I'll write it on a piece of paper. You can read it after I leave."

I gave her the paper and got ready to leave. I could see the water coming into her eyes. That made my eyes water a little, too.

"Good-bye," she says. "I'll do just what you told me. If I don't ever see you again, I won't ever forget you. I'll think of you a lot. I'll pray for you, too." Then she was gone.

Pray for me! I reckoned if she knew me, she'd take on a job nearer her size. But I'll bet she did it anyway. She had the grit to pray for a devil if she set her mind to it.

A Second Pair of Uncles

They held the auction in the public square.

The two frauds sold off everything that old Peter owned.

Right after that, a steamboat landed. Then up comes a crowd whooping and yelling and laughing.

"Now Peter Wilks has two sets of brothers!" somebody yells.

The crowd was leading a nice-looking old gentleman and a younger one. The younger one had his right arm in a sling.

The old man began to speak, and I could tell he was an Englishman. He didn't say words the king's way at all. I can't give you the old gent's words. But he says something like this:

"This is a surprise to me. I am Harvey Wilks, and this is my brother William. He can't hear nor speak. Because of his broken arm, he can't make signs, either. We are Peter Wilks's brothers. I will be able to prove it when our baggage arrives. It was taken off the boat by mistake at a town last night."

"A broken arm?" the king yells. "That would be very convenient for a fraud who doesn't know how to make signs. Lost baggage? That would be very convenient, I'd say."

Then the king laughed, and most of the crowd laughed with him. One person who didn't laugh was Dr. Robinson.

"Neighbors," the doctor says, "I don't know if these two new men are frauds. But if the first two aren't frauds, then I'm an idiot. I say they should let us keep the gold till they prove who they are."

Everybody agreed with that.

The king says, "I would like to do as the doctor suggests. But, I'm sorry to say, I don't have that money. I hid it in my room, but a household servant must have taken it." Then, pointing at me, he says, "My servant here can tell you about it."

Nobody really believed what he said. One man asked me if I had seen a servant steal the money. I said no, but I saw one sneaking out of the room early one morning. I said I reckoned he was just trying not to wake up my master.

Then the doctor says to me, "Are you English, too?"

When I said I was, everybody laughed.

I began to tell them about Sheffield in England but I didn't get very far before the doctor began to laugh.

"I wouldn't strain myself if I were you," he says. "I reckon you aren't used to lying. What you need is practice."

I didn't care for the compliment. But I was glad to be let off anyway.

A Trip to the Graveyard

Then the old gentleman who had just arrived says, "I've thought of something. Is there anybody who helped to prepare Peter Wilks for burying?"

"I did," a voice answers. "My name's Ab Turner."

The old gentleman turned to the king. "Perhaps," he says, "you can tell us what was tattooed on Peter's chest."

"Now," I says to myself, "the rascal will give up and throw in the sponge. There's no use trying to fake his way out of this one."

Well, a body can hardly believe it, but he didn't throw in the sponge. I reckon he meant to keep it up till they all got tired of asking questions. Then he and the duke could break loose and get away.

"I'll tell you what's tattooed on his chest," the king says. "It's a small, thin, blue arrow. If you don't look closely, you can't see it."

The old gentleman turned to Ab Turner. "Did you see any such mark on Peter's chest?" he asks.

"I did not," Ab answers.

"There!" the old gentleman says. "What you saw were his initials — P.B.W."

"No, I didn't," Ab says. "I didn't see any marks at all."

Well, that put everybody in a state of mind.

"They're all frauds!" somebody yells. "Let's drown them!"

But the lawyer yells, "Listen to me! There's still a way to check! Let's go and dig up Peter and look!"

"We'll do it!" somebody shouts. "And if we don't find those marks, we'll lynch the whole gang!"

I was scared now, I tell you. But there was no getting away. They grabbed us and marched us to the graveyard, carrying on like wildcats.

To make it more scary, the sky was darkening. Lightning was beginning to wink and flitter. The wind shivered among the leaves.

This was the most awful trouble I'd ever been in. But a big man had me by the wrist, and I couldn't run.

When we got to the graveyard, they found they had plenty of shovels. But nobody had thought to fetch a lantern. So they started digging by the flicker of the lightning.

They dug and dug. It got awful dark, and the rain started. The lightning came faster and faster, and the thunder boomed.

One second you could see the crowd and the dirt piling up around the grave. The next second you couldn't see a thing.

At last they got out the coffin and took off the lid. People crowded around to get a look. In the dark that way, it was an awful sight. Then the lightning suddenly lit up the place.

Somebody sings out, "By jingo! Here's the bag of gold on his chest!"

I Light Out in the Storm

Everybody let out a whoop, including the man who was holding my wrist. He forgot me and let go. I lit out and ran for the road in the dark.

I had the road all to myself, and I fairly flew. It was just me and the lightning and the rain and the thunder. As sure as you're born, I did clip along!

As I sailed by Mary Jane's house, I saw her in a window. She was waiting, just as I told her. She wouldn't tell on those frauds till she knew I was safe and away.

My heart swelled up, almost ready to bust. In a second, the house was behind me. I wasn't ever going to see that girl again in this world. She was the best girl I've ever seen, and she had the most grit.

At last I reached the raft and jumped aboard. "Jim," I calls. "Set her loose! Glory be to goodness, we're rid of those two!"

After all this time, Jim was so glad to see me. Of course, he wanted to hear about what had happened.

"Not now," I says. "We'll talk later. Cut loose and let her slide."

So in two seconds, away we went, sliding down the river. It was good to be free again, all by ourselves on the river, with nobody to bother us. I had to jump up and crack my heels together a few times. I couldn't help it. I was that happy about being back with Jim and being on the river.

READING COMPREHENSION

Summarizing. Choose the best phrase and write the complete sentence on your paper.

1. Huck and Jim let the con artists travel with them because they _____ (were amused by the two men, needed some money, were afraid they would report Jim as a runaway slave in order to collect a reward).

2. The king and the duke, pretending to be Peter Wilks's brothers, gave the bag of gold to the girls, because they _____ (pitied the girls, didn't want anyone

to suspect their con game, felt guilty keeping the money).

3. Mary Jane asked the king to invest the gold for her to prove she _____ (trusted him, liked him, needed the help of a wise investor).

4. Huck took the gold because he wanted to _____ (keep it, play a joke on the con artists, help Mary Jane).

5. Huck escaped after the real brothers arrived and _____ (proved their identity, the con artists were tarred and feathered, the gold was found).

Interpreting. Write the answer to each question on your paper.

1. How did the king learn about Peter Wilks's nieces and the money left for his two brothers?

2. Why didn't Dr. Robinson believe that the king and the duke were Peter Wilks's brothers?

3. The duke thought that he and the king should slip away with the bag of gold before they got caught. Why did the king persuade him to stay on?

4. Why did the Wilks's neighbors dig up Peter Wilks's coffin?

5. Why didn't Huck want Mary Jane to tell on the con artists before he could get back to the raft?

For Thinking and Discussing. Huck told Mary Jane the truth because he trusted her. But Mary Jane felt she could trust the king and the duke. Is there a way to know whether or not you can trust someone?

UNDERSTANDING LITERATURE

Theme. You have learned many ways to discover the theme, or the most important idea, of a story. The title, plot, characters, setting, and mood may all be important to understanding the author's message. Sometimes, two or three ideas are connected to make up the theme This is true in "The Dead Man and His Gold." Answer the questions below. They will help you discover the important ideas in the story.

1. In "The Dead Man and His Gold," what does Mark Twain show about trusting others?

2. What does he show about protecting someone you care about? Was Jim right to trust Huck?

3. What do you think Mark Twain wanted to show about human nature?

4. In some parts of the story, there is a mood of humor, a feeling of, "Oh, no! What next?" Why do you think humor is important in the story?

5. Which events in the story could happen today? Which events could *not* happen today? Why?

WRITING

Think of a theme for a story of your own. It can be anything you like. For example: crime does not pay; or, the love of people who are close to you is the most important thing of all. Write your theme at the top of your paper. Then tell what the story would be about.

The Waxwork

by A.M. Burrage

A reporter is spending the night in a wax museum's "Murderers' Den" so that he can write about the experience. Is it his imagination, or is one of the "wax figures" actually alive?

While the guards of Marriner's Museum of Waxworks were ushering the last stragglers through the glass-paneled double doors, the manager sat in his office interviewing Raymond Hewson.

The manager was a youngish man, stout, blond, and of medium height. He wore his clothes well and contrived to look extremely smart without appearing overdressed. Raymond Hewson looked the opposite. His clothes, which had been good when new and which were still carefully pressed, were beginning to show signs of their owner's losing battle with the world. He was a small, spare, pale man, with brown hair, and he had the defensive air of a man who was used to being turned down. He was a man who had talent, but was a failure because he did not assert himself.

The manager was speaking. "There is nothing new about your request," he said. "In fact we turn people down about three times a week. We have nothing to gain and something to lose by letting people spend the night in our Murderers' Den. If I allowed it, and some young idiot lost his senses, I'd lose my job. But the fact that

you're a reporter somewhat changes the case."

Hewson smiled. "I suppose you mean that reporters have no senses to lose."

"No, no," laughed the manager, "but one imagines them to be responsible people. Besides, here we have something to gain: publicity and advertisement."

"Exactly," said Hewson, "and there I thought we might come to terms."

"What paper do you work for, Mr. Hewson?"

"I am working on my own at present," Hewson confessed, "submitting articles to several papers. However, I will have no trouble getting the story printed. The *Morning Echo* would use it like a shot. 'A Night with Marriner's Murderers.' No paper could turn it down."

The manager rubbed his chin. "And how do you propose to treat it?"

"I shall make it gruesome, of course; gruesome with a saving touch of humor."

The other nodded. "Very well, Mr. Hewson. Get your story printed in the *Morning Echo,* and there will be a 50-pound note waiting for you here when you care to come and call for it. But first,

I'd like to be quite sure about you. I confess I wouldn't care to do what you're proposing. Those wax figures don't bother me while the museum is open, but I would hate to have to sleep down there alone with them."

"Why?" asked Hewson.

"I don't know. I don't believe in ghosts. If I did, I would expect them to haunt the scene of their crimes, not a cellar which happens to contain their figures in wax. It's just that I couldn't sit alone among them all night, with their eyes seeming to stare at me in the way they do. After all, they represent the lowest types of humanity. The whole atmosphere of the place is unpleasant. If atmosphere affects you, you will have a very uncomfortable night."

Hewson had known that from the moment the idea first occurred to him. He felt sick, even while he smiled at the manager. But he had a wife and family to support. Here was a chance to earn the price of a special story in the *Morning Echo*, plus 50 pounds from the museum. That would keep him going for two weeks. Besides, if he wrote the story well, it might lead to a full-time job.

"The way of newspaper men is hard," Hewson said. "I expect to have an uncomfortable night, for the Murderers' Den is not a hotel room. But I don't think your waxworks will worry me much."

"You're not superstitious?"

"Not a bit." Hewson laughed.

"But you're a writer. You must have a strong imagination."

"The news editors I've worked for have always complained that I haven't any. Readers of newspapers, you see, want more than just plain facts."

The manager smiled. "Right," he said. "I think the last of the visitors have gone. I'll let the night watchmen know that you'll be here. Then I'll take you down and show you around."

He made a brief phone call. Then he remarked, "I must ask you not to smoke while you're here. We had a fire scare down in the Murderers' Den today. It turned out to be a false alarm. Still, we must be careful. And now, if you're ready, we'll go downstairs."

Hewson followed the manager through half a dozen rooms, past the wax figures of kings and queens, generals and statesmen and other famous people. The manager stopped once and spoke to a man in uniform, saying something about an armchair in the Murderers' Den.

"It's the best we can do for you, I'm afraid," he said to Hewson. "I hope you'll be able to get some sleep."

He led the way down some dark stairs. Beyond a dark passage was the Murderers' Den.

It was a room of irregular shape and high ceiling. It was dimly lit on purpose. The waxwork murderers stood on low pedestals with numbered tickets at their feet. Recent murderers stood next to old "favorites." The manager pointed out a few of them to Hewson.

"That's Crippen; I expect you recognize him. He looks as if he couldn't bear to step on a worm. That's Armstrong. He looks like a harmless gentleman, doesn't he? And there's —"

"Who's that?" Hewson interrupted in a whisper, pointing.

"Oh, I was coming to him," said the manager. "This is our star. He's the only one of the bunch that hasn't been hanged."

The figure was of a small man wearing a cape. Hewson did not know why the face seemed so horrible to him. He had to force himself to look at it.

"But who is he?" he asked.

"That," said the manager, "is Dr. Bourdette."

"I think I've heard the name," Hewson said, "but I can't remember what he did."

"You'd remember if you were a Frenchman," the manager said. "For some time that man was the terror of Paris. He was a doctor who healed people by day, and cut throats by night. He killed for the sheer devilish pleasure it gave him to kill, and always in the same way — with a razor. After his last crime he left a clue behind which set the police on his track. One clue led to another, and before long they had enough evidence to have him hanged — or sent to the madhouse.

"But even then our friend here was too clever for them. When he realized that they were closing in on him, he disappeared. Ever since, police all over the world have been looking for him. It is believed that he killed himself, but he did it in such a way that his body was never found. One or two crimes that look like his work have taken place since his disappearance, but experts believe they were the work of an imitator."

Hewson shuddered. "I don't like him at all," he confessed. "What eyes he's got!"

"Yes, this figure is a masterpiece. Do you find the eyes biting into you? Bourdette used to hypnotize his victims with his eyes before cutting their throats. There were never any signs of a struggle."

"I thought I saw him move," said Hewson, with a catch in his voice.

The manager smiled. "Your eyes will

play a number of tricks on you before the night is over, I expect. You won't be locked in. You can go upstairs when you've had enough of it. There are watchmen around, so you'll find company. Don't be alarmed if you hear them moving about. I'm sorry I can't give you any more light, because all the lights are on. And now it's time for me to leave. One of the watchmen will bring a chair down here for you to use. I wish you well, Mr. Hewson."

The night watchman who brought down an armchair for Hewson was amused.

"Where shall I put it, sir?" he asked, grinning. "Would you like it here, so you can have a little talk with Crippen? Or there's old Mother Dyer over there, looking as if she would like a bit of company. Say where, sir."

Hewson smiled. The man's joking pleased him because it made everything seem normal.

"I'll place it myself, thanks," he said.

"Well, good night, sir. I'll be upstairs. Don't let them sneak up behind you and touch your neck with their cold and clammy hands."

Hewson laughed and wished the man good night. He turned the armchair around so its back was toward the figure of Dr. Bourdette. For some reason he did not like this waxwork.

The rows of figures in the dim light looked so human that the silence seemed unreal. He missed the sound of breathing and the rustling of clothes. Here nothing moved, and all was silent.

"It must be like this at the bottom of the sea," he thought. Then he decided to work that idea into his story for the newspaper.

He faced the figures boldly. They were only waxworks. Still, he felt uncomfortable. He knew that Dr. Bourdette was staring at the back of his head. The eyes of the little doctor haunted him, and he felt he must turn and look.

"No," he thought. "If I turn and look, I will be admitting my fear."

Then another voice in his brain spoke to him. "It's because you're afraid that you won't turn and look at him."

The two voices argued silently for a moment or two. Then Hewson turned and looked behind him.

The figure of the dreadful little doctor stood out from all the others. Perhaps this was because a beam of light fell straight down upon it. Hewson looked into the eyes for one painful second, and turned again to face the other direction.

"He's only a waxwork like the rest of you," Hewson muttered.

They were only waxworks, yes, but waxworks don't move. He hadn't seen them actually move, but he felt there had been a slight change in their positions when his back was turned. Hewson held his breath for a moment, and then drew his courage back to him. He remembered the words of his editors, and he laughed bitterly.

"And they tell me I've got no imagination!" he said beneath his breath.

He took a notebook from his pocket and wrote: "It's like being at the bottom of the sea. Dr. Bourdette's eyes are hyp-

notic. The figures seem to move when not being watched."

He closed the notebook and looked around quickly over his right shoulder. He hadn't *seen* anything move, but he was sure something *had*. He stared straight into the face of one of the figures, and it looked back as if to say, "I wasn't the one who moved."

Of course it wasn't he, or any of them. It was his own nerves. Or was it? Hadn't Crippen moved just now when he wasn't looking? You couldn't trust that man! Once you took your eyes off him, he shifted his position. That was what they were all doing. He started to get up from the chair. He wasn't going to spend the night with a lot of waxworks which moved while he wasn't looking.

Hewson sat down again. This was silly. They were only waxworks and they couldn't move. Then why was he sure that something was happening — just out of his sight?

He swung around quickly to meet the stare of Dr. Bourdette. Then he jerked back his head to stare at Crippen. Ha! He had almost caught Crippen that time!

"You'd better be careful, Crippen— and all the rest of you! If I see one of you move, I'll smash you to pieces! Do you hear?"

He told himself he ought to leave. Already he had experienced enough to write his story, or ten stories. The *Morning Echo* would not care how long he stayed here, as long as his story was good.

Yes, but that night watchman upstairs would laugh at him. And the manager might not give him the 50-pound note which he needed so badly. He wondered if his wife were asleep. She would laugh when he told her what he had imagined.

Wait! Somebody was breathing. Or was it the sound of his own breath? He sat still and held his breath. Finally he let it out with a sign. It was his own breathing he had heard, after all. Or was somebody breathing only when *he* breathed?

He must stop this! He must get his mind on something normal. He was Raymond Hewson, an unsuccessful newspaper writer. These figures around him were only made of wax and sawdust. That was better! Now, what was that funny story he had heard at lunch yesterday?

He recalled part of it, but not all, for the gaze of Dr. Bourdette challenged him to turn around.

Now Hewson was staring into those dreadful hypnotic eyes. His own eyes were open wide and his mouth was twisted in a snarl.

"You moved!" he cried. "Yes, you did! I saw you!"

Then he sat quite still, staring straight ahead, like a man found frozen in the snow.

Dr. Bourdette moved slowly. He stepped off his pedestal. Then he stepped

off the platform and sat down on the edge, facing Hewson. He nodded and said, "Good evening."

He continued to speak in perfect English. "I did not know that I would have the pleasure of your company tonight until I heard you speaking with the manager of this museum. You cannot move or speak unless I tell you to, but you can hear me perfectly well. Please do not be nervous. I am not a waxwork that has come to life. I am Dr. Bourdette himself."

He paused and stretched his legs. Then he went on.

"Pardon me. I am a little stiff. Let me explain. For certain reasons I must live in England. I was close to this building this afternoon when I saw a policeman staring at me. I thought he might ask me some questions, so I mingled with the crowd and came in here. When I entered this room, I had a wonderful idea.

"I cried out, 'Fire!' Then when all the fools had rushed upstairs, I took the cape off the waxwork of myself. I put it around my shoulders and hid the waxwork under the platform at the back. Then I took its place on the pedestal.

"I have spent a very tiring evening there. But when I was not being watched, I could breathe. One small boy screamed and said he saw me moving. I heard his parents say he would be punished when he got home.

"The manager's description of me was not entirely correct. I am not dead, although it is just as well that the world thinks I am. And the manager did not describe my hobby very well. You see, the world is filled with collectors. They collect anything, from money to stamps, from moths to matchboxes. I collect throats."

He paused and looked at Hewson's throat. Then he went on.

"I am thankful for the good fortune that brought us together tonight, and I should not complain. But you have a skinny neck, sir. I like thick necks."

From an inside pocket, he took out a small razor.

"This is a little French razor," he remarked. "The blade is very narrow. It does not cut very deeply, but deeply enough. In just one moment, you will see for yourself. I shall ask you the question that all polite barbers ask: Does the razor suit you, sir?"

He stood up and walked over to Hewson.

"Please raise your chin a little. Thank you. Just a little more. Ah, thank you!"

After sunrise, a few weak rays of sun entered a window of the room. These rays mixed with the dim light of the electric bulbs. This mixture of light added to the horror of an already horrible scene.

The waxwork figures stood in their places. In their midst, Hewson sat still, leaning far back in the armchair. His chin was tilted up, as if he were waiting for a barber to shave him. There was not a scratch on his throat — nor anywhere else on his body. But he was cold and dead. The editors he used to work for were wrong in thinking he had no imagination.

Dr. Bourdette was on his pedestal. He did not move, nor was he able to move. After all, he was only a waxwork.

READING COMPREHENSION

Summarizing. Choose the best phrase and write the complete sentence on your paper.

1. Raymond Hewson spent a night in the museum because he _____ (was fearless, had a family to support, wanted to test his courage).

2. Dr. Bourdette used to hypnotize people before he _____ (cured them, strangled them, cut their throats).

3. The doctor seemed to come to life and asked Hewson to _____ (stand up, turn around, raise his chin).

4. The next day, Hewson was found dead — _____ (with a gun in his hand, his throat cut, without a scratch on him).

5. You can conclude that Hewson died _____ (by his own hand, at the hand of Dr. Bourdette, of fright).

Interpreting. Write the answer to each question on your paper.

1. Which part of Dr. Bourdette's face frightened Hewson the most?

2. Why did Hewson think he couldn't move unless Bourdette told him to?

3. Were Hewson's editors right in saying that he had no imagination?

For Thinking and Discussing. When a person is frightened, what may happen physically to him or her? Could a person be frightened to death?

UNDERSTANDING LITERATURE

Theme. The characters, setting, mood, plot, and title of a story may all help you understand the theme, or most important idea. Ask yourself what the author of "The Waxwork" wanted to show about a person's imagination. Then answer the following questions.

1. What did Raymond Hewson's editors think of his imagination?

2. Why do you suppose Hewson didn't let them know they were wrong? Was he the sort of man who speaks up?

3. The manager of the museum seemed self-confident, but he admitted he wouldn't want to spend a night in the Murderer's Den. How did he describe the atmosphere of it to Hewson?

4. In the Murderer's Den, what effects did the dim light and silence have upon Hewson?

5. What actual facts did Hewson's imagination work into his imagined encounter with Dr. Bourdette?

6. What is the connection between the title "The Waxwork" and Hewson's imagination?

WRITING

Imagine that you are the manager of the museum. The police want to question you about Hewson, whose body has just been found. How would you describe to the police Hewson's character and motive for spending the night in the museum?

Section Review

VOCABULARY

Expressions. The statements that follow are taken from "The Dead Man and His Gold." In your own words, write the meaning of each expression written in italics.

1. "But they *play along with* them to avoid trouble."

2. "So they *worked their brains* for a while, but they couldn't come up with a plan."

3. "It was *enough to make a body ashamed* of the human race."

4. " 'Mary Jane, *turn these rascals out.*' "

5. "They made me feel so *low down* and mean."

6. " 'I'll steal that money back for them or *bust!*' "

7. "The king *talked him blind.*"

8. "That *put me in a fix.*"

9. "I reckon if she knew me, she'd *take on a job nearer her size.*"

10. " 'Now,' I say to myself, 'the rascal will give up and *throw in the sponge.*' "

11. " '*Cut loose and let her slide.*' "

12. "As sure as you're born, I did *clip along!*"

READING

Inference/Critical Reading. Sometimes it is important to ask yourself questions as you read. When an author presents facts in a story, are the facts correct? Do the events take place long ago, or in the present? In the stories you have read, the characters often draw conclusions. Are the characters thinking clearly? Do their conclusions make sense?

Read each paragraph below and ask yourself questions like these as you read. Then write the answers to the questions that follow on your paper.

> And Nimuk, he told himself, would soon be looking for food. "One of us will soon be eating the other," Noni thought.

1. In "Two Were Left," what facts led Noni to the conclusion that he or his dog would die? Did his conclusion make sense? Why or why not?

> I knew the terror the old man felt. I pitied him, although I laughed inside. I knew he had been lying awake ever since the first slight noise. His fears had grown ever since. He tried to tell himself, "It is nothing but the wind in the chimney. . . . It is only a mouse crossing the floor. . . . It is just a cricket."

2. In "The Tell-Tale Heart," did the narrator know how the old man felt? Was he a good judge of other people's feelings? Could you trust what the narrator told you in the story?

> She clawed a larger hole, using both hands. It was very narrow. . . .Her body would not fit through. If it was too narrow for her head, too, she would die.

3. If Priscilla could not get her head above the ice, do you think she would

die? Was she thinking clearly? Does her conclusion make sense?

In his store clothes, that liar looked about as honest as anybody. He wanted me to paddle him back up the river in our canoe. There was a steamboat taking on freight back there.

4. In "The Dead Man and His Gold," when do the events take place? How can you tell? What facts about this time in history could be important to understanding the story?

"Keep your hands off me!" the doctor says. "You don't sound like an Englishman. It's the worst imitation I've ever heard. You're a fraud!"

5. In "The Dead Man and His Gold," the doctor does not believe that the king and the duke are Peter Wilks's brothers. What led the doctor to this conclusion? What might he have known that the other townspeople didn't know?

Hadn't Crippen moved just now when he wasn't looking? You couldn't trust that man! Once you took your eyes off him, he shifted his position. That was what they were all doing. He started to get up from the chair. He wasn't going to spend the night with a lot of waxworks which moved while he wasn't looking.

6. In "The Waxwork," were the waxworks moving when Raymond Hewson wasn't looking? Was Hewson a calm person? Was he looking forward to spending the night in the Murderer's Den? Was the atmosphere of the place good for clear thinking? Was Hewson imaginative?

WRITING

Answers on Essay Test. When you write an answer on an essay test, your task seems straightforward enough. But there are common traps that people fall into, and there are techniques that let you avoid the traps. These techniques help you organize a clear and convincing essay.

Step 1: Set Your Goal

People often do not read the question carefully. Then they answer the wrong question. The first rule is to read carefully, looking for *key words* that tell you the kind of answer needed.

Read these essay test questions.

a. <u>Summarize</u> the plot of "Priscilla in the Pond."

b. <u>Compare</u> the characters Noni and Nimuk in "Two Were Left."

c. <u>Explain</u> why the narrator alone hears the heart in "The Tell-Tale Heart."

d. <u>Discuss</u> the importance of greed in "The Dead Man and His Gold."

Each of the underlined key words signals that a different kind of answer is called for.

When you *summarize*, you write a shortened version of the main events.

When you *compare*, you look for similarities and differences.

You *explain* by writing why or how, backing it up with details and examples.

When you *discuss*, you tell your

thoughts about the topic, giving facts, reasons, and examples.

Choose one of the essay test questions on page 387 to write an essay on.

Step 2: Make a Plan
Once you know the kind of essay needed, organize your answer. On your paper, jot down the points you want to cover.

Next, make a rough outline of your answer by narrowing your list to about five major points and putting them in a sensible order.

This is a rough outline of your answer. The opening sentence of the essay is very important. It should include important words from the question and the first point you wish to make. For example, an essay on "The Waxwork" might begin, "In 'The Waxwork,' Hewson is cursed with an imagination that is, at the same time, not very good *and* far too good."

Remember that when you are writing an answer to an essay question, you may not have time to revise your first draft in a major way. That is why it is so important to do Steps 1 and 2 carefully.

Step 3: Write your First Draft
Using your rough outline, expand on each point you wish to make. Think ahead, and stay with the organization you have decided on.

Step 4: Revise Your Essay
Reread your answer critically. Is the opening sentence clear? Have you made the points you want to make? Are they clear

and logical? Is your answer convincing?

When you are satisfied with the content of your answer, proofread it carefully for mistakes in spelling, grammar, and punctuation.

QUIZ

The following is a quiz for Section 10. Write the answers in complete sentences on your paper.

Reading Comprehension

1. How were Noni and Nimuk saved in "Two Were Left"?

2. At the end of "The Tell-Tale Heart," what did the narrator think he heard? What do you think he heard?

3. In "Priscilla in the Pond," how did Priscilla "earn her way to a better death"?

4. In "The Dead Man and His Gold," what did the king and the duke plan to steal besides the gold?

5. In "The Waxwork," how did Raymond Hewson die?

Understanding Literature

6. In "Two Were Left," what did Noni learn?

7. How is the title a key, or a clue, to the theme of "The Tell-Tale Heart"?

8. In "Priscilla in the Pond," what does the author show about courage and facing danger?

9. In "The Dead Man and His Gold," is it important that the events seem true to life? Is this important in "Priscilla in the Pond"? Give reasons to support your opinion.

10. In "The Waxwork," what does the author show about the human imagination?

ACTIVITIES

Word Attack

1. Below are some words from this section. Each word contains a suffix. Write each suffix on your paper. Then use all the words (including suffixes) in a paragraph about a camper who gets lost in the woods.

   nervous   providence

   defensive   superstitious

   description   straggler

2. These two words from "The Waxwork" have something in common: *unpleasant* and *irregular*. They both begin with prefixes that mean *not*. Think of at least three other prefixes that mean *not*. Then think of at least one word that has each prefix.

Speaking and Listening. "The Tell-Tale Heart" is written as though the mad killer were telling his story to someone. Practice reading the story out loud as though you were the mad killer and you were speaking the words for the first time as they came to you. Pretend you are speaking directly to one other person. Be prepared to read part of the story aloud in class. Try to stay in character when you do.

Researching. Go to the library and read about Eskimos. Write two paragraphs telling what kind of food Noni in "Two Were Left" probably ate and what kind of clothing he probably wore.

Creating

1. Look at some of the biographies in this book. Think about the facts they contain. Then use reference books in the library to write a one-page biography of either Robert Frost or Mark Twain.

2. A floor plan is a diagram of a room or building as seen from above. Draw a floor plan of the old man's bedroom in "The Tell-Tale Heart." Show where the door and the bed are and where the body is buried. Also show the other furniture in the room.

THE NOVEL

*A novel is a book-length
story. Its plot is usually richer and its
characters more fully developed than
they are in a short story.*

Introduction

The final section of this book is a novel. A novel, like a short story, is a piece of fiction. But a novel is longer than a short story. An author can use the length of a novel to do things that would be very difficult or impossible to do in a short story.

Characterization

A short story, for example, usually takes place within a fairly short amount of time — a day, a month, or a year. A novel, though, can take place over a long period of time.

A short story can focus on more than one character, but usually not more than two characters. And even then, usually only one character is portrayed in much detail. A novel, on the other hand, can present a large cast of characters. And while it may feature only one main character, other characters often play improtant roles.

In a short story, the main character may change in some way. Suppose the character adopts a new belief about human nature. This new belief may make a big difference in the character's life. But it must come about fairly suddenly. And there is seldom enough space in a short story to let the character test this new belief.

The main character of a novel may also adopt a new belief about human nature. But adopting the belief usually comes in stages. The character may have some doubts at first. Or the character may act upon this new belief — and fail for some reason. But, later, the character may try again — and succeed this time. Then the belief becomes stronger than ever.

Setting

The setting of a short story can be important to its message. It can make a difference, for instance, whether a story takes place in a city or on a farm. It can matter whether the action takes place in 1800 or the year 2000.

Setting is usually more important in a novel than in a short story. In some short stories, the setting does not matter at all. But in most novels, the reader is told where and when the action takes place. This information is usually necessary for the reader to appreciate the challenges facing the characters.

Theme

A short story and a novel can have the same theme. That is, an author can deliver the same message to readers in both forms of fiction. But it is easier for an author to repeat a theme — or to offer several versions of a theme — in a novel than in a short story. This is because there is more space in a novel.

Why would an author repeat a theme, or offer several versions of a theme? It is a way of making sure that the theme gets across to the reader. It allows the reader to appreciate the theme *while* the plot is unfolding and the characters are being developed.

Old Yeller

The novel you are about to read is *Old Yeller*. The title of the book is the name of a dog, and the young narrator of the book tells you right away how the dog got his name:

> We called him Old Yeller. The name had a sort of double meaning. One part meant that his short hair was a dingy yellow, a color that we called "yeller" in those days. The other meant that when he opened his throat, the sound he let out came closer to being a yell than a bark.

Now, even though the title of the novel is the name of a dog, the novel is not just the story of a dog. It is the story of the narrator, a 14-year-old boy named Travis who is suddenly expected to be the "man" of his family.

To learn what that means, you will want to find out who the members of Travis' family are and what they are like. You will want to learn what role Old Yeller plays in Travis's life. And to appreciate what Travis is up against, you will want to find out where he is living — and when.

This will not be hard. The author gives you all the information you need and while parts of this novel are serious, other parts are funny. None of it is dull.

Old Yeller

by Fred Gipson

Chapter 1

We called him Old Yeller. The name had a sort of double meaning. One part meant that his short hair was a dingy yellow, a color that we called "yeller" in those days. The other meant that when he opened his head, the sound he let out came closer to being a yell than a bark.

I remember like yesterday how he strayed in out of nowhere to our log cabin on Birdsong Creek. He made me so mad at first that I wanted to kill him. Then later, when I had to kill him, it was like having to shoot some of my own folks. That's how much I'd come to think of the big yeller dog.

He came in the late 1860's, the best I remember. Anyhow, it was the year that Papa and a bunch of other Salt Licks settlers formed a "pool herd" of their little separate bunches of steers and trailed them to the new cattle market at Abilene, Kansas.

This was to get "cash money," a thing that all Texans were short of in those years right after the Civil War. We lived then in a new country and a good one. As Papa pointed out the day the men talked over making the drive, we had plenty of grass, wood, and water. We had wild game for the killing, fertile ground for growing bread corn, and the Indians had been put onto reservations with the return of federal soldiers to the Texas forts.

"In fact," Papa wound up, "all we lack having a tight tail-holt on the world is a little cash money. And we can get that at Abilene."

Well, the idea sounded good, but some of the men still hesitated. Abilene was better than six hundred miles north of the Texas hill country we lived in. It would take months for the men to make the drive and ride back home. And all the time the womenfolks and children of Salt Licks would be left in a wild frontier settlement to make out the best they could.

Still, they needed money, and they realized that whatever a man does, he's bound to take some risks. So they talked it over with each other and with their women and decided it was the thing to do. They told their folks what to do in case the Indians came off the reservation or the coons got to eating the corn or the bears got killing too many hogs. Then they gathered their cattle, burned a trail brand on their hips, and pulled out on the long trail to Kansas.

I remember how it was the day Papa left. I remember him standing in front of the cabin with his horse saddled, his gun in his scabbard, and his bedroll tied on back of the saddle. I remember how tall and straight and handsome he looked, with his high-crowned hat and his black mustaches drooping in cow-horn curves past the corners of his mouth. And I remember how Mama was trying to keep from crying because he was leaving and how Little Arliss, who was only five and didn't know much, wasn't trying to keep from crying at all. In fact, he was howling his head off; not because Papa was leaving, but because he couldn't go, too.

I wasn't about to cry. I was 14 years old, pretty near a grown man. I stood back and didn't let on for a minute that I wanted to cry.

Papa got through loving up Mama and Little Arliss and mounted his horse. I looked up at him. He motioned for me to come along. So I walked beside his horse down the trail that led under big live-oaks and past the spring.

When he'd gotten out of hearing of the house, Papa reached down and put a hand on my shoulder.

"Now, Travis," he said, "you're getting to be a big boy, and while I'm gone, you'll be the man of the family. I want you to act like one. You take care of Mama and Little Arliss. You look after the work and don't wait around for your mama to point out what needs to be done. Think you can do that?"

"Yessir," I said.

"Now, there's the cows to milk and wood to cut and young pigs to mark and fresh meat to shoot. But mainly there's the corn patch. If you don't work it right or if you let the varmints eat up the roasting ears, we'll be without bread corn for the

© 1957 The Walt Disney Company

winter."

"Yessir," I said.

"All right, boy. I'll be seeing you this fall."

I stood there and let him ride on. There wasn't any more to say.

Suddenly I remembered and went running down the trail after him, calling for him to wait.

He pulled his horse and twisted around in the saddle. "Yeah, boy," he said. "What is it?"

"That horse," I said.

"What horse?" he said, like he'd never heard me mention it before. "You mean you're wanting a horse?"

"Now, Papa," I complained. "You know I've been aching all over for a horse to ride. I've told you time and again."

I looked up to catch him grinning at me and felt foolish that I hadn't realized he was teasing.

"What you're needing worse than a horse is a good dog."

"Yessir," I said, "but a horse is what I'm wanting the worst."

"All right," he said. "You act a man's part while I'm gone, and I'll see that you get a man's horse to ride when I sell the cattle. I think we can shake on that deal."

He reached out his hand, and we shook. It was the first time I'd ever shaken hands like a man. It made me feel big and solemn and important in a way I'd never felt before. I knew then that I could handle whatever needed to be done while Papa was gone.

I turned and started back up the trail toward the cabin. I guessed maybe Papa was right. I guessed I could use a dog. All the other settlers had dogs. They were big fierce cur dogs that the settlers use for catching hogs and driving cattle and fighting coons out of the cornfields. They kept them as watchdogs against the depredations of loafer wolves, bears, panthers,

and raiding Indians. There was no question about it: for the sort of country we lived in, a good dog around the place was sometimes worth more than two or three men. I knew this as well as anybody, because the summer before I'd a good dog.

His name was Bell. He was nearly as old as I was. We'd had him ever since I could remember. He'd protected me from rattlesnakes and bad hogs while I was little. He'd hunted with me when I was bigger. Once he'd dragged me out of Bird-song Creek when I was about to drown, and another time he'd given warning in time to keep some raiding Comanches from stealing and eating our mule, Jumper.

Then he'd had to go act a fool and get himself killed.

It was while Papa and I were cutting wild hay in a little patch of prairie back of the house. A big diamond-back rattler struck at Papa and Papa chopped his head off with one quick lick of his scythe. The head dropped to the ground three or four feet away from the writhing body. It lay there, with the ugly mouth opening and shutting, still trying to put its fangs into something.

As smart as Bell was, you'd have thought he'd have better sense than to go up and nuzzle that rattler's head. But he didn't, and a second later, he was falling back, howling and slinging his own head till his ears popped. But it was too late then. That snake mouth had snapped shut on his nose, driving the fangs in so deep that it was a full minute before he could sling the bloody head loose.

He died that night, and I cried for a

week. Papa tried to make me feel better by promising to get me another dog right away, but I wouldn't have it. It made me mad just to think about other dog's trying to take Bell's place.

And I still felt the same about it. All I wanted now was a horse.

The trail I followed led along the bank of Birdsong Creek through some bee myrtle bushes. The bushes were blooming white and smelled sweet. In the top of one a mockingbird was singing. That made me recollect how Birdsong Creek had got its name. Mama had named it the first day she and Papa came to settle. Mama had told me about it. She said she named it the first day she and Papa got there, with Mama driving the ox cart loaded with our house plunder, and with Papa driving the cows and horses. They'd meant to build closer to the other settlers, over on Salt Branch. But they'd camped there at the spring; and the bee myrtle had been blooming white that day, and seemed like in every bush there was a mockingbird, singing his fool head off. It was all so pretty and the singing birds made such fine music that Mama wouldn't go on.

"We'll build right here," she'd told Papa.

And that's what they'd done. Built themselves a home right here on Birdsong Creek and fought off the Indians and cleared a corn patch and raised me and Little Arliss and lost a sister who died of fever.

Now it was my home, too. And while Papa was gone, it was up to me to look after it.

I came to our spring that gushed clear cold water out of a split in a rock ledge. The water poured into a pothole about the size of a wagon bed. In the pothole, up to his ears in the water, stood Little Arliss. Right in our drinking water!

I said: "*Arliss!* You get out of that water."

Arliss turned and stuck out his tongue at me.

"I'll cut me a sprout!" I warned.

All he did was stick out his tongue at me again and splash water in my direction.

I got my knife out and cut a green mesquite sprout. I trimmed all the leaves and thorns off, then headed for him.

Arliss saw then that I meant business. He came lunging up out of the pool, knocking water all over his clothes lying on the bank. He lit out for the house, running naked and screaming bloody murder. To listen to him, you'd have thought the Comanches were lifting his scalp.

Mama heard him and came rushing out of the cabin. She saw Little Arliss running naked. She saw me following him with a mesquite sprout in one hand and his clothes in the other. She called out to me.

"Travis," she said, "what on earth have you done to your little brother?"

I said, "Nothing yet. But if he doesn't keep out of our drinking water, I'm going to wear him to a frazzle!"

That's what Papa always told Little Arliss when he caught him in the pool. I figured if I had to take Papa's place, I might as well talk like him.

Mama stared at me for a minute. I thought she was fixing to argue that I was getting too big for my britches. Lots of times she'd tell me that. But this time she didn't. She just smiled suddenly and grabbed Little Arliss by one ear and held on. He went to hollering and jumping up and down and trying to pull away, but she held on till I got there with his clothes. She put them on him and told him: "Look here, young squirrel. You better listen to your big brother Travis if you want to keep out of trouble." Then she made him go sit still awhile in the dog run.

The dog run was an open roofed-over space between the two rooms of our log cabin. It was a good place to eat watermelons in the hot summer or to sleep when the night breezes weren't strong enough to push through the cracks between the cabin logs. Sometimes we hung up fresh-killed meat there to cool out.

Little Arliss sat in the dog run and sulked while I packed water from the spring. I packed the water in a bucket that Papa had made out of the hide of a cow's leg. I poured the water into the ash hopper that stood beside the cabin. That was so the water could trickle down through the wood ashes and become lye water. Later Mama would mix this lye water with hog fat and boil it in an iron pot when she wanted to make soap.

When I went to cut wood for Mama, though, Little Arliss left the dog run to come watch me work. Like always, he stood in exactly the right place for the chips from my axe to fly up and maybe knock his eyeballs out. I said, "You better skin out for that house, you little scamp!" He skinned out, too. Just like I told him. Without even sticking out his tongue at me this time.

And he sat right there till Mama called us to dinner.

After dinner, I didn't wait for Mama to tell me that I needed to finish running out the corn middles. I got right up from the table and went out and hooked Jumper to the double shovel. I started plowing where Papa had left off the day before. I figured that if I got an early start, I could finish the corn patch by sundown.

Jumper was a dun mule with a narrow black stripe running along his backbone between his mane and tail. Papa had named him Jumper because nobody yet had ever built a fence he couldn't jump over. Papa claimed Jumper could clear the moon if he took a notion to see the other side of it.

Jumper was a pretty good mule, though. He was gentle to ride: you could pack in fresh meat on him; and he was willing about pulling a plow. Only, sometimes when I plowed him and decided quitting time had come, he'd stop work right then. Maybe we'd be out in the middle of the field when Jumper got the notion that it was time to quit for dinner. Right then, he'd swing around and head for the cabin, dragging down corn with the plow and paying no mind whatever to my hauling back on the reins and hollering "Whoa!"

Late that evening, Jumper tried to pull that stunt on me again, but I was laying for him. With Papa gone, I knew I had to teach Jumper a good lesson. I'd been plowing all afternoon, holding a green cedar club between the plow handles.

I still lacked three or four corn rows being finished when sundown came and Jumper decided it was quitting time. He let out a long bray and started wringing his tail. He left the middle he was traveling in. He struck out through the young corn, headed for the cabin.

I didn't even holler "Whoa!" at him. I just threw the looped reins off my shoulder and ran up beside him. I drew back my green cedar club and whacked him so hard across the jawbone that I nearly dropped him in his tracks.

You never saw a worse surprised mule. He snorted, started to run, then just stood there and stared at me. Like maybe he couldn't believe that I was man enough to club him that hard.

I drew back my club again. "Jumper," I said, "if you don't get back there and finish this plowing job, you're going to get more of the same. You understand?"

I guess he understood, all right. Anyhow, from then on till we were through, he stayed right on the job. The only thing he did different from what he'd have done with Papa was to travel with his head turned sideways, watching me every step of the way.

When finally I got to the house, I found that Mama had done the milking and she and Little Arliss were waiting supper on me. Just like we generally waited for Papa when he came in late.

I crawled into bed with Little Arliss that night, feeling pretty satisfied with myself. Our bed was a cornshuck mattress laid over a couple of squared-up cowhides that had been laced together. The cowhides stood about two feet off the dirt floor, stretched tight inside a pole frame Papa had built in one corner of the room.

I lay there and listened to the corn shucks squeak when I breathed and to the owls hooting in the timber along Birdsong Creek. I guessed I'd made a good start. I'd done my work without having to be told. I'd taught Little Arliss and Jumper that I wasn't to be triffled with. And Mama could already see that I was man enough to wait supper on.

I guessed that I could handle things while Papa was gone just about as good as he could.

Chapter 2

It was the next morning when the big yeller dog came.

I found him at daylight when Mama told me to step out to the dog run and cut down a side of middling meat hanging to the pole rafters.

The minute I opened the door and looked up, I saw that the meat was gone. It had been tied to the rafter with bear-grass blades braided together for string. Now nothing was left hanging to the pole but the frazzled ends of the snapped blades.

I looked down then. At the same instant, a dog rose from where he'd been curled up on the ground beside the barrel that held our cornmeal. He was a big, ugly, slick-haired, yeller dog. One short ear had been chewed clear off and his tail had been bobbed so close to his rump that there was hardly stub enough left to wag. But the most noticeable thing to me about him was how thin and starved-looking he was, all but for his belly. His belly was swelled up as tight and round as a pumpkin.

It wasn't hard to tell how come that belly was so full. All I had to do was look at the piece of curled-up rind lying in the dirt beside him, with all the meat gnawed off. That side of meat had been a big one, but now there wasn't enough meat left on the rind to interest a pack rat.

Well, to lose the only meat we had left from last winter's hog butchering was bad enough. But what made me even madder was the way the dog acted. He didn't even have the manners to feel ashamed of what he'd done. He rose to his feet, stretched, yawned, then came romping toward me, wiggling that stub tail and yelling *Yow! Yow! Yow!* Just like he belonged there and I was his best friend.

"Why, you thieving rascal!" I shouted and kicked at him as hard as I could.

He ducked, just in time, so that I missed him by a hair. But nobody could have told I missed, after the way he fell over on the ground and lay there, with his belly up and his four feet in the air, squawling and bellering at the top of his voice. From the racket he made, you'd have thought I had a club and was breaking every bone in his body.

Mama came running to stick her head through the door and say, "What on earth, Travis?"

"Why, this old stray dog has come and

eaten our middling meat clear up," I said.

I aimed another kick at him. He was quick and rolled out of reach again, just in time, then fell back to the ground and lay there, yelling louder than ever.

Then out came Little Arliss. He was naked, like he always slept in the summer. He was hollering "A dog! A dog!" He ran past me and fell on the dog and petted him till he quit howling, then turned on me, fighting mad.

"You quit kicking my dog!" he yelled fiercely. "You kick my dog, and I'll wear you to a frazzle!"

The battling stick that Mama used to beat the dirt out of clothes when she washed stood leaning against the wall. Now, Little Arliss grabbed it up in both hands and came at me, swinging.

It was such a surprise move, Little Arliss making fight at me that way, that I just stood there with my mouth open and let him clout me a good one before I thought to move. Then Mama stepped in and took the stick away from him.

Arliss turned on her, ready to fight with his bare fists. Then he decided against it and ran and put his arms around the big dog's neck. He began to yell, "He's my dog. You can't kick him. He's my dog!"

The big dog was back up on his feet now, wagging his stub tail again and licking the tears off Arliss's face with his pink tongue.

Mama laughed. "Well, Travis," she said, "it looks like we've got us a dog."

"But, Mama," I said. "You don't mean we'd keep an old, ugly dog like that. One that will come in and steal meat right out of the house."

"Well, maybe we can't keep him," Mama said. "Maybe he belongs to somebody around here who'll want him back."

"He doesn't belong to anybody in the settlement," I said. "I know every dog at Salt Licks."

"Well, then," Mama said. "If he's a stray, there's no reason why Little Arliss can't claim him. And you'll have to admit he's a smart dog. Mighty few dogs have sense enough to figure out a way to reach a side of meat hanging that high. He must have climbed up on top of that meal barrel and jumped from there."

I went over and looked at the wooden lid on top of the meal barrel. Sure enough, in the thin film of dust that had settled over it were dog tracks.

"Well, all right," I admitted. "He's a smart dog. But I still don't want him."

"Now, Travis," Mama said. "You're not being fair. You had you a dog when you were little, but Arliss has never had one. He's too little for you to play with, and he gets lonely."

I didn't say any more. When Mama got her mind set a certain way, there was no use in arguing with her. But I didn't want that meat-thieving dog on the place, and I didn't aim to have him. I might have to put up with him for a day or so, but sooner or later, I'd find a way to get rid of him.

Mama must have guessed what was going on in my mind, for she kept handing me sober looks all the time she was getting breakfast.

She fed us cornmeal mush cooked in a pot swung over the fireplace. She sweetened it with wild honey that Papa and I had cut out of a bee tree last fall, and added cream skimmed off last night's milk. It was good eating; but I'd my appetite whetted for fried middling meat to go with it.

Mama waited till I was done, then said, "Now, Travis, as soon as you've milked the cows, I think you ought to get your gun and try to kill us a fat young doe for meat. And while you're gone, I want you to do some thinking on what I said about Little Arliss and this stray dog."

Chapter 3

All right, I was willing to go make a try for a fat doe. I was generally more than willing to go hunting. And while I was gone, I might do some thinking about Little Arliss and that thieving stray dog. But I didn't much think my thinking would take the turn Mama wanted.

I went and milked the cows and brought the milk in for Mama to strain. I got my rifle and went out to the lot and caught Jumper. I tied a rope around his neck, half-hitched a noose around his nose and pitched the rest of the rope across his back. This was the rope I'd rein him with. Then I got me a second rope and tied it tight around his middle, just back of his withers. This second rope I'd use to tie my deer onto Jumper's back — if I got one.

Papa had shown me how to tie a deer's

feet together and pack it home across my shoulder, and I'd done it. But to carry a deer very far like that was a sweat-popping job that I'd rather leave to Jumper. He was bigger and stronger.

I mounted Jumper bareback and rode him along Birdsong Creek and across a rocky hog-back ridge. I thought how fine it would be if I was riding my own horse instead of an old mule. I rode down a long sweeping slope where a scattering of huge, ragged-topped liveoaks stood about in grass so tall that it dragged against the underside of Jumper's belly. I rode to within a quarter of a mile of the Salt Licks, then left Jumper tied in a thicket and went on afoot.

I couldn't take Jumper close to the Licks for a couple of reasons. In the first place, he'd get to swishing his tail and stomping his feet at flies and maybe scare off my game. On top of that, he was gun shy. Fire a gun close to Jumper, and he'd fall to staves. He'd snort and wheel to run and fall back against his tie rope, trying to break loose. He'd bawl and paw the air and take on like he'd been shot. When it came to gunfire Jumper didn't have any more sense than a red ant in a hot skillet.

It was a fine morning for hunting with the air still and the rising sun shining bright on the tall green grass and the greener leaves of the timber. There wasn't enough breeze blowing for me to tell the wind direction, so I licked one finger and held it up. Sure enough, the side next to me cooled first. That meant that what little push there was to the air was away from me, toward the Salt Licks. Which wouldn't do at all. No deer would come to the Licks if he caught wind of me first.

I half circled the Licks till I had the breeze moving across them toward me and took cover under a wild grapevine that hung low out of the top of a gnarled oak. I sat down with my back against the trunk of the tree. I sat with my legs crossed and my rifle cradled on my knees. Then I made myself get as still as the tree.

Papa had taught me that, way back when I was little, the same as he'd taught me to hunt downwind from my game. He always said, "It's not your shape that catches a deer's eye. It's your moving. If a deer can't smell you and can't see you move, he won't ever know you're there."

So I sat there, holding as still as a stump, searching the clearing around the Licks.

The Licks were a scattered outcropping of dark rocks with black streaks in them. The black streaks held the salt that Papa said had got mixed up with the rocks a jillion years ago. I don't know how he knew what had happened so far back, but the salt was there, and all the hogs and cattle and wild animals in that part of the country came there to lick it.

One time, Papa said, when he and Mama had first settled there, they'd run clean out of salt and had to beat up pieces of the rock and boil them in water. Then they'd used the salty water to season their meat and cornbread.

Wild game generally came to lick the rocks in the early mornings or late evenings, and those were the best times to come for meat. The killer animals, like bear and panther and bobcats, knew this and came to the Licks at the same time.

Sometimes we'd get a shot at them. I'd killed two bobcats and a wolf there while waiting for deer; and once Papa shot a big panther right after it had leaped on a mule colt and broken its neck with one slap of its heavy forepaw.

I hoped I'd get a shot at a bear or panther this morning. The only thing that showed up, however, was a little band of javelina hogs, and I knew better than to shoot them. Make a bad shot and wound one so that he went to squealing, and you had the whole bunch after you, ready to eat you alive. They were small animals. Their tushes weren't as long as those of the range hogs we had running wild in the woods. They couldn't cut you as deep, but once javelinas got after you, they'd keep after you for a lot longer time.

Once Jed Simpson's boy Rosal shot into a bunch of javelinas and they took after him. They treed him up a mesquite and kept him there from early morning till long after suppertime. The mesquite was a small one, and they nearly chewed the trunk of it in two trying to get to him. After that Rosal was willing to let the javelinas alone.

The javelinas moved away, and I saw some bobwhite quail feed into the opening around the Licks. Then here came three cows with young calves and a roan bull. They stood and licked at the rocks. I watched them awhile, then got to watching a couple of squirrels playing in the top of a tree close to the one I sat under.

The squirrels were running and jumping and chattering and flashing their tails in the sunlight. One would run along a tree branch, then take a flying leap to the next branch. There it would sit, fussing, and wait to see if the second one had the nerve to jump that far. When the second squirrel did, the first one would set up an excited chatter and make a run for a longer leap. Sure enough, after a while, the leader tried to jump a gap that was too wide. He missed his branch, clawed at some leaves, and came tumbling to the ground. The second squirrel went to dancing up and down on his branch then, chattering louder than ever. It was plain that he was getting a big laugh out of how that show-off squirrel had made such a fool of himself.

The sight was so funny that I laughed, myself, and that's where I made my mistake.

Where the doe had come from and how she ever got so close without my seeing, I don't know. It was like she'd suddenly lit down out of the air like a buzzard or risen right up out of the bare ground around the rocks. Anyhow, there she stood, staring straight at me, sniffling and snorting and stomping her forefeet against the ground.

She couldn't have scented me, and I hadn't moved; but I had laughed out loud a little at those squirrels. And that sound had warned her.

Well, I couldn't lift my gun then, with her staring straight at me. She'd see the motion and take a scare. And while Papa was a good enough shot to down a running deer, I'd never tried it and didn't much think I could. I figured it smarter to wait. Maybe she'd quit staring at me after a while and give me a chance to lift my gun.

But I waited, and still she kept looking at me, trying to figure me out. Finally, she started coming toward me. She'd take one dancing step and then another and bob her head and flap her long ears about, then start moving toward me again.

I didn't know what to do. It made me nervous, the way she kept coming at me. Sooner or later she was bound to make out what I was. Then she'd whirl and be gone before I could draw a bead on her.

She kept doing me that way till finally my heart was flopping around inside my chest like a catfish in a wet sack. I could feel my muscles tightening up all over. I knew then that I couldn't wait any longer. It was either shoot or bust wide open, so I whipped my gun up to my shoulder.

Like I figured, she snorted and wheeled, so fast that she was just a brown blur against my gunsights. I pressed the trigger, hoping my aim was good.

After I fired, the black powder charge in my gun threw up such a thick fog of blue smoke that I couldn't see through it. I reloaded, then leaped to my feet and went running through the smoke. What I saw when I came into the clear again made my heart drop down into my shoes.

There went the frightened, snorting cattle, stampeding through the trees with their tails in the air like it was heel-fly time. And right beside them went my doe, running all humped up and with her white, pointed tail clamped tight to her rump.

Which meant that I'd hit her but hadn't made a killing shot.

I didn't like that. I never minded killing for meat. Like Papa had told me, every creature has to kill to live. But to wound an animal was something else. Especially one as pretty and harmless as a deer. It made me sick to think of the doe's escaping, maybe to hurt for days before she finally died.

I swung my gun up, hoping yet to get a killing shot. But I couldn't fire on account of the cattle. They were too close to the deer. I might kill one of them.

Then suddenly the doe did a surprising thing. Way down in the flat there, nearly out of sight, she ran head on into the trunk of a tree. Like she was stone blind. I saw the flash of her light-colored belly as she went down. I waited. She didn't get up. I tore out, running through the chin-tall grass as fast as I could.

When finally I reached the place, all out of breath, I found her lying dead, with a bullet hole through her middle, right where it had to have shattered the heart.

Suddenly I wasn't sick anymore. I felt big and strong and sure of myself. I hadn't made a bad shot. I hadn't caused an animal a lot of suffering. All I'd done was get meat for the family, shooting it on the run, just like Papa did.

I rode toward the cabin, sitting behind the gutted doe that I'd tied across Jumper's back. I rode, feeling proud of myself as a hunter and a provider for the family. Making a killing shot like that on a moving deer made me feel bigger and more important. Too big and important, I guessed, to fuss with Little Arliss about that old yeller dog. I still didn't think much of the idea of keeping him, but I guessed that when you are nearly a man, you have to learn to put up with a lot of aggravation from little bitty kids. Let Arliss keep the thieving rascal. I guessed I could provide enough meat for him, too.

That's how I was feeling when I crossed Birdsong Creek and rode up to the spring under the trees below the house. Then suddenly, I felt different. That's when I found Little Arliss in the pool again. And in there with him was the big yeller dog. That dirty, stinking rascal, romping around in our drinking water.

"Arliss!" I yelled at Little Arliss. "You get that nasty old dog out of the water!"

They hadn't seen me ride up, and I guess it was my sudden yell that surprised them both so bad. Arliss went tearing out of the pool on one side and the dog on the

other. Arliss was screaming his head off, and here came the big dog with his wet fur rising along the ridge of his backbone, baying me like I was a panther.

I didn't give him a chance to get to me. I was too quick about jumping off the mule and grabbing up some rocks.

I was lucky. The first rock I threw caught the big dog right between the eyes, and I was throwing hard. He went down, yelling and pitching and wallowing. And just as he came to his feet again, I caught him in the ribs with another one. That was too much for him. He turned tail then and took out for the house, squawling and bawling.

But I wasn't the only good rock thrower in the family. Arliss was only five years old, but I'd spent a lot of time showing him how to throw a rock. Now I wished I hadn't. Because about then, a rock nearly tore my left ear off. I whirled around just barely in time to duck another that would have caught me square in the left eye.

I yelled, "Arliss, you quit!" but Arliss wasn't listening. He was too scared and too mad. He bent over to pick up a rock big enough to brain me with if he'd been strong enough to throw it.

Well, when you're 14 years old, you can't afford to mix in a rock fight with your five-year-old brother. You can't do it, even when you're in the right. You just can't explain a thing like that to your folks. All they'll do is point out how much bigger you are, how unfair it is to your little brother.

All I could do was turn tail like the yeller dog and head for the house, yelling for Mama. And right after me came Little Arliss, naked and running as fast as he could, doing his dead-level best to get close enough to hit me with the big rock he was packing.

I outran him, of course; and then here came Mama, running so fast that her long skirts were flying, and calling out, "What on earth, boys!"

I hollered, "You better catch that Arliss!" as I ran past her. And she did; but Little Arliss was so mad that I thought for a second he was going to hit her with the rock before she could get it away from him.

Well, it all wound up about like I figured. Mama switched Little Arliss for playing in our drinking water. Then she blessed me out good and proper for being so bossy with him. And the big yeller dog that had caused all the trouble got off scot free.

It didn't seem right and fair to me. How could I be the man of the family if nobody paid any attention to what I thought or said?

I went and led Jumper up to the house. I hung the doe in the live oak tree that grew beside the house and began skinning it and cutting up the meat. I thought of the fine shot I'd made and knew it was worth bragging about to Mama. But what was the use? She wouldn't pay me any mind — not until I did something she thought I shouldn't have done. Then she'd treat me like I wasn't any older than Little Arliss.

I sulked and felt sorry for myself all the time I worked with the meat. The more I thought about it, the madder I got at the big yeller dog.

I hung the fresh cuts of venison up in the dog run, right where Old Yeller had stolen the hog meat the night he came. I did it for a couple of reasons. To begin with, that was the handiest and coolest place we had for hanging fresh meat. On top of that, I was looking for a good excuse to get rid of that dog. I figured if he stole more of our meat, Mama would see that he was too sorry to keep.

But Old Yeller was too smart for that. He gnawed around on some of the deer's leg bones that Mama threw away; but not once did he ever even act like he could smell the meat we'd hung up.

Chapter 4

A couple of days later, I had another and better reason for wanting to get rid of Old Yeller. That was when the two longhorn range bulls met at the house and pulled off their big fight.

We first heard the bulls while we were eating our dinner of cornbread, roasted venison, and green watercress gathered from below the spring. One bull came from off a high rocky ridge to the south of the cabin. We could hear his angry rumbling as he moved down through the thickets of catclaw and scrub oak.

Then he lifted his voice in a wild brassy blare that sent echoes clamoring in the draws and canyons for miles around.

"That old bull's talking fight," I told Mama and Little Arliss. "He's bragging that he's the biggest and toughest and meanest. He's telling all the other bulls that if they've got a lick of sense, they'll take to cover when he's around."

Almost before I'd finished talking, we heard the second bull. He was over about the Salt Licks somewhere. His bellering was just as loud and braggy as the first one's. He was telling the first bull that his fight talk was all bluff. He was saying that *he* was the bull of the range, that *he* was the biggest and toughest.

We sat and ate and listened to them. We could tell by their rumblings and bawlings that they were gradually working their way down through the brush toward each other and getting madder by the minute.

I always liked to see a fight between bulls or bears or wild boars or almost any wild animals. Now, I got so excited that I jumped up from the table and went to the door and stood listening. I'd made up my mind that if the bulls met and started a fight, I was going to see it. There were still plenty of careless weeds and crabgrass that needed hoeing out of the corn, but I guessed I could let them go long enough to see a bullfight.

Our cabin stood on a high knoll about a hundred yards above the spring. Years ago, Papa had cleared out all the brush and trees from around it, leaving a couple

of live-oaks near the house for shade. That was so he could get a clear shot at any Comanches or desperadoes coming to raid us. And while I stood there at the door, the first bull entered the clearing.

He was a leggy, mustard-colored bull with black freckles speckling his jaws and the underside of his belly. He had one great horn set for hooking, while the other hung down past his jaw like a tallow candle that had drooped in the heat. He was what the Mexicans called a *chongo* or "droop horn."

He trotted out a little piece into the clearing, then stopped to drop his head low. He went to snorting and shaking his horns and pawing up the dry dirt with his forefeet. He flung the dirt back over his neck and shoulders in great clouds of dust.

I couldn't see the other bull yet, but I could tell by the sound of him that he was close and coming in a trot. I hollered back to Mama and Little Arliss.

"They're fixing to fight right here, where we can all see it."

There was a split-rail fence around our cabin. I ran out and climbed up and took a seat on the top rail. Mama and Little Arliss came and climbed up to sit beside me.

Then, from the other side of the clearing came the second bull. He was the red roan I'd seen at the Salt Licks the day I shot the doe. He wasn't as tall and long-legged as the *chongo* bull, but every bit as heavy and powerful. And while his horns were shorter, they were both curved right for hooking.

Like the first bull, he came blaring out into the clearing, then stopped, to snort and sling his wicked horns and paw up clouds of dust. He made it plain that he wanted to fight just as bad as the first bull.

About that time, from somewhere behind the cabin, came Old Yeller. He charged through the rails, bristled up and was roaring almost as loud as the bulls. All their bellering and snorting and dust pawing sounded like a threat to him. He'd come out to run them away from the house.

I hollered at him. "Get back there, you rascal," I shouted. "You're fixing to spoil our show."

That stopped him, but he still wasn't satisfied. He kept baying the bulls till I jumped down and picked up a rock. I didn't have to throw it. That sent him flying back into the yard and around the corner of the cabin, yelling like I'd murdered him.

That also put Little Arliss on the fight.

He started screaming at me. He tried to get down where he could pick up a rock.

But Mama held him. "Hush, now, baby," she said. "Travis isn't going to hurt your dog. He just doesn't want him to scare off the bulls."

Well, it took some talking, but she finally got Little Arliss's mind off hitting me with a rock. I climbed back up on the fence. I told Mama that I was betting on Chongo. She said she was betting her money on Roany because he had two fighting horns. We sat there and watched the bulls get ready to fight and talked and laughed and had ourselves a real good

time. We never once thought about being in any danger.

When we learned different, it was nearly too late.

Suddenly, Chongo quit pawing the dirt and flung his tail into the air.

"Look out!" I shouted. "Here it comes."

Sure enough, Chongo charged, pounding the hardpan with his feet and roaring his mightiest. And here came Roany to meet him, charging with his head low and his tail high in the air.

I let out an excited yell. They met head on, with a loud crash of horns and a jar so solid that it seemed like I could feel it clear up there on the fence. Roany went down. I yelled louder, thinking Chongo was winning.

A second later, though, Roany was back on his feet and charging through the cloud of dust their hoofs had churned up. He caught Chongo broadside. He slammed his sharp horns up to the hilt in the shoulder of the mustard-colored bull. He drove against him so fast and hard that Chongo couldn't wheel away. All he could do was barely keep on his feet by giving ground.

And here they came, straight for our rail fence.

"Land sakes!" Mama cried suddenly and leaped from the fence, dragging Little Arliss down after her.

But I was too excited about the fight. I didn't see the danger in time. I was still astride the top rail when the struggling bulls crashed through the fence, splintering the posts and rails, and toppling me to the ground almost under them.

I lunged to my feet, wild with scare, and got knocked flat on my face in the dirt.

I sure thought I was a goner. The roaring of the bulls was right in my ears. The hot, reeking scent of their blood was in my nose. The bone-crushing weight of their hoofs was stomping all around and over me, churning up such a fog of dust that I couldn't see a thing.

Then suddenly Mama had me by the hand and was dragging me out from under, yelling in a scared voice, "Run, Travis, run!"

Well, she didn't have to keep hollering at me. I was running as fast as I ever hoped to run. And with her running faster and dragging me along by the hand, we scooted through the open cabin door just about a quick breath before Roany slammed Chongo against it.

They hit so hard that the whole cabin shook. I saw great big chunks of dried-mud chinking fall from between the logs.

There for a second, I thought Chongo was coming through that door, right on top of us. But turned broadside like he was, he was too big to be shoved through such a small opening. Then a second later, he got off Roany's horns somehow and wheeled on him. Here they went, then, down alongside the cabin wall, roaring and stomping and slamming their heels against the logs.

I looked at Mama and Little Arliss. Mama's face was white as a bed sheet. For once, Little Arliss was so scared that he couldn't scream. Suddenly, I wasn't scared anymore. I was just plain mad.

I reached for a braided rawhide whip that hung in a coil on a wooden peg driven between the logs.

That scared Mama still worse. "Oh, no, Travis," she cried. "Don't go out there!"

"They're fixing to tear down the house, Mama," I said.

"But they might run over you," Mama argued.

The bulls crashed into the cabin again. They grunted and strained and roared. Their horns and hoofs clattered against the logs.

I turned and headed for the door. Looked to me like they'd kill us all if they ever broke through those log walls.

Mama came running to grab me by the arm. "Call the dog!" she said. "Put the dog after them!"

Well, that was a real good idea. I was half aggravated with myself because I hadn't thought of it. Here was a chance for that old yeller dog to pay back for all the trouble he'd made around the place.

I stuck my head out the door. The bulls had fought away from the house. Now they were busy tearing down more of the yard fence.

I ducked out and around. I ran through the dog run toward the back of the house, calling, "Here, Yeller! Here Yeller! Get 'em, boy! Sic 'em!"

Old Yeller was back there, all right. But he didn't come and he didn't sic 'em. He took one look at me running toward him with that bullwhip in my hand and knew I'd come to kill him. He tucked his tail and lit out in a yelling run for the woods.

If there had been any way I could have done it, right then is when I would have killed him.

But there wasn't time to mess with a fool dog. I had to do something about those bulls. They were wrecking the place, and I had to stop it. Papa had left me to look after things while he was gone, and I wasn't about to let two mad bulls tear up everything we had.

I ran up to the bulls and went to work on them with the whip. It was a heavy 16-footer and I'd practiced with it a lot. I could crack that rawhide popper louder than a gunshot. I could cut a branch as thick as my little finger off a green mesquite with it.

But I couldn't stop those bulls from fighting. They were too mad. They were hurting too much already; I might as well have been spitting on them. I yelled and whipped them till I gave clear out. Still they went right on with their roaring bloody battle.

I guess they would have kept on fighting till they leveled the house to the ground if it hadn't been for a freak accident.

We had a heavy two-wheeled Mexican cart that Papa used for hauling wood and hay. It happened to be standing out in front of the house, right where the ground broke away in a sharp slant toward the spring and creek.

It had just come to me that I could get my gun and shoot the bulls when Chongo crowded Roany up against the cart. He ran that long single horn clear under Roany's belly. Now he gave such a big heave that he lifted Roany's feet off the ground and rolled him in the air. A second later, Roany landed flat on his back inside the bed of that dump cart, with all four feet sticking up.

I thought his weight would break the cart to pieces, but I was wrong. The cart was stronger than I'd thought. All the bull's weight did was tilt it so that the wheels started rolling. And away the cart went rolling down the hill, carrying Roany with it.

When that happened, Chongo was suddenly the silliest-looking bull you ever saw. He stood with his tail up and his head high, staring after the runaway cart. He couldn't for the life of him figure out what he'd done with the roan bull.

The rolling cart rattled and banged and careened its way down the slope till it was right beside the spring. There, one wheel struck a big boulder, bouncing that side of the cart so high that it turned over and skidded to a stop. The roan bull spilled right into the spring. Water flew in all directions.

Roany got his feet under him. He scrambled up out of the hole. But I guess that cart ride and sudden wetting had taken all the fight out of him. Anyhow, he headed for the timber, running with his tail tucked. Water streamed down out of his hair, leaving a dark wet trail in the dry dust to show which way he'd gone.

Chongo saw Roany then. He snorted and went after him. But when he got to the cart, he slid to a sudden stop. The cart, lying on its side now, still had that top wheel spinning around and around. Chongo had never seen anything like that. He stood and stared at the spinning wheel. He couldn't understand it. He lifted his nose up close to smell it. Finally he reached out his long tongue to lick and taste it.

That was a bad mistake. I guess the iron tire of the spinning wheel was roughed up pretty badly and maybe had chips of broken rock and gravel stuck to it. Anyhow, from the way Chongo acted, it must have scraped all the hide off his tongue.

Chongo bawled and went running backward. He whirled away so fast that he lost his footing and fell down. He came to his feet and took out in the opposite direction from the roan bull. He ran, slinging his head and flopping his long tongue around, bawling like he'd stuck it into a bear trap. He ran with his tail clamped just as tight as the roan bull's.

It was enough to make you laugh your head off, the way both those bad bulls had gotten the wits scared clear out of them, each one thinking he'd lost the fight.

But they sure had made a wreck of the yard fence.

READING COMPREHENSION

Summarizing. Choose the best phrase to complete each sentence. Then write the complete statements on your paper.

1. Travis's father left home in order to _____ (find a better place to live, sell some cattle, hunt for food).

2. That night, Travis felt good because he had _____ (found Old Yeller, made Little Arliss and Jumper mind him, taught Old Yeller not to steal food).

3. Travis became angry when he _____ (missed shooting a deer, found Arliss and Old Yeller in the drinking water, found Old Yeller stealing more meat).

4. When Travis wanted Old Yeller to scare off the two fighting bulls, the dog _____ (chased them away, saved Arliss's life, ran away).

Interpreting. Write the answer to each question on your paper.

1. Why was Travis suddenly expected to be "the man of the family"?

2. Why did all the settlers have dogs?

3. Why didn't Travis want a dog?

4. Why did Travis hang fresh deer meat in the dog run? After all, that's where Old Yeller stole the hog meat.

For Thinking and Discussing. If you were Travis and had been left in charge of the family, what would you consider your toughest task?

UNDERSTANDING LITERATURE

Characterization. Authors reveal characters to the reader in several ways. They may describe how a character looks, acts, thinks, and what the character says. They may also describe what other characters say or think about this character.

Read the following passages from *Old Yeller*. For each passage, write on your paper which character is being described, and what you learn about the character.

1. "I remember how tall and straight and handsome he looked, with his high-crowned hat and his black mustaches, drooping in cow-horn curves. . . ."

2. "I was 14 years old, pretty near a grown man. I didn't let on for a minute that I wanted to cry."

3. "All he did was stick his tongue out at me . . . ."

4. "He began to yell: 'He's my dog. You can't kick him. He's my dog!'"

5. "Mama switched Little Arliss for playing in our drinking water. Then she blessed me out good and proper for being so bossy with him."

6. "How could I be the man of the family if nobody paid any attention to what I thought or said?"

WRITING

Write a brief conversation between Arliss and Mama, in which Arliss complains about the way Travis treats him.

Chapter 5

That Little Arliss! If he wasn't a mess! From the time he'd grown up big enough to get out of the cabin, he'd made a practice of trying to catch and keep every living thing that ran, flew, jumped, or crawled.

Every night before Mama let him go to bed, she'd make Arliss empty his pockets of whatever he'd captured during the day. Generally, it would be a tangled-up mess of grasshoppers and worms and praying bugs and little rusty tree lizards. One time he brought in a horned toad that got so mad he swelled out round and flat as a Mexican *tortilla* and bled at the eyes. Sometimes it was stuff like a young bird that had fallen out of its nest before it could fly, or a green-speckled spring frog or a striped water snake. And once he turned out of his pocket a wadded-up baby copperhead that nearly threw Mama into spasms. We never did figure out why the snake hadn't bitten him, but Mama took no more chances on snakes. She switched Arliss hard for catching that snake. Then she made me spend better than a week, taking him out and teaching him to throw rocks and kill snakes.

That was all right with Little Arliss. If Mama wanted him to kill his snakes first, he'd kill them. But that still didn't keep him from sticking them in his pockets along with everything else he'd captured that day. The snakes might be stinking by the time Mama called on him to empty his pockets, but they'd be dead.

Then, after the yeller dog came, Little Arliss started catching even bigger game. Like cottontail rabbits and chaparral birds and a baby possum that sulked and lay like dead for the first several hours until he finally decided that Arliss wasn't going to hurt him.

Of course, it was Old Yeller that was doing the catching. He'd run the game down and turn it over to Little Arliss. Then Little Arliss could come in and tell Mama a big fib about how he caught it himself.

I watched them one day when they caught a blue catfish out of Birdsong Creek. The fish had fed out into water so shallow that his top fin was sticking out. About the time I saw it, Old Yeller and

Little Arliss did, too. They made a run at it. The fish went scooting away toward deeper water, only Yeller was too fast for him. He pounced on the fish and shut his big mouth down over it and went romping to the bank, where he dropped it down on the grass and let it flop. And here came Little Arliss to fall on it like I guess he'd been doing everything else. The minute he got his hands on it, the fish finned him and he went to crying.

But he wouldn't turn the fish loose. He just grabbed it up and went running and squawling toward the house, where he gave the fish to Mama. His hands were all bloody by then, where the fish had finned him. They swelled up and got mighty sore; not even a mesquite thorn hurts as bad as a sharp fish fin when it's run deep into your hand.

But as soon as Mama had wrapped his hands in a poultice of mashed-up prickly-pear root to draw out the poison, Little Arliss forgot all about his hurt. And that night when we ate the fish for supper, he told the biggest windy I ever heard about how he'd dived 'way down into a deep hole under the rocks and dragged that fish out and nearly got drowned before he could swim to the bank with it.

But when I tried to tell Mama what really happened, she wouldn't let me. "Now, this is Arliss's story," she said. "You let him tell it the way he wants to."

I told Mama then, I said, "Mama, that old yeller dog is going to make the biggest liar in Texas out of Little Arliss."

But Mama just laughed at me, like she always laughed at Little Arliss's big windies after she'd gotten off where he couldn't hear her. She said for me to let Little Arliss alone. She said that if he ever told a bigger whopper than the ones I used to tell, she had yet to hear it.

Well, I hushed then. If Mama wanted Little Arliss to grow up to be the biggest liar in Texas, I guessed it wasn't any of my business.

All of which, I figure, is what led up to Little Arliss's catching the bear. I think Mama had let him tell so many big yarns about his catching live game that he'd begun to believe them himself.

When it happened, I was down the creek a ways, splitting rails to fix the yard fence where the bulls had torn it down. I'd been down there since dinner, working in a stand of tall slim post oaks. I'd chop down a tree, trim off the branches as far up as I wanted, then cut away the rest of the top. After that I'd start splitting the log lengthways.

I'd split the log by driving steel wedges into the wood. I'd start at the big end and hammer in a wedge with the back side of my axe. This would start a little split running lengthways of the log. Then I'd take a second wedge and drive it up into this split. This would split the log further along and, at the same time, loosen the first wedge. I'd then knock the first wedge loose and move it up in front of the second one.

Driving one wedge ahead of the other like that, I could finally split a log in two halves. Then I'd go to work on the halves, splitting them apart. That way, from each log, I would come out with four rails.

Swinging that chopping axe was sure hard work. The sweat poured off me. My back muscles ached. The axe got so heavy I could hardly swing it. My breath got harder and harder to breathe.

An hour before sundown, I was worn down to a nub. It seemed like I couldn't hit another lick. Papa could have lasted till past sundown, but I didn't see how I could. I shouldered my axe and started toward the cabin, trying to think up some excuse to tell Mama to keep her from knowing I was played clear out.

That's when I heard Little Arliss scream.

Well, Little Arliss was a screamer by nature. He'd scream when he was happy and scream when he was mad and a lot of times he'd scream just to hear himself make a noise. Generally, we paid no more mind to his screaming than we did to the gobble of a wild turkey.

But this time was different. The second I heard his screaming, I felt my heart flop clear over. This time I knew Little Arliss was in real trouble.

I tore up the trail leading toward the cabin. A minute before, I'd been so tired out with my rail splitting that I couldn't have struck a trot. But now I raced through the tall trees in that creek bottom, covering ground like a scared wolf.

Little Arliss's second scream, when it came, was louder and shriller and more frantic-sounding than the first. Mixed with it was a whimpering crying sound that I knew didn't come from him. It was a sound I'd heard before and seemed like I ought to know what it was, but right then I couldn't place it.

Then, from way off to one side came a sound that I would have recognized any-where. It was the coughing roar of a charging bear. I'd just heard it once in my life. That was the time Mama had shot and wounded a hog-killing bear and Papa had had to finish it off with a knife to keep it from getting her.

My heart went to pushing up into my throat, nearly choking off my wind. I strained for every lick of speed I could get out of my running legs. I didn't know what sort of fix Little Arliss had got himself into, but I knew that it had to do with a mad bear, which was enough to send me running.

The way the late sun slanted through the trees had the trail all cross-banded with streaks of bright light and dark shade. I ran through these bright and dark patches so fast that the changing light nearly blinded me. Then suddenly, I raced out into the open where I could see ahead. And what I saw sent a chill clear through to the marrow of my bones.

There was Little Arliss, down in that spring hole again. He was lying half in and half out of the water, holding onto the hind leg of a little black bear cub no bigger than a small coon. The bear cub was out on the bank, whimpering and crying and clawing the rocks with all three of his other feet, trying to pull away. But Little Arliss was holding on for all he was worth, scared now and screaming his head off. Too scared to let go.

How the bear cub ever came to prowl close enough for Little Arliss to grab him, I don't know. And why he didn't turn on him and bite loose, I couldn't figure out, either. Unless he was like Little Arliss, too scared to think.

But all of that didn't matter now. What mattered was the bear cub's mama. She'd heard the cries of her baby and was coming to save him. She was coming so fast that she had the brush popping and breaking as she crashed through and over it. I could see her black heavy figure piling off down the slant on the far side of Birdsong Creek. She was roaring mad and ready to kill.

And worst of all, I could see that I'd never get there in time!

Mama wouldn't either. She'd heard Arliss, too, and here she came from the cabin, running down the slant toward the spring, screaming at Arliss, telling him to turn the cub bear loose. But Little Arliss wouldn't do it. All he'd do was hang onto that hind leg and let out one shrill shriek after another.

Now the she bear was charging across the shallows in the creek. She was knocking sheets of water high in the bright sun, charging with her fur up and her long teeth bared, filling the canyon with that awful coughing roar. And no matter how fast Mama ran or how fast I ran, the she bear was going to get there first!

I think I nearly went blind then, picturing what was going to happen to Little Arliss. I know that I opened my mouth to scream and not any sound came out.

Then, just as the bear went lunging up the creek bank toward Little Arliss and her cub, a flash of yellow came streaking out of the brush.

It was that big yeller dog. He was roaring like a mad bull. He wasn't one-third as big and heavy as the she bear, but when he piled into her from one side, he rolled her clear off her feet. They went down in a wild roaring tangle of twisting bodies and scrambling feet and slashing fangs.

As I raced past them, I saw the bear lunge up to stand on her hind feet like a man while she clawed at the body of the yeller dog hanging to her throat. I didn't wait to see more. Without ever checking my stride, I ran in and jerked Little Arliss loose from the cub. I grabbed him by the wrist and yanked him up out of that water and slung him toward Mama like he was a half-empty sack of corn. I screamed at Mama, "Grab him, Mama! Grab him and run!" Then I swung my chopping axe high and wheeled, aiming to cave in the she bear's head with the first lick.

But I never did strike. I didn't need to. Old Yeller hadn't let the bear get close enough. He couldn't handle her; she was too big and strong for that. She'd stand there on her hind feet, hunched over, and take a roaring swing at him with one of those big front claws. She'd slap him head over heels. She'd knock him so far that it didn't look like he could possibly get back there before she charged again, but he always did. He'd hit the ground rolling, yelling his head off with the pain of the blow; but somehow he'd always roll to his feet. And here he'd come again, ready to tie into her for another round.

I stood there with my axe raised, watching them for a long moment. Then from up toward the house, I heard Mama calling, "Come away from there, Travis. Hurry, son! Run!"

That spooked me. Up till then, I'd been ready to tie into that bear myself. Now, suddenly, I was scared out of my wits again. I ran toward the cabin.

But like it was, Old Yeller nearly beat me there. I didn't see it, of course; but Mama said that the minute Old Yeller saw we were all in the clear and out of danger, he threw the fight to that she bear and lit out for the house. The bear chased him for a little piece, but at the rate Old Yeller was leaving her behind, Mama said it looked like the bear was backing up.

But if the big yeller dog was scared or hurt in any way when he came dashing into the house, he didn't show it. He sure didn't show it like we all did. Little Arliss had hushed his screaming, but he was trembling all over and clinging to Mama like he'd never let her go. And Mama was sitting in the middle of the floor, holding him up close and crying like she'd never stop. And I was close to crying myself.

Old Yeller, though, all he did was come bounding in to jump on us and lick us in the face and bark so loud that there, inside the cabin, the noise nearly made us deaf.

The way he acted, you might have thought that bear fight hadn't been anything more than a rowdy romp that we'd all taken part in for the fun of it.

Chapter 6

Till Little Arliss got us mixed up in that bear fight, I guess I'd been looking on him about like most boys look on their little brothers. I liked him, all right, but I didn't have a lot of use for him. What with his always playing in our drinking water and getting in the way of my chopping axe and howling his head off and chunking me with rocks when he got mad, it didn't seem to me like he was hardly worth the bother putting up with.

But that day when I saw him in the spring, so helpless against the angry she bear, I learned different. I knew then that I loved him as much as I did Mama and Papa, maybe in some ways even a little bit more.

So it was only natural for me to come to love the dog that saved him.

After that, I couldn't do enough for Old Yeller. What if he was a big, ugly, meat-stealing rascal? What if he did fall over and yell bloody murder every time I looked crossways at him? What if he had run off when he ought to have helped with the fighting bulls? None of that made a lick of difference now. He'd pitched in and saved Little Arliss when I couldn't possibly have done it, and that was enough for me.

I petted him and made over him till he was wiggling all over to show how happy he was. I felt mean about how I'd treated him and did everything I could to let him know. I searched his feet and pulled out a long mesquite thorn that had become embedded between his toes. I held him down and had Mama hand me a stick

with a coal of fire on it, so I could burn off three big bloated ticks that I found inside one of his ears. I washed him with lye soap and water, then rubbed salty bacon grease into his hair all over to rout the fleas. And that night after dark, when he sneaked into bed with me and Little Arliss, I let him sleep there and never said a word about it to Mama.

I took him and Little Arliss squirrel hunting the next day. It was the first time I'd ever taken Little Arliss on any kind of hunt. He was such a noisy pest that I always figured he'd scare off the game.

As it turned out, he was just as noisy and pesky as I'd figured. He'd follow along, keeping quiet like I told him, till he saw maybe a pretty butterfly floating around in the air. Then he'd set up a yell you could have heard a mile off and go chasing after the butterfly. Of course, he couldn't catch it; but he would keep yelling at me to come help him. Then he'd get mad because I wouldn't and yell still louder. Or maybe he'd stop to turn over a flat rock. Then he'd stand yelling at me to come back and look at all the yellow ants and centipedes and crickets and stinging scorpions that went scurrying away, hunting new hiding places.

Once he got hung up in some briars and yelled till I came back to get him out. Another time he fell down and struck his elbow on a rock and didn't say a word about it for several minutes — until he saw blood seeping out of a cut on his arm. Then he stood and screamed like he was being burnt with a hot iron.

With that much racket going on, I knew we'd scare all the game clear out of the country. Which, I guess we did. All but the squirrels. They took to the trees where they could hide from us. But I was lucky enough to see which tree one squirrel went up; so I put some of Little Arliss's racket to use.

I sent him in a circle around the tree, beating on the grass and bushes with a stick, while I stood waiting. Sure enough, the squirrel got to watching Little Arliss and forgot me. He kept turning around the tree limb to keep it between him and Little Arliss, till he was on my side in plain sight. I shot him out of the tree the first shot.

After that, Old Yeller caught onto what game we were after. He went to work then, trailing and treeing the squirrels that Little Arliss was scaring up off the ground. From then on, with Yeller to tree the squirrel and Little Arliss to turn them on the tree limbs, we had pickings. Wasn't long before I'd shot more than enough to make us a good squirrel fry for supper.

A week later, Old Yeller helped me catch a wild gobbler that I'd have lost without him. We had gone up to the corn patch to pick a bait of black-eyed peas. I was packing my gun. Just as we got up to the slab-rock fence that Papa had built around the corn patch, I looked over and spotted this gobbler doing our pea-picking for us. The pea pods were still green yet, most of them no further along than snapping size. This made them hard for the gobbler to shell, but he was working away at it, pecking and scratching so hard that he was raising a big dust out in the field.

"Why, that old rascal," Mama said.

"He's just clawing those pea vines all to pieces."

"Hush, Mama," I said. "Don't scare him." I lifted my gun and laid the barrel across the top of the rock fence. "I'll have him ready for the pot in just a minute."

It wasn't a long shot, and I had him sighted in, dead to rights. I aimed to stick a bullet right where his wings hinged to his back. I was holding my breath and already squeezing the trigger when Little Arliss, who had strayed behind us, came running up.

"Whatcha shootin' at, Travis?" he yelled at the top of his voice. "Whatcha shootin' at?"

Well, that made me and the gobbler both jump up. The gun fired, and I saw the gobbler go down. But a second later, he was up again, streaking through the tall corn, dragging a broken wing.

For a second, I was so mad at Little Arliss I could have wrung his neck like a frying chicken's. I said, "*Arliss!* Why can't you keep your mouth shut? You've made me lose that gobbler!"

Well, Little Arliss didn't have sense enough to know what I was mad about. Right away, he puckered up and went to crying and leaking tears all over the place. Some of them splattered clear down on his bare feet, making dark splotches in the dust that covered them. I always did say that when Little Arliss cried he could shed more tears faster than any crier I ever saw.

"Wait a minute!" Mama put it. "I don't think you've lost your gobbler. Look!"

She pointed, and I looked, and there was Old Yeller jumping the rock fence and racing toward the pea patch. He ran up to where I'd knocked the gobbler down. He circled the place one time, smelling the ground and wiggling his stub tail. Then he took off through the corn the same way the gobbler went, yelling like I was beating him with a stick.

When he barked "treed" a couple of minutes later, it was in the woods the other side of the corn patch. We went to him. We found him jumping at the gobbler that had run up a stooping live-oak and was perched there, panting, just waiting for me.

So in spite of the fact that Little Arliss had caused me to make a bad shot, we had us a real sumptuous supper that night. Roast turkey with cornbread dressing and watercress and wild onions that Little Arliss and I found growing down in the creek next to the water.

But when we tried to feed Old Yeller some of the turkey, on account of his saving us from losing it, he wouldn't eat. He'd lick the meat and wiggle his stub tail to show how greatful he was, but he didn't swallow down more than a bite or two.

That puzzled Mama and me because, when we remembered back, we realized that he hadn't been eating anything we'd fed him for the last several days. Yet he was fat and with hair as slick and shiny as a dog eating three square meals a day.

Mama shook her head. "If I didn't know better," she said, "I'd say that dog was sucking eggs. But I've got three hens setting and one with biddy chickens, and I'm getting more eggs from the rest of them than I've gotten since last fall. So he can't be robbing the nests."

Well, we wondered some about what Old Yeller was living on, but didn't worry about it. That is, not until the day Bud Searcy dropped by the cabin to see how we were making out.

Bud Searcy was a red-faced man with a bulging middle who liked to visit around the settlement and sit and talk hard times and spit tobacco juice all over the place and wait for somebody to ask him to dinner.

I never did have a lot of use for him and my folks didn't, either. Mama said he was shiftless. She said that was the reason the rest of the men left him at home to sort of look after the womenfolks and kids while they were gone on the cow drive. She said the men knew that if they took Bud Searcy along, they'd never get to Kansas before the steers were dead with old age. It would take Searcy that long to get through visiting and eating with everybody between Salt Licks and Abilene.

But he did have a little light-haired granddaughter that I sort of liked. She was 11 and different from most girls. She would hang around and watch what boys did, like showing how high they could climb in a tree or how far they could throw a rock or how fast they could swim or how good they could shoot. But she never wanted to mix in or try to take over and boss things. She just went along and watched and didn't say much, and the only thing I had against her was her eyes. They were big, solemn brown eyes and right pretty to look at; only when she fixed them on me, it always seemed like they looked clear through me and saw everything I was thinking. That always

made me sort of jumpy, so that when I could, I never would look right straight at her.

Her name was Lisbeth and she came with her grandpa the day he visited us. They came riding up on an old shad-bellied pony that didn't look like he'd had a fill of corn in a coon's age. She rode behind her grandpa's saddle, holding to his belt in the back, and her light hair was all curly and rippling in the sun. Trotting behind them was a blue-ticked she dog that I always figured was one of Bell's pups.

Old Yeller went out to bay them as they rode up. I noticed right off that he didn't go about it like he really meant business. His yelling bay sounded a lot more like he was just barking because he figured that's what we expected him to do. And the first time I hollered at him, telling him to dry up all that racket, he hushed. Which surprised me, as hard-headed as he generally was.

By the time Mama had come to the door and told Searcy and Lisbeth to get down and come right in, Old Yeller had started a romp with the blue-ticked dog.

Lisbeth slipped to the ground and stood staring at me with those big, solemn eyes while her grandpa dismounted. Searcy told Mama that he believed he wouldn't come in the house. He said that as hot as the day was, he figured he'd like it better sitting in the dog run. So Mama had me bring out our four cowhide bottom chairs. Searcy picked the one I always liked to sit in best. He got out a twist of tobacco and bit off a chew big enough to bulge his cheek and went to chewing and talking and spitting juice right where we'd all be bound to step in it and pack it around on the bottoms of our feet.

First he asked Mama if we were making out all right, and Mama said we were. Then he told her that he'd been left to look after all the families while the men were gone, a mighty heavy responsibility that was nearly working him to death, but that he was glad to do it. He said for Mama to remember that if the least little thing went wrong, she was to get in touch with him right away. And Mama said she would.

Then he leaned his chair back against the cabin wall and went to telling what all was going on around in the settlement. He told about how dry the weather was and how he looked for all the corn crops to fail and the settlement folks to be scraping the bottoms of their meal barrels long before the next spring. He told how the cows were going dry and the gardens were failing. He told how Jed Simpson's boy

Rosal was sitting at a turkey roost, waiting for a shot, when a fox came right up and tried to jump on him, and Rosal had to club it to death with his gun butt. This sure looked like a case of hydrophobia to Searcy, as anybody knew that no fox in his right mind was going to jump on a hunter.

Which reminded him of an uncle of his that got mad-dog bit down in the piney woods of East Texas. This was 'way back when Searcy was a little boy. As soon as the dog bit him, the man knew he was bound to die; so he went and got a big log chain and tied one end around the bottom of a tree and the other end to one of his legs. And right there he stayed till the sickness got him and he lost his mind. He slobbered at the mouth and moaned and screamed and ran at his wife and children, trying to catch them and bite them. Only, of course, the chain around his leg held him back, which was the reason he'd chained himself to that tree. He finally died and they buried him under the same tree.

Bud Searcy sure hoped that we wouldn't have an outbreak of hydrophobia in Salt Licks and all die before the men got back from Kansas.

Then he talked awhile about a panther that had caught and killed one of Joe Anson's colts and how the Anson boys had put their dogs on the trail. They ran the panther into the cave and Jeff Anson followed in where the dogs had more sense than to go and got pretty badly panther-mauled for his trouble; but he did get the panther.

Searcy talked till dinnertime, said not a

word all through dinner, and then went back to talking as quick as he'd swallowed down the last bite.

He told how some strange varmint that wasn't a coyote, possum, skunk, or coon had recently started robbing the settlement blind. Or maybe it was even some-*body*. Nobody could tell for sure. All they knew was that they were losing meat out of their smokehouses, eggs out of their hens' nests, and sometimes even whole pans of cornbread that the womenfolks had set out to cool. Ike Fuller had been barbecuing some meat over an open pit and came back to find that a three- or four-pound chunk of beef ribs had disappeared like it had gone up in smoke.

Salt Licks folks were getting pretty riled about it, Searcy said, and guessed it would go hard with whatever or whoever was doing the raiding if they ever learned what it was.

Listening to this, I got an uneasy feeling. The feeling got worse a minute later when Lisbeth motioned me to follow her off down to the spring.

We walked clear down there, with Old Yeller and the blue-ticked dog following with us, before she finally looked up at me and said, "It's him."

"What do you mean?" I said.

"I mean it's your big yeller dog," she said. "I saw him."

"Do what?" I asked.

"Steal that bait of ribs," she said. "I saw him get a bunch of eggs, too. From one of our nests."

I stopped then and looked straight at her and she looked straight back at me and I couldn't stand it and had to look down.

"But I'm not going to tell," she said.

I didn't believe her. "I bet you do," I said.

"No, I won't," she said, shaking her head. "I wouldn't, even before I knew he was your dog."

"Why?"

"Because Miss Prissy is going to have pups."

"Miss Prissy?"

"That's the name of my dog, and she's going to have pups and your dog will be their papa, and I wouldn't want their papa to get shot."

I stared at her again, and again I had to look down. I wanted to thank her, but I didn't know the right words. So I fished around in my pocket and brought out an Indian arrowhead that I'd found the day before and gave that to her.

She took it and stared at it for a little bit, with her eyes shining, then shoved it deep into a long pocket she had sewn to her dress.

"I won't never, never tell," she said, then whirled and tore out for the house, running as fast as she could.

I went down and sat by the spring awhile. It seemed like I liked Bud Searcy a lot better than I ever had before, even if he did talk too much and spit tobacco juice all over the place. But I was still bothered. If Lisbeth had caught Old Yeller stealing stuff at the settlement, then somebody else might, too. And if they did, they were sure liable to shoot him. A family might put up with one of its own dogs stealing from them if he was a good dog. But for a dog that left home to steal from everybody else — well, I didn't see much chance for him if he ever got caught.

After Bud Searcy had eaten a hearty supper and talked awhile longer, he finally rode off home, with Lisbeth riding behind him. I went then and gathered the eggs and held three back. I called Old Yeller off from the house and broke the eggs on a flat rock, right under his nose, and tried to get him to eat them. But he wouldn't. He acted like he'd never heard tell that eggs were fit to eat. All he'd do was stand there and wiggle his tail and try to lick me in the face.

It made me mad. "You thievin' rascal," I said. "I ought to get a club and break your back — in 14 different places."

But I didn't really mean it, and I didn't say it loud and ugly. I knew that if I did, he'd fall over and start yelling like he was dying. And there I'd be — in a fight with Little Arliss again.

"When they shoot you, I'm going to laugh," I told him.

But I knew that I wouldn't.

Chapter 7

I did considerable thinking on what Lisbeth Searcy had told me about Old Yeller and finally went and told Mama.

"Why, that old rogue," she said. "We'll have to try to figure some way to keep him from prowling. Everybody in the settlement will be mad at us if we don't."

"Somebody'll shoot him," I said.

"Try tying him," she said.

So I tried tying him. But we didn't have any bailing wire in those days, and he could chew through anything else before you could turn your back. I tied him with rope and then with thick rawhide string that I cut from a cowhide hanging across the top rail of the yard fence. It was the same thing in both cases. By the time we could get off to bed, he'd done chewed them in two and was gone.

"Let's try the corncrib," Mama said on the third night.

Which was a good idea that might have worked if it hadn't been for Little Arliss.

I took Old Yeller out and put him in the corncrib and the second that he heard the door shut on him, he set up a yelling and a howling that brought Little Arliss on the run. Mama and I both tried to explain to him why we needed to shut the dog up, but Little Arliss was too mad to listen. You can't explain things very well to somebody who is screaming his head off and chunking you with rocks as fast as he can pick them up. So that didn't work, either.

"Well, it looks like we're stumped," Mama said.

I thought for a minute and said, "No, Mama. I believe we've got one other chance. That's to shut him up in the same room with me and Little Arliss every night."

"But he'll sleep in the bed with you boys," Mama said, "and the first thing

Old Yeller and I were kept busy nearly all night long.

It was the coons, mainly. The corn was ripening into roasting ears now, and the coons would come at night and strip the shucks back with their little hands, and gnaw the milky kernels off the cob. Also, the watermelons were beginning to turn red inside and the skunks would come and open little round holes in the rinds and reach in with their forefeet and drag out the juicy insides to eat. Sometimes the coyotes would come and eat watermelons, too; and now and then a deer would jump into the field and eat corn, melons, and peas.

So Old Yeller and I took to sleeping in the corn patch every night. We slept on the cowhide that Yeller never would sleep on at the house. That is, we did when we got to sleep. Most of the night, we'd be up fighting coons. We slept out in the middle of the patch, where Yeller could scent a coon clear to the fence on every side. We'd lie there on the cowhide and look

you know, you'll both be scratching fleas and breaking out with ringworms."

"No, I'll put him a cowhide on the floor and make him sleep there," I said.

So Mama agreed and I spread a cowhide on the floor beside our bed and we shut Old Yeller in and didn't have a bit more trouble.

Of course, Old Yeller didn't sleep on the cowhide. And once, a good while later, I did break out with a little ringworm under my left arm. But I rubbed it with turpentine, just like Mama always did, and it soon went away. And after that, when we fed Old Yeller cornmeal mush or fresh meat, he ate it and never one time bothered our chicken nests.

About that time, too, the varmints got to pestering us so much that a lot of times up at the stars and listen to the warm night breeze rustling the corn blades. Sometimes I'd wonder what the stars were and what kept them hanging up there so high and bright and if Papa, 'way off up yonder in Kansas, could see the same stars I could see.

I was getting mighty lonesome to see Papa. With the help of Old Yeller, I was taking care of things all right; but I was sure beginning to wish that Papa would come back home.

Then I'd think awhile about the time when I'd get big enough to go off on a cow drive myself, riding my own horse, and see all the big new country of plains and creeks and rivers and mountains and timber and new towns and Indian camps. Then, finally, just about the time I started drifting off to sleep, I'd hear Old Yeller rise to his feet and go padding off through the corn. A minute later, his yelling bay would lift from some part of the corn patch, and I'd hear the fighting squawl of some coon caught stealing corn. Then I'd jump to my feet and go running through the corn, shouting encouragement to Old Yeller.

"Git him, Yeller," I'd holler. "Tear him up!"

And that's what Old Yeller would be trying to do; but a boar coon isn't an easy thing to tear up. For one thing, he'll fight you from sundown till sunup. He's not big for size, but the longer you fight him, the bigger he seems to get. He fights you with all four feet and every tooth in his head and enough courage for an animal five times his size.

On top of that, he's fighting inside a thick hide that fills a dog's mouth like a wad of loose sacking. The dog has a hard time ever really biting him. He just squirms and twists around inside that hide and won't quit fighting even after the dog's got enough and is ready to throw the fight to him. Plenty of times, Papa and I had seen a boar coon whip Bell, run him off, then turn on us and chase us clear out of a cornfield.

It was easy for me to go running through the dark cornfields, yelling for Old Yeller to tear up a thieving coon, but it wasn't easy for Old Yeller to do it. He'd be yelling and the coon would be squawling and they'd go wallowing and clawing and threshing throught the corn, popping the stalks as they broke them off, making such an uproar in the night that it sounded like murder. But, generally, when the fight was all over, the coon went one way and Old Yeller the other, both of them pretty well satisfied to call it quits.

We didn't get much sleep of a night while all this was going on, but we had us a good time and saved the corn from the coons.

The only real bad part of it was the skunks. What with all the racket we made coon fighting, the skunks didn't come often. But when one did come, we were in a mess.

Old Yeller could handle a skunk easy enough. All he had to do was rush in, grab it by the head and give it a good shaking. That would break the skunk's neck, but it wouldn't end the trouble. Because not even a hoot owl can kill a skunk without getting sprayed with his scent. And skunk scent is a smell that won't quit. After every skunk killing, Old Yeller would get so sick that he could hardly stand it. He'd snort and drool and slobber and vomit. He'd roll and wallow in the dirt and go dragging his body through tall weeds, trying to get the scent off; but he couldn't. Then finally, he'd give up and come lie down on the cowhide with me. And of course he'd smell so bad that I couldn't stand him and I'd have to go off and try to sleep somewhere else. Then he'd follow me and get his feelings hurt because I wouldn't let him sleep near me.

Papa always said that breathing skunk scent was the best way in the world to cure a head cold. But this was summertime, when Old Yeller and I didn't have head colds. We would just as soon that the skunks stayed out of the watermelons and let us alone.

Working there, night after night, guarding our precious bread corn from the varmints, I came to see what I would have been up against if I'd had it to do without the help of Old Yeller. By myself, I'd have been run to death and still probably wouldn't have saved the corn. Also, look at all the fun I would have missed if I'd been alone, and how lonesome I would have been. I had to admit Papa had been right when he'd told me how bad I needed a dog.

I saw that even more clearly when the spotted heifer had her first calf.

Our milk cows were all old-time longhorn cattle and didn't give a lot of milk. It was real hard to find one that would give much more than her calf could take.

What we generally had to do was milk five or six cows to get enough milk for just the family.

But we had one crumpled-horn cow named Rose that gave a lot of milk, only she was getting old, and Mama kept hoping that each of her heifer calves would turn out to be as good a milker as Rose. Mama had tried two or three, but none of them proved to be any good. And then along came this spotted one that was just raw-boned and ugly enough to make a good milk cow. She had the bag for it, too, and Mama was certain this time that she'd get a milk cow to replace Rose.

The only trouble was, this heifer Spot, as we called her, had been snaky wild from the day she was born. Try to drive her with the other cattle, and she'd run off and hide. Hem her up in a corner and try to get your hands on her, and she'd turn on you and make fight. Mama had been trying all along to get Spot gentled before she had her first calf, but it was no use. Spot didn't want to be friends with anybody. We knew she was going to give us a pile of trouble when we set out to try to milk her.

I failed to find Spot with the rest of our milk cows one evening, and when I went to drive them up the next day, she was still gone.

"It's time for her to calve," Mama said, "and I'll bet she's got one."

So the next morning I went further back in the hills and searched all over. I finally came across her, holed up in a dense thicket of bee myrtle close to a little seep spring. I got one brief glimpse of a wobbly, long-legged calf before Spot snorted and took after me. She ran me clear to the top of the next high ridge before she turned back.

I made another try. I got to the edge of the thicket and picked me up some rocks. I went to hollering and chunking into the brush, trying to scare her and the calf out. I got her out, all right, but she wasn't scared. She came straight for me with her horns lowered, bawling her threats as she came. I had to turn tail a second time, and again she chased me clear to the top of that ridge.

I tried it one more time, then went back to the house and got Old Yeller. I didn't know if he knew anything about driving cattle or not, but I was willing to bet that he could keep her from chasing me.

And he did. I went up to the edge of the thicket and started hollering and chunking rocks into it. Here came the heifer, madder than ever, it looked like. I yelled at Old Yeller. "Get her, Yeller," I hollered. And Yeller got her. He pulled the neatest trick I ever saw a dog pull on a cow brute.

Only I didn't see it the first time. I was getting away from there too fast. I'd stumbled and fallen to my knees when I turned to run from Spot's charge, and she was too close behind for me to be looking back and watching what Old Yeller was doing. I just heard the scared bawl she let out and the crashing of brush as Old Yeller rolled her into it.

I ran a piece further, then looked back. The heifer was scrambling to her feet in a cloud of dust and looking like she didn't know any more about what had happened than I did. Then she caught sight of Old Yeller. She snorted, stuck her tail in the air and made for him. Yeller ran like he was scared to death, then cut back around a thicket. A second later, he was coming in behind Spot.

Without making a sound, he ran up beside her, made his leap and set his teeth in her nose.

I guess it was the weight of him that did it. I saw him do it lots of times later, but never did quite understand how. Anyway, he just set his teeth in her nose, doubled himself up in a tight ball, and hung on. That turned the charging heifer into a flip. Her heels went straight up in the air over her head. She landed flat on her back with all four feet sticking up. She hit the ground so hard that it sounded like she ought to bust wide open.

I guess she felt that way about it, too. Anyhow, after taking that second fall, she didn't have much fight left in her. She just scrambled to her feet and went trotting back into the thicket, lowing to her calf.

I followed her, with Old Yeller beside me, and we drove her out and across the hills to the cow lot. Not one time did she turn on us again. She did try to run off a couple of times, but all I had to do was send Old Yeller in to head her off. And the second she caught sight of him, she couldn't turn fast enough to get headed back in the right direction.

It was the same when we got her into the cowpen. Her bag was full of milk. Mama said we needed to get that milk out. She came with a bucket and I took it, knowing I had a big kicking fight on my hands if I hoped to get any milk.

The kicking fight started. The first time I even touched Spot, she reached out with

429

a flying hind foot, aiming to kick my head off and coming close to doing it. Then she wheeled on me and put me on top of the rail fence as quick as a squirrel could have made it.

Mama shook her head. "I was hoping she wouldn't be that way," she said. "I always hate to have to tie up a heifer, to break her for milking. But I guess there's no other way with this one."

I thought of all the trouble it would be, having to tie up that Spot heifer, head and feet, twice a day, every day, for maybe a month or more. I looked at Old Yeller, standing just outside the pen.

"Yeller," I said, "you come in here."

Mama said, "Why, son, you can't teach a heifer to stand with a dog in the pen. Especially one with a young calf. She'll be fighting at him, thinking he's a wolf or something trying to get her calf."

I laughed. "Maybe it won't work," I said, "but I bet you one thing. She won't be fighting Old Yeller."

She didn't, either. She lowered her horns and rolled her eyes as I brought Old Yeller up to her.

"Now, Yeller," I said, "you stand here and watch her."

Old Yeller seemed to know just what I wanted. He walked right up to where he could almost touch his nose to hers and stood there, wagging his stub tail. And she didn't charge him or run from him. All she did was stand there and sort of tremble. I went back and milked her and she didn't offer to kick me one time, just flinched and drew up a little when I first touched her.

"Well, that does beat all," Mama marveled. "Why, at that rate, we'll have her broke to milk in a week's time."

Mama was right. Within three days after we started, I could drive Spot into the pen, go right up and milk her, and all she'd do was stand there and stare at Old Yeller. By the end of the second week, she was standing and belching and chewing her cud — the gentlest cow I ever milked.

After all that, I guess you can see why I nearly died when a man rode up one day and claimed Old Yeller.

Chapter 8

The man's name was Burn Sanderson. He was a young man who rode a good horse and was mighty nice and polite about taking his hat off to Mama when he dismounted in front of our cabin. He told Mama who he was. He said he was a newcomer to Salt Licks. He said that he'd come from down San Antonio way with a little bunch of cattle that he was grazing over in the Devil's River country. He said he couldn't afford to hire riders, so he'd brought along a couple of dogs to help him herd his cattle. One of these dogs, the best one, had disappeared. He'd inquired around about it at Salt Licks, and Bud Searcy had told him that we had the dog.

"A big yeller dog?" Mama asked, looking sober and worried.

"Yessum," the man said, then added with a grin, "and the worse egg sucker and camp robber you ever laid eyes on. Steal you blind, that old devil will; but there was never a better cow dog born."

Mama turned to me. "Son, call Old Yeller," she said.

I stood frozen in my tracks. I was so full of panic that I couldn't move or think.

"Go on, son," Mama urged. "I think he and Little Arliss must be playing down about the creek somewhere."

"But, Mama!" I gasped. "We can't do without Old Yeller. He's —"

"Travis!"

Mama's voice was too sharp. I knew I was whipped. I turned and went toward the creek, so mad at Bud Searcy that I couldn't see straight. Why couldn't he keep his blabber mouth shut?

"Come on up to the house," I told Little Arliss.

I guess the way I said it let him know

that something real bad was happening. He didn't argue or stick out his tongue or anything. He just got out of the water and followed me back to the house and embarrassed Mama and the young man nearly to death because he came packing his clothes in one hand instead of wearing them.

I guess Burn Sanderson had gotten an idea of how much we thought of Old Yeller, or maybe Mama had told some things about the dog while I was gone to the creek. Anyhow, he acted uncomfortable about taking the dog off. "Now, Mrs. Coates," he said to Mama, "your man is gone, and you and the boys don't have much protection here. Bad as I need that old dog, I can make out without him until your man comes."

But Mama shook her head.

"No, Mr. Sanderson," she said. "He's your dog; and the longer we keep him, the harder it'll be for us to give him up. Take him along. I can make the boys understand."

The man tied his rope around Old Yeller's neck and mounted his horse. That's when Little Arliss caught onto what was happening. He threw a wall-eyed fit. He screamed and hollered. He grabbed up a bunch of rocks and went throwing them at Burn Sanderson.

One hit Sanderson's horse in the flank. The horse bogged his head and went to pitching and bawling and grunting. This excited Old Yeller. He chased after the horse, baying him at the top of his voice. And what with Mama running after Little Arliss, hollering for him to shut up and quit throwing those rocks, it was the biggest and loudest commotion that had taken place around our cabin for a good long while.

When Burn Sanderson finished riding the pitch out of his scared horse, he hollered at Old Yeller. He told him he'd better hush up that racket before he got his brains beat out. Then he rode back toward us, wearing a wide grin.

His grin got wider as he saw how Mama and I were holding Little Arliss. We each had him by one wrist and were holding him clear off the ground. He couldn't get at any more rocks to throw that way, but it sure didn't keep him from dancing up and down in the air and screaming.

"Turn him loose," Sanderson said with a big laugh. "He's not going to throw any more rocks at me."

He swung down from his saddle. He came and got Little Arliss and loved him up till he hushed screaming. Then he said, "Look, boy, do you really want that thieving old dog?"

He held Little Arliss off and stared him straight in the eyes, waiting for Arliss to answer. Little Arliss stared straight back at him and didn't say a word.

"Well, do you?" he insisted.

Finally, Little Arliss nodded, then tucked his chin and looked away.

"All right," Burn Sanderson said. "We'll make a trade. Just between you and me. I'll let you keep the old rascal, but you've got to do something for me."

He waited till Little Arliss finally got up the nerve to ask what, then went on, "Well, it's like this. I've hung around over there in that cow camp, eating my own cooking till I'm so starved out, I don't hardly throw a shadow. Now if you could talk your mama into feeding me a real jam-up meal of woman-cooked grub, I think it would be worth at least a one-eared yeller dog. Don't you?"

I didn't wait to hear any more. I ran off. I was so full of relief that I was about to pop. I knew that if I didn't get out of sight in a hurry, this Burn Sanderson was going to catch me crying.

Mama cooked the best dinner that day I ever ate. We had roast venison and fried catfish and stewed squirrel and blackeyed peas and cornbread and flour gravy and butter and wild honey and hog-plum jelly and fresh buttermilk. I ate till it seemed like my eyeballs would pop out of my head, and still didn't make anything like the showing that Burn Sanderson made. He was a slim man, not nearly as big as Papa, and I never could figure out where he was putting all that grub. But long before he finally sighed and shook his head at the last of the squirrel stew, I was certain of one thing: he sure wouldn't have any trouble throwing a shadow on the ground for the rest of that day.

After dinner, he sat around for a while, talking to me and Mama and making Little Arliss some toy horses out of dry cornstalks. Then he said his thank-yous to Mama and told me to come with him. I followed with him while he led his horse down to the spring for water. I remembered how Papa had led me away from the house like this the day he left and knew by that that Burn Sanderson had something he wanted to talk to me about.

At the spring, he slipped the bits out of his horse's mouth to let him drink, then turned to me.

"Now, boy," he said, "I didn't want to tell your mama this. I didn't want to worry her. But there's a plague of hydrophobia making the rounds, and I want you to be on the lookout for it."

I felt scare run through me. I didn't know much about hydrophobia, but after what Bud Searcy had told about his uncle that died, chained to a tree, I knew it was something bad. I stared at Burn Sanderson and didn't say anything.

"And there's no mistake about it," he said. "I've done shot two wolves, a fox, and one skunk that had it. And over at Salt Licks, a woman had to kill a bunch of house cats that her younguns had been playing with. She wasn't sure, but she couldn't afford to take any chances. And you can't, either."

"But how will I know what to shoot and what not to?" I wanted to know.

"Well, you can't hardly tell at first," he said. "Not until they have already gone to foaming at the mouth and are reeling with the blind staggers. Any time you see a critter acting that way, you know for sure. But you watch for others that aren't that far along. You take a pet cat. If he takes to spitting and fighting at you for no reason, you shoot him. Same with a dog. He'll get mad at nothing and want to bite you. Take a fox or a wildcat. You know they'll run from you; when they don't run, and try to make fight at you, shoot 'em. Shoot anything that acts unnatural, and don't fool around about it. It's too late after they've already bitten or scratched you."

433

Talk like that made my heart jump up in my throat till I could hardly get my breath. I looked down at the ground and went to kicking around some rocks.

"You're not scared, are you, boy? I'm only telling you because I know your papa left you in charge of things. I know you can handle whatever comes up. I'm just telling you to watch close and not let anything — *anything* — get to you with hydrophobia. Think you can do it?"

I swallowed. "I can do it," I told him. "I'm not scared."

The sternness left Burn Sanderson's face. He put a hand on my shoulder, just as Papa had the day he left.

"Good boy," he said. "That's the way a man talks."

Then he gripped my shoulder real tight, mounted his horse and rode off through the brush. And I was so scared and mixed up about the danger of hydrophobia that it was clear into the next day before I even thought about thanking him for giving us Old Yeller.

READING COMPREHENSION

Summarizing. Choose the best phrase to complete each sentence. Then write the complete statements on your paper.

1. When a bear went after Arliss, Old Yeller _____ (ran off, barked for help, attacked the bear).

2. Travis was able to save the corn, melon, and peas from varmints, with the help of _____ (Mama, Little Arliss, Old Yeller).

3. Travis was able to turn Spot into a milking cow, thanks to _____ (Mama, Bud Searcy, Old Yeller).

4. Burn Sanderson agreed to trade Old Yeller for a _____ (home-cooked meal, cow, rifle).

Interpreting. Write the answer to each question on your paper.

1. Why did a bear try to attack Arliss?

2. What kind of fighter was Old Yeller?

3. How did Travis stop Old Yeller from stealing food from the settlement?

4. Who was Burn Sanderson, and why did he let Arliss keep Old Yeller?

5. What did Burn Sanderson do that made Travis think of his father?

For Thinking and Discussing. Why do you think Little Arliss and Old Yeller like playing together so much? In what ways are they alive?

UNDERSTANDING LITERATURE

Plot. The plot of a novel is the sequence of events. The events are planned to get the reader involved and to make a point.

Here are some of the events in *Old Yeller*, so far. But they are not in the right order. On your paper, write the events in the correct order. Look back at the story if you want to.

1. Burn Sanderson agreed to let Arliss keep Old Yeller.

2. Travis learned from Lisbeth Searcy that Old Yeller was stealing food from the settlement.

3. Old Yeller helped Travis guard the corn patch from varmints at night.

4. Burn Sanderson claimed that Old Yeller was *his* dog.

5. Old Yeller stopped a bear from attacking Little Arliss.

6. Travis found that a stray dog had eaten the family's hog meat, which had been hanging in the dog run.

7. Travis got Old Yeller to stop stealing food from the settlement by keeping him in his bedroom at night.

8. Burn Sanderson warned Travis to shoot any animals that might have hydrophobia.

WRITING

Write a paragraph in which you describe two or more events which *might* occur before the story is over.

Chapter 9

A boy, before he really grows up, is pretty much like a wild animal. He can get the wits scared clear out of him today, and by tomorrow he will have forgotten all about it.

At least, that's the way it was with me. I was plenty scared of the hydrophobia plague that Burn Sanderson told me about. I could hardly sleep that night. I kept picturing in my mind mad dogs and mad wolves reeling about with the blind staggers, drooling slobbers and snapping and biting at everything in sight. Maybe biting Mama and Little Arliss, so that they got the sickness and went mad, too. I lay in bed and shuddered and shivered and dreamed all sorts of nightmare happenings.

Then, the next day, I went to rounding up and marking hogs and forgot all about the plague.

Our hogs ran loose on the range in those days, the same as our cattle. We fenced them out of the fields, but never into a pasture; we had no pastures. We never fed them, unless maybe it was a little corn that we threw to them during a bad spell in the winter. The rest of the time, they rustled for themselves.

They slept out and ate out. In the summertime, they slept in the cool places around the water holes, sometimes in the water. In the winter, they could always tell at least a day ahead of time when a blizzard was on the way; then they'd gang up and pack tons of leaves and dry grass and sticks into some dense thicket or cave. They'd pile all this into a huge bed and sleep on it until the cold spell blew over.

They ranged all over the hills and down into the canyons. In season, they fed on acorns, berries, wild plums, prickly-pear apples, grass, weeds, and bulb plants, which they rooted out of the ground. They especially liked the wild black persimmons that the Mexicans called chapotes.

Sometimes, too, they'd eat a newborn calf if the mama cow couldn't keep them horned away. Or a baby fawn that the doe had left hidden in the tall grass. Once, in a real dry time, Papa and I saw an old sow standing belly deep in a drying up pothole of water, catching and eating perch that were trapped in there and couldn't get away.

Most of these meat eaters were old hogs, however. Starvation, during some bad drought or extra cold winter, had forced them to eat anything they could get hold of. Papa said they generally started out by feeding on the carcass of some deer or cow that had died, then going from there to catching and killing live meat. He told a tale about how one old range hog had caught him when he was a baby and his folks got there just barely in time to save him.

It was that sort of thing, I guess, that always made Mama so afraid of wild hogs. The least little old biting shoat could make her take cover. She didn't like it a bit when I started out to catch and mark all the pigs that our sows had raised that year. She knew we had it to do, else we couldn't tell our hogs from those of the neighbors. But she didn't like the idea of my doing it alone.

"But I'm not working hogs alone, Mama," I pointed out. "I've got Old Yeller, and Burn Sanderson says he's a real good hog dog."

"That doesn't mean a thing," Mama said. "All hog dogs are good ones. A good one is the only kind that can work hogs and live. But the best dog in the world won't keep you from getting cut all to pieces if you ever make a slip."

Well, Mama was right. I'd worked with Papa enough to know that any time you messed with a wild hog, you were asking for trouble. Let him alone, and he'll generally snort and run from you on sight, the same as a deer. But once you corner him, he's the most dangerous animal that ever lived in Texas. Catch a squealing pig out of the bunch, and you've got a battle on your hands. All of them will turn on you at one time and here they'll come, roaring and popping their teeth, cutting high and fast with gleaming white tushes that they keep whetted to the sharpness of knife points. And there's no bluff to them, either. They mean business. They'll kill you if they can get to you; and if you're not fast-footed and don't keep a close watch, they'll get to you.

They had to be that way to live in a country where the wolves, bobcats, panther, and bear were always after them trying for a bait of fresh hog meat. And it was because of this that nearly all hog owners usually left four or five old barrows, or "bar' hogs," as we called them, to run with each bunch of sows. The bar' hogs weren't any more vicious than the boars, but they'd hang with the sows and help them protect the pigs and shoats, when generally the boars pulled off to range alone

I knew all this about range hogs, and plenty more; yet I still wasn't bothered about the job facing me. In fact, I sort of looked forward to it. Working wild hogs was always exciting and generally proved to be a lot of fun.

I guess the main reason I felt this way was because Papa and I had figured out a quick and nearly fool-proof way of doing it. We could catch most of the pigs we needed to mark without ever getting in reach of the old hogs. It took a good hog dog to pull off the trick; but the way Burn Sanderson talked about Old Yeller, I was willing to bet that he was that good.

He was, too. Old Yeller caught on right away.

We located our first bunch of hogs at a seep spring at the head of a shallow dry wash that led back toward Birdsong Creek. There were seven sows, two long-tushed old bar' hogs, and 14 small shoats.

They'd come there to drink and to wallow around in the potholes of soft cool mud.

They caught wind of us about the same time I saw them. The old hogs threw up their snouts and said "Woo-oof!" Then they all tore out for the hills, running through the rocks and brush almost as swiftly and silently as deer.

"Head 'em, Yeller," I hollered. "Go get 'em, boy!"

But it was a waste of words. Old Yeller was done gone.

He streaked down the slant, crossed the

draw, and had the tail-end pig caught by the hind leg before the others knew he was after them.

The pig set up a loud squeal. Instantly, all the old hogs wheeled. They came at Old Yeller with their bristles up, roaring and popping their teeth. Yeller held onto his pig until I thought for a second they had him. Then he let go and whirled away, running toward me, but running enough that the old hogs kept chasing him, thinking every second that they were going to catch him the next.

When they finally saw that they couldn't, the old hogs stopped and formed a tight circle. They faced outward around the ring, their rumps to the center, where all the squealing pigs were gathered. That way, they were ready to battle anything that wanted to jump on them. That's the way they were used to fighting bear and panther off from their young, and that's the way they aimed to fight us off.

But we were too smart, Old Yeller and I. We knew better than to try to break into that tight ring of threatening tushes. Anyhow, we didn't need to. All we needed was just to move the hogs along to where we wanted them, and Old Yeller already knew how to do this.

Back he went, right up into their faces, where he pestered them with yelling bays and false rushes till they couldn't stand it. With an angry roar, one of the barrows broke the ring to charge him. Instantly, all the others charged, too.

They were right on Old Yeller again. They were just about to get him. Just let them get a few inches closer, and one of

them would slam a four-inch tush into his soft belly.

The thing was, Old Yeller never would let them gain that last few inches on him. They cut and slashed at him from behind and both sides, yet he never was quite there. Always he was just a little bit beyond their reach, yet still so close that they couldn't help thinking that the next try was sure to get him.

It was a blood-chilling game Old Yeller played with the hogs, but one that you could see he enjoyed by the way he went at it. Give him time, and he'd take that bunch of angry hogs clear down out of the hills and into the pens at home if that's where I wanted them — never driving them, just leading them along.

But that's where Papa and I had other hog hunters out-figured. We almost never took our hogs to the pens to work them anymore. That took too much time. Also, after we got them penned, there was still the dangerous job of catching the pigs away from the old ones.

I hollered at Old Yeller. "Bring 'em on, Yeller," I said. Then I turned and headed for a big gnarled live-oak tree that stood in a clear patch of ground down the draw apiece.

I'd picked out that tree because it had a huge branch that stuck out to one side. I went and looked the branch over and saw that it was just right. It was low, yet still far enough above the ground to be out of reach of the highest-cutting hog.

I climbed up the tree and squatted on the branch. I unwound my rope from where I'd packed it coiled around my waist and shook out a loop. Then I hollered for Old yeller to bring the hogs over to me.

He did what I told him. He brought the fighting hogs to the tree and rallied them in a ring around it. Then he stood back, holding them there while he cocked his head sideways at me, wanting to know what came next.

I soon showed him. I waited till one of the pigs came trotting under my limb. I dropped my loop around him, gave it a quick yank, and lifted him, squealing and kicking, up out of the shuffling and roaring mass of hogs below. I clamped him between my knees, pulled out my knife, and went to work on him. First I folded his right ear and sliced out a three-cornered gap in the top side, a mark that we called an overbit. Then, from the under side of his left ear, I slashed off a long strip that ran clear to the point. That is what we called an underslope. That had

him marked for me. Our mark was overbit the right and underslope the left.

Other settlers had other marks, like crop the right and underbit the left, or two underbits in the right ear, or an overslope in the left and an overbit in the right. Everybody knew the hog mark of everybody else and we all respected them. We never butchered or sold a hog that didn't belong to us, or marked a pig following a sow that didn't wear our mark.

Cutting marks in a pig's ear is bloody work, and the scared pig kicks and squeals like he's dying. . . .

The squealing of the pig and the scent of his blood made the hogs beneath me go nearly wild with anger. You never heard such roaring and teeth-popping, as they kept circling the tree and rearing up on its trunk, trying to get to me. The noise they made and the hate and anger that showed in their eyes was enough to chill your blood. Only, I was used to the feeling and didn't let it bother me. That is, not much. Sometimes I'd let my mind slip for a minute and get to thinking how they'd slash me to pieces if I happened to fall out of the tree, and I'd feel a sort of cold shudder run all through me. But Papa had told me right from the start that fear was a right and natural feeling for anybody, and nothing to be ashamed of.

"It's a thing of your mind," he said, "and you can train your mind to handle it just like you can train your arm to throw a rock."

Put that way, it made sense to be afraid; so I hadn't bothered about that. I'd put in all my time trying to train my mind not to let fear stampede me. Sometimes it still did, of course, but not when I was working hogs. I'd had enough experience at working hogs that now I could generally look down and laugh at them.

I finished with the first pig and dropped it to the ground. Then, one after another, I roped the others, dragged them up into the tree, and worked them over.

A couple of times, the old hogs on the ground got so mad that they broke ranks and charged Old Yeller. But right from the start, Old Yeller had caught onto what I wanted. Every time they chased him from the tree, he'd just run off a little way and circle back, then stand off far enough away that they'd rally around my tree again.

In less than an hour, I was done with the job, and the only trouble we had was getting the hogs to leave the tree after I was finished. After going to so much trouble to hold the hogs under the tree, Old Yeller had a hard time understanding that I finally wanted them out of the way. And even after I got him to leave, the hogs were so mad and so suspicious that I had to squat there in the tree for nearly an hour longer before they finally drifted away into the bush, making it safe for me to come down.

Chapter 10

With hogs ranging in the woods like that, it was hard to know for certain when you'd found them all. But I kept a piece of ear from every pig I marked. I carried the pieces home in my pockets and stuck them on a sharp-pointed stick which I kept hanging in the corn crib. When the count reached 46 and I couldn't seem to locate any new bunches of hogs, Mama and I decided that was all the pigs the sows had raised that year. So I had left off hog hunting and started getting ready to gather corn when Bud Searcy paid us another visit. He told me about one bunch of hogs I'd missed.

"They're clear back in that bat cave country, the yonder side of Salt Branch," he said. "Rosal Simpson ran into them a couple of days ago, feeding on pear apples in them prickly-pear flats. Said there was five pigs following three sows wearing your mark. Couple of old bar' hogs ranging with them."

I'd never been that far the other side of Salt Branch before, but Papa had told me about the bat cave. I figured I could find the place. So early the next morning, I set out with Old Yeller, glad for the chance to hunt hogs a while longer before starting in on the corn gathering. Also, if I was lucky and found the hogs early, maybe I'd have time left to visit the cave and watch the bats come out.

Papa had told me that was a real sight, the way the bats come out in the late afternoon. I was sure anxious to go see it. I always like to go see strange sights.

Like one place on Salt Branch that I'd

found. There was a high, undercut cliff there and some birds building their nests against the face of it. They were little gray, sharp-winged swallows. They gathered sticky mud out of a hog wallow and carried it up and stuck it to the bare rocks of the cliff, shaping the mud into little bulging nests with a single hole in the center of each one. The young birds hatched out there and stuck their heads out through the holes to get at the worms and bugs the grown birds brought to them. The mud nests were so thick on the face of the cliff that, from a distance, the wall looked like it was covered with honeycomb.

There was another place I liked, too. It was a wild, lonesome place, down in a deep canyon that was bent in the shape of a horsehoe. Tall trees grew down in the canyon and leaned out over a deep hole of clear water. In the trees nested hundreds of long-shanked herons, blue ones and white ones with black wing tips. The herons built huge ragged nests of sticks and trash and sat around in the trees all day long, fussing and staining the tree branches with their white droppings. And beneath them, down in the clear water, yard-long catfish lay on the sandy bottom, waiting to gobble up any young birds that happened to fall out of the nests.

The bat cave sounded like another of those wild places I liked to see. I sure hoped I could locate the hogs in time to pay it a visit while I was close by.

We located the hogs in plenty of time; but before we were done with them, I didn't want to go see a bat cave or anything else.

Old Yeller struck the hogs' trail at a water hole. He ran the scent out into a regular forest of prickly pear. Bright red apples fringed the edges of the pear pads. In places where the hogs had fed, bits of peel and black seeds and red juice stain lay on the ground.

The sight made me wonder again how a hog could be tough enough to eat prickly-pear apples with their millions of little hairlike spines. I ate them, myself, sometimes; for pear apples are good eating. But even after I'd polished them clean by rubbing them in the sand, I generally wound up with several stickers in my mouth. But the hogs didn't seem to mind the stickers. Neither did the wild turkeys or the pack rats or the little big-eared ringtail cats. All of those creatures came to the pear flats when the apples started turning red.

Old Yeller's yelling bay told me that he'd caught up with the hogs. I heard their rumbling roars and ran through the pear clumps toward the sound. They were the hogs that Rosal Simpson had sent word about. There were five pigs, three sows, and a couple of bar' hogs, all but the pigs wearing our mark. Their faces bristled with long pear spines that they'd got stuck with, reaching for apples. Red juice stain was smeared all over their snouts. They stood, backed up against a big prickly-pear clump. Their anger had their bristles standing in high fierce ridges along their backbones. They roared and popped their teeth and dared me or Old Yeller to try to catch one of the squealing pigs.

I looked around for the closest tree. It stood better than a quarter of a mile off. It was going to be rough on Old Yeller, trying to lead them to it. Having to duck and dodge around in those prickly pears, he was bound to come out bristling with more pear spines than the hogs had in their faces. But I couldn't see any other place to take them. I struck off toward the tree, hollering at Old Yeller to bring them along.

A deep cut-bank draw ran through the pear flats between me and the huge mesquite tree I was heading for, and it was down in the bottom of this draw that the hogs balked. They'd found a place where the flood waters had undercut one of the dirt banks to form a shallow cave.

They'd backed up under the bank, with the pigs behind them. No amount of barking and pestering by Old Yeller could get them out. Now and then, one of the old bar' hogs would break ranks to make a quick cutting lunge at the dog. But when Yeller leaped away, the hog wouldn't follow up. He'd go right back to fill the gap he'd left in the half circle his mates had formed at the front of the cave. The hogs knew they'd found a natural spot for making a fighting stand, and they didn't aim to leave it.

I went back and stood on the bank above them, looking down, wondering what to do. Then it came to me that all I needed to do was go to work. This dirt bank would serve as well as a tree. There were the hogs right under me. They couldn't get to me from down there, not without first having to go maybe 50 yards down the draw to find a place to get out. And Old Yeller wouldn't let them do that. It wouldn't be easy to reach beneath that undercut bank and rope a pig, but I believed it could be done.

I took my rope from around my waist and shook out a loop. I moved to the lip of the cut bank. The pigs were too far back under me for a good throw. Maybe if I lay down on my stomach, I could reach them.

I did. I reached back under and picked up the first pig, slick as a whistle. I drew him up and worked him over. I dropped him back and watched the old hogs sniff his bloody wounds. Scent of his blood made them madder, and they roared louder.

I lay there and waited. A second pig moved out from the back part of the cave that I couldn't quite see. He still wasn't quite far enough out. I inched forward and leaned further down, to where I could see better. I could reach him with my loop now.

I made my cast, and that's when it happened. The dirt bank broke beneath my weight. A wagon load of sand caved off and spilled down over the angry hogs. I went with the sand.

I guess I screamed. I don't know. It happened too fast. All I can really remember is the wild heart-stopping scare I knew as I tumbled, head over heels, down among those killer hogs.

The crumbling sand all but buried the hogs. I guess that's what saved me, right at the start. I remember bumping into the back of one old bar' hog, then leaping to my feet in a smothering fog of dry dust. I jumped blindly to one side as far as I could. I broke to run, but I was too late.

A slashing tush caught me in the calf of my right leg.

A searing pain shot up into my body. I screamed. I stumbled and went down. I screamed louder then, knowing I could never get to my feet in time to escape the rush of angry hogs roaring down upon me.

It was Old Yeller who saved me. Just like he'd saved Little Arliss from the she bear. He came in, roaring with rage. He flung himself between me and the killer hogs. Fangs bared, he met them head on, slashing and snarling. He yelled with pain as the savage tushes ripped into him. He took the awful punishment meant for me, but held his ground. He gave me that one-in-a-hundred chance to get free.

I took it. I leaped to my feet. In wild terror, I ran along the bed of that dry wash, cut right up a sloping bank. Then I took out through the forest of prickly pear. I ran till a forked stick tripped me and I fell.

It seemed like that fall, or maybe it was the long prickly-pear spines that stabbed me in the hip, brought me out of my scare. I sat up, still panting for breath and with the blood hammering in my ears. But I was all right in my mind again. I yanked the spines out of my hip, then pulled up my slashed pants to look at my leg. Sight of so much blood nearly threw me into another panic. It was streaming out of the cut and clear down into my shoe.

I sat and stared at it for a moment and shivered. Then I got hold of myself again. I wiped away the blood. The gash was a bad one, clear to the bone, I could tell, and plenty long. But it didn't hurt much;

not yet, that is. The main hurting would start later, I guessed, after the bleeding stopped and my leg started to get stiff. I guessed I'd better hurry and tie up the place and get home as quick as I could. Once that leg started getting stiff, I might not make it.

I took my knife and cut a strip off the tail of my shirt. I bound my leg as tight as I could. I got up to see if I could walk with the leg wrapped as tight as I had it, and I could.

But when I set out, it wasn't in the direction of home. It was back along the trail through the prickly pear.

I don't quite know what made me do it. I didn't think to myself, "Old Yeller saved my life and I can't go off and leave him. He's bound to be dead, but it would look mighty shabby to go home without finding out for sure. I have to go back, even if my hurt leg gives out on me before I can get home."

I didn't think anything like that. I just started walking in that direction and kept walking till I found him.

He lay in the dry wash, about where I'd left it to go running through the prickly pear. He'd tried to follow me, but was too hurt to keep going. He was holed up un-

der a broad slab of red sandstone rock that had slipped off a high bank and now lay propped up against a round boulder in such a way as to form a sort of cave. He'd taken refuge there from the hogs. The hogs were gone now, but I could see their tracks in the sand around the rocks, where they'd tried to get at him from behind. I'd have missed him, hidden there under that rock slab, if he hadn't whined as I walked past.

I knelt beside him and coaxed him out from under the rocks. He grunted and groaned as he dragged himself toward me. He sank back to the ground, his blood-smeared body trembling while he wiggled his stub tail and tried to lick my hog-cut leg.

A big lump came up into my throat. Tears stung my eyes, blinding me. Here he was, trying to lick my wound, when he was bleeding from a dozen worse ones. And worst of all was his belly. It was ripped wide open and some of his insides were bulging out through the slit.

It was a horrible sight. It was so horrible that for a second I couldn't look at it. I wanted to run off. I didn't want to stay and look at something that filled me with such a numbing terror.

But I didn't run off. I shut my eyes and made myself run a hand over Old Yeller's head. The stickiness of the blood on it made my flesh crawl, but I made myself do it. Maybe I couldn't do him any good, but I wasn't going to run off and leave him to die all by himself.

Then it came to me that he wasn't dead yet and maybe he didn't have to die.

Maybe there was something that I could do to save him. Maybe if I hurried home, I could get Mama to come back and help me. Mama'd know what to do. Mama always knew what to do when somebody got hurt.

I wiped the tears from my eyes with my shirt sleeves and made myself think what to do. I took off my shirt and tore it into strips. I used a sleeve to wipe the sand from the belly wound. Carefully, I eased his entrails back into place. Then I pulled the lips of the wound together and wound strips of my shirt around Yeller's body. I wound them tight and tied the strips together so they couldn't work loose.

All the time I worked with him, Old Yeller didn't let out a whimper. But when I shoved him back under the rock where he'd be out of the hot sun, he started whining. I guess he knew that I was fixing to leave him, and he wanted to go, too. He started crawling back out of his hole.

I stood and studied for a while. I needed something to stop up that opening so Yeller couldn't get out. It would have to be something too big and heavy for him to shove aside. I thought of a rock and went looking for one. What I found was even better. It was an uprooted and dead mesquite tree, lying on the bank of the wash.

The stump end of the dead mesquite was big and heavy. It was almost too much for me to drag in the loose sand. I heaved and sweated and started my leg to bleeding again. But I managed to get that tree stump where I wanted it.

I slid Old Yeller back under the rock

slab. I scolded him and made him stay there till I could haul the tree stump into place.

Like I'd figured, the stump just about filled the opening. Maybe a strong dog could have squeezed through the narrow opening that was left, but I didn't figure Old Yeller could. I figured he'd be safe in there till I could get back.

Yeller lay back under the rock slab now, staring at me with a look in his eyes that made that choking lump come into my throat again. It was a begging look, and Old Yeller wasn't the kind to beg.

I reached in and let him lick my hand. "Yeller," I said, "I'll be back. I'm promising that I'll be back."

Then I lit out for home in a limping run. His howl followed me. It was the most mournful howl I ever heard.

Chapter 11

It looked like I'd never get back to where I'd left Old Yeller. To begin with, by the time I got home, I'd traveled too far and too fast. I was so hot and weak and played out that I was trembling all over. And that hog-cut leg was sure acting up. My leg hadn't gotten stiff like I'd figured. I'd used it too much. But I'd strained the cut muscle. It was jerking and twitching long before I got home, and after I got there, it wouldn't stop.

That threw a big scare into Mama. I argued and fussed, trying to tell her what bad shape Old Yeller was in and how we needed to hurry back to him. But she wouldn't pay me any mind.

She told me, "We're not going anywhere until we've cleaned up and doctored that leg. I've seen hog cuts before. Neglect them, and they can be as dangerous as snakebite. Now, you just hold still till I get through."

I saw that it wasn't any use, so I held still while she got hot water and washed out the cut. But when she poured turpentine into the place, I couldn't hold still. I jumped and hollered and screamed. It was like she'd burnt me with a red-hot iron. It hurt worse than when the hog slashed me. I hollered with hurt till Little Arliss tuned up and went to crying, too. But when the pain finally left my leg, the muscle had quit jerking.

Mama got some clean white rags and bound up the place. Then she said, "Now, you lie down on that bed and rest. I don't want to see you take another step on that leg for a week."

I was so stunned that I couldn't say a word. All I could do was stare at her. Old Yeller, lying 'way off out there in the hills, about to die if he didn't get help, and Mama telling me I couldn't walk.

I got up off the stool I'd been sitting on. I said to her, "Mama, I'm going back after Old Yeller. I promised him I'd come back, and that's what I aim to do." Then I walked out to the lot.

By the time I got Jumper caught, Mama had her bonnet on. She was ready to go, too. She looked a little flustered, like she didn't know what to do with me, but all she said was, "How'll we bring him back?"

"On Jumper," I said. "I'll ride Jumper and hold Old Yeller in my arms."

"You know better than that," she said. "He's too big and heavy. I might lift him up to you, but you can't stand to hold him in your arms that long. You'll give out."

"I'll hold him," I said. "If I give out, I'll rest. Then we'll go on again."

Mama stood tapping her foot for a minute while she gazed off across the hills. She said, like she was talking to herself, "We can't use the cart. There aren't any roads, and the country is too rough."

Suddenly she turned to me and smiled. "I know what. Get that cowhide off the fence. I'll go get some pillows."

"Cowhide?"

"Tie it across Jumper's back," she said. "I'll show you later."

I didn't know what she had in mind, but it didn't much matter. She was going with me.

I got the cowhide and slung it across Jumper's back. It rattled and spooked him so that he snorted and jumped from under it.

"You, Jumper!" I shouted at him. "You hold still."

He held still the next time. Mama brought the pillows and a long coil of rope. She had me tie the cowhide to Jumper's back and bind the pillows down on top of it. Then she lifted Little Arliss up

© 1957 The Walt Disney Company

and set him down on top of the pillows.

"You ride behind him," she said to me. "I'll walk."

We could see the buzzards gathering long before we got there. We could see them wheeling black against the blue sky and dropping lower and lower with each circling. One we saw didn't waste time to circle. He came hurtling down at a long-slanted dive, his ugly head outstretched, his wings all but shut against his body. He shot past, right over our heads, and the whooshing sound his body made in splitting the air sent cold chills running all through me. I guessed it was all over for Old Yeller.

Mama was walking ahead of Jumper. She looked back at me. The look in her eyes told me that she figured the same thing. I got so sick that it seemed like I couldn't stand it.

But when we moved down into the prickly-pear flats, my misery eased some. For suddenly, up out of a wash ahead rose a flurry of flapping wings. Something had disturbed those buzzards and I thought I knew what it was.

A second later, I was sure it was Old Yeller. His yelling bark sounded thin and weak, yet just to hear it made me want to holler and run and laugh. He was still alive. He was still able to fight back!

The frightened buzzards had settled back to the ground by the time we got there. When they caught sight of us, though, they got excited and went to trying to get off the ground again. For birds that can sail around in the air all day with hardly more than a movement of their wing tips, they sure were clumsy and awkward about getting started. Some had to keep hopping along the wash for 50 yards, beating the air with their huge wings, before they could finally take off. And then they were slow to rise. I could have shot a dozen of them before they got away if I'd thought to bring my gun along.

There was a sort of crazy light shining in Old Yeller's eyes when I looked in at him. When I reached to drag the stump away, he snarled and lunged at me with bared fangs.

I jerked my hands away just in time and shouted "Yeller!" at him. Then he knew I wasn't a buzzard. The crazy light went out of his eyes. He sank back into the hole with a loud groan like he'd just had a big load taken off his mind.

Mama helped me drag the stump away. Then we reached in and rolled his hurt body over on its back and slid him out into the light.

Without bothering to examine the blood-caked cuts that she could see all over his head and shoulders, Mama started unwinding the strips of cloth from around his body.

Then Little Arliss came crowding past me, asking in a scared voice what was the matter with Yeller.

Mama stopped. "Arliss," she said, "do you think you could go back down this sandy wash here and catch Mama a pretty green-striped lizard? I thought I saw one down there around that first bend."

Little Arliss was as pleased as I was surprised. Always before, Mama had just sort of put up with his lizard-catching. Now she was wanting him to catch one just for her. A delighted grin spread over his face. He turned and ran down the wash as hard as he could go.

Mama smiled up at me, and suddenly I understood. She was just getting Little Arliss out of the way so he wouldn't have to look at the terrible sight of Yeller's slitted belly.

She said to me, "Go jerk a long hair out of Jumper's tail, son. But stand to one side, so he won't kick you."

I went and stood to one side of Jumper and jerked a long hair out of his tail. Sure enough, he snorted and kicked at me, but he missed. I took the hair back to Mama, wondering as much about it as I had about the green-striped lizard. But when Mama pulled a long sewing needle from her dress front and poked the small end of the hair through the eye, I knew then.

"Horse hair is always better than thread for sewing up a wound," she said. She didn't say why, and I never did think to ask her.

Mama asked me if any of Yeller's entrails had been cut and I told her that I didn't think so.

"Well, I won't bother them then," she said. "Anyway, if they are, I don't think I could fix them."

It was a long, slow job, sewing up Old Yeller's belly. And the way his flesh would flinch and quiver when Mama poked the needle through, it must have hurt. But if it did, Old Yeller didn't say anything about it. He just lay there and licked my hands while I held him.

We were wrapping him up in some clean rags that Mama had brought along when here came Little Arliss. He was running as hard as he'd been when he left. He was grinning and hollering at Mama. And in his right hand he carried a green-striped lizard, too.

How on earth he'd managed to catch anything as fast running as one of those green-striped lizards, I don't know; but he sure had one.

You never saw such a proud look as he wore on his face when he handed the lizard to Mama. And I don't guess I ever saw a more helpless look on Mama's face as she took it. Mama had always been squeamish about lizards and snakes and bugs and things, and you could tell that it just made her flesh crawl to have to touch this one. But she took it and admired it and thanked Arliss. Then she asked him if he'd keep it for her till we got home. Which Little Arliss was glad to do.

"Now, Arliss," she told him, "we're going to play a game. We're playing like Old Yeller is sick and you are taking care of him. We're going to let you both ride on a cowhide, like the sick Indians do sometimes."

It always pleased Little Arliss to play any sort of game, and this was a new one that he'd never heard about before. He was so anxious to get started that we could hardly keep him out from underfoot till Mama could get things ready.

As soon as she took the cowhide off Jumper's back and spread it hair-side down upon the ground, I began to get the idea. She placed the soft pillows on top of the hide, then helped me to ease Old Yeller's hurt body onto the pillows.

"Now, Arliss," Mama said, "you sit there on the pillows with Old Yeller and help hold him on. But remember now, don't play with him or get on top of him. We're playing like he's sick, and when your dog is sick, you have to be real careful with him."

It was a fine game, and Little Arliss fell right in with it. He sat where Mama told him to. He held Old Yeller's head in his lap, waiting for the ride to start.

It didn't take long. I'd already tied a rope around Jumper's neck, leaving the loop big enough that it would pull back against his shoulders. Then, on each side of Jumper, we tied another rope into the one knotted about his shoulders, and carried the ends of them back to the cowhide.

I took my knife and cut two slits into the edge of the cowhide, then tied a rope into each one. We measured to get each rope the same length and made sure they were far enough back that the cowhide wouldn't touch Jumper's heels. Like most mules, Jumper was mighty fussy about anything touching his heels.

"Now, Travis, you ride him," Mama said, "and I'll lead him."

"You better let me walk," I argued. "Jumper's liable to throw a fit with that hide rattling along behind him, and you might not can hold him by yourself."

"You ride him," Mama said. "I don't want you walking on that leg anymore. If Jumper acts up one time, I'll take a club to him!"

We started off, with Little Arliss crowing at what a fine ride he was getting on the dragging hide. Sure enough, at the first sound of that rattling hide, old Jumper acted up. He snorted and tried to lunge to one side. But Mama yanked down on his bridle and said, "Jumper, you wretch!" I whacked him between the ears with a dead stick. With the two of us coming at him like that, it was more than Jumper wanted. He settled down and went to traveling as quiet as he generally pulled a plow, with just now and then bending his neck around to take a look at what he was dragging. You could tell he didn't like it, but I guess he figured he'd best put up with it.

Little Arliss never hd a finer time than he did on that ride home. He enjoyed every long hour of it. And a part of the time, I don't guess it was too rough on Old Yeller. The cowhide dragged smooth and even as long as we stayed in the sandy wash. When we left the wash and took out across the flats, it still didn't look bad. Mama led Jumper in a long roundabout way, keeping as much as she could to the openings where the tall grass grew. The grass would bend down before the hide, making a soft cushion over which the hide slipped easily. But this was a rough country, and try as hard as she could, Mama couldn't always dodge the rocky places. The hide slid over the rocks, the same as over the grass and sand, but it couldn't do it without jolting the riders pretty much.

Little Arliss would laugh when the hide raked along over the rocks and jolted him till his teeth rattled. He got as much fun out of that as the rest of the ride. But the jolting hurt Old Yeller till sometimes he couldn't hold back his whinings.

When Yeller's whimperings told us he was hurting too bad, we'd have to stop and wait for him to rest up. At other times, we stopped to give him water. Once we got water out of a little spring that trickled down through the rocks. The next time was a Birdsong Creek.

Mama'd pack water to him in my hat. He was too weak to get up and drink; so Mama would hold the water right under his nose and I'd lift him up off the pillows and hold him close enough that he could reach down and lap the water up with his tongue.

Having to travel so far and so slow and with so many halts, it looked like we'd never get him home. But we finally made it just about the time it got dark enough for the stars to show.

By then, my hurt leg was plenty stiff,

never get him home. But we finally made it just about the time it got dark enough for the stars to show.

By then, my hurt leg was plenty stiff, stiff and numb. It was all swelled up and felt as dead as a chunk of wood. When I slid down off Jumper's back, it wouldn't hold me. I fell clear to the ground and lay in the dirt, too tired and hurt to get up.

Mama made a big to-do about how weak and hurt I was, but I didn't mind. We'd gone and brought Old Yeller home, and he was still alive. There under the starlight, I could see him licking Little Arliss's face.

Little Arliss was sound asleep.

Chapter 12

For the next couple of weeks, Old Yeller and I had a rough time of it. I lay on the bed inside the cabin and Yeller lay on the cowhide in the dog run, and we both hurt so bad that we were wallowing and groaning and whimpering all the time. Sometimes I hurt so bad that I didn't quite know what was happening. I'd hear grunts and groans and couldn't tell if they were mine or Yeller's. My leg had swelled up till it was about the size of a butter churn. I had such a wild hot fever that Mama nearly ran herself to death, packing fresh cold water from the spring, which she used to bathe me all over, trying to run my fever down.

When she wasn't packing water, she was out digging prickly-pear roots and hammering them to mush in a sack, then binding the mush to my leg for a poultice.

We had lots of prickly pear growing close to the house, but they were the big tall ones and their roots were no good. The ones that make a good poultice are the smaller size. They don't have much top, but lots of knotty roots, shaped sort of like sweet potatoes. That kind didn't grow close to the house. Along at the last,

Mama had to go clear over to the Salt Licks to locate that kind.

When Mama wasn't waiting on me, she was taking care of Old Yeller. She waited

on him just like she did me. She was getting up all hours of the night to doctor our wounds, bathe us in cold water, and feed us when she could get us to eat. On top of that, there were the cows to milk, Little Arliss to look after, clothes to wash, wood to cut, and old Jumper to worry with.

The bad drought that Bud Searcy predicted had come. The green grass all dried up till Jumper was no longer satisfied to eat it. He took to jumping the field fence and eating the corn that I'd never yet gotten around to gathering.

Mama couldn't let that go on; that was our bread corn. Without it, we'd have no bread for the winter. But it looked like for a while that there wasn't any way to save it. Mama would go to the field and run Jumper out; then before she got her back turned good, he'd jump back in and go to eating corn again.

Finally, Mama figured out a way to keep Jumper from jumping. She tied a drag to him. She got a rope and tied one end of it to his right forefoot. To the other end, she tied a big heavy chunk of wood. By pulling hard, Jumper could move his drag along enough to graze and get to water; but any time he tried to rear up for a jump, the drag held him down.

The drag on Jumper's foot saved the corn, but it didn't save Mama from a lot of work. Jumper was always getting his chunk of wood hung up behind a bush or rock, so that he couldn't get away. Then he'd have himself a big scare and rear up, fighting the rope and falling down and pitching and bawling. If Mama didn't hear him right away, he'd start braying, and he'd keep it up till she went and lossened the drag.

Altogether, Mama sure had her hands full, and Little Arliss wasn't any help. He was too little to do any work. And with neither of us to play with, he got lonesome. He'd follow Mama around every step she made, getting in the way and feeling hurt because she didn't have time to pay him any mind. When he wasn't pestering her, he was pestering me. A dozen times a day, he'd come in to stare at me and say, "Whatcha doin' in bed, Travis? Why doncha get up? Why doncha get up and come play with me?"

He nearly drove me crazy till the day Bud Searcy and Lisbeth came, bringing the pup.

I didn't know about the pup at first. I didn't even know that Lisbeth had come. I heard Bud Searcy talk to Mama when they rode up, but I was hurting too bad even to roll over and look out the door. I remember just lying there, being mad at Searcy for coming. I knew what a bother he'd be to Mama. For all his talk of looking after the women and children of Salt Licks while the men were gone, I knew he'd never turn a hand to any real work. You wouldn't catch him offering to chop wood or gather in a corn crop. All he'd do was sit out under the dog run all day, talking and chewing tobacco and spitting juice all over the place. On top of that, he'd expect Mama to cook him up a good dinner and maybe a supper if he took a notion to stay that long. And Mama had 10 times too much to do, like it was.

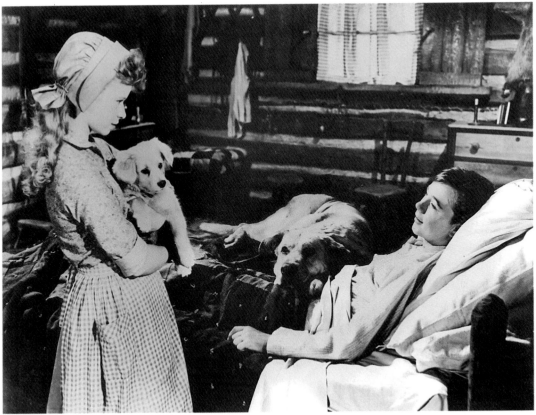

In a little bit, though, I heard a quiet step at the door. I looked up. It was Lisbeth. She stood with her hands behind her back, staring at me with her big solemn eyes.

"You hurting pretty bad?" she asked.

I was hurting a-plenty, but I wasn't admitting it to a girl. "I'm doing all right," I said.

"We didn't know you'd got hog cut, or we'd have come sooner," she said.

I didn't know what to say to that, so I didn't say anything.

"Well, anyhow," she said, "I brung you a surprise."

I was too sick and worn out to care about a surprise right then; but there was such an eager look in her eyes that I knew I had to say "What?" or hurt her feelings, so I said, "What?"

"One of Miss Prissy's pups!" she said.

She brought her hands around from behind her back. In the right one she held a dog pup about as big as a year-old possum. It was dirty white in color and speckled all over with blue spots about the size of cow ticks. She held it by the slack hide at the back of its neck. It hung there, half asleep, sagging in its own loose hide like it was dead.

"Born in a badger hole," she said. "Seven of them. I brung you the best one!"

I thought: If that puny-looking thing is the best one, Miss Prissy must have had a sorry litter of pups. But I didn't say so. I said, "He sure looks like a dandy."

"He is," Lisbeth said. "See how I've been holding him, all this time, and he hasn't said a word."

I'd heard that one all my life — that if a pup didn't holler when you held him up by the slack hide of his neck, he was sure to turn out to be a gritty one. I didn't think much of that sign. Papa always put more stock in what color was inside a pup's mouth. If the pup's mouth was black inside, Papa said that was the one to choose. And that's the way I felt about it.

But right now I didn't care if the pup's mouth was pea-green on the inside. All I wanted was just to quit hurting.

I said, "I guess Little Arliss will like it," then knew I'd said the wrong thing. I could tell by the look in her eyes that I'd hurt her feelings, after all.

She didn't say anything. She just got real still and quiet and kept staring at me till I couldn't stand it and had to look away. Then she turned and went out of the cabin and gave the pup to Little Arliss.

It made me mad, her looking at me like that. What did she expect, anyhow? Here I was laid up with a bad hog cut, hurting so bad I could hardly get my breath, and her expecting me to make a big to-do over a puny speckled pup.

I had me a dog. Old Yeller was all cut up, worse than I was, but he was getting well. Mama had told me that. So what use did I have for a pup? Be all right for Little Arliss to play with. Keep him occupied and out from underfoot. But when Old Yeller and I got well and took to the woods again, we wouldn't have time to wait around on a fool pup, too little to follow.

I lay there in bed, mad and fretful all day, thinking how silly it was for Lisbeth to expect me to want a pup when I already had me a full-grown dog. I lay there, just waiting for a chance to tell her so, too; only she never did come back to give me a chance. She stayed outside and played with Little Arliss and the pup till her grandpa finally wound up his talking and tobacco spitting and got ready to leave. Then I saw her and Little Arliss come past the door, heading for where I could hear her grandpa saddling his horse. She looked in at me, then looked away, and suddenly I wasn't mad at her anymore. I felt sort of mean. I wished now I could think of the right thing to say about the pup, so I could call her back and tell her. I didn't want her to go off home with her feeling still hurt.

But before I could think of anything, I hear her grandpa say to Mama, "Now Mrs. Coates, you all are in a sort of bind here, with your man gone and that boy crippled up. I been setting out here all evening, worrying about it. That's my responsibility, you know, seeing that everybody's taken care of while the men are gone, and I think now I've got a way figured. I'll just leave our girl Lisbeth here to help you all out."

Mama said in a surprised voice, "Why,

Mr. Searcy, there's no need for that. It's mighty kind of you and all, but we'll make out all right."

"No, Mrs. Coates, you got too big a load to carry, all by yourself. My Lisbeth, she'll be proud to help out."

"But," Mama argued, "she's such a little girl, Mr. Searcy, She's probably never stayed away from home of a night."

"She's little," Bud Searcy said, "but she's stout and willing. She's like me; when folks are in trouble, she'll pitch right in and do her part. You just keep her here now. You'll see what a big help she'll be."

Mama tried to argue some more, but Bud Searcy wouldn't listen. He just told Lisbeth to be a good girl and help Mama out, like she was used to helping out at home. Then he mounted and rode on off.

READING COMPREHENSION

Summarizing. Choose the best phrase to complete each sentence. Then write the complete statements on your paper.

1. Travis had to catch the pigs that the sows had raised that year in order to _____ (pen them up, mark their ears, sell them).

2. Old Yeller got the hogs to Travis by _____ (having them chase him, herding them, driving them one by one).

3. Old Yeller saved Travis from being killed by _____ (a bear, two bulls, some wild hogs).

4. Old Yeller's life was saved by _____ (Arliss and Lisbeth Searcy, Burn Sanderson, Travis and Mama).

Interpreting. Write the answer to each question on your paper.

1. When both Travis and Old Yeller were badly wounded, why did Travis limp home, leaving the dog behind?

2. How did Travis and Mama manage to get Old Yeller home?

3. Why did Lisbeth give Travis the pup? why didn't Travis want it?

For Thinking and Discussing. Travis tells the reader, "A boy, before he really grows up . . . can get the wits scared out of him today and by tomorrow have forgotten all about it." How might he define a man? Do you agree with these definitions?

UNDERSTANDING LITERATURE

Setting. The setting of a novel is the time and place of the events. It is *when* and *where* the events take place.

Here are some passages from *Old Yeller*. On your paper, answer the questions that follow the passages.

> Our hogs ran loose in those days, the same as our cattle. We fenced them out of the fields, but never into a pasture; we had no pastures.

1. If the story took place today, would Travis have had to hunt for the hogs?

> "Horse hair is always better than thread for sewing up a wound," she [Mama] said.

2. Would Mama be apt to know this information if she lived in a city today?

> When she [Mama] wasn't packing water, she was out digging prickly-pear roots and hammering them to mush in a sack, then binding the mush to my leg for a poultice.

3. Would Mama be doing these chores if she lived in a modern city?

Now, write the answer to this question.

4. Travis's family lived pretty much alone, away from the settlement. How does this affect the story?

WRITING

Pretend you are Travis. Would you like to live in a different setting? Write a paragraph telling how you feel about the time and place in which you live.

Chapter 13

I was like Mama. I didn't think Lisbeth Searcy would be any help around the place. She was too little and too skinny. I figured she'd just be an extra bother for Mama.

But we were wrong. Just like Bud Searcy said, she was a big help. She could tote water from the spring. She could feed the chickens, pack in wood, cook cornbread, wash dishes, wash Little Arliss, and sometimes even change the prickly-pear poultice on my leg.

She didn't have to be told, either. She was right there on hand all the time, just looking for something to do. She was a lot better about that than I ever was. She wasn't as big and she couldn't do as much as I could, but she was more willing.

She didn't even back off when Mama hooked Jumper to the cart and headed for the field to gather in the corn. That was a job I always hated. It was hot work, and the corn shucks made my skin itch and sting till sometimes I'd wake up at night scratching like I'd stumbled into a patch of bull nettles.

But it didn't seem to bother Lisbeth. In fact, it looked like she and Mama and Little Arliss had a real good time gathering corn. I'd see them drive past the cabin, all three of them sitting on top of a cart-load of corn. They would be laughing and talking and having such a romping big time, playing with the speckled pup, that before long I half wished I was able to gather corn, too.

In a way, it sort of hurt my pride for a little old girl like Lisbeth to come in and take over my jobs. Papa had left me to look after things. But now I was laid up, and here was a girl handling my work about as good as I could. Still, she couldn't get out and mark hogs or kill meat or swing a chopping axe.

Before they were finished gathering corn, however, we were faced with a trouble a whole lot too big for any of us to handle.

The first hint of it came when the Spot heifer failed to show up one evening at milking time. Mama had come in too late from the corn gathering to go look for her before dark, and the next morning she didn't need to. Spot came up, by herself; or rather, she came past the house.

I heard her first. The swelling in my leg was about gone down. I was weak as a rain-chilled chicken, but most of the hurting had stopped. I was able to sit up in bed a lot and take notice of things.

I heard a cow coming toward the house. She was bawling like cows do when they've lost a calf or when their bags are stretched too tight with milk. I recognized Spot's voice.

Spot's calf recognized it, too. It had stood hungry in the pen all night and now it was nearly crazy for a bait of milk. I could hear it blatting and racing around in the cowpen, so starved it could hardly wait.

I called to Mama. "Mama," I said, "you better go let old Spot in to her calf. I hear her coming."

"That pesky Spot," I heard her say impatiently. "I don't know what's got into her, staying out all night like that and letting her calf go hungry."

I heard Mama calling to Spot as she went out to the cowpen. A little later, I heard Spot beller like a fighting bull, then Mama's voice rising high and sharp. Then here came Mama, running into the cabin, calling for Lisbeth to hurry and bring in Little Arliss. There was scare in Mama's voice. I sat up in bed as Lisbeth came running in, dragging Little Arliss after her.

Mama slammed the door shut, then turned to me. "Spot made fight at me," she said. "I can't understand it. It was like I was some varmint that she'd never seen before."

Mama turned and opened the door a crack. She looked out, then threw the door wide open and stood staring toward the cowpen.

"Why, look at her now," she said. "She's not paying one bit of attention to her calf. She's just going on past the cowpen like her calf wasn't there. She's acting as crazy as if she'd got hold of a bit of pea vine."

There was a little pea vine that grew wild all over the hills during wet winters and bloomed pale lavender in the spring. Cattle and horses could eat it, mixed with grass, and get fat on it. But sometimes when they got too big a bait of it alone, it poisoned them. Generally, they'd stumble around with the blind staggers for a while, then gradually get well. Sometimes, though, the pea vine killed them.

I sat there for a moment, listening to Spot. She was bawling again, like when I first heard her. But now she was heading off into the brush again, leaving her calf to starve. I wondered where she'd gotten enough pea vine to hurt her.

"But, Mama," I said, "she couldn't have eaten pea vine. The pea vine is all dead and gone this time of year."

Mama turned and looked at me, then looked away. "I know," she said. "That's what's got me so worried."

I thought of what Burn Sanderson had told me about animals that didn't act right. I said, "Cows don't ever get hydrophobia, do they?"

I saw Lisbeth start at the word. She stared at me with big solemn eyes.

"I don't know," Mama said. "I've seen dogs with it, but I've never heard of a cow brute having it. I just don't know."

In the next few days, while Old Yeller and I healed fast, we all worried and watched.

All day and all night, Spot kept right on doing what she did from the start: she walked and she bawled. She walked mostly in a wide circle that brought her pretty close to the house about twice a day and then carried her so far out into the hills that we could just barely hear her. She walked with her head down. She walked slower and her bawling got weaker as she got weaker; but she never stopped walking and bawling.

When the bull came, he was worse, and a lot more dangerous. He came two or three days later. I was sitting out under the dog run at the time. I'd hobbled out to sit in a chair beside Old Yeller, where I could scratch him under his chewed-off ear. That's where he liked to be scratched

best. Mama was in the kitchen, cooking dinner. Lisbeth and Little Arliss had gone off to the creek below the spring to play with the pup and to fish for catfish. I could see them running and laughing along the bank, chasing after grasshoppers for bait.

Then I heard this moaning sound and turned to watch a bull come out of the brush. He was the roan bull, the one that the droopy-horned *chongo* had dumped into the Mexican cart the day of the fight. But he didn't walk like any bull I'd ever seen before. He walked with his head hung low and wobbling. He reeled and staggered like he couldn't see where he was going. He walked head on into a mesquite tree like it wasn't there, and fell to his knees when he hit it. He scrambled to his feet and came on, grunting and staggering and moaning, heading toward the spring.

Right then, for the first time since we'd brought him home, Old Yeller came up off his cowhide bed. He'd been lying there beside me, paying no attention to sight or sound of the bull. Then, I guess the wind must have shifted and brought him the bull's scent; and evidently that scent told him for certain what I was only beginning to suspect.

He rose, with a savage growl. He moved out toward the bull, so trembly weak that he could hardly stand. His loose lips were lifted in an ugly snarl, baring his white fangs. His hackles stood up in a ragged ridge along the back of his neck and shoulders.

Watching him, I felt a prickling at the back of my own neck. I'd seen him act like that before, but only when there was the greatest danger. Never while just facing a bull.

Suddenly, I knew that Mama and I had been fooling ourselves. Up till now, we'd been putting off facing up to facts. We'd

460

kept hoping that the heifer Spot would get over whatever was wrong with her. Mama and Lisbeth had kept Spot's calf from starving by letting it suck another cow. They'd had to tie the cow's hind legs together to keep her from kicking the calf off; but they'd kept it alive, hoping Spot would get well and come back to it.

Now, I knew that Spot wouldn't get well, and this bull wouldn't, either. I knew they were both deathly sick with hydrophobia. Old Yeller had scented that sickness in this bull and somehow sensed how fearfully dangerous it was.

I thought of Lisbeth and Little Arliss down past the spring. I came up out of my chair, calling for Mama. "Mama!" I said. "Bring me my gun, Mama!"

Mama came hurrying to the door. "What is it, Travis?" she wanted to know.

"That bull!" I said, pointing. "He's mad with hydrophobia and he's heading straight for Lisbeth and Little Arliss."

Mama took one look and said, "Oh, no!" in almost a whisper. She didn't wait to get me my gun or anything else. She just tore out for the creek, hollering for Lisbeth and Little Arliss to run, to climb a tree, to do anything to get away from the bull.

I called after her, telling her to wait, to give me a chance to shoot the bull. I don't guess she ever heard me. But the bull heard her. He tried to turn on her, stumbled and went to his knees. Then he was back on his feet again as Mama went flying past. He charged straight for her. He'd have gotten her, too, only the sickness had his legs too wobbly. This time, when he fell, he rooted his nose into the ground and just lay there, moaning, too weak even to try to get up agian.

By this time, Old Yeller was there, baying the bull, keeping out of his reach, but ready to eat him alive if he ever came to his feet again.

I didn't wait to see more. I went and got my gun. I hobbled down to where I couldn't miss and shot the roan bull between the eyes.

Chapter 14

We couldn't leave the dead bull to lie there that close to the cabin. In a few days, the scent of rotting flesh would drive us out. Also, the carcass lay too close to the spring. Mama was afraid it would foul up our drinking water.

"We'll have to try to drag it further from the cabin and burn it," she said.

"Burn it?" I said in surprise. "Why can't we just leave it for the buzzards and varmints to clean up?"

"Because that might spread the sickness," Mama said. "If the varmints eat it, they might get the sickness, too."

Mama went to put the harness on Jumper. I sent Lisbeth to bring me a rope.

I doubled the rope and tied it in a loop around the bull's horns. Mama brought Jumper, who snorted and shied away at the sight of the dead animal. Jumper had smelled deer blood plenty of times, so I guess it was the size of the bull that scared him. Or maybe like Yeller, Jumper could scent the dead bull's sickness. I had to talk mean and threaten him with a club before we could get him close enough for Mama to hook the singletree over the loop of rope I'd tied around the bull's horns.

Then the weight of the bull was too much for him. Jumper couldn't drag it. He leaned into his collar and dug in with his hoofs. He grunted and strained. He pulled till I saw the big muscles of his haunches flatten and start quivering. But the best he could do was slide the bull carcass along the ground for about a foot before he gave up.

I knew he wasn't throwing off. Jumper was full of lot of a pesky, aggravating mule tricks; but when you called on him to move a load, he'd move it or bust something.

I called on him again. I drove him at a different angle from the load, hoping he'd have better luck. He didn't. He threw everything he had into the collar, and all he did was pop a link out of his right race chain. The flying link whistled past my ear with the speed of a bullet. It would have killed me just as dead if it had hit me.

Well, that was it. There was no moving the dead bull now. We could patch up that broken trace chain for pulling an ordinary load. But it would never be strong enough to pull this one. Even if Jumper was.

I looked at Mama. She shook her head.

"I guess there's nothing we can do but burn it here," she said. "But it's going to take a sight of wood gathering."

It did, too. We'd lived there long enough to use up all the dead wood close to the cabin. Now, Mama and Lisbeth had to go 'way out into the brush for it. I got a piece of rawhide string and patched up the race chain, and Mama and Lisbeth used Jumper to drag up big dead logs. I helped them pile the logs on top of the bull. We piled them up till we had the carcass completely covered, then set fire to them.

In a little bit, the fire was roaring. Sheets of hot flame shot high into the air. The heat and the stench of burnt hair and scorching hide drove us back.

It was the biggest fire I'd ever seen. I thought there was fire enough there to burn three bulls. But when it began to die down a couple of hours later, the bull carcass wasn't half burnt up. Mama and Lisbeth went back to dragging up more wood.

It took two days and nights to burn up that bull. We worked all day long each day, with Mama and Lisbeth dragging up the wood and me feeding the stinking fire. Then at night, we could hardly sleep. This was because of the howling and snarling and fighting of the wolves lured to the place by the scent of the roasting meat. The wolves didn't get any of it; they were too afraid of the hot fire. But that didn't keep them from gathering for miles around and making the nights hideous with their howlings and snarlings.

And all night long, both nights, Old Yeller crippled back and forth between the fire and the cabin, baying savagely, warning the wolves to keep away.

Both nights, I lay there, watching the eyes of the shifting wolves glow like live mesquite coals in the firelight, and listening to the weak moaning bawl of old Spot still traveling in a circle. I lay there, feeling shivery with a fearful dread that brought up pictures in my mind of Bud Searcy's uncle.

I sure did wish Papa would come home.

As soon as the job of burning the bull was over, Mama told us we had to do the same for Spot. That was all Mama said about it, but I could tell by the look in her eyes how much she hated to give up. She'd had great hopes for Spot's making us a real milk cow, especially after Old Yeller had gentled her so fast; but that was all gone now.

Mama looked tired, and more worried than I think I'd ever seen her. I guess she couldn't help thinking what I was thinking — that if hydrophobia had sickened one of our cows, it just might get them all.

"I'll do the shooting," I told her. "But I'm going to follow her out a ways from the house to do it. Close to some wood."

"How about your leg?" Mama asked.

"That leg's getting all right," I told her. "Think it'll do it some good to be walked on."

"Well, try to kill her on bare ground," Mama cautioned. "As dry as it is now, we'll be running a risk of setting the woods afire if there's much old grass around the place."

I waited till Spot circled past the cabin again, then took my gun and followed her, keeping a safe distance behind.

By now, Spot was so sick and starved I could hardly stand to look at her. She didn't look like a cow; she looked more like the skeleton of one. She was just skin and bones. She was so weak that she stumbled as she walked. Half a dozen times she went to her knees and each time I'd think she'd taken her last step. But she'd always get up and go on again — and keep bawling.

I kept waiting for her to cross a bare patch of ground where it would be safe to build a fire. She didn't; and I couldn't drive her, of course. She was too crazy mad to be driven anywhere. I was afraid to mess with her. She might be like the bull. If I ever let her know I was anywhere about, she might go on the fight.

I guess she was a mile from the cabin before I saw that she was about to cross a dry sandy wash, something like the one where Yeller and I had got mixed up with the hogs. That would be a good place, I knew. It was pretty far for us to have to come to burn her, but there was plenty of dry wood around. And if I could drop her out there in that wide sandy wash, there'd be no danger of a fire getting away from us.

I hurried around and got ahead of her. I hid behind a turkey-pear bush on the far side of the wash. But as sick and blind as she was, I think I could have stood out in the broad open without her ever seeing me. I waited till she came stumbling across the sandy bed of the wash, then fired, dropping her in the middle of it.

I'd used up more of my strength than I knew, following Spot so far from the cabin. By the time I got back, I was dead beat. The seat was pouring off me and I was trembling all over.

Mama took one look at me and told me to get to bed. "We'll go start the burning," she said. "You stay on that leg any longer, and it'll start swelling again."

I didn't argue. I knew I was too weak and tired to take another walk that far without rest. So I told Mama where to find Spot and told her to leave Little Arliss with me, and watched her and Lisbeth head out, both mounted on Jumper. Mama was carrying a panful of live coals to start the fire with.

At the last minute, Yeller got up off his cowhide. He stood watching them a minute, like he was trying to make up his mind about something; then he went trotting after them. He was still thin and rough-looking and crippled pretty badly in one leg. But I figured he knew better than I did whether or not he was able to travel. I didn't call him back.

As it turned out, it's a good thing I didn't. Only, afterward, I wished a thousand times that I could have had some way of looking ahead to what was going to happen. Then I would have done everything I could to keep all of them from going.

With Little Arliss to look after, I sure didn't mean to drop off to sleep. But I did and slept till sundown when suddenly I jerked awake, feeling guilty about leaving him alone so long.

I needn't have worried. Little Arliss was right out there in the yard, playing with the speckled pup. They had themselves a game going. Arliss was racing around the cabin, dragging a short piece of frayed rope. The pup was chasing the rope. Now and then he'd get close enough to pounce on it. Then he'd let out a growl and set his teeth into it and try to shake it and hang on at the same time. Generally, he got jerked off his feet and turned a couple of somersets, but that didn't seem to bother him. The next time Arliss came racing past, the pup would tie into the rope again.

I wondered if he wouldn't get some of his baby teeth jerked out at such rough play, but guessed it wouldn't matter. He'd soon be shedding them, anyhow.

I wondered, too, what was keeping Mama and Lisbeth so long. Then I thought how far it was to where the dead

cow lay and how long it would take for just the two of them to drag up enough wood and get a fire started, and figured they'd be lucky if they got back before dark.

I went off to the spring after a bucket of fresh water and wondered when Papa would come back. Mama had said a couple of days ago that it was about that time, and I hoped so. For one thing, I could hardly wait to see what sort of horse Papa was going to bring me. But mainly, this hydrophobia plague had me scared. I'd handled things pretty well until that came along. Of course, I'd gotten a pretty bad hog cut, but that could have happened to anybody, even a grown man. And I was about to get well of that. But if the sickness got more of our cattle, I wouldn't know what to do.

Chapter 15

It wasn't until dark came that I really began to get uneasy about Mama and Lisbeth. Then I could hardly stand it because they hadn't come home. I knew in my own mind why they hadn't: it had been late when they'd started out; they'd had a good long piece to go; and even with wood handy, it took considerable time to drag up enough for the size fire they needed.

And I couldn't think of any real danger to them. They weren't far enough away from the cabin to be lost. And if they were, Jumper knew the way home. Also, Jumper was gentle; there wasn't much chance that he'd scare and throw them off. On top of all that, they had Old Yeller along. Old Yeller might be pretty weak and crippled yet, but he'd protect them from just about anything that might come their way.

Still, I was uneasy. I couldn't help having the feeling that something was wrong. I'd have gone to see about them if it hadn't been for Little Arliss. It was past his suppertime; he was getting hungry and sleepy and fussy.

I took him and the speckled pup inside the kitchen and lit a candle. I settled them on the floor and gave them each a bowl of sweet milk into which I'd crumbled cold cornbread. In a little bit, both were eating out of the same bowl. Little Arliss knew better than that and I ought to have paddled him for doing it. But I didn't. I didn't say a word; I was too worried.

I'd just about made up my mind to put Little Arliss and the pup to bed and go look for Mama and Lisbeth when I heard a sound that took me to the door in a hurry. It was the sound of dogs fighting. The sound came from 'way out there in the dark; but the minute I stepped outside, I could tell that the fight was moving toward the cabin. Also, I recognized the voice of Old Yeller.

It was the sort of raging yell he let out when he was in a fight to the finish. It was the same savage roaring and snarling and squawling that he'd done the day he fought the killer hogs off me.

The sound of it chilled my blood. I stood, rooted to the ground, trying to think what it could be, what I ought to do.

Then I heard Jumper snorting keenly and Mama calling in a frightened voice. "Travis! Travis! Make a light, son, and get your gun. And hurry!"

I came alive then. I hollered back at her, to let her know that I'd heard. I ran back into the cabin and got my gun. I couldn't think at first what would make the sort of light I needed, then recollected a clump of bear grass that Mama'd recently grubbed out, where she wanted to start a new fall garden. Bear grass has an oily sap that makes it burn bright and fierce for a long time. A pile of it burning would make a big light.

I ran and snatched up four bundles of the half-dried bear grass. The sharp ends of the stiff blades stabbed and stung my arms and chest as I grabbed them up. But I had no time to bother about that. I ran and dumped the bunches in a pile on the bare ground outside the yard fence, then hurried to bring a live coal from the fireplace to start them burning.

I fanned fast with my hat. The bear-grass blades started to smoking, giving off their foul smell. A little flame started, flickered and wavered for a moment, then bloomed suddenly and leaped high with a roar.

I jumped back, gun held ready, and caught my first glimpse of the screaming, howling battle that came wheeling into the circle of light. It was Old Yeller, all right, tangled with some animal as big and savage as he was.

Mama called from outside the light's rim. "Careful, son. And take close aim; it's a big loafer wolf, gone mad."

My heart nearly quit on me. There weren't many of the gray loafer wolves in our part of the country, but I knew about them. They were big and savage enough to hamstring a horse or drag down a full-grown cow. And here was Old Yeller, weak and crippled, trying to fight a mad one!

I brought up my gun, then held fire while I hollered at Mama. "Y'all get in the cabin," I yelled. "I'm scared to shoot till I know you're out of the line of fire!"

I heard Mama whacking Jumper with a stick to make him go. I heard Jumper snort and the clatter of his hoofs as he went galloping in a wide circle to come up behind the cabin. But even after Mama called from the door behind me, I still couldn't fire. Not without taking a chance on killing Old Yeller.

I waited, my nerves on edge, while Old Yeller and the big wolf fought there in the firelight, whirling and leaping and snarling and slashing, their bared fangs gleaming white, their eyes burning green in the half light.

Then they went down in a tumbling roll that stopped with the big wolf on top, his huge jaws shut tight on Yeller's throat. That was my chance, and one that I'd better make good. As weak as Old Yeller was, he'd never break that throat hold.

There in the wavering light, I couldn't get a true bead on the wolf. I couldn't see my sights well enough. All I could do was guess-aim and hope for a hit.

I squeezed the trigger. The gunstock slammed back against my shoulder, and such a long streak of fire spouted from the gun barrel that it blinded me for a second; I couldn't see a thing.

Then I realized that all the growling and snarling had hushed. A second later, I was running toward the two, still, gray forms lying side by side.

For a second, I just knew that I'd killed Old Yeller, too. Then, about the time I bent over him, he heaved a big sort of sigh and struggled up to start licking my hands and wagging that stub tail.

I was so relieved that it seemed like all the strength went out of me. I slumped to the ground and was sitting there, shivering, when Mama came and sat down beside me.

She put one arm across my shoulders and held it there while she told me what had happened.

Like I'd figured, it had taken her and Lisbeth till dark to get the wood dragged up and the fire to going around the dead cow. Then they'd mounted old Jumper and headed for home. They'd been without water all this time and were thirsty.

When they came to the crossing on Bird-song Creek, they'd dismounted to get a drink. And while they were lying down, drinking, the wolf came.

He was right on them before they knew it. Mama happened to look up and see the dark hulk of him come bounding toward them across a little clearing. He was snarling as he came, and Mama just barely had time to come to her feet and grab up a dead chinaberry pole before he sprang. She whacked him hard across the head, knocking him to the ground. Then Old Yeller was there, tying into him.

Mama and Lisbeth got back on Jumper and tore out for the house. Right after them came the wolf, like he had his mind fixed on catching them, and nothing else. But Old Yeller fought him too hard and too fast. Yeller wasn't big and strong enough to stop him, but he kept him slowed down and fought away from Jumper and Mama and Lisbeth.

He had to've been mad, son," Mama wound up. "You know that no wolf in his right senses would have acted that way. Not even a big loafer wolf."

"Yessum," I said, "and it's sure a good thing that Old Yeller was along to keep him fought off." I shuddered at the thought of what could have happened without Old Yeller.

Mama waited a little bit, then said in a quiet voice, "It was a good thing for us, son; but it wasn't good for Old Yeller."

The way she said that gave me a cold feeling in the pit of my stomach. I sat up straighter. "What do you mean?" I said. "Old Yeller's all right. He's maybe chewed up some, but he can't be bad hurt. See, he's done trotting off toward the house."

Then it hit me what Mama was getting at. All my insides froze. I couldn't get my breath.

I jumped to my feet, wild with hurt and scare. "But, Mama!" I cried out. "Old Yeller's just saved your life! He's saved my life. He's saved Little Arliss's life! We can't —"

Mama got up and put her arm across my shoulders again. "I know, son," she said. "But he's been bitten by a mad wolf."

I stared off into the blackness of the night while my mind wheeled and darted this way and that, like a scared rat trying to find its way out of a trap.

"But, Mama," I said. "We don't know for certain. We could wait and see. We could tie him or shut him up in the corn-crib or some place till we know for sure!"

Mama broke down and went to crying then. She put her head on my shoulder and held me so tight that she nearly choked off my breath.

"We can't take a chance, son," she sobbed. "It would be you or me or Little Arliss or Lisbeth next. I'll shoot him if you can't, but either way, we've got it to do. We just can't take the chance!"

It came clear to me then that Mama was right. We couldn't take the risk. And from everything I had heard, I knew that there was very little chance of Old Yeller's escaping the sickness. It was going to kill something inside me to do it, but I knew then that I had to shoot my big yeller dog.

Once I knew for sure I had it to do, I don't think I really felt anything. I was just numb all over, like a dead man walking.

Quickly, I left Mama and went to stand in the light of the burning bear grass. I reloaded my gun and called Old Yeller back from the house. I stuck the muzzle of the gun against his head and pulled the trigger.

Chapter 16

Days went by, and I couldn't seem to get over it. I couldn't eat. I couldn't sleep. I couldn't cry. I was all empty inside, but hurting. Hurting worse than I'd ever hurt in my life. Hurting with a sickness there didn't seem to be any cure for. Thinking every minute of my big yeller dog, how we'd worked together and romped together, how he'd fought the she bear off Little Arliss, how he'd saved me from the killer hogs, how he'd fought the mad wolf off Mama and Lisbeth. Thinking that after all this, I'd had to shoot him the same as I'd done the roan bull and the Spot heifer.

Mama tried to talk to me about it, and I let her. But while everything she said made sense, it didn't do a thing to that dead feeling I had.

Lisbeth talked to me. She didn't say

469

much; she was too shy. But she pointed out that I had another dog, the speckled pup.

"He's part of Old Yeller," she said. "And he was the best one of the bunch."

But that didn't help, either. The speckled pup might be part of Old Yeller, but he wasn't Old Yeller. He hadn't saved all our lives and then been shot down like he was nothing.

Then one night it clouded up and rained till daylight. That seemed to wash away the hydrophobia plague. At least, pretty soon afterward, it died out completely.

But we didn't know that then. What seemed important to us about the rain was that the next morning after it fell, Papa came riding home through the mud.

The long ride to Kansas and back had Papa drawn down till he was as thin and knotty as a fence rail. But he had money in his pockets, a big shouting laugh for everybody, and a saddle horse for me.

The horse was a cat-stepping blue roan with a black mane and tail. Papa put me on him the first thing and made me gallop him in the clearing around the house. The roan had all the pride and fire any grown man would want in his best horse, yet was as gentle as a pet.

"Now, isn't he a dandy?" Papa asked.

I said, "Yessir!" and knew that Papa was right and that I ought to be proud and thankful. But I wasn't. I didn't feel one way or another about the horse.

Papa saw something was wrong. I saw him look a question at Mama and saw Mama shake her head. Then late that evening, just before supper, he called me off down to the spring, where we sat and he talked.

"Your mama told me about the dog," he said.

I said, "Yessir," but didn't add anything.

"That was rough," he said. "That was as rough a thing as I ever heard tell of happening to a boy, and I'm mighty proud to learn how my boy stood up to it. You couldn't ask any more of a grown man."

He stopped for a minute. He picked up some pebbles and thumped them into the water, scattering a bunch of hairy-legged water bugs. The bugs darted across the water in all directions.

"Now the thing to do," he went on, "is to try to forget it and go on being a man."

"How?" I asked. "How can you forget a thing like that?"

He studied me for a moment, then shook his head. "I guess I don't quite mean that," he said. "It's not a thing you can forget. What I mean is, things like that happen. They may seem mighty cruel and unfair, but that's how life is a part of the time.

"But that isn't the only way life is. A part of the time, it's mighty good. And a man can't afford to waste all the good parts, worrying about the bad parts. That makes it all bad . . . . You understand?"

"Yessir," I said. And I did understand. Only, it still didn't do me any good. I still felt just as dead and empty.

That went on for a week or better, I guess, before a thing happened that brought me alive again.

It was right at dinnertime. Papa had sent me out to the lot to feed Jumper and the horses. I'd just started back when I heard a commotion in the house. I heard Mama's voice lifted high and sharp. "Why, you thieving little whelp!" she cried out. Then I heard a shrieking yelp, and out the kitchen door came the speckled pup with a big chunk of cornbread clutched in his mouth. He raced around the house, running with his tail clamped. He was yelling and squawling like somebody was beating him to death. But that still didn't keep him from hanging onto that piece of cornbread that he'd stolen from Mama.

Inside the house, I heard Little Arliss. He was fighting and screaming his head off at Mama for hitting his dog. And above it all, I could hear Papa's roaring laughter.

Right then, I began to feel better. Sight of that little old pup, tearing out for the brush with that piece of cornbread, seemed to loosen something inside me.

I felt better all day. I went back and rode my horse and enjoyed it. I rode 'way off out in the brush, not going anywhere especially, just riding and looking and beginning to feel proud of owning a real horse of my own.

Then along about sundown, I rode up into Birdsong Creek, headed for the house. Up at the spring, I heard a splashing and hollering. I looked ahead. Sure enough, it was Little Arliss. He was stripped naked and romping in our drinking water again. And right in there, romping with him, was that bread-stealing

speckled pup.

I started to holler at them. I started to say, "*Arliss!* You get that nasty old pup out of our drinking water."

Then I didn't. Instead, I went to laughing. I sat there and laughed till I cried. When all the time I knew that I ought to beat them to a frazzle for messing up our drinking water.

When finally I couldn't laugh and cry another bit, I rode on up to the lot and turned my horse in. Tomorrow, I thought, I'll take Arliss and that pup out for a squirrel hunt. The pup was still mighty little. But the way I figured it, if he was big enough to act like Old Yeller, he was big enough to start earning his keep.

471

READING COMPREHENSION

Summarizing. Choose the best phrase to complete each sentence. Then write the complete statements on your paper.

1. Travis shot Spot and the roan bull because _____ (they were starving from the drought, they had hydrophobia, the family needed meat).

2. Mama and Lisbeth would have been killed by a wolf if it hadn't been for _____ (Travis, Burn Sanderson, Old Yeller).

3. After Old Yeller was bitten by a mad wolf, he had to be _____ (trained not to attack wolves, shot, cured of hydrophobia).

Interpreting. Write the answer to each question on your paper.

1. Why did Travis and Mama suspect that Spot had hydrophobia?

2. Why did Mama, Lisbeth, and Travis burn the dead roan bull?

3. Why wasn't Travis happy at first to get the horse from his father?

4. At the end, why did Travis laugh when he found Little Arliss and the pup playing in the drinking water?

For Thinking and Discussing. Travis tells the reader, "It was going to kill something inside me to do it, but I knew then that I had to shoot my big yeller dog." What inside him was going to be killed?

UNDERSTANDING LITERATURE

Theme. The theme of a novel is the most important idea in the story. It is the author's message to the reader, and it is often about the way people deal with life.

What is the theme of *Old Yeller*? The statements below will help you think about this. In each case, choose the best phrase and write the complete sentence on your paper.

1. While his father was away on the cattle drive, Travis learned _____.
   a. how to handle wild hogs, bulls, bears, and wolves
   b. what it took to be a man
   c. how to provide the family with food

2. Having to kill the dog he loved so much taught Travis that _____.
   a. dogs count for nothing in this life
   b. growing up is nothing but grief
   c. life is sometimes cruel and unfair

3. When Travis decided to teach Old Yeller's pup how to hunt squirrels, he seemed to realize that _____.
   a. he didn't want to waste the good parts of life, worrying about the bad parts
   b. his family needed some food
   c. if the pup learned to hunt, maybe he wouldn't steal food from Mama's kitchen

WRITING

Pretend you are Travis. Write a paragraph telling what you expect in general from life from now on.

Section Review

VOCABULARY

Similes. A *simile* is a comparison in which a signal word (*like, as,* or *than*) separates the things being compared. For example: "Mama's face was as white as a bed sheet." The signal word is *as*. Mama's face is compared to a white bed sheet.

Here are some similes from *Old Yeller*. On your paper, write the signal word and the two things being compared in each simile.

1. "His belly was swelled up as tight and round as a pumpkin."

2. "When it came to gunfire Jumper didn't have any more sense than a red ant in a hot skillet."

3. ". . . my heart was flopping around inside my chest like a catfish in a wet sack."

4. "But now I raced through the tall trees in that creek bottom, covering ground like a scared wolf."

5. "Then they [the hogs] all tore out for the hills, running through the rocks and brush almost as swiftly and silently as deer."

6. "I was as weak as a rain-chilled chicken. . . ."

7. "I started off into the blackness of the night while my mind wheeled and darted this way and that, like a scared rat trying to find its way out of a trap."

READING

Cloze Exercise. In some reading tests, words are left out of a selection. If you understand what you are reading, you will be able to fill in the blanks correctly. Each word you fill in will make sense in the context of the selection.

Here are some lines from *Old Yeller*. On your paper, write the word which best completes each sentence.

1. "He [Old Yeller] made me so _____ at first that I wanted to kill him."
   a. curious
   b. mad
   c. proud

2. "Then, later, when I had to shoot him [Old Yeller], it was like having to _____ some of my own folks."
   a. hate
   b. save
   c. shoot

3. "She [Mama] was getting up at all hours of the night to doctor our wounds, bathe us in cold water, and _____ us when she could get us to eat."
   a. cook
   b. feed
   c. heat

4. " 'A part of the time [life] is mighty good. And a man can't afford to waste all the good parts, worrying about the _____ parts.' "
   a. bad
   b. great
   c. small

WRITING

A Story. You have read many stories in this book. You have learned many things about the different elements of a story: plot, characters, conflict, setting, point of view, theme, and mood. Now it is time to write a story of your own.

Step 1: Set Your Goal

Think of an event you would like to write about. It can be something that actually happened to you or someone you know. It can be an idea that came from something you read — a newspaper article, perhaps, or another story. After reading "The Dead Man and His Gold," for example, you might wonder how Peter Wilks got the gold. You could write a story telling how it might have happened.

You can also begin by thinking of a character, setting, or theme you want to write about, or a mood you want to get across. But if you begin with any of these things, you should decide on the main events of the story before going on to Step Two. After all, something important has to happen in a story, or it isn't a story at all.

Step 2: Make a Plan

To make a plan for your story, write each of the following headings on your paper. Then fill in the information shown under the heading.

Plot: List the events that take place. Which event is the turning point? How is the story resolved?

Characters: Describe each major character. Include what the person looks like, how he or she behaves, and his or her personality traits. Tell how the characters are related to each other.

Conflict: What is the major conflict in the story?

Setting: Where and when does the story take place?

Point of View: Who is telling the story?

Theme: What message do you want to get across?

Mood: What feeling do you want the story to give the reader?

Step 3. Write Your First Draft

Now it's time to begin. But where? Try using this approach:

☐ Start with a description of your setting.

☐ Describe each important character when he or she first appears.

☐ Start the action and introduce the conflict as early as possible.

☐ Tell the events in chronological order.

☐ End the story by telling what, if anything, has changed because of the story's events.

As you write, remember that there are different ways to give information to the reader. You have read stories in this book that follow a variety of methods. You may want to review some of them now. Your story will probably contain a mixture of description, action, and dialogue.

Step 4. Revise Your Story

Put your story away for a few days before you revise it. Then try to read it as if you've never seen it before. Will your readers get from the story what you want them to get? Will they become caught up in it and want to read it to the end? If not, why not? You may find you need to change something as basic as the behavior of a central character. Or you may just need to take out some unnecessary descriptions or add more dialogue. It's your story and you're free to do whatever you please with it. You can even turn it into a totally different story.

You should probably go over the story several times over a number of days. Once you are satisfied with it, proofread it and copy it over neatly.

QUIZ

The following is a quiz for Section 11. Write your answers on your paper in complete sentences.

Reading Comprehension

1. When Travis's father left home, what did he tell Travis he expected the boy to do?

2. Why did Old Yeller suddenly appear at Travis's home, and why did Travis want to get rid of the dog at first?

3. Why did Travis come to love and value Old Yeller?

4. Why did Travis finally have to shoot Old Yeller?

5. Why didn't Travis appreciate his new horse or the speckled pup at first? What changed his mind?

Understanding Literature

6. In what ways did the character of Travis change between the beginning and the end of the novel?

7. Which of these two characters was better suited to life on the frontier: Bud Searcy or Travis's mother? Why?

8. If the setting of this novel had been a city in 1980, would the plot have been basically the same?

9. Is it important that the events seem true to life? Why or why not?

10. What does the author show about dealing with life — the bad parts *and* the good parts?

ACTIVITIES

Word Attack

As Travis explains in Chapter One, "Yeller" in Old Yeller has two meanings: "yellow," and "one who yells." Below are six other words from the story. Look them up in the dictionary and write down two meanings for each of them.

reservation	shake	spring
stick	fair	strain

Speaking and Listening. Imagine that you are Travis, visiting a school. You have been invited to make a speech about Old Yeller, a wonderful dog you once had. What would Travis say? Make a speech for Travis. Be prepared to give the speech in class.

Research. Hydrophobia plays a central role in *Old Yeller*. What is hydrophobia? Do research to find out what it is, how it spreads, and how it is treated and controlled.

Creating. In the story, Papa and other men of Salt Licks, Texas, undertook a cattle drive that ended up 600 miles away in Abilene, Kansas. Such cattle drives are a well-remembered part of the American past. Do some research and then draw a map of the trail that Travis's father took on the cattle drive to Abilene.

PRONUNCIATION KEY

ă	pat	j	**j**ud**g**e	sh	di**sh**, **sh**ip
ā	**ai**d, f**ey**, p**ay**	k	**c**at, **k**i**ck**, pi**que**	t	**t**igh**t**
â	**air**, c**are**, w**ear**	l	**l**id, need**le**	th	pa**th**, **th**in
ä	f**a**ther	m	a**m**, **m**an, **m**u**m**	*th*	ba**th**e, **th**is
b	**b**i**b**	n	**n**o, sudde**n**	ŭ	c**u**t, r**ou**gh
ch	**ch**ur**ch**	ng	thi**ng**	û	c**ir**cle, f**ir**m, h**ear**d, t**er**m,
d	**d**ee**d**	ŏ	h**o**rrible, p**o**t		t**ur**n, **ur**ge, w**or**d
ĕ	p**e**t, pl**ea**sure	ō	g**o**, h**oa**rse, r**ow**, t**oe**	v	ca**v**e, **v**al**v**e, **v**ine
ē	b**e**, b**ee**, **ea**sy, l**ei**sure	ô	**a**lter, c**au**ght, f**o**r, p**aw**	w	**w**ith
f	**f**ast, **f**i**f**e, o**ff**, **ph**ase, rou**gh**	oi	b**oy**, n**oi**se, **oi**l	y	**y**es
g	**g**a**g**	ou	c**ow**, **ou**t	yo͞o	ab**u**se, **u**se
h	**h**at	o͝o	t**oo**k	z	ro**s**e, **s**i**z**e, **x**ylophone, **z**ebra
hw	**wh**ich	o͞o	b**oo**t, fr**ui**t	zh	gara**g**e, plea**s**ure, vi**s**ion
ĭ	p**i**t	p	**p**o**p**	ə	**a**bout, sil**e**nt, penc**i**l, lem**o**n,
ī	b**y**, g**uy**, p**ie**	r	**r**oa**r**		circ**u**s
î	d**ear**, d**eer**, f**ier**ce, m**ere**	s	mi**ss**, **s**au**c**e, **s**ee	ər	butt**er**

PART OF SPEECH LABELS

n.	(noun)	*conj.*	(conjunction)
adj.	(adjective)	*prep.*	(preposition)
adv.	(adverb)	*v.*	(verb)
pron.	(pronoun)	*interj.*	(interjection)

The additional italicized labels below are used as needed to show inflected forms:

pl.   (plural)   *sing.*   (singular)

STRESS

Primary stress ′
   bi · ol′o · gy | bī ŏl′əjē |
Secondary stress ′
   bi′o · log′i · cal | bī′ə lŏj′ĭ kəl |

In this glossary, definitions were chosen to show the meanings of the words as they are used in the selections. Unless otherwise indicated, entries based on © 1977 by Houghton Mifflin Company. Reprinted by permission from The American Heritage School Dictionary.

ac·cent | ăk′ sĕnt′ | *n.* **3.** A style of speech or pronunciation that is typical of a certain region or country: *She speaks with a French accent.*

ac·count·ant | ə koun′ tənt | *n.* A person who keeps or inspects the financial records of business concerns or individuals.

ag·gra·vate | ăg′rə vāt′ | *v.* **ag·gra·vat·ed, ag·gra·vat·ing. 1.** To make worse: *aggravate an injury.* **2.** To irritate; provoke.

a·li·as | ā′ lē əs | *n.* An assumed name used by a person wishing to conceal his identity.

am·bi·tion | ăm bĭsh′ən | *n.* **1.a.** A strong desire to get or become something: *His ambition was to become a fearless detective.* **b.** The thing desired: *He spent a lot of money to achieve his one great ambition.* **2.** Initiative; drive: *people of great energy and ambition.*

an·a·lyze | ăn′ ə līz′ | *v.* **1.** To perform or prepare an analysis of: *They analyzed the ore and found iron in it.* **2.** To examine in detail.

an·ces·tor | ăn sĕs′ tər | *n.* **1.** Any person from whom one is descended, especially if of a generation earlier than a grandparent.

an·cient | ān′ shənt | *adj.* **1.** Very old; aged. **2.** Of times long past, especially belonging to the historical period before the fall of Rome in A.D. 476.

an·them | ăn′them | *n.* **1.** A song of praise or loyalty: *a national anthem.* **2.** A choral composition, usually of moderate length, with a sacred text.

an·tique | ăn tēk′ | *n.* **1.** Something made at a period much earlier than the present: *The car was old enough to be an antique.* **2.** Something having special value because of its age, especially a work of art or handicraft that is over 100 years old: *treasured antiques such as the Windsor chair.*

ap·pear·ance | ə pîr′ əns | *n.* **3.** The way something or someone looks or appears; outward aspect: *A good appearance makes other people wish to know you better.*

a·shamed | ə shāmd′ | *adj.* **1.** Feeling shame or guilt: *He was very much ashamed of his fear of drowning.* **2.** Reluctant through fear of shame or embarrassment: *ashamed to tell anyone that a little girl had kicked him in the face.*

at·mos·phere | ăt′ mə sfîr′ | *n.* **1.** The gas that surrounds a body in space, especially the air that surrounds the earth, and is held by the body's gravitational field. **2.** A unit of pressure equal to the pressure of the atmosphere at sea level, about 14.7 pounds per square inch. **3.** The air or climate of a place: *the dry atmosphere of the desert.* **4.** Environment or surroundings regarded as having a psychological, physical, or other influence: *A hospital should have a quiet atmosphere.* **5.** A general feeling or mood: *the atmosphere of a story.*

at·ti·tude | ăt′ ĭ tōod′ | *or* | tyōod′ | *n.* **1.** A state of mind with regard to someone or something; a point of view: *What is the speaker's attitude toward the kind of life he is describing?*

auc·tion | ôk′ shən | *n.* A public sale in which goods or property is sold to the highest bidder.

bam·boo | băm bōo′ | *n.* **1.** A tall, treelike tropical grass with hollow, jointed stems.

bar·gain | bâr′ gĭn | *n.* **1.** An arrangement or agreement between two sides, often involving payment or a trade; a deal: *We made a bargain that he would cut the grass for two dollars.*

bog | bôg | *or* | bŏg | *n.* Soft, water-soaked ground; a marsh; swamp.

book·keep·er | bŏok′ kē′pər | *n.* The person who keeps records of money received, owed, etc., by a business.*

bough | bou | *n.* A large branch of a tree.

cap·i·tal | kăp′ ĭ tl | *n.* **1.** A city that is the

---

*© 1983 by Scholastic Inc.

seat of a state or national government.

ca·tas·tro·phe | kə tăs′ trə fē | *n.* A great and sudden calamity, such as an earthquake or flood.

cen·taur | sĕn′ tôr′ | *n.* In Greek mythology, a creature having the head, arms, and trunk of a man and the body and legs of a horse.

cen·tu·ry | sĕn′ chə rē | *n., pl.* **cen·tu·ries.** **1.** A period of 100 years.

com·bi·na·tion | kŏm′ bə nā′ shən | *n.* **4.** The sequence of numbers or letters that opens a combination lock.

com·pas·sion | kəm păsh′ ən | *n.* The feeling of sharing the suffering of another, together with a desire to give aid or show mercy.

con·ti·nent | kŏn′ tə nənt | *n.* One of the main land masses of the earth, including Africa, Antarctica, Asia, Australia, Europe, North America, and South America.

con·tract | kŏn′ trăkt′ | *n.* **1.** A formal agreement, enforceable by law, between two or more persons or groups. **2.** A document stating the terms of such an agreement.

cour·age | kûr′ĭj | *or* | kŭr′- | *n.* The quality of mind or spirit that enables one to face danger or hardship with confidence, resolution, and firm control of oneself; bravery.

crit·ic | krĭt′ ĭk | *n.* **1.** A person who forms and expresses judgments of the good and bad qualities of anything. **2.** A person whose job is judging and reporting on the worth of something intended as an artistic work or on its performance: *a book critic; a music critic.*

cul·ture | kŭl′ chər | *n.* **3.** The arts, beliefs, customs, institutions, and all other products of human work and thought created by a people or group at a particular time: *The culture of Western Europe owes much to Greece.*

cus·tom | kŭs′ təm | *n.* **1.** An accepted practice or convention followed by tradition: *tribal customs. Shaking hands when meeting someone is an ancient custom.*

di·a·lect | dī′ ə lekt′ | *n.* A regional variety of a language, distinguished from other varieties by pronunciation, vocabulary, etc.: *Cockney is a dialect of English.*

di·lem·ma | dĭ lĕm′ ə | *n.* A situation that requires a person to choose between courses of action that are equally difficult or unpleasant: *He faced the dilemma of giving in or losing his job.*

dis·dain | dĭs dān′ | *n.* A feeling, attitude, or show of scornful superiority; aloof contempt

drench | drĕnch | *v.* To wet through and through; saturate: *Occasionally a cloudburst will drench the desert.*

duke | dook | *or* | dyook | *n.* **1.** A member of the highest level of the British peerage, holding a title and rank above that of a marquis.

dumb | dŭm | *adj.* **1.** Unable to speak; mute: *A deaf and dumb person.*

en·chant·ed | ĕn chăn′ tĭd | *adj.* Cast under a spell; bewitched.*

fate | fāt | *n.* **1.** The invisible force or power that is supposed to determine the course of events. **2.** Something that happens to or befalls a person or thing: *The fate of the plane's passengers is yet unknown.*

fig·ured | fĭg′ yərd | *v.* **1. b.** To reach a conclusion about; decide on.

flus·ter | flŭs′ ter | *v.* To make nervous, excited, or confused: *The staring faces flustered her.* —*n.* A nervous, excited, or confused condition.

frag·ment | frăg′ mənt | *n.* **1.** A piece or part broken off or detached from a whole: *a fragment of a china plate.*

fra·grant | frā′ grənt | *adj.* Having a pleasant odor; sweet-smelling: *a fragrant rose.*

freight | frāt | *n.* **1. a.** Goods carried by a vessel or vehicle, especially goods transported as cargo. **b.** The charge for transporting such goods.

head·line | hĕd′ līn′ | *n.* A group of words that is printed in large type over a newspaper article and tells what the article is about.

herb | ûrb | or | hûrb | *n.* **1.** A plant with leaves, roots, or other parts used to flavor food or as medicine.

her·i·tage | hĕr′ ĭ tĭj | *n.* **2.** Something other than property passed down from preceding generations; legacy; tradition: *Every country has its heritage of folk music.*

he·ro | hîr′ ō | *n., pl.* **he·roes. 1.** A man noted for his courage, special achievements, etc.: *a war hero; a sports hero.* **2.** The main male character in a novel, poem, movie, etc.

her·o·ine | hĕr′ ō ĭn | *n.* **1.** The female counterpart of a hero. **2.** The main female character in a novel, poem, movie, etc.

hid·e·ous | hĭd′ ē əs | *adj.* **1.** Horribly ugly; revolting: *a hideous mask.*

hu·mil·i·ate | hyōō mĭl′ē āt′ | *v.* **hu·mil·i·at·ed, hu·mil·i·at·ing.** To lower the pride or status of; humble or disgrace.

im·mi·grant | ĭm′ ĭ grənt | *n.* A person who leaves his native country or region to settle in another.

in·so·lent | ĭn′ sə lənt | *adj.* Disrespectfully arrogant; impudent; rude; *an insolent reply.*

in·vest | ĭn vĕst′ | *v.* **1.** To put (money) into something, such as property, stocks, or a business, in order to earn interest or make a profit: *She invested $18,000 in bonds.*

in·ves·ti·gate | ĭn vĕs′ tĭ gāt′ | *v.* **1.** To look into or examine carefully in a search for facts, knowledge, or information: *investigate a burglary.*

judg·ment, also **judge·ment** | jŭj′ mənt | *n.* **1.** A decision reached after a careful weighing of evidence or choices, as in a court of law: *a judgment holding an act of Congress unconstitutional.* **2.** The ability to choose wisely; good sense: *trust his judgment.*

king·dom | kĭng′ dəm | *n.* **1.** A country that is ruled or headed by a king or queen.

knight | nīt | *n.* **1.** In feudal times, a mounted man-at-arms giving service to a king or other superior, especially such a man raised to an order of chivalry after training as a page and squire.

la·goon | lə gōōn′ | *n.* A body of water, usually connecting with the ocean, especially one bounded by sandbars or coral reefs.

lec·ture | lĕk′ chər | *n.* **1.** A speech providing information about a given subject, delivered before an audience or class. **2.** A serious, lengthy warning or reproof.

lig·a·ment | lĭg ə mənt | *n.* A sheet or band of tough, fibrous tissue that connects bones or cartilage or holds a muscle or body organ in place.

ma·roon | mə rōōn′ | *v.* To abandon or isolate (someone), as on a deserted island, with little hope of rescue or escape.

me·chan·i·cal | mə kăn′ĭ kəl | *adj.* **1.** Of or involving machines or tools. **2.** Operated, produced, or performed by machine. **3.** Suitable for performance by a machine: *dull, routine mechanical tasks.* **4.** Of, involving, or involved in the science of mechanics. **5.** Like a machine in operation; showing no emotion: *He spoke in a mechanical way, as if nothing had happened.* —**me·chan′i·cal·ly** *adv.*

mis·er·y | mĭz′ə rē | *n., pl.* **mis·er·ies. 1.** Prolonged suffering or distress: *Dad has been in misery for days with a pain in his* *shoulder.* **2.** Miserable conditions of life; dire poverty: *millions of people living in misery.*

mis·for·tune | mĭs fôr′chən | *n.* **1.** Bad luck or fortune: *Be brave in times of misfortune.* **2.** An unfortunate occurrence: *The hurricane was a great misfortune for the fishermen of the area.*

mis·sion·ar·y | mĭsh′ ə nĕr′ ē | *n., pl.* **mis·sion·ar·ies.** A person sent to do religious or charitable work in some territory or foreign country.

mor·tal | môr′ tl | *adj.* **1.** Subject to death: *All human beings are mortal and so will someday die.*

no·ble | nō′ bəl | *adj.* **2.** Having or showing qualities of high moral character, as courage, generosity, self-sacrifice, etc.: *a noble spirit.*

of·fi·cial | ə fĭsh′ əl | *adj.* **2. a.** Arising from authority: *an official document.* **b.** Designated as authorized: *The official language.*

or·chard | ôr′ chərd | *n.* **1.** A piece of land on which trees are grown for their fruit. **2.** A group of such trees.

pan·ic | păn′ĭk | *n.* **1.** A sudden, overwhelming terror. **2.** A sudden fear of financial loss among investors. —*adj.* Of panic: *a panic reaction.* —*v.* **pan·icked, pan·ick·ing, pan·ics. 1.** To be stricken with panic: *The troops panicked and retreated in disorder.* **2.** To cause panic in: *Gunshots panicked the cattle.*

phar·ma·cist | fär′ mə sĭst | *n.* Someone who specializes in pharmacy: a druggist.

phe·nom·e·na | fĭ nŏm′ ə nə′ | *n. pl.* **2.** Unusual, significant, or unaccountable facts or occurrences; marvels

plan·ta·tion | plăn tā′ shən | *n.* **1.** A large farm or estate on which crops such as cotton, sugar, or rubber are tended and gathered by workers who often live on the same property.

pov·er·ty | pŏv′ ər tē | *n.* **1.** The condition of being poor and in need; lack of sufficient food, shelter, etc.

pre·cious | prĕsh′ əs | *adj.* **1.** Of high price; valuable: *precious metals.* **2.** Highly prized or esteemed; cherished: *thanked the old man for his precious advice.*

prey | prā | *n.* **1.** An animal or animals hunted or seized by another for food.

pride | prīd | *n.* **1.** A sense of one's own proper dignity or worth; self respect. **2.** Pleasure or satisfaction in one's accomplishments or possessions: *My aunt takes a great deal of pride in her furniture.* **3.** Someone or something that is a source or cause of pride: *The painting was the pride of his collection.* **4.** An excessively high opinion of oneself; conceit: *Pride is one of the seven deadly sins.* **5.** A group of lions. —*v.* **prid·ed, prid·ing.** —**pride (oneself) on.** To be proud of: *She prided herself on her eloquence.*

pri·vate | prī′ vĭt | *adj.* **1. a.** Of or confined to one person: *private opinion.* **b.** Intimate; secret: *a private thought.* **2.** Owned by a person or group of persons rather than the public or government: *a private house; private property.* **3.** Not available for public use or participation: *a private party.* **4.** Not known publicly; secret: *private negotiations.* **5.** Not holding public office: *a private citizen.* **6.** Secluded; isolated: *a private corner.* —*n.* An enlisted man of the lowest rank in the Army or Marine Corps. A **private first class** ranks above a private. —**pri′vate·ly** *adv.* **Idiom. in private.** Secretly; confidentially.

pub·lic·i·ty | pŭ blĭs′ ĭ tē | *n.* **1.** Information given out, as to the press, as a means of attracting public notice to a person or thing. **2.** Public notice directed toward someone or something.

pub·lish | pŭb′ lĭsh | *v.* **1.** To prepare and issue (printed matter) for distribution or sale to the public.

raise | rāz | *n.* An increase in wages: *ask for a raise.*

real estate. Land and anything on it, as buildings and other property.

reck·less | rĕk′lĭs | *adj.* Without care or caution; careless: *reckless driving.* —**reck′less·ly** *adv.*

rep·re·sent | rĕp′ rĭ zĕnt′ | *v.* To act as a speaker for, especially in a legislative body.*

rep·tile | rĕp′ tīl′ | *n.* Any of a group of cold-blooded animals that have a backbone and are covered with scales or horny plates, such as a snake, turtle, or dinosaur.

res·er·va·tion | rĕz′ ər vā′ shən | *n.* **3.** A tract of land set apart by the Federal government for a certain purpose: *an Indian reservation.*

rev·o·lu·tion | rĕv′ ə loo′ shən | *n.* **1.** A sudden political overthrow from within a given system.

sa·cred | sā′ krĭd | *adj.* **1.** Regarded or treated with special reverence as belonging to, coming from, or being associated with God or a divine being or power; holy: *a sacred place; a sacred book.*

scent | sĕnt | *n.* **1.** A distinctive odor: *the scent of pine.*

schol·ar·ship | skŏl′ ər shĭp′ | *n.* **1.** A grant of money awarded to a student seeking further education, usually based on personal achievement or need.

sense·less | sĕns′lĭs | *adj.* **1.** Deprived of sensation; unconscious: *knocked senseless.* **2.** Without meaning; pointless: *muttering senseless words.* **3.** Lacking good judgment; foolish. —**sense′less·ly** *adv.* —**sense′less·ness** *n.*

shrewd | shrood | *adj.* **shrewd·er, shrewd·est. 1.** Clever and practical; *a shrewd person.* **2.** Sharp; penetrating; searching: *a shrewd glance.* —**shrewd′ly** *adv.* —**shrewd′ness** *n.*

skep·ti·cism | skĕp′ tə sĭz′ əm | *n.* **1.** A doubting or questioning attitude or state of mind

so·ci·e·ty | sə sī′ ĭ tē | *n.* **1.** A group of living things, usually of the same kind, living and functioning together: *human societies; a society of bees forming a single hive; plant societies.*

sol·emn | sŏl′əm | *adj.* **1.** Impressive; serious; grave: *a solemn occasion; solemn tones.* **2.** Having the force of a religious ceremony; sacred: *a solemn oath.* **3.** Performed with full ceremony: *a solemn mass.* **4.** Gloomy: *She looked solemn today.* —**sol′emn·ly** *adv.* —**sol′emn·ness** *n.*

spe·cial·ty | spesh′ əl tē | *n.* **1.** A special pursuit, occupation, service, etc.: *His specialty is portrait painting.*

sym·pa·thy | sĭm′ pə thē | *n.* **2. a.** The act of or capacity for sharing or understanding the feelings of another. **b.** A feeling or expression of pity or sorrow for the distress of another; compassion.

sym·pho·ny | sĭm′ fə nē | *n.* **1. a.** A usually long and elaborate sonata for orchestra, usually consisting of four movements. **b.** An instrumental passage or movement of a vocal piece, such as an opera or oratorio.

tra·di·tion | trə dĭsh′ ən | *n.* **1.** The passing down of elements of a culture from generation to generation, especially orally. **2.** A custom or usage handed down this way.

tra·gic | trăj′ ĭk | *adj.* **2.** Bringing or involving great misfortune, suffering, or sadness.

trai·tor | trā′ tər | *n.* A person who betrays his country, a cause, or a trust, especially one who has committed treason.

tro·phy | trō′ fē | *n., pl.* **tro·phies.** A prize or memento received as a symbol of victory.

vic·tim | vĭk′ tĭm | *n.* **2.** Someone made to suffer or undergo difficulty, as by trickery, unfair practices, or misunderstanding: *the victim of a hoax.*

*© 1983 by Scholastic Inc.

vow | vou | *v.* **1.** To promise or pledge solemnly: *She vowed that she would return to that place someday.*

voy·age | voi′ ĭj | *n.* A long journey to a distant place, made on a ship, boat, etc., or sometimes an aircraft or spacecraft: *Columbus' four voyages to the New World; a voyage up the Hudson; a voyage to the moon.*

vul·ture | vul′chər | *n.* **1.** Any of several large birds that generally have dark feathers and a bare head and neck and that feed on the flesh of dead animals. **2.** A greedy, grasping, ruthless person.

wan·der | wŏn′ dər | *v.* **2.** To stray from a given place, path, group, or subject: *One hiker wandered away from the others. The speaker's droning voice caused the listener's attention to wander.*

yield | yēld | *v.* **3.** To allow to another; concede: *yield the right of way.* **4.** To give up; surrender: *yielded the fort to the enemy.*

Handbook
of Literature, Reading, Vocabulary, and Research Skills and Terms

The following pages contain information about skills and terms that you will find helpful as you read the selections in this book and other materials as well. The terms are arranged alphabetically, with a brief definition or explanation for each. Examples from this book are used, and the section where a term is taught is indicated.

act   A part of a play. Acts may be divided into *scenes.*

almanac   A book containing many facts. Almanacs are published every year so that the facts will be up to date. The subjects almanacs cover include government leaders of the world, sports records, weather records, awards like the Nobel Prize, and the size and population of different countries. The facts may be given in the form of lists and charts.

When to use an almanac.   Almanacs give facts, but they do not discuss or explain them. Use an almanac when you are looking for a particular name or date, especially if the information is too recent to be in an encyclopedia. For example, if you wanted to find out who won the Nobel Prize for literature in 1986, an almanac would be the best place to find the information.

How to use an almanac.   To find the topic you want in an almanac, look it up in the index. The *index* is a section at the back of the book that lists topics alphabetically. If you were looking for Nobel Prize winners, you would look under *n* for *Nobel.* The index would tell you what page or pages the information is on.

Use the newest almanac you can get to be sure of finding the most recent information.

alphabetical order   The order of the letters in the alphabet. To put words in alphabetical order, look at the first letter of each word first. If the first letters are the same, look at the second letters, and so on.

Many research materials are arranged in alphabetical order, including *card catalogs, dictionaries, encyclopedias*, and *indexes.*

Remember, if you are looking for a

person's name in alphabetical order, look for the last name first. If you are looking for a book title, ignore the articles *a, an,* and *the.*

antonyms Words that have opposite meanings. *Up* and *down* are antonyms. [Section 3]

article A short, nonfiction work; not a made-up story. Articles appear in newspapers, magazines, and books. (See also news story.)

atlas A book of maps. Some atlases also give other geographical information, such as the products of various regions, countries, or states.

When to use an atlas. Use an atlas when you need information on a map, including directions, locations of particular places, and distances between places. For example, if you wanted to know how far Miami, Florida is from Gainesville, Florida, you would use an atlas.

How to use an atlas. Most atlases have an *index*, a section at the back of the book where the places shown on the maps are arranged in alphabetical order. The indexes will usually tell you both the number of the map you need and the particular section of the map that shows the place you are looking for.

For example, if you look up *Gainesville, Florida*, in the index, you might see a notation like this after it: "42 E 4." You would turn to map number 42 in the atlas. You would see that the

map is divided into squares. You would look along the top of the page until you found the square marked *E*. Then you would look along the side of the page for the square marked *4*. Where the two squares meet, in square E 4, you would find Gainesville.

author The writer of an article, a story, a play, a poem, or a book. If you know who wrote a book, you can find the book in the library by looking at the *author card* in the *card catalog.*

author card A card in the library's *card catalog* that has the author's name at the top. Author cards are arranged alphabetically by the author's last name. (See also catalog cards.)

author's purpose The author's goal in writing. Authors may wish to *entertain* readers by making them laugh as in "Animal Poems" (page 265), or by scaring them as in "The Tell-Tale Heart" (page 349). Or an author may want to give readers a serious message about life as in "The Telegram" (page 89), explain something to readers, or tell a true story about a person as in "Muhammad Ali's African Battle" (page 138). (See also theme)   [Section 3]

autobiograpy Someone's true account of his or her own life. An autobiography is usually written from the *first-person point of view*, using the pronouns *I* and *me.* It tells important events from the author's life and says how the author feels about those events. "Once Upon a Christmas" (page 158) is an example of an autobiography. [Section 5]

bibliography   A list of writings. Many books contain lists of other books and articles on the same subject. Here is part of a bibliography from a book about zoos. Notice that the entries are arranged alphabetically by the authors' last names. After each author's name comes the title of the book, the place where it was published, the publisher, and the date:

Crandall, Lee S. *Management of Wild Mammals in Captivity*. Chicago: University of Chicago Press, 1964.

Elgin, Robert. *The Tiger Is My Brother*. New York: Morrow, 1980.

Bibliographies are usually at the end of a book, although sometimes short bibliographies are given at the end of each chapter.

By looking at a bibliography, you can find the authors and titles of other books that may give you more information about the subject you are interested in.

For a list of bibliographies, look up your subject in *The Bibliographic Index*. It will tell you which publications contain bibliographies on the subject.

biographical dictionary   A special dictionary that gives information about famous people. Some biographical dictionaries are *Webster's Biographical Dictionary*, which includes information about people from many nations; the *Dictionary of American Biography*; and *Who's Who in America*, which is revised every second year and includes only people living at the time of publication.

When to use a biographical dictionary. Use a biographical dictionary when you need brief, factual information about a famous person. Biographical dictionaries usually give information such as birth (and death) dates, birthplaces, and important accomplishments. Many biographical dictionaries do not include details about a person's life. You may be able to find more details in an *encyclopedia*. If there is a *biography*, or book about the person's life, it would contain the most information of all.

How to use a biographical dictionary. If the person you are looking up became famous recently, make sure the biographical dictionary you are using is new enough to list him or her. Check to see whether the dictionary includes people from your person's country.

In most biographical dictionaries, people are listed in alphabetical order by their last names. If you wanted information about George Washington, you would look for *Washington, George*. However, if you wanted information about Queen Victoria, you would look for *Victoria*. People are not listed by their titles.

biography   A true story about a person's life written by another person. A book-length biography will give you a lot of information about a person. "Cheryl Toussaint" (page 124) is a short biography.   [Section 4]

To find out whether your library has any biographies about the person you are interested in, look for the person's name in the *subject cards* in the *card catalog*. The person would be listed there in alphabetical order, last name first. On library shelves, biographies are arranged together, alphabetically by subject's names.

Books in Print A list of books that are available for purchase from publishers doing business in this country. *Books in Print* is published every year in three sets. One set lists books alphabetically by author; another set lists books alphabetically by title; and a third set, *The Subject Guide to Books in Print*, lists books alphabetically by subject.

Books in Print is excellent for finding out what books are available at regular bookstores. Remember, though, that there are millions of books that are no longer "in print" but can still be found in libraries and second-hand bookstores.

call number The *Dewey Decimal Classification* number. A number written on library books and at the upper-left hand corner of *catalog cards* to show where the books are placed on the library shelves.

card catalog A large cabinet in the library whose drawers, called trays, contain filing cards listing all the books in the library. There are three types of *catalog cards*: author, title, and subject. All are usually combined in the cabinet in

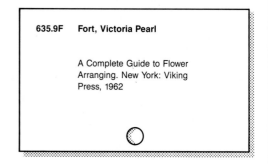

alphabetical order. Letters on the front of each drawer, or tray, show which section of the alphabet it contains. The trays themselves are placed in the cabinet in alphabetical order, from top to bottom.

Here is what the card catalog looks like:

When to use the card catalog. Use the card catalog when you want to find out whether your library has a book whose title you know, or when you want to see what books your library has by a particular author or on a particular subject.

How to use the card catalog. See the next section, catalog card, for information on how to use the card catalog.

catalog card There are at least three cards in the *card catalog* for every non-fiction book in the library: an author card, a title card, and a subject card. Here is an example of an author card:

635.9F   **Fort, Victoria Pearl**

A Complete Guide to Flower Arranging. New York: Viking Press, 1962

The top of this card tells you the author's name. Her name is Victoria Pearl Fort, but last names are listed first on catalog cards. Below the author's name are the title of the book, the place where it was published, the publisher's

name, and the date of publication. At the top of the card is the call number that you should look for on the shelf in order to find the book: 635.9F. This card is called the *author card* because it has the author's name at the top

The other two catalog cards contain the same information in a different order. Here is an example of a title card for the same book:

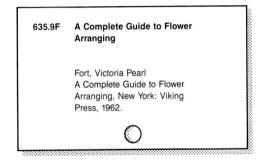

635.9F   A Complete Guide to Flower
          Arranging

          Fort, Victoria Pearl
          A Complete Guide to Flower
          Arranging, New York: Viking
          Press, 1962.

This is called a *title card* because it has the title at the top. Otherwise, the information is the same as on the author card.

Here is an example of a subject card:

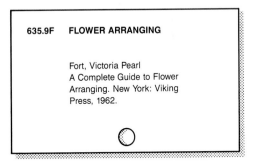

635.9F   FLOWER ARRANGING

          Fort, Victoria Pearl
          A Complete Guide to Flower
          Arranging. New York: Viking
          Press, 1962.

This is the *subject card* because it has the subject of the book at the top. If a book covers several subjects, it will have a separate subject card for each subject. Fiction books usually do not have subject cards.

When to use catalog cards. Use catalog cards to find out what books your library has and where they are located on the shelves.

How to use catalog cards. If you know the title of a book, you can look in the card catalog for the title card. Remember, all the cards are arranged in alphabetical order. If you were looking for *A Complete Guide to Flower Arranging*, you would look in the catalog drawer containing the letter *c* (for *Complete*), because the articles *a, an,* and *the* are ignored in alphabetizing titles. If you find the card, your library has the book. Note the call number given in the upper left-hand corner of the card. It will help you find the book on the shelves.

If you are looking for books by a particular author, look for author cards with that author's name. In this case, you would look in the *f* drawer *Fort, Victoria Pearl*. There will be a separate card for each book the library has by that author. Make notes of the titles and call numbers.

If you are looking for books on a particular subject, look for subject cards. If you were interested in flower arranging, for example, you would look in the *f* drawer for cards with this heading. There will be a card for each book the library has on the subject. Note the titles, authors, and call numbers.

Now you can find the books on the library shelves. Look at the call numbers you wrote down. For the book we have been discussing, it is *635.9F*. This book would probably be on a shelf marked *635*. It would come after books with the call number *635.8*. (In a library, call numbers are marked on the side of the books, or *spines.*) The *F* in the call number is the initial of the author's name.

There are some exceptions to the rule. *Fiction* books are arranged on the shelves not by call number but alphabetically by the author's last name. *Biographies* are shelved together alphabetically by the subject's name. *Reference books*, including *dictionaries* and *encyclopedias*, are kept on special shelves.

cause Something that makes something else happen. (See also cause and effect.)   [Section 4]

cause and effect In some stories and some sentences, there is a cause-and-effect relationship. The *cause* is something that makes another thing happen. What happens is called the *effect*. In "The Safecracker" (page 17), when May was locked in the vault, Jimmy used his tools to open it. That May became locked in the safe is the cause, that Jimmy used his tools and opened the safe is the effect.

Effects may have more than one cause. Jimmy opened the safe because he had the tools to do it, and also because he wanted to save the child's life. Similarly, causes may have more than one effect.

Think about cause and effect relationships as you read. Noticing clue words and phrases such as *because, since, so, so that, as a result of,* and *for this reason* will help you.   [Section 4]

character A person or an animal in a story. (See also flat character and round character.)

characterization The way an author informs readers about characters. *Direct characterization* is when the author describes the character directly. For example, in "The Telegram" (page 89), in describing Homer, the author states "He felt compassion . . . " *Indirect characterization* is when the author lets readers find out about a character through the character's own thoughts, speech, or actions. For example, the reader can tell Homer was compassionate from his actions. The author states "But he knew he would stay. He didn't know what else to do to make the woman less unhappy."

Pay attention to the characters' thoughts, words, and actions when you read a story. They may be related to the message or *theme* that the author wants you to discover.   [Sections 1, 2, 3, 11]

chart An orderly list of facts. Here is an example of a chart:

Noun	Adjective
Danger	Dangerous
Beauty	Beautiful
Remark	Remarkable

You can read this chart down or across. If you read down each column, you see a list of nouns and a list of adjectives. If you read across, you see which nouns and adjectives are similar.

climax The highest point of action in a story. The climax is the same as the *turning point.*

cloze exercise A reading test in which words are left out of a selection and the reader is asked to fill in the blanks. [Section 1]

compare and contrast When you compare people or things, you state the similarities and differences between them. When you contrast people or things, you state only the differences. Teachers sometimes use the words *compare* and *contrast* in test questions to make sure that you include both similarities and differences in your answer.

There are three ways to organize a comparison in your writing. One way is to use one paragraph to describe all the similarities between the two items you are comparing, and another paragraph to describe all their differences.

The second way to organize a comparison is to discuss the two things being compared in two separate paragraphs.

A third way to compare items is to decide on the points you want to compare, and then give the similarities and differences for each point.   [Sections 1, 2, 6]

comparison of unlike things See figurative language.

composition See writing.

compound word A word made up of two or more smaller words. *Cowboy* is an example of a compound word. It is made up of the words *cow* and *boy*. Notice that the meaning of the compound word is different from the meaning of each word alone.   [Section 7]

conclusion 1. The end of an article, a story, a play, a poem, or a book. 2. An opinion or judgement. To find out how to form opinions about stories and characters, see drawing conclusions.

conflict A struggle or fight. Many selections contain conflict, because conflict helps make a story interesting. Readers want to find out who or what will win the struggle.

There are several types of conflict: (1) *Conflict of a person against another person or group.* For example, in Pancakes (page 28), Jud and Jackson Bird have a conflict. (2)*Conflict of a person against nature.* This type of conflict is found in "Priscilla in the Pond" (page 356). (3) *Inner conflict.* A person struggles with his or her own different feelings. Swede in "There Must Be a Losing Coach" (page 132), has this type of conflict.   [Section 4]

contents See table of contents.

context The selection or part of a selection that contains a particular word or group of words. The context can affect the meaning of words or sentences. If you just read the sentence "Laura was hurt," you might think that Laura had been injured. However, if the sentence was in a story about someone refusing a present Laura had bought, you would know it meant she was insulted.   [Section 4]

context clues Other words in a sentence, a paragraph, or lines of poetry that help you figure out the meaning of a word you do not know. Here is an example: "The teacher's *lucid* explanation helped the students understand." The explanation helped the students understand, so it must have been clear. [Sections 8, 9]

contrast To say how two or more people or things are different. (See also comparison and contrast.)

copyright date The date a book was published. The date is usually printed like this: © 1987. If you need up-to-date information, be sure the book was published recently.

critical reading Making judgments about what you read. To read critically, you must try to find the author's message and understand how the characters think and feel. You must read the author's descriptions and the characters' words and actions.

Here are some of the questions you might think about as you read critically:

What is the *author's purpose*, and how well does he or she accomplish it?

In a story, does the *plot* make the message clear?

If *facts* are presented, are they correct?

Are the *characters* in a story believable?   [Sections 8, 10]

decoding Figuring out unfamiliar words from the sounds of the letters they contain. Knowing the sounds that different letters and groups of letters may make is important in decoding. Here are some examples:

a The letter *a* usually stands for the short *a* sound when it is followed by two consonants, as in *batter*, or by one consonant and no vowel, as in *tag*. *A* usually stands for the long *a* sound when it is followed by i, y, or a consonant and a vowel, as in *daily*, *day*, and *race*.

ch When the letters *ch* come together in a word, they may stand for the sounds at the beginning of *child*. That is the sound they always make when a *t* comes before the *ch*, as in *patch*. At other times, though, the letters *ch* together make a sound like *k*, as in *character*. If you are not sure which sound *ch* stands for, try saying the word both ways. See which way sounds like a word you know.

ea When the vowels *ea* come together, they usually stand for the long *e* sound, as in *teach*. However, sometimes they stand for the short *e* sound *thread*, the long *a* sound *great*, the vowel sound in *her*, *heard*, or the vowel sound in *here*, *beard*. If you are not sure which sound *ea* makes in a word you are reading, try pronouncing the word different ways until one pronunciation sounds like a word you know.

-ed Many words end with the suffix *-ed*. Sometimes the suffix is pronounced like a *t*, as in *skipped*. Sometimes it sounds like a *d*, as in *demand*. At other times it stands for the *ed* sound, as in *batted*. If you know the base word, you can figure out which sound *-ed* has.

g The letter *g* usually stands for the sound at the beginning of *go*. However, when *g* is followed by an *e*, *i*, or *y*, it may make a *j* sound, as in *badge*, *giant*, or *gym*. Often when a *g* and an *h* come together, they are both silent, as in *night*.

i The letter *i* usually stands for the long *i* sound when it is followed by a consonant and then a vowel, as in *kite*. It usually stands for the short *i* sound when it is followed by two consonants, as in *kitten*, or by one consonant and no vowel, as in *him*. When *i* is followed by the letters *gh*, the *i* usually stands for the long *i* sound, as in *night*.

-ly Some words end with the suffix *-ly*. When the letters *-ly* come together at the end of a word, they make the sounds *lee*, as in *slowly*.

-ous When the letters *-ous* come together at the end of a word, the suffix is usually pronounced like the word *us*. *Dangerous* is an example.

-tion Some words end with the suffix *-tion*. The letters *-tion* almost always make the sound *shun*, which rhymes with *run*. *Perfection* is an example.

y When the letter *y* comes at the beginning of the word, it usually stands for the sound you hear at the beginning of *yes*. When *y* comes at the end or in the middle of a word, it may stand for a vowel sound, as in *my, flying,* or *city.* When *y* comes after a vowel, it usually helps the vowel make a vowel sound, as in *say, joy,* or *saying.*

definition The meaning of a word or term. Definitions are given in *dictionaries.*

description A word picture of what someone or something is like. Authors include details about the person, place, or thing being described to help the readers form pictures in their minds.

detail A small piece of information. In a paragraph, the *main idea* tells what the paragraph is about, and the details give information to support or explain the main idea.

Sometimes important details are called *significant details. Significant* means "important" or "meaningful." For example, a significant detail in "The Safecraker" (page 17), is that Jimmy took a suitcase containing burglar's tools from a wall.

Dewey Decimal Classification System A system of arranging books according to their subject matter that was invented by Melvil Dewey. The subjects are divided into nine main classes and many sub-classes. The *call number* that is written on library books and *catalog cards* is the number the book is given in this system.

diagram A drawing that shows the parts of something or shows how something works.

dialect The way a character would speak in person. Spoken language is often different from standard written language. It is informal. It may contain expressions, slang, or pronunciations that are casual. (See also expressions) [Section 7]

dialogue The conversation in a story or a play. The exact words the characters say. In a story, quotation marks point out the dialogue.

dictionary A book that lists words in alphabetical order and gives their meanings, pronunciations, and other information.

When to use a dictionary. Use a dictionary to find out any of the following things: the meaning of a word; how a word is spelled; how it is pronounced; where it is divided into syllables; where it comes from; synonyms (words that mean the same) and antonyms (opposites) for a word; the meanings of prefixes (word parts added to the beginning of a word) and the meanings of suffixes (word parts added to the ending of a word).

How to use a dictionary. Look up your word in alphabetical order. Guide words at the top of each dictionary page will tell you the first and last words contained on that page. Following a word are letters and symbols that tell you how to pronounce it. If you are not sure what the symbols stand for; turn to the pronunciation key at the beginning of the dictionary. That explains the meanings of the symbols.

direct characterization An author's direct description of a person or an animal in the story. Readers do not have to form an opinion about the character from his or her thoughts, speech, or actions, because the author says what the character is like. An example is in "The Cop and The Anthem" (page 38), when the author says that "Soapy's ambitions were not great . . . Three months of food, a bed, and good company was his desire."

drawing conclusions Making your own decisions about a story and its characters. The happenings and details in a story help you draw conclusions. For example, in "The Safecracker (page 17), when Ben Prince tells Jimmy "I don't believe I know you." you can safely conclude that he has decided Jimmy is no longer a criminal. [Section 5]

editorial An item in a newspaper or magazine that expresses the opinions or beliefs, of the editors.

effect Something that happens as a result of a cause. (See also cause and effect.) [Section 4]

elements of plot The plot is the sequence, or order, of important events in a story or a play. The plot usually has four elements, or parts: (1) the *problem* that the characters face; (2) the *rising action* as the characters try to solve the problem; (3) the *turning point*, the highest point of the action, as the characters find a solution; and (4) the *resolution*, when readers learn how the solution affects the characters. (See also plot.)

encyclopedia A book or set of books containing information about many topics.

When to use an encyclopedia. Use an encyclopedia when you need a lot of information about a subject. For example, if you wanted to find out the history of libraries, the names of some famous modern libraries, and how libraries arrange their books, it would be a good idea to look up *library* in an encyclopedia.

How to use an encyclopedia. The articles in encyclopedias are arranged in alphabetical order. If the encyclopedia you are using is in more than one book or *volume*, be sure to look in the volume that includes the letter you are looking for.

entertain To give readers enjoyment by making them laugh or by scaring them. An *author's purpose* in writing may be to entertain readers.   [Sections 1, 4]

essay A brief discussion of a particular subject or idea.   [Section 5]

explain To state how or why something happens. An *author's purpose* may be to explain.   [Section 1]

explanation An account of how or why something happens. When you write an explanation, help your readers understand by stating the events clearly and in the correct order.

expression A word or a group of words with a specific meaning; an idiom. For example, *hanging around* is an expression that means "waiting".   [Section 10]

495

fact Something that can be proved or observed. For example, in "Muhammad Ali's African Battle" (page 138), the author says that Zaire is the third largest country in Africa. This is a fact that can be proved. You can look up Zaire in an encyclopedia and see if the author's definition is correct. The author also says that Forman "fell to the canvas." This is a fact that was observed.   [Section 6]
When you read, think about which statements are facts and which are *opinions* (ideas, beliefs, or feelings that cannot be proved.)

fiction Made up stories. Many of the stories in this book are fiction. Fiction that contains imaginary characters and events that are very much like people and happenings in real life is called *realistic fiction*. "The Sound of Annie's Silence" (page 52) is an example of realistic fiction.

"The Golden Fleece"(page 306) is not realistic fiction because it contains a character that could not exist in real life.   [Section 3]

figurative language Words used in a fresh, new way to appeal to the imagination. The words take on more than their usual meanings.

Figurative language often compares two things that are not usually thought of as alike. Here are some examples:

The man's hair was as smooth as velvet. (The man's hair is compared to velvet.)

His voice was thunder. (His voice is compared to thunder.)

The clouds frowned at the earth. (The clouds' appearance is compared to a person's frown.) (See also *simile*, *metaphor*, and *personification*.)   [Section 6]

first-person point of view Telling a story by using the pronouns *I* and *me*. Some stories told from the first-person point of view are *autobiographies*, or true accounts of a person's life. "Once Upon A Christmas" (page 158) is an example. Other stories told in this way are *fiction*, or made-up stories, but the author pretends to be a character in the story and writes as if the events had happened to him or her. "The Sound of Annie's Silence" (page 52) is an example.   [Section 6]

finding facts First decide what kind of fact you are looking for. For facts about words, you would look in a *dictionary*. For facts about places, you might use an *atlas*, an *encyclopedia*, or an *almanac*. For facts about people, you might use a *biography*, an *autobiography*, a *biographical dictionary*, an *encyclopedia*, or a *newspaper*. Sometimes you will want to read a *nonfiction* book to find facts. The *catalog cards* in the library's *card catalog* will tell you what books the library has and where to find them on the shelves.

flat character A person in a story who is described only briefly. The author does not provide much information about the character. Sometimes that is because the character does not have a big part in the story. Other characters are more important. In "Pancakes" (page 28), Jose is an example of this. At other times, even the main characters in a story are flat, because the author wants readers to concentrate on other things.

folktale   A story that has been handed down from generation to generation. Originally, folktales were spoken rather than written. Many folktales contain these elements:

They happened long ago and far away.

They contain unusual characters.

There is a *moral*, or lesson, to be learned from the story.

foreshadowing   Clues in a story that hint at what is to happen at the end. In "A Service of Love" (page 23), clues in the story hint at the discovery Joe and Delia finally make.

form   The particular way in which an author chooses to write a story, an article, or a poem. For example, an author may choose to write a modern story as though it were an old folktale. Or an author may choose to write an article by stating the main idea and then giving examples that support it.

glossary   A list of important or hard words in a book, with their meanings. A glossary is usually at the end of a book. Not every book has a glossary.

graph   A drawing that shows how two kinds of information are related. There are several kinds of graphs. Here is a bar graph that shows average summer temperatures in Juneau, Alaska.

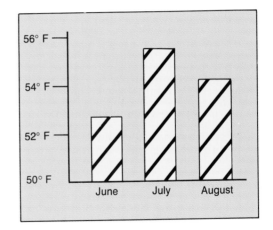

The two kinds of information that are related on this graph are the months, shown at the bottom of the graph, and the temperatures, shown at the left.

Here is a line graph that shows the same things:

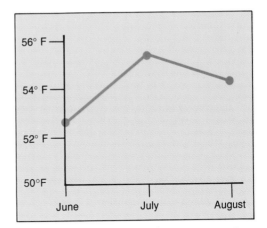

guide words   Words printed at the top of dictionary and encyclopedia pages to let you know the first and last words or topics on that page.

homophone   Words that sound alike but are spelled differently. The words whole and hole in the following sentences are homophones:

497

The whole family will be here.

Be careful you don't fall into the hole.

[Section 3]

humor   The quality of being funny. An *author's purpose* or goal may be to entertain readers by making them laugh. In other cases, the author's main purpose may be to teach readers a message about life, but he or she uses humor to keep readers interested. In "Pancakes" (page 28), the characters speak with humor. Through these characters, the author gives the reader the message about the value of clever thinking.

Authors can create humor in several ways. They may use funny events or situations. They may use funny characters. They may use *word play*, such as nonsense words and words with double meanings. "Animal Poems" (page 265) contains humorous charcters, and word play.

imagery   Words that appeal to the senses of sight, hearing, taste, touch, or smell. "The saw screeched through the wood," for example, is an image that appeals to the sense of hearing. Imagery is used in all forms of writing, but it is most common in poetry.

index   A section at the back of a nonfiction book that lists the topics in the book in alphabetical order and tells what pages they are on. Use an index to see if facts you need are in the book.

Indexes in atlases usually give map numbers and sections instead of page numbers; see *atlas* to find out how to use this type of index. Indexes in newspapers are usually printed on the first page. They list sections and pages of regular features in the newspaper, such as the crossword puzzle.

indirect characterization   Instead of describing a character directly, the author tells about the character's thoughts, speech, and actions and leaves it up to the reader to decide what the person is like.

For example, in indirect characterization, an author would not say, "Ken was helpful." He or she might say, "When Ken had finished eating, he immediately cleared the table." Readers should be able to see for themselves that Ken was helpful.

inference   A conclusion or guess based on the information presented. When you make an inference, you recognize clues the author gives as well as information he or she presents directly.

For example, in "The Safecracker" (page 17), after Jimmy opened the safe you read that "Jimmy walked out toward the front door. He heard a voice behind him calling 'Ralph!' But he did not stop." You could infer that Jimmy thought it was more important to save the child than to hide his identity, and that he thought Ben Price would arrest him.

inform   To give readers information about some topic. An *author's purpose* may be to inform.

inner conflict   A person's struggle with his or her own different feelings. If you love pizza but you are on a diet, you may have an inner conflict when you are offered a slice of pizza. (See also conflict.)

interview   A meeting in order to get information from a person.

When to use an interview.   Interviews are a good way of getting first-hand information from somebody with special experience or knowledge. For example, if you were interested in becoming a teacher, you might interview one of your teachers and ask about the advantages and disadvantages of teaching as a career.

How to interview.   Before the interview, make a list of the questions you want to ask. Make an appointment for the interview, and tell the person what the purpose of the interview is. Ask permission to take notes. Notes will help you remember what the person said. If you have a recorder, you can use that instead of taking notes, but again you will need the person's permission. Ask permission to use the person's name if you are going to write about the interview or speak.

ironic turn of events   When something happens that is different from what was expected. For example, in "The Cop and the Anthem" (page 38), Soapy tries to get arrested by not paying a restaurant bill. When he decides to change his life, he is arrested.

joint author   A book with more than one author is said to have joint authors. There is an author card for each author in the *card catalog.*

journal   1. A diary.   2. A magazine, newspaper, or other work that is published every day, every week, or at other intervals.

judgment   An opinion based on facts. Your own knowledge and experience help you make good judgments. (See also critical reading)   [Section 8]

legend   A story handed down from earlier times that tries to explain how or why something in nature came to be. Every country and group of people has legends. "The Legend of King Arthur" (page 317), is from England. [Section 9]

librarian   A person who works in a library.

library   1. A collection of books and/or other materials.   2. The place where such a collection is kept. For information on finding books in a library, see catalog card.

library card   A card that allows a person to borrow books from a library.

Library of Congress system   A way of classifying and arranging books that is used in the National Library in Washington, D.C., and some other large libraries. The system is different from the *Dewey Decimal Classification System,* which is used in most school libraries.

magazine   A publication that contains stories, articles, pictures, and/or other features written by different authors. Magazines are published weekly, monthly, or at other intervals.

main idea The most important idea in a paragraph; the sentence that tells what the paragraph is about. The main idea may be at the beginning, the middle, or the end of a paragraph. In this paragraph from "The Safecracker" (page 17) the main idea is given in the first sentence: "Everything in his room was the way he left it. There on the floor was Ben Price's shirt button. It was torn off when the famous detective arrested Jimmy."

map A drawing or diagram of a place. Here is a map of California.

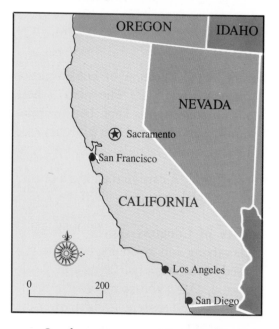

On the map, a special symbol stands for the capital city. You can tell that the capital of California is Sacramento.

Most maps contain a *compass rose* that shows directions. You can tell that San Diego is southeast of Sacramento.

The above map is called a *political map*. Political maps show divisions such as countries, states, and boundaries. There are other kinds of maps as well. For example, *physical maps* show physical features of the earth's surface, such as mountains and valleys.

For information about books of maps, see atlas.

meaning in poetry Because poets often use words in special ways that appeal to your senses and allow you to form mental pictures, it is important to read the whole poem and examine all the words and ideas carefully so that you can understand the full meaning of the poem. [Section 4]

message An important idea about life that the author wants to tell readers. An author's purpose in writing may be to give readers such a message. (See also theme.) [Section 1]

metaphor A comparison of two things that are not usually thought of as alike. Metaphors do not contain words such as like or as. Here is an example of a metaphor: "The football player's legs were tree trunks." The author does not mean the legs were really tree trunks. He or she is just comparing them to tree trunks.

Metaphors are a type of *figurative language*.

mood The strongest feeling or emotion in a work of literature. Plots, descriptions, conversations, and actions contribute to the mood. Examples of mood are *humor* and *suspense*. [Section 8]

moral A message or lesson about right

and wrong. In some works, the moral is stated directly. In other works, readers can figure it out for themselves from the plot and the actions, thoughts, and speeches of the characters. Not every work has a moral.

multiple meaning of words   Some words have more than one meaning. From the context clues, or the way a word is used in a sentence, you can decide which meaning is correct. For example, *bat* can mean "a flying mammal" or "a stick." In the sentence "Joanne stepped up to the mound and lifted her bat," you can tell that *bat* means "a stick."

mystery   A story or a play that contains a puzzle that the characters and the readers try to solve.

myth   A story told by people in ancient times to explain life and nature. Many myths, including the Greek myths, are about gods and goddesses. "The Golden Fleece" (page 306) tells about some Greek myths.   [Section 9]

narration   Writing or speaking that tells a story.

narrative essay   See personal narrative essay.

narrative poem   A poem that tells a story. Like a story, a narrative poem has characters and a *plot* (a sequence of important events). The events occur in a particular order, or *sequence*. The poem has a beginning, a middle, and an end.

narrator   A person who tells a story.

Some stories, poems, and plays have a narrator who is a character in the work. For example, the narrator in "The Tell-Tale Heart" (page 349) is the major character as well. On the stage, an actor or actress would play the part of the narrator.

newspaper   A paper that contains news, editorials, (writings giving the editors' opinions), features, and that usually is published every day or every week.

When to use a newspaper.   Use a newspaper to find out about important recent happenings and about sports and entertainment events. Use newspaper advertisements to find out products for sale and jobs that are available.

How to use a newspaper.   Most newspapers have indexes on the front page that tell the sections and the pages of regular features, such as movie listings.

Libraries usually have old copies of newspapers. Sometimes they have been reduced in size and copied on film called *microfilm*. Libraries have special machines for viewing these films.

news story   A nonfiction story that appears in a newspaper or news magazine; an article. A news story should answer these questions: *Who? What? When? Where? Why? How?*   [Section 9]

nonfiction   Writing about real people and real events. Articles, essays, biographies, and autobiographies are examples of nonfiction. Some nonfiction works such as encyclopedias and dictionaries, give information used for reference.

Among the nonfiction selections in this book are "Cheryl Toussaint" (page 124) and "Harriet Tubman: The Moses of Her People" (page 237).

notes When you are doing research, it helps to take notes on what you read so that you will remember it. Write down the important information and the title, author, and page number of the book where you got it.

novel A book-length piece of writing that tells a story. Novels are *fiction*; that is, they are made-up stories.

numbers In alphabetical order, numbers appear as though they were spelled out. For example, if you were looking for a catalog card for a book title that started with *12*, you would look under *t* for *twelve*.

opinion A statement about a person's ideas, beliefs, or feelings. Opinions cannot be proved true or false. Another person may have a different opinion. For example, in "President Cleveland, Where Are You?" (page 58), the author says, "I thought that love was really dumb." This statement is an opinion. You may agree or disagree.

Authors often support their opinions with *facts* (statements that can be proved) that they hope will convince readers to share their beliefs. [Section 6]

out-of-print book A book that is no longer available for sale from the publisher or regular bookstores. You can often find out-of-print books in libraries or second-hand bookshops.

parts of a book The front cover of a book gives the title and author and perhaps the person who did the pictures. The *spine* of the book is the side that shows on the library shelves. The spine also gives the title and author. In libraries, the call number of the book is marked on the spine so that you can find the book on the shelf. Here is a picture of a book's spine:

Inside the book, one of the first pages is the *title page*, which again gives the title and author. Next to it is the *copyright page*, which tells when the book was published. If you need up-to-date facts, be sure the book was published recently.

Two parts of a book help you find out what topics are covered in the book. The *table of contents*, which is in the front of many books, lists all the chapters in the book. The index, which is at the back of many nonfiction books, is an alphabetical list of the topics in the book and the pages they are on. Use the table of contents to find out what broad subjects are covered in the book. Use the index to see whether facts you need are in the book.

periodical A publication that comes out daily, weekly, monthly, or at other intervals. Magazines are periodicals.

personal narrative essay A brief, nonfiction work in which an author expresses his or her own beliefs about a particular subject or idea.

personification Writing about a nonhuman thing as if it were human. For example, an author might say, "The wind grabbed at my coat." Personification really compares a nonhuman thing to a human being. In the example, the wind is compared to a person, who can grab a coat.

Personification is a type of *figurative language.*

persuasion   Convincing people to share your beliefs.

persuasive writing   Writing that tries to convince people to share the author's beliefs. The author usually states his or her opinions, or beliefs, and then supports them with facts, or true statements, and examples that may convince readers.   [Section 7]

places   You can find information about places in *atlases, encyclopedias,* and *almanacs.*

play   Something written to be performed before an audience. A play may be divided into parts called *acts.* The acts are often divided into smaller parts called *scenes. Stage directions* tell the director or actors how the stage should look and how the characters should act, move, and speak.

Like stories, plays have plots, characterization, and settings. The *plot* is the sequence, or order, of important events. *Characterization* is the way an author informs the reader or the audience about the characters. In a play, you can learn about the characters through their speech and actions or through a narrator's descriptions. *Setting* is the time when and the place

where the events of the story happen. The characters' speeches, the narrator's descriptions, and the stage directions all may give information about the setting.

The play in this book is "Pancakes" (page 28).

plot   The sequence, or order, of important events in a story, that makes a point or brings out a reaction in the reader. The plot has a beginning, a middle, and an end. The events are planned to get the reader interested and to show what the *theme,* or most important idea in the selection, is.

Usually the events that make up the plot can be divided into three elements, or parts:

1. *Rising Action* is the part of the plot where a problem situation develops and the action builds up. In "A Service of Love" (page 23), Delia and Joe have a busy and happy life together. But they begin to have a problem in paying for both their art and music classes.

2. The *turning point* is the highest point of the action. The characters find a way to solve the problem. In "A Service of Love" both Joe and Delia bring money home from jobs they get.

3. The *resolution* is the last part of the plot. The problem is solved, and readers learn how the characters react. In "A Service of Love," Delia and Joe learn the truth about each other's job. They find it funny that each tried to help the other in the same way.   [Sections 1, 11]

poem A written or spoken work with language chosen for its sound, beauty, and power to express feelings. (See also poetry.)

poet The author of a poem.

poetry Poems. Poetry looks and sounds different from other forms of writing. It looks different because poets arrange their words in lines instead of sentences and group these lines into stanzas instead of paragraphs. It sounds different because poets often use rhythm, rhyme, imagery, and figurative language.

Rhythm is the arragement of the syllables in a line to make a particular sound pattern, or beat, as in music. You can hear the rhythm of a line of poetry best when you read it aloud. The punctuation and capitalization in a poem will help you decide when to pause and what to stress in order to hear the rhythm.

Rhyme is an element that many poems have. Two words rhyme when they end with the same sound: *cat, fat.* Two lines rhyme when they end with rhyming words. Here are rhyming lines from "The Panther" (page 265):

"The panther is like a leopard
Except it hasn't been peppered."

Imagery is language that appeals to the senses of sight, hearing, taste, touch, or smell.

Figurative language means words that are used in a new way to appeal to the imagination. Two things that do not seem alike may be compared. In "Mother to Son" (page 244), for example, life is compared to a staircase.

There are other elements poets may use. For instance, *humor.*

The words and elements a poet chooses are part of the poet's *style.*

point of view The position from which a story is told. In the *first-person point of view*, an author tells a true story about his or her own life; or, in a made-up story, the author pretends to be one of the characters. The first-person point of view uses the pronouns *I* and *me* in telling the story. In the *third-person point of view*, the story-teller is not a character in the story. The author uses the pronouns *he, she*, and *they* to tell the story.

"The Sound of Annie's Silence" (page 52) is an example of a story told from the first-person point of view. "The Safecracker" (page 17) is an example of a story told from the third-person point of view.   [Section 6]

predicting outcomes Guessing what will happen next in a story. You have a better chance of being right if you keep in mind what has already happened and what the characters are like.

prefix A word part added to the beginning of a word. Each prefix has its own meaning. For example, the prefix *un-* means "not." If you add a prefix to a word, you change the meaning of the word. For example, *done* means finished. Add the prefix *un-* and you get *undone*, meaning "not finished."

If you do not know a word, look at the word parts. The meaning of each part can help you figure out the word. [Sections 5, 7, 10]

problem   A difficult situation that the characters in a story have to solve. The problem is the first part of the *plot*. In "Ta-Na-E-Ka" (page 66), for example, the problem is how to survive the endurance ritual.

prose   Written work that is not poetry.

pun   A humorous play on words, usually using a word or phrase with a double meaning.   [Section 4]

publisher   A person or company that prints and sells books, newspapers, magazines, and/or other written materials.

realistic fiction   Stories that contain made-up characters and events that are similar to people and happenings in real life. "President Cleveland, Where Are You?" (page 58) is an example of realistic fiction.

Readers' Guide to Periodical Literature
A guide that comes out once or twice a month and lists recent magazine articles by their subjects. If you wanted to see what magazine articles had been written recently about whales, you would take a recent copy of the *Readers' Guide* and look under *w* for *whales*. If you wanted to read one of the listed articles, you might be able to borrow the magazine from the library. Large libraries have copies of many old and new magazines.

reference books   Books that are not meant to be read from cover to cover like a story but instead are used to look up particular facts. *Dictionaries, encyclopedias, atlases, almanacs*, and *biographical dictionaries* are important types of reference books.
Reference books are kept on special shelves in the library.

research   Investigation to find facts.

resolution   The last part of the *plot*, when the problem is solved, and you learn how the solution affects the characters. In "Ta-Na-E-Ka" (page 66), the resolution comes when Mary tells her grandfather, "There's no reason in 1947 to eat grasshoppers when you can eat a hamburger." Mary's grandfather thought she could survive anything.

rhyme   An element found in many, though not all, poems. Words rhyme when they end with the same sound. Lines rhyme when they end with rhyming words.

rhythm   The arrangement of the syllables in a line of poetry so that they make a particular sound pattern, or beat, as in music. When you read poetry aloud, listen for the rhythm. The punctuation and capitalization in a poem will help you decide when to pause and what words to stress to make the rhythm clear.

rising action   The first part of a *plot*. The action builds up and a problem situation develops. In "Ta-Na-E-Ka," (page 66), Mary must find a way to survive her upcoming endurance ritual.

root word   A word from which other words can be made. By adding a *prefix* to the beginning of a root word or a *suffix* to the end, you can change the word's meaning. For example, if you add the prefix *re-* to the root word *play*, you form the word replay, which means "play again." If you add the suffix *-ful* to the end of the root word, you get *playful*, which means "full of play" or "fun-loving."

round character   A character that is described fully. The author includes details that help you understand how the character thinks, acts, looks, and feels. Cheryl Toussaint in "Cheryl Toussaint" (page 124) is a round character.

scene   Part of a play. Plays are often divided into parts called *acts*, which, in turn, may be divided into smaller parts, the scenes.

sensory imagery   Words that appeal to the senses of sight, hearing, taste, touch, or smell.

sequence of events   The order in which events occur in a story or play. The events are put in a particular order, or sequence, so that the reader will understand what the story is about. The order of important events in a story makes up the *plot*.

setting   The time when and the place where the events of the story happen. You can tell what the setting is by looking for words or phrases that tell when and where.

Pay attention to time and place words throughout the selection, because the setting may change as the story or play goes on. For example, in "Once Upon a Christmas" (page 158), the setting shifts from America to North China and back again. It also shifts in time from present to past and back again.   [Sections 5, 11]

short story   A brief work of *fiction* (made-up story).

significant detail   A small but important bit of information. (See also detail.)

simile   A comparison. Usually similes contain the word *like* or the word *as*. Examples of similes are "her hands were like ice" and "her hands were as cold as ice."   [Section 11]

speaking and listening   (See decoding.)

speech   A formal talk given in public before an audience. Speeches may present facts or opinions or both.   [Section 9]

spine   The part of a book that shows on the library shelf. The spine tells the book's title and author and, in a library, is marked with the book's *call number*.

stanza   A division of a poem that is longer than a line. Lines in poetry are grouped into stanzas in much the same way that sentences in other works are grouped into paragraphs.

The following stanza is part of the poem "Grandfather" (page 75):

"Grandfather sings I dance.
Grandfather speaks I listen.

Now I sing, who will dance?
I speak, who will listen?"

stage directions   Directions in a play that tell the director or actors how the stage should look and how the characters are to act, move, and speak. Stage directions are not meant to be spoken out loud to the audience.

style   The words an author uses and the type of sentences he or she writes. For example, some authors use more *imagery*, or words that appeal to the senses, than other authors. Some authors write in short sentences, while others prefer to use long sentences. An author may change his or her style for different types of writing. In poetry, for instance, the author might use more imagery than when he or she was writing a non-fiction article.

suffix   A word part added to the ending of a word. Each suffix has its own meaning. For example, the suffix *-less* means "without." If you add a suffix to a word, you change the meaning of the word. For example, *care* means "concern." Add the suffix *-less* and you get *careless*, which means "without concern."

If you do not know a word, look at the word parts. The meaning of each part can help you figure out the word. Here are some other examples of suffixes: *less*, "without" *-ful*, "filled with" and *-able*, "able."   [Sections 7, 9, 10]

subject card   A card in the library's *card catalog* that has the subject at the top.

The subject tells what the book is about. Subject cards are arranged alphabetically in the card catalog. *Fiction* books do not have subject cards.

(For more information about subject cards, see catalog cards.)

summary   A brief retelling of a story. A summary tells the main events. In order for people who have not read the story to understand it, the events should be in the correct order, or *sequence*.

surprise ending   An ending that is different from what readers have been led to believe would happen. In most stories, the ending follows logically from the rest of the plot, or sequence of events. However, in stories with a surprise ending, the story takes an unexpected twist at the end.

In "The Cop and The Anthem" (page 38), the ending comes as a surprise both to the readers and to the characters in the story.   [Section 1]

suspense   A quality that produces feelings of curiosity and tension in the reader, because the reader is not sure what will happen next. The suspense keeps you reading the story. The stories in Section 10 are written with suspense.

synonyms   Synonyms are words that have the same or almost the same meaning. *Try* and *attempt* are synonyms.   [Sections 2, 5]

symbol   Something that stands for something else. For example, a heart may be a symbol of love. In "The Shirt" (page 76), Rodge's shirt is a symbol of his brother.   [Section 9]

table of contents   A section at the front of many books that lists all the chapters in the order in which they appear in the book. The table of contents tells you what broad subjects are covered in the book.

telephone directory   A list of names, addressess, and telephone numbers.

theme   The author's message; the most important idea in a written work. The *plot*, or sequence of important events in a story, helps to show what the theme is. So does the *characterization*, or what the author lets readers know or discover about the characters. Even if the author does not state the theme directly, you can figure out the message by thinking about the events in the story and the characters' thoughts, words and actions.

In "The Shirt" (page 76), the theme is that other people can feel the way you feel. The events in the story lead the readers to understand that Melody cares about Rodge in the same way that Hank does.

In "Ta-Na-E-Ka" (page 66), one theme is that using your head and planning will help you to survive.

In some stories readers learn a lesson about life while laughing at the characters or the situations. The author uses humor to develop the theme. "Pancakes" (page 28) is an example of this. One theme of the story is that cleverness usually wins out over physical threats. Amusing incidents teach readers the value of being clever.   [Sections 7, 10, 11]

third-person point of view   Telling a story by using the pronouns *he, she,* and *they*. Most *biographies*, or true accounts of another person's life, are written from the third-person point of view. "Cheryl Toussaint" (page 124) is an example. Most (though not all) made-up stories are also written in a third-person point of view. (See also first-person point of view.)   [Section 6]

title card   A card in the library's *card catalog* that has the book's title at the top. Title cards are arranged alphabetically in the card catalog. The articles *a, an,* and *the* are ignored in alphabetizing the cards. (For more information about title cards, see catalog cards.)

title page   A page at the beginning of a book that gives the book's title and author.

turning point   The highest point of the action in a story. At the turning point, the characters finally find a way to solve the problem they have been facing. In "Ta-Na-E-Ka" (page 66), the turning point comes when Mary borrows $ 5 to take care of herself on her endurance ritual. (See also plot.)

volume   1. A book. 2. One book in a set of books. 3. A group of issues of a magazine or other periodical.

word meaning   A definition. The best place to find the meaning of a word is in a dictionary. (See also context)   [Sections 4, 9]

word origin   Where a word comes from. Most   dictionaries   include   this information.   [Sections 8, 9]

word parts   Root words, prefixes, and suffixes. A *root word* is a word from which other words can be made. A *prefix* is a word part added to the beginning of a word. A *suffix* is a word part added to the ending of a word. If you know the meaning of each word part, you can figure out the word.

For example, in the word *prepayable*, the prefix *pre-* means "before;" the root word *pay* means "to give money;" and the suffix -able means "able to be." By putting all these meanings together, you can see that *prepayable* means "able to be given money for, in advance."   [Section 3]

word play   A humorous use of words. In order to be funny, authors sometimes use nonsense words and *puns*, or words with double meanings.

writing   These four steps will help you in your writing:

Step 1: Set Your Goal
Choose the topic that you will write about.

Step 2: Make a Plan
Plan what you are going to say. Often this involves making a list.

Step 3: Write the First Draft
Use your plan to write a first draft.

Step 4: Revise
Read what you have written. Make sure that it says what you want to say in a clear way. Correct any errors in spelling, grammar and punctuation. Make a final, neat copy.

Here are the main writing assignments given in this book:

comparison and contrast of two characters   For step 2, you make one list of examples from the story that shows how the characters or homes, are alike, and another list that shows how they are different.   [Section 6]

composition   For step 2, you list important events and organize them into paragraphs of similar ideas.   [Section 5]

description of a sports event or story character   For step 2, you list details that describe your subject.   [Section 9]

persuasive letter   For step 2, you list facts (true statements) and examples that support your opinion.   [Section 7]

a story review   For step 2, you decide your standards and apply them.   [Section 8]

social letter   For step 2, you list the facts and ideas you want to tell your friend.   [Section 3]

speech   For step 2, you organize using chronological order, spatial order, or topical order   [Section 9]

story   For step 2, you list the elements of plot, characters, conflict, setting, point of view, theme, and mood.   [Section 10]

ILLUSTRATION & PHOTOGRAPHY CREDITS

Illustrations: pp. 18, 19, 20, 21, 356, 357, 358, 359, 360, Tom Leonard; p. 25, Gwen Connelly; pp. 39, 41, Tom Lulevitch; p. 51, Linda Y. Miyamoto; pp. 53, 54, 98, 99, Lyle Miller; pp. 67, 69, 70, 71, 72, 73, 349, 350, 351, 352, Arvis Stewart; pp. 76-77, 79, Roger Roth; pp. 90, 134, 135, Jas Szygiel; p. 94, Rosekrans Hoffman; pp. 103, 105, Ivan Powell; pp. 109, 112, Paul Frame; p. 123, Barbara Maslen; pp. 145, 146, 147, 345, Narda Lebo; p. 159, Kathryn Yingling; pp. 162, 163, 167, 168, 207, Robert Steele; pp. 170, 171, 172, Ron Himler; pp. 175, 177, Donna Ayers; p. 187, Armen Kojoyian; pp. 188, 189, 190, 193, 194, 195, Phil Huling; pp. 211, 215, 216, 217, 219, 220, Nicholas Wilton; pp. 238, 239, Barbara Samuels; pp. 256, 257, Bryce Lee; pp. 259, 261, 262, 263, John Wallner; pp. 265, 266, 267, Don Madden; pp. 269, 270, 271, 272, 273, Arieh Zeldich; pp. 276-277, 279, Dave Allen; pp. 283, 285, 288, 291, 292, 293, 294, Steve Tanis; pp. 304, 305, Frank Mayo; pp. 306, 307, 308, 309, 311, 313, 314, Gerry Hoover; pp. 318, 321, 322, 323, 325, 326, 332, 333, 334, 335, Walter Brooks; pp. 363, 365, 366, 367, 368, 370, 371, 374, Konrad Hack; pp. 378, 381, 382, David Celsi; p. 392, Ray Lago; pp. 402, 406, 410, 414, 422, 426, 431, 438, 443, 451, 453, 455, 460, 464, Paul Frame; pp. 488, 489, Rose Mary Slader; p. 500, Joe Le Monnier.

Photography: pp. 14, 29, 30, 33, 34, 35, 88, The Bettman Archives; p. 57, Brian Brake/Photo Researchers, Inc.; p. 75, Lowell Georgia/Photo Researchers, Inc.; pp. 126, 127, Wide World Photos; p. 129, Neil Leifer/Sports Illustrated; p. 140, Tony Triolo/Sports Illustrated; p. 142, Neil Leifer/Photo Researchers, Inc.; p. 156, Culver Pictures; pp. 199, 200, 201, Richard Hutchings/Photo Researchers, Inc.; pp. 204, 205, Jack Tauss; pp. 222, 234, 235, Richard Hutchings/Photo Researchers, Inc.; p. 230, Henri-Cartier-Bresson/Magnum Photos; p. 243, Eric Wheater/The Image Bank; pp. 244, 245, Nathan Benn/Woodfin Camp & Assoc.; p. 281, M. Philip Kahl/Bruce Coleman, Inc.; p. 347, Winter Prather/Photo Researchers, Inc.; p. 355, James Lester/Photo Researchers, Inc.; Photo Hand Coloration: pp. 419, 434, 443, 444, 447, 453, 456, 467, 469, Christen Rodin.

Section Openers: pp. 13, 49, 87, 121, 155, 185, 229, 255, 303, 343. Photography: Jack George Tauss. Photo Coloration: Marc Tauss.

ACKNOWLEDGMENTS (continued from page 4)

Thomas Y. Crowell Company, Inc. for the adaptation from *The Good Earth* by Pearl S. Buck (The John Day Company), copyright 1931, 1949, copyright © 1958 by Pearl S. Buck.

The John Day Company, Publishers, for the adaptation of "Once Upon a Christmas" by Pearl S. Buck. Copyright © 1962 by Creativity, Inc.; the adaptation of "Begin to Live" from *Fourteen Stories* by Pearl S. Buck, copyright © 1943, 1945, 1948, 1956, 1957, 1960, 1961 by Pearl S. Buck.

Borden Deal Family Trust for "Antaeus" (slightly adapted) by Borden Deal. Copyrightt © 1961 by Southern Methodist University Press.

Dodd, Mead and Company, Inc. for the adaptation of "Harriet Tubman" from *Famous American Negroes* by Langston Hughes, copyright 1954 by Langston Hughes.

Esquire, Inc. for the adaptation of "There Must Be a Losing Coach" by Samuel W. Taylor, copyright © 1948 by Esquire, Inc.

Estate of William Saroyan (Bohnert, McCarthy, Flowers, Roberts & Damir) for "The Parsley Garden" by William Saroyan and adaptations of "Where I Come From People Are Polite," "Laughing Sam," and "The Coldest Winter Since 1954" by William Saroyan. Copyright 1937 by Harcourt Brace Jovanovich, Inc., renewed 1965 by William Saroyan.

Harcourt Brace Jovanovich, Inc. for "Dance of the Animals" from *The African Saga* by Blaise Cendrars.

Harper & Row, Publishers, Inc. for the novel *Old Yeller* by Fred Gipson, copyright © 1956 by Fred Gipson; for the adaptation of "Zlateh the Goat" from *Zlateh the Goat and Other Stories* by Isaac Bashevis Singer, text copyright © by Isaac Bashevis Singer.

Hart Book Company for "The Golden Fleece" from *Myths and Legends of the Ages* by Marion N. French. Copyright © 1956 by Hart Book Company.

Hill and Wang, a division of Farrar, Straus and Giroux, Inc. for "Early Autumn" from *Something in Common* by Langston Hughes. Copyright © 1963 by Langston Hughes.

Holt, Rinehart and Winston, Publishers, for "House Fear" from *The Poetry of Robert Frost* edited by Edward Connery Lathem. Copyright 1916, © 1969 by Holt, Rinehart, and Winston. Copyright 1944 by Robert Frost.

Houghton Mifflin Company for an adaptation of Chapters 4 and 5 from *Carlota* by Scott O'Dell. Copyright © 1977 by Scott O'Dell.

Alfred A. Knopf, Inc. for "Dream Deferred" from *The Panther and the Lash* by Langston Hughes, copyright 1951 by Langston Hughes; "Mother to Son" from *Selected Poems* by Langston Hughes, copyright 1926 by Alfred A. Knopf, Inc. and renewed by Langston Hughes, copyright © 1932 by Alfred A. Knopf, Inc. and renewed 1960 by Langston Hughes; an excerpt from *A Day No Pigs Would Die* by Robert Newton Peck, copyright © 1972 by Robert Newton Peck.

Little, Brown and Company for "The Panther," "The Canary," and "The Shrew" from *Family Reunion* by Ogden Nash, copyright 1940 by Curtis Publishing Company; "The Termite" from *Family Reunion* by Ogden Nash, copyright 1942 by Curtis Publishing Company.

McGraw-Hill Book Company for the adaptation of "No Hero" from *The Jesse Stuart Reader*, copyright © 1963 by McGraw-Hill Book Company, Inc.

Harold Matson Company, Inc. for the adaptation of "Weep No More, My Lady" by James Street, copyright 1941, renewed 1969 by James Street.

Harold Ober Associates, Inc. for British Commonwealth rights to the adaptation of "Begin to Live" by Pearl S. Buck; British Commonwealth rights to "Dream Deferred" by Langston Hughes; "Thank You, M'am" by Langston Hughes; British Commonwealth rights to the adaptation of "Harriet Tubman" by Langston Hughes; "Christmas Day in the Morning" by Pearl S. Buck, copyright © 1955 by Pearl S. Buck, copyright renewed 1983; British Commonwealth rights to the adaptation of "Begin to Live" by Pearl S. Buck.

Pantheon Books, A Division of Random House, Inc. for an adaptation of "President Cleveland, Where Are You?" by Robert Cormier from *8 Plus 1* by Robert Cormier. Copyright © 1965, 1966, 1967, 1968, 1969, 1971, 1973, 1975, 1980 by Robert Cormier. "President Cleveland, Where Are You?" was originally published in *Redbook*.

Penguin Books, Ltd. for British Commonwealth rights to the adaptation of "Zlateh the Goat" translated by Isaac Bashevis Singer and Elizabeth Shub.

Random House, Inc. for an adaptation of "Cheryl Toussaint" from *Women Who Win* by Francene Sabin, copyright © 1975 by Francene Sabin; "Alone" from *Oh Pray My Wings Are Gonna Fit Me Well* by Maya Angelou, copyright © 1975 by Maya Angelou.

Marian Reiner for "Thumbprint" from *It Doesn't Always Have to Rhyme* by Eve Merriam. Copyright © 1964 by Eve Merriam. All rights reserved.

Scholastic Inc. for "Alligators" by Jennifer Blathley; "Ta-Na-E-Ka" by Mary Whitebird; "Me" by Linda Sue Estes; "Winning . . . and Losing!" by Sarah Thonney; "The Sound of Annie's Silence" by Phyllis Fair Cowell; "The Antique Sale" by Cyndy Hecht; adaptation of "The Dead Man and His Gold" by Mark Twain; "The Legend of King Arthur"; "The Shirt" by Susan E. Kirby. Copyright © 1966, 1967, 1969, 1974, 1978, 1979, 1981, 1983. Adaptation of *Carlota* by Les Purificación.

The Jesse Stuart Foundation for "The Slipover Sweater" by Jesse Stuart from *Woman's Home Companion*, Vol. 76, January 1949.

John K. Terres for an adaptation of "Hitchhikers in the Sky," copyright © 1987 by John K. Terres. Originally published in *National Wildlife* Magazine, October-November 1987.